Perspectives on
Elementary Reading

Preface

This book of selected readings is intended to present those rationales and treatments of the teaching of elementary reading in which I have some confidence and which I included in my basic textbook *Teaching Elementary Reading: Principles and Strategies*. Because of its comprehensive nature and its organization, this book can also supplement other textbooks on teaching reading in elementary school, or it can be used as a primary source of information on that subject.

One of the real frustrations I have experienced is the failure of both university and public libraries to make available to students the wide range of literature on teaching reading. Invariably, particularly useful descriptive and research reports supposedly contained in cataloged volumes disappear (whole volumes are sometimes lost), or limited funds prevent the purchase of specialized publications. While a book of carefully selected articles does not completely replace those sources, it does make it possible for students to sample materials that might not be available to them otherwise.

This book is divided into ten sections, which parallel the organization of *Teaching Elementary Reading: Principles and Strategies*. As a rule, the articles are more comprehensive than those ordinarily found in books of readings, since many have been drawn from conference proceedings, bulletins, and monographs. While a number of pieces have been published since 1970, they have been selected for their relevancy, high quality, and lucid style rather than for their recent publication. Recognized scholars and authorities who have made significant contributions to reading instruction are represented in this collection.

I believe that practice should have a strong foundation in principle. Therefore, each section contains some selections that establish rationales for reading instruction drawn from psychology, linguistics, and other related disciplines. Research in reading is represented too. Students will benefit from the host of practical teaching suggestions that appear in many of the articles. Both students and teachers need help in closing the gap between principle and practice; thus each section contains guidelines and specific teaching plans that are applications of the understanding gained from study and research.

I am grateful to the reading experts who reviewed the table of contents and offered valuable suggestions for improving it. I also wish to thank the authors and publishers who gave me permission to reprint their articles, the editors who helped plan the book and assumed responsibility for its production, and the students who helped clarify my views about reading and reading instruction.

Robert Karlin

Contents

1

EMERGING CONCEPTS
IN TEACHING READING

What shall be the content of reading instruction? How shall it be taught? The answers to both these questions are by no means simple; in fact, they have been the subject of debate for more years than most of us realize. It was more than one hundred fifty years ago that Horace Mann stated his firm conviction that whole words, not individual letters, should be the vehicles by which children are taught to read. And since that time other convictions, some based on feelings and others based on less tenuous grounds, have been offered and, as is so often the case, embraced without reservations by one group or another.

Times have not changed much. Plans and programs for reading instruction flood the marketplace, and each one apparently finds its coterie of avid supporters. There is one difference however: those who wish to examine the extent to which present-day proposals are built on firm foundations now have a body of knowledge against which they can assess the validity of these proposals. This is not to say that we can view what we know about reading and reading instruction in the same way as we accept the truths revealed by scientists. But we do have an accumulation of information that emerges from the results of research—though admittedly this information is often less solid than one would hope for—and that permits us to identify trends and thereby evaluate proposals. Moreover, theoretical frameworks from several disciplines, particularly psychology and linguistics, enable us to view the act of reading in more than simplistic terms and offer some insights into its nature and possible treatments. While these structures still need to be tested more fully, they do suggest avenues through which teachers might work with pupils. Thus a combination of some factual observations and theoretical insights can provide bases (not one base) on which reading programs may rest. This is the point of view that prompted the selection of the six articles that appear in this section; they have been drawn from the literature of reading research, learning psychology, and linguistics. Each article puts forth qualified justification for

1

placing confidence in some reading proposals and withholding approval from others.

In the first selection Robert Karlin points out the limitations in reading research but offers the view that some tentative guidelines can be discerned from the results of this research. He reviews some of the more relevant studies on basal reading instruction and summarizes what he considers to be the possible implications for elementary reading programs. He further examines the findings on individualized instruction and ability grouping and suggests that in the final analysis it is teacher "know-how" that makes the difference in any organizational plan. He interprets the results of research on several aspects of reading readiness including form, letter, and word discrimination, early reading instruction and early detection of learning difficulties, and the assessment for instructional purposes of the difficulty levels of materials. Content and methodology are the subjects of other investigations that Karlin reviews and from which he makes explicit recommendations for classroom practices. The results of most recent findings do not challenge the positions he takes on these issues.

Jean Piaget's longitudinal studies of perceptual and cognitive development support some of the conclusions and implications that Karlin draws from the research in reading. In a summary of Piaget's theory of intellectual development Ronald J. Raven and Richard T. Salzer explain the behaviors of children during each of their four developmental stages and then relate these stages to reading instruction. During the sensori-motor period (birth to age two) wide opportunities for manipulative experiences rather than reading instruction (as some would suggest) are desirable. Piaget divides the pre-operational period (age two to seven) into the preconceptual and intuitive phases. It is during the intuitive phase that reading instruction is undertaken, building on the "readiness" developed during the earlier, preconceptual, phase. The authors suggest that during the preoperational period most children will not succeed in a reading program with a heavy decoding emphasis based on the memorization of rules. They also find support in Piagetian theory for the use of materials that others have questioned. During the concrete-operational period (age seven to eleven) the child masters the concept of reversibility, a development that allows him to cope with modifications in original understandings. Raven and Salzer point out how reading strategies can take advantage of this ability as well as of those abilities developed during the formal-operational period (beginning at age eleven or twelve), which follows. Throughout the discussion the authors emphasize the importance of sequence in perceptual and cognitive development with its implied meaning for reading instruction.

In contrast with judgments based on extended study, Kenneth S. Goodman hypothesizes that, contrary to popular belief, reading is not a precise process of perceiving letters or words; instead, it is a "psycholinguistic guessing game" that involves the interaction of thought and language. This he deduces from a series of errors (which he prefers to call miscues) that children make as they read orally somewhat difficult material. He makes a case for helping children to use graphic cues more effectively by utilizing materials and methods that capitalize on their knowledge of language structure, experiences, and concepts.

In a related vein Richard L. Venezky also underscores the primacy of language structures in reading. His concern, however, is not with the typical English-speaking child but with the speaker of nonstandard English—especially the Northern urban black, Appalachian, Spanish-American, American Indian, Hawaiian, and rural Southerner (black and white). His major premise is that children who speak nonstandard dialects and who generally are in the lowest socioeconomic groups are failing to learn to read as well as children who speak standard English because of their inability to cope with unfamiliar language structures found in reading materials. Venezky examines three possible ways to overcome this widespread problem: make available printed materials in the dialect beginning readers speak; teach standard English as a second language before introducing reading instruction; or develop materials in standard English that minimize dialect and cultural differences. He discusses the pros and cons of each proposal and concludes, interestingly enough, that none by itself will suffice, although he does favor the adoption of one method, alone or in combination with another.

No discipline in the sixties has aroused those interested in reading instruction—teachers, researchers, publishers—as much as linguistics. Today we still have with us "linguistic methods" and "linguistic materials" that essentially involve the adoption of spelling patterns in teaching children phoneme-grapheme correspondences. Such a system for beginning reading was the product of Bloomfield's and Fries' concern with improving instruction. These linguists believed that reading is mainly a decoding process and that comprehension involves thinking and not reading. Hence their minimal concern with meaningful sentences as they developed materials containing words that reflected consistency in sound-letter relationships.

Ronald Wardhaugh questions the assumptions underlying these and other procedures attributed to linguistic knowledge because "the problems are not exclusively linguistic." He goes on to say that there are not linguistic methods, that reading is not linguistics, but that any method for teaching reading ought to utilize sound linguistic knowledge. A successful reader is one who possesses linguistic competence (that is, he knows the grammar of the language though he is not necessarily able to describe it) as well as perceptual and cognitive competences. "The teaching of reading must be clearly distinguished from the teaching of speaking," but "it should be possible to teach [children] to read by drawing upon the language competence they exhibit in [their] dialect." Wardhaugh believes that the teaching of reading should be part of a total language program and that it "should emphasize the discovery of how language is used." This task he leaves to those who are familiar with psychological and pedagogical principles.

In the last article in this section, Ernest Hilton sets forth the ground rules on strategy and content for elementary reading programs in the seventies. It is a kind of summary of the implications drawn from research and theoretical considerations and from the results of programs that schools have used during the previous decade. One message is clear: schools must provide more and better teaching than they have in the past. Another is that "the quality of the teaching will continue to be the most important factor in reading programs." A third supports a strong reading curriculum for the middle grades that stresses "learning to read to learn," the appreciation of literature, and the development of positive attitudes toward reading. Acceptance of these tenets is likely to give strong impetus to the "Right To Read" campaign to which federal, state, and local units appear dedicated.

Research Results
and Classroom Practices

ROBERT KARLIN

Attempts to identify guidelines for good practices in reading from research results lead to a number of problems, not the least of which are quantity and quality of reading research. Reviews in various sources would tend to indicate that a list covering reading research since 1930 would be exceedingly long. But when one seeks direction for classroom practice, the fact that there is a great deal of research from which to draw does not mean that answers to all significant questions will be found through reading investigations. There are areas in which little or no research has been conducted; for example, vocabulary control and vocabulary repetition. To what extent is it necessary to repeat words in books for young learners—two, three, four times or more? At what point do reading materials become frustrating—when pupils can't recognize what percentage of the words and understand what portion of the content? There are many gray areas in which there are few answers except those based upon experiences and hunches.

Then there is the question of separating from the research those studies whose design and treatment will permit one to view with some degree of confidence their results, conclusions and implications. Reading research suffers from a basic limitation—having to work through humans to predict human behavior. Such a limitation places a premium upon the research sophistication, lack of which is apparent in so many investigations. Added to these problems is the failure of most published studies to offer sufficient information that they might be evaluated intelligently and possibly replicated. The fact that a study, regardless of its merit, obtains a given set of results is no guarantee that similar results will be achieved a second and third time.

Does this state of affairs suggest a desert from which no guides for classroom practice can spring? By no means. It does mean that one must sort, sift and then recognize that few definitive answers have fallen into the hopper of truth. In most cases results can support trends, but not dogmas. Furthermore, one must recognize that some strong beliefs may fall as research yields more clues to the reading process and to productive procedures.

RESEARCH RESULTS AND CLASSROOM PRACTICES by Robert Karlin. From *The Reading Teacher*, 21 (December 1967), pp. 211–26. Reprinted with permission of the International Reading Association and Robert Karlin.

BASAL READING

With these conditions, what ideas can one gain from the research on the basal approach to reading methods and materials. Incidentally, it is barely possible to separate basal reading methods from basal reading materials as they are presently constituted. A review of the first-grade USOE and other studies shows how related both are.

In a study conducted in Chesapeake, Virginia, Bliesmer and Yarborough (1965) compared ten different beginning reading programs in first grade, five of which were based on the belief that children should be taught to recognize words by the analytic method and five by the synthetic method. The scores on the *Stanford Achievement Test* showed significant differences in the majority of the means—these differences in favor of the synthetic programs. All differences in word meaning and word study skills favored the synthetic group though not all were significant. Twenty out of twenty-five comparisons in paragraph reading revealed significant differences in favor of the synthetic group.

Two studies which sought to measure the values of a basal set of materials which stresses a synthetic program and another which follows the typical sequences of most basal reading materials produced different results. Henderson (1959) reported that children in the first three grades taught by the former approach were significantly superior in word recognition and comprehension to children in the latter program and retained superiority. On the other hand, Sparks and Fay (1957) found that by the time children reached the fourth grade there were no significant differences in reading ability regardless of the program followed.

Grimes (1958) sought to determine how different kinds of children fared with synthetic and analytic programs. He found that lower I.Q. children did not do as well as higher I.Q. children in synthetic programs and that highly anxious children did better than less anxious children in synthetic programs.

Chall and Feldmann (1966) attacked the problem in another way. They were interested in determining the extent to which the kinds of teaching and teacher characteristics in an eclectic basal reader approach influenced reading achievement. Teachers of twelves classes were rated on their views of teaching reading—sound, symbol and meaning, as well as classroom practices. They found that teacher competence, a thinking approach to learning, a sound-symbol emphasis and adaptation to appropriate difficulty levels were related to reading achievement. They concluded that teachers using a method vary in their implementation of the method and that teacher variables influence reading achievement.

Studies to test the effectiveness of typical basal reading programs and "linguistic" oriented reading programs produced mixed results. Sheldon and Lashinger (1966) reported no significant differences on the *Stanford Achievement Test*. Schneyer (1966) reported significant differences favoring the linguistic group on the linguistic reading test and favoring the typical group on four of five subtests of the *Stanford Achievement Test.* However, these differences were not consistent at all ability levels. A study by Wyatt (1966) did not produce results which led to definitive conclusions.

Studies involving typical basal reading programs and atypical orthography produced mixed results too. Mazurkiewicz (1966) reported significantly higher scores on word reading for children taught with different orthography. Children in the typical program obtained significantly higher scores in spelling. There were no significant differences in paragraph meaning, word study and vocabulary. Hayes (1966) found that children receiving reading instruction through a program using unconventional orthography generally scored higher in word reading, paragraph reading, and word study skills than did children taught through the usual basal reading program. However, Fry (1966) reported no significant differences in these tests of scores obtained by similar groups of children.

In comparing a basal reader method with a language-experience approach Harris and Serwer (1966) reported an advantage in favor of the former with disadvantaged children. McCanne (1966) found that for children from Spanish-speaking homes the basal reader approach developed higher achievement in reading skills than the language-experience approach. Stauffer (1966) concluded that the language arts approach is an effective method for beginning reading instruction for all children.

Other studies involving basal approaches to reading with and without the use of additional materials and approaches have been conducted. Miller (1963), Ungaro (1965), and Sister Mary Edward (1964) found that the introduction of supplementary activities tends to produce better readers.

What conclusions might be drawn from this research?

1. That one type of program does not seem to be overwhelmingly superior to another.
2. That differences in program effectiveness might be attributed to teacher variables.
3. That any one program fails to provide for all reading requirements.
4. That no single program is best for all children.

What recommendations might one, from these research findings and experience, suggest? Any program which purports to be basic and beats the drums for one and only one approach to reading success should be suspect. A given program might produce excellent results under one set of conditions but not under another. In evaluating basal reading programs one should determine the extent to which each, through variety of skills and content, covers the reading experiences which most children require, realizing that a single program is not likely to cover all. A comprehensive basal reading program might be viewed as a jumping off point from which to move to instruction in reading varieties of materials including newspapers, magazines, encyclopedias and other reference sources as well as such writing as plays, poetry, biography and fiction. It is an established fact that few programs presently provide for extensive reading in the content fields. Obviously, basic instruction must make provisions for dealing with this type of material.

Furthermore, one can not assume basal reading programs through their manuals offer the best possible use of the materials. Just as too many teachers have failed to use to fullest advantage some excellent suggestions found in manuals, so have others relied almost exclusively upon these guides. Knowledgeable teachers are discriminating in their adoption and extension of ideas offered them. They know that quality of materials and quality of use are mutually dependent.

There is one important additional point. Not all children profit to the same extent from any one set of procedures. What is desirable for average readers might not be equally good for poorer ones or for superior readers. The study by Saxton (1957) suggests that the majority of the last group do not have to follow highly organized programs in order to develop necessary reading skills. Perhaps not all superior readers need the basal program, or at least, all aspects of it.

ORGANIZATION

How shall teachers organize for reading instruction? Is it desirable to teach the class as a whole? Is group instruction within a classroom a better procedure for meeting individual differences? How effective is intra-class grouping? What about individualized reading? What does research say on some of these questions?

Sister M. Marita (1966) compared reading achievements under three classroom procedures: a modified individualized pattern in which children received group instruction (three to five groups) and participated in individualized reading; three to five groups; and whole class instruction. The latter involved a whole array of activities including the use of audio-visual materials. The superiority of one treatment over another was not constant and the investigator concluded that the whole-class pattern might be as useful an approach to teaching reading as the other patterns.

McCracken (1953) and others found it is possible to teach the class as a whole by centering its attention on visual materials paralleling the basal text. However, McRobbie (1961) concluded that such a program had shortcomings and that it did not guarantee improved reading achievement.

Individual versus group instruction has been studied. McDonald and others (1966) found that first-grade children who were taught individually did not surpass the reading achievement of others taught in groups, both groups using basal reading materials. MacKinnon (1959), concluded that first-grade children taught in groups surpassed in oral reading others who were taught individually. He found also that the materials used with each seemed to influence outcomes.

Individualized reading has been compared to ability grouping. Several persons have reviewed the research in this area. Vite (1961) reported that, of seven controlled studies, four showed results favoring individualized reading while three obtained results definitely in favor of grouping. Groff (1963) reported results, some of which were in favor of individualized reading and others for grouping. Greenman (1959) reported that the children in her study did not do uniformly well in individualized reading, the best pupils making the greatest gains and some slow pupils little or no gains. Sartain (1960) found no significant differences for average and better readers. Poor readers seemed to do better in group instruction.

Joplin plans (inter-class grouping) have been compared with other forms of grouping. Hillson and others (1964) reported after one and one-half years that children in a non-graded plan scored significantly higher on word and paragraph meaning than children grouped on the basis of ability. Carson and Thompson (1964) reported no significant differences in reading achievement for children taught in self-contained classrooms or in the Joplin pattern. No real differences for slow or fast learners were found in the two plans.

Green and Riley (1963) found that Joplin plans were more effective than traditional grouping. Kierstead (1963) found no significant differences between groups while Ramsey (1962) reported that the Joplin plan was effective for the upper third but not effective for the lower third of the class. Balow (1962, 1963) compared homogeneous and heterogeneous grouping for reading and found no significant differences in growth. He concluded on the basis of two experiments that grouping per se does not insure achievement.

Another form of grouping which has not received as much attention as others is pupil teams. Under this pattern two, three, or four pupils, having received an assignment, work together without the teacher. One pupil might be assigned a leadership role, seeing to it that all members of the team were profitably engaged and giving help where able. Lambert conducted one study (1965) involving over 600 pupils in grades one through six and reported significant gains in reading and study skills for the regular groups over the team groups in the first year. In the second year the team groups showed greater gains. Studies by Murphy (1966) and Spencer (1966) reported the use of pupil teams with other procedures and materials. Murphy made no specific recommendations regarding their worth; Spencer reached the conclusion that "pupil-team learning activities should be part of any classroom organization." Studies conducted under the sponsorship of Boston University by Batty (1959) and Clapper (1958) demonstrated some values of pupil teams although the results have not been conclusive.

It is evident that no clear-cut advantages of one grouping plan over another or of individual over group forms have been found. What implications, then, might be drawn from these and other studies?

1. There are times when it is feasible to teach a class of children as a whole, providing all can benefit from the offering.

2. Grouping can narrow but not completely eliminate the range of reading abilities. Recognizing the difficulties in providing for individual differences, teachers might function more effectively if the range were not too great.
3. Combinations of individual and group instruction seem to be more productive than either alone. Teachers can take advantage of any organizational patterns which assist them in meeting the learning requirements of all their pupils.
4. No organizational plan will insure reading success. The "know-how" the teacher brings to the plan is what counts.

Dependence upon inter-class grouping, intra-class grouping, pupil teams, or other plans to solve instructional problems fails to take into account differences in pupils and in teachers. Some pupils and some teachers function better under one set of conditions than another. A plan of organization is not a method of teaching. It is a facilitator of method, perhaps, but no more.

CLASSROOM AND SCHOOL PRACTICES

What classroom and school practices are likely to reduce reading difficulties? The answers to this question are not clearcut; nor are they found completely in the results of research. Few investigations indeed set out to determine whether or not a given set of practices could reduce reading difficulties. Perhaps the best approach, then, is to seek implications from research which is related to the problem as well as draw upon empirical findings for guidance. In the past this author has taken the position that knowledge of the learner and the learning process adequately translated into teaching strategies is more likely to promote reading success than any plan which might be adopted. The findings of research have not destroyed the belief that some roads to reading growth are longer and harder than others and thus ought to be avoided wherever possible. Promising practices should emerge from an examination of different facets of the reading-learning act.

Readiness

For years now, there has been exploration of ways to identify children who do not seem good prospects for formal reading instruction with the view to assisting them overcome weaknesses that are tied to reading and thereby avoid failure. Schools ordinarily use reading-readiness tests for these purposes. Can these tests sort out the children who need special help in developing skills requisite for reading success? Powell and Parsley (1961) used the *Lee-Clark Reading Readiness Test* with 711 children and found that while it was able to predict the general reading achievement of the total group, the results were not sufficiently good to enable the schools to predict the growth of individual children and group them for instruction. Karlin (1957) studied children with the *Metropolitan Readiness Test* and found a very small relationship between scores on the test and reading growth at the end of the first grade. Studies by Zingle and Hohol (1964) and Mitchell (1962) as well as others show that while it might be possible to predict the behavior of a group of children, it is virtually impossible to predict the reading achievement of individual members in the group.

It appears that the results of readiness tests cannot be used alone to group children for reading instruction. Performances on certain aspects of the tests which seem to be related to reading growth, such as letter and word matching, were found by Barrett (1965) and others to make the greatest contributions to predicting reading success.

De Hirsch (1966) and her colleagues have been working on a series of tests to be used in identifying children who are likely to experience real difficulties in learning to read. Although their results are tentative, there seem to be some indications that the prevention of some reading failures might be realized by analyzing responses on a battery of test items and treating the causes of improper responses.

However, the thought that what happens to children during instruction is as important as what they bring to the reading task opens up a related area—the use of readiness materials for developing visual skills which seem to be lacking or partially developed in some children. Some materials require children to see likenesses and differences in shapes and objects. To what extent there is a relationship between discrimination among shapes and objects and word discrimination is a matter of question. Obviously, one precedes the other in the normal course of development. But ability in one does not necessarily mean ability in the other. Can it be assumed that the child who is able to differentiate between three rabbits who show two ears and one with a single ear can readily distinguish between such words as run and ran or where and when? Although the research on this specific question is meager indeed, there are indications that attention specifically paid to weaknesses in word discrimination is more productive than practice with shape and form. Both Goins (1959) and Vernon (1959), who studied visual perception in young children, seem to have reached this same conclusion. Allen (1959) and Muehl (1960) also reached this conclusion on the basis of their research.

A series of investigations sought to determine the relationship between knowledge of letter names and their sounds and reading success. Olson (1963) concluded that both are necessary to the development of a sight vocabulary. A large number of children were studied by Durrell (1958) and his students, who found that such knowledge was important and that the majority of reading failures in first grade could be prevented by early instruction in letter names and their sounds. Muehl (1962), on the other hand, reported that knowledge of letter names interfered with associating nonsense words with pictures.

It appears that knowledge of letters and sounds has some importance for the perceptual act in reading. The results of the research suggest some beefing up of programs which are weak in phonic analysis. They do not suggest a preference of one phonic program over another.

Early Learning and Instruction

What effect does early reading have on later achievement? Durkin (1966) followed the progress of thirty pairs of bright early and non-early readers over a three-year period and reported a significantly higher reading achievement for the early readers. Brzeinski (1964) studied the Denver Public Schools' efforts to provide reading instruction in kindergarten and at home. He reported a significant advantage for children who had beginning reading activities in kindergarten as well as no more adverse effects on children with physical or emotional handicaps. Parents were able to help children whose mental ages were at least $4\frac{1}{2}$ years.

It is apparent that children who are ready for an early start in reading do not seem to suffer from adverse effects when taught; in fact, they appear to profit from activities which stimulate and feed their interests in reading.

Corrective Efforts

The early detection of children who are having difficulty in learning to read needs greater attention. Occasionally, one reads a glowing report of a youngster in the middle or upper grades, who, after continuous reading failure, is taught to read so well that he becomes an academic success. However, larger numbers of older children fail to grow in this same way. On the basis of a comparison of younger and older children with reading problems, Robeck (1964) concluded that there should be no delay of the study into the causes of reading failures once observed. Two studies by Scott (1959) and Farrelly (1960) with second-grade children who were poor readers produced results which indicated that a carefully planned and systematic remedial program could raise significantly the reading levels of such children. Mc-Connell (1956) with fourth-grade pupils reached a similar conclusion.

It is entirely possible that early treatment of reading difficulties will contribute significantly to a reduction of reading failures. One community in California was able to salvage approximately 50 per cent of beginning second and third graders with serious reading problems by providing special help for them early in their school careers.

Appropriate Materials

The study of materials which are too difficult can be expected to be just as profitable for a child as efforts by an adult to read narrative or expository materials written in a foreign language with which he had a mere acquaintance would be. Elder (1963) conducted an investigation among children in grades two through six to determine to what extent they could tolerate material. He found that they could manage those in which they knew 88 to 99 per cent of the words. This more recent study tended to support an earlier one by Killgallon (1942) who found that children who knew about 95 per cent of the words could use such materials for instructional purposes.

It has been known for some time that the results of standardized reading tests fail to place children in materials with which they can function satisfactorily. In order to select materials which are neither too simple nor too difficult, greater reliance should be placed upon the results of informal inventories instead of standardized reading test scores. This recommendation can be supported by the results of a number of studies, among which are those of McCracken (1962), Sipay (1964) and Williams (1963). McCracken studied sixth-grade pupils and found that 93 per cent of the pupils would meet many difficulties in reading books chosen to match standardized test scores. Comprehension scores over two years higher than levels at which the students were able to read were obtained from the standardized test. Sipay reported that two of three reading tests underestimated by one grade the frustration level of fourth graders and overestimated their instructional levels by one or more years. Williams' results led her to conclude that standardized tests placed pupils of intermediate grades in materials too difficult for them to use. In some cases there was a discrepancy of as much as four years difference between reading test scores and actual reading ability.

It would be reasonable to conclude that the application of properly designed informal reading inventories would lead to selecting materials that more appropriately fit the reading needs of students. Proper fit is one of the ingredients of successful reading programs and concomitantly successful reading achievement.

Discovery Methods

Suchman in science and others in different subject areas have demonstrated the values that accrue to children who have had an opportunity to explore situations from which they draw conclusions and generalizations. There is some evidence that discovery applied to the teaching of reading could be an avenue through which children might learn reading skills and be in a better position to apply them. Loban (1963) in an extensive longitudinal study of children's oral language and reading came to the conclusion, among others, that oral language seems to be the basis for reading ability and that instruction should stress inductive reasoning. Catterson (1962) compared deductive methods with inductive methods for teaching word-attack skills. She studied the relative merits of each approach using 1200 words ranging in difficulty from third to eighth grade. She found that her low achievers learned to recognize words better through classifications than by memorization of rules governing them.

It might be wise to extend these findings to other aspects of reading. Comprehension skills involving word meanings and interpretation and study skills covering selection, organization and location of information can be developed through discovery procedures. Memorization has never been proved to be a superior way to learn when compared to understanding.

Use of Various Modalities

The majority of children who become clinical cases in reading suffer from an inability to recognize and identify words readily. Many would be able to understand the material they read were it not for this serious deficiency. One consideration in relation to this problem is the modality of word presentation. Is there a best single way to present words?

Perry (1960) through a learning methods test, sought to determine whether one modality of word presentation was superior to another with first graders and concluded that none is best for all children. Rivkind (1958) found no significant differences for individuals and groups who were taught by visual, phonic or auditory, kinesthetic or combinations of these methods. Roberts and Coleman (1958) found that children who have difficulty recognizing words learn more efficiently when not taught by visual presentations alone. Budoff and Quinlan (1964) found that second graders achieved better results through aural than visual presentations. The poorest readers showed little preference for either. Geiger (1964), McNeil and Keisler (1963), and Mills (1956) found that multiple means of presentation and response produce better results than single modes.

The conclusions that might be drawn from this series of studies seem clear. Reliance upon a single method of teaching word recognition is not warranted. All children do not respond in the same way. Superior results should be achieved through multiple forms and presentations.

Vocabulary Development

One area of continuing concern is vocabulary development. There is general agreement that a limited vocabulary stands in the way of reading with comprehension. Three ways to build vocabulary for reading comprehension have been suggested: direct vocabulary instruction, incidental attention in building word meanings, and wide reading. Although it appears that persons who do wide reading have large meaning vocabularies, there is little evidence to support the conclusion that wide reading alone leads to increased vocabulary. Both Traxler (1938) and Sachs (1943) came to this judgment some years ago.

Several studies provide support for direct vocabulary instruction. Mc-Cullough (1957), in a review of research on this question, recommended that high school students receive such instruction. Wozencraft (1964) concluded on the basis of her study of word meaning and paragraph meaning that children of lower ability in upper grades do require vocabulary instruction. Jackson and Dizney (1963) also reported significant vocabulary gains for students receiving direct instruction over those not receiving instruction.

Perhaps of greater importance are the forms this direct instruction might take. Should pupils get lists of words whose meanings are to be sought? From what sources should these words come? What forms of presentation appear to be more valid than others?

Lawless (1961) reported significant gains for fourth graders who studied words taken from social studies, science and arithmetic. Vanderlinde (1964), selecting words from a fifth-grade arithmetic book, this vocabulary study being a part of the regular arithmetic program, found that pupils receiving this instruction were able to solve verbal problems better than pupils receiving no special attention in vocabulary. Pupils with average and superior ability profited more from the instruction than below-average students. Otterman (1955) taught seventh graders prefixes and roots and concluded that only students of high ability were able to apply what they had learned to new words. The students did not show any improvement in vocabulary or comprehension. Severson (1963) found that tenth grade biology students who were given lists of biological terms with their etymology showed greater improvement in vocabulary than did students not receiving such a list. Nelson (1961) had pupils in the middle grades work individually using words and meaning exercises, others in pairs working on words and sentences, and a third group working individually on writing sentences. He found the first two plans produced vocabulary growth significantly higher than the last. Serra (1953) surveyed research results and concluded that independent use of the dictionary by pupils produces poorer results than programs which include teacher explanation and illustration. Eichholz and Barbe (1961) combined modified programing with informal talk about words and concluded that repetition influences the learning of word meanings.

These and other studies on vocabulary development, while they do not demonstrate procedures guaranteed to be effective, suggest dependence upon no single method. Words which students have immediate need to use seem to be better candidates for study than words drawn from sources unrelated to current tasks. A combination of methods should produce better achievement in vocabulary development than any one method alone. Meaningful dictionary work; word study in context rather than isolation; possible uses of context clues for specific word meanings; attention to multiple meanings and figurative language; study of the history and etymology of words relevant to current reading; application of new words in oral and written language—

these efforts together with wider reading might prove truly effective. Many vocabulary programs fail to produce results over short periods of time. Vocabulary development is an on-going affair and product of all learning experiences. To expect great and lasting achievements in vocabulary growth through intermittent and quick shock treatments is unrealistic and wasteful.

Comprehension

The improvement of reading comprehension in narrative and expository materials is a major concern. Concept development plays an important role in this improvement. What guiding principles should govern efforts to develop and strengthen concepts? Direct experiences are important, especially during the beginning stages of their development. Hazy and incomplete understandings are the products of ideas gained mainly from books. These conclusions are supported by Diederich (1944), Serra (1953), and Carner and Sheldon (1954). Serra pointed out the impossibility of providing first-hand experiences in all learning situations. Buchanan (1959) concluded that demonstrations to clarify concepts before reading in science were of great help to both good and poor students. Still pictures, film, explanation, discussion, experimentation, and dramatization can offer vicarious experiences where first-hand experiences cannot be realized. Unfortunately, teachers tend to assume that students grasp the ideas with which they deal and neglect opportunities to clarify them.

Handling Content Materials

Does general reading ability insure the ability to read and understand content materials? While no one will deny that general reading skills are needed to comprehend these materials, there is evidence to support direct instruction in reading content. Traxler (1946) summarized a series of investigations and concluded that instruction in reading skills peculiar to each field is necessary. Koehn (1960) found a high relation between sixth grade general reading ability and social studies reading in the ninth grade for gifted students. However, the relationship for general reading ability and reading in science was low. Shores (1960) concluded that sixth graders should be taught to read science materials for different purposes. In two companion studies Maney (1958) in science and Sochor (1958) in social studies found that higher-level interpretation abilities such as finding the central and key ideas, drawing conclusions and recognizing author's purpose appeared to be independent of general and literal reading ability.

The implications of the research are clear. It is important to analyze the materials students read for organization and special difficulties and offer help in reading them. Subject-matter teacher involvement should be encouraged since the knowledge of content is his, and it is through content that the skills of reading are taught. The teacher of English will teach reading through the content of literature. Would it not be consistent to expect similar treatment by teachers of other content?

Skill Practice

A cursory examination of materials presently available for teaching reading skills will reveal that they are mainly practice materials rather than teaching materials. If pupils can perform the tasks required of them by these workbooks or boxed materials or other sets, they will strengthen the skills they bring to bear upon the tasks. However, if they lack the abilities needed to perform the tasks, no amount of exposure to these materials will help them overcome their weaknesses. Such materials may be used for diagnostic and practice purposes. Such emphases as these require closer teacher guidance as well as deeper teacher understanding. Perhaps the mixed findings of research on the use of materials reflect differences in the ways they have been used. Jones (1961) found no significant differences between fourth-grade groups who used a reading laboratory and who did not. Both groups made significant gains in reading over a five month period. Walker (1961) used a variety of reading materials including a reading laboratory, a single text and workbook and did not realize significant gains among three groups of seventh graders. Sartain (1961) reported no differences in progress between third-grade groups who used and did not use workbooks. Doctor (1962) reported gains in favor of the workbook groups in grades two and three, superior gains for non-workbook groups in grades one and four, and no differences between groups in grades five and six.

These are the representative findings on the use of skill-building materials. They appear to support the view that materials are less crucial than teacher sophistication.

SUMMARY

Explorations into the research on reading take one along different avenues, some of which permit firmer judgments about practices than others. There are few definitive conclusions. However, some trends appear sharper than others and some practices seem more promising than others. Through weighing and comparing plans and patterns for teaching, signs are likely to emerge. And these signs could lead to better teaching programs.

References

Allen, Ruth, *et al.* The relationship of readiness factors to January first-grade reading achievement. Master's thesis, Boston University, 1959.

Balow, I. Does homogeneous grouping give homogeneous results? *Elementary School Journal*, 1962, 28-32.

Balow, I., and Ruddell, A. The effects of three types of grouping on achievement. *California Journal of Educational Research*, 1963, *14*, 108–117.

Barrett, T. Visual discrimination tasks as predictors of first grade reading achievement. *The Reading Teacher*, 1965, *18*, 276–282.

Batty, Dorothy. Comparison of individual and paired practice at primer level. Unpublished master's thesis, Boston University, 1959.

Bliesmer, E., and Yarborough, Betty. A comparison of ten different beginning reading programs in first grade. *Phi Delta Kappan*, 1965, *46*, 500–504.

Brzeinski, J. Beginning reading in Denver. *The Reading Teacher*, 1964, *18*, 16–21.

Buchanan, Sidney. A study of growth in kowledge of important terms and concepts, understanding of concepts, and application of concepts through reading and demonstrations in the science program. Unpublished master's thesis, University of Minnesota, 1959.

Budoff, M., and Quinlan, D. Reading progress as related to efficiency of visual and aural learning in the primary grades. *Journal of Educational Psychology*, 1964, *55*, 247–252.

Carner, R., and Sheldon, W. Problems in the development of concepts through reading. *Elementary School Journal*, 1954, *55*, 226–229.

Carson, R., and Thompson, J. The Joplin plan and traditional reading groups. *Elementary School Journal*, 1964, *65*, 38–43.

Catterson, Jane. Inductive versus deductive methods in teaching word-attack skills. Challenge and experiment in reading. *Proceedings of the International Reading Association*, 1962, 121–123.

Chall, Jeanne, and Feldmann, Shirley. First grade reading: an analysis of the interactions of professed methods, teacher implementation and child background. *The Reading Teacher*, 1966, *19*, 569–575.

Clapper, Harriet, *et al.* The effectiveness of paired learning on a reading program in grades II and III. Unpublished master's thesis, Boston University, 1958.

DeHirsch, Katrina. Predicting reading failure. New York: Harper and Row, 1966.

Diederich, P. B. Relationships among experience, language and reading. Reading in relation to experience and language. *Supplementary Educational Monographs, No. 58*. Chicago: University of Chicago Press, 1944, 12–15.

Doctor, R. Reading workbooks: boon or busywork? *Elementary English*, 1962, *39*, 224–228.

Durkin, Dolores. The achievement of pre-school readers: two longitudinal studies. *Reading Research Quarterly*, 1966, *1*, 5–36.

Durrell, D. (Ed.) Success in first grade reading. *Journal of Education*, 1958, *140*, 1–48.

Edward, Sister Mary. A modified linguistic versus a composite basal reading program. *The Reading Teacher*, 1964, *17*, 511–515, 527.

Eichholz, G., and Barbe, R. An experiment in vocabulary development. *Educational Research Bulletin*, 1961, *40*, 1–7, 28.

Elder, R. Behavioral criteria and pupil achievement. *Michigan Educational Journal*, 1963, *40*, 502, 536.

Farrelly, Mary. The construction and evaluation of a series of lesson plans in phonics to be used with the reluctant readers in the second grade. Unpublished master's thesis, Rhode Island College, 1960.

Fry, E. B. Comparing the diacritical marking system, ITA and a basal reading series. *Elementary English*, 1966, *43*, 607–611.

Geiger, Alice. A study of learning utilizing visual-visual and visual-auditory stimuli. *Reading Horizons*, 1964, *4*, 51–54.

Goins, Jean. Visual and auditory perception in reading. *The Reading Teacher*, 1959, *13*, 9–13.

Green, D., and Riley, Hazel. Interclass grouping for reading instruction in the middle grades. *Journal of Experimental Education*, 1963, *31*, 273–278.

Greenman, Ruth. Individual reading in the third and fourth grade. *Elementary English*, 1959, *35*, 234–237.

Grimes, J. The interaction of certain pupil personality characteristics with methods of teaching reading in determining primary grade achievement. Unpublished doctoral dissertation, Harvard University, 1958.

Groff, P. Comparisons of individualized and ability grouping approaches to reading achievement. *Elementary English*, 1963, *40*, 258–264, 276.

Harris, A., and Serwer, Blanche. Comparing reading approaches in first grade teaching disadvantaged children. *The Reading Teacher*, 1966, *19*, 631–635.

Hayes, R. B. ITA and three other approaches to reading in first grade. *The Reading Teacher*, 1966, *19*, 627–630.

Henderson, Margaret. A six year experimental study of two methods of teaching reading in the elementary school. Paper presented to AERA, February, 1959.

Hillson, Maurie, *et al.* A controlled experiment evaluating the effects of a nongraded organization on pupil achievement. *Journal of Educational Research,* 1964, *77*, 548–550.

Jackson, Jeanne, and Dizney, H. Intensive vocabulary training. *Journal of Developmental Reading,* 1963, *6*, 221–229.

Jones, R., and Van Why, E. The SRA reading laboratory and fourth grade pupils. *Journal of Developmental Reading,* 1961, *5*, 36–46.

Karlin, R. The prediction of reading success and reading readiness tests. *Elementary English*, 1957, *34*, 320–322.

Kierstead, R. A comparison and evaluation of two methods of organization for the teaching of reading. *Journal of Educational Research,* 1963, *56*, 317–321.

Killgallon, P. A. A study of relationships among certain pupil adjustments in reading situations. Doctoral dissertation, Pennsylvania State College, 1942.

Koehn, Edna. The relationship of the basic skill development of sixth grade gifted children to ninth grade achievement in the content fields. Unpublished doctoral dissertation, University of Minnesota, 1960.

Lambert, P., *et al.* A comparison of pupil achievement in team and self-contained organizations. *Journal of Experimental Education,* 1965, *33*, 217–224.

Lawless, Lillian. An evaluation of a fourth grade program for the enrichment of vocabulary in three content areas. Unpublished master's thesis, Rhode Island College, 1961.

Loban, W. The language of elementary school children. Champaign: National Council of Teachers of English, 1963.

McCanne, R. Approaches to first grade English reading instruction for children from Spanish-speaking homes. *The Reading Teacher*, 1966, *19*, 670–675.

McConnell, Elsie. A study of the reading difficulties of children in Alnwick School, Blount County, Tennessee. Unpublished master's thesis, University of Tennessee, 1956.

McCracken, G. The New Castle reading experiment: a terminal report. *Elementary English*, 1953, *30*, 13–21.

McCracken, R. Standardized reading tests and informal reading inventories. *Education*, 1962, *82*, 366–369.

McCullough, Constance. What does research reveal about practices in teaching reading? *English Journal*, 1957, *66*, 475–490.

McDonald, J., Harris, T., and Mann, J. Individual versus group instruction in first grade reading. *The Reading Teacher*, 1966, *19*, 643–646.

MacKinnon, A. R. How do children learn to read? Toronto: Copp Clark, 1959.

McNeil, J., and Keisler, E. Value of the oral response in beginning reading: an experimental study using programmed instruction. *British Journal of Educational Psychology*, 1963, *33*, 162–169.

McRobbie, K. A. The Toronto New Castle text-film reading experiment. *Ontario Journal of Educational Research*, 1961, *3*, 133–168.

Maney, Ethel. Literal and critical reading in science. *Journal of Experimental Education*, 1958, *27*, 57–64.

Marita, Sister M. Beginning reading achievement in three classroom organizational patterns. *The Reading Teacher*, 1966, *20*, 12–17.

Mazurkiewicz, A. ITA and TO reading achievement when methodology is controlled. *The Reading Teacher*, 1966, *19*, 606–610.

Miller, Billie. A comparison of three types of reading programs—S.R.A., individualized, and Scott-Foresman. *The Inter-Institutional Seminar in Child Development, Collected Papers*. Dearborn: Edison Institute, 1963.

Mills, R. An evaluation of techniques for teaching word recognition. *Elementary School Journal*, 1956, *56*, 221–225.

Mitchell, Blythe. The *Metropolitan Readiness Tests* as predictors of first grade achievement. *Educational and Psychological Measurement*, 1962, *22*, 765–772.

Muehl, S. The effects of letter-name knowledge on learning to read a word list in kindergarten children. *Journal of Educational Psychology*, 1960, *51*, 217–221.

Murphy, Helen. Growth in perception of word elements in three types of beginning reading instruction. *The Reading Teacher*, 1966, *79*, 585–589, 600.

Nelson, M. An experimental study of three methods of vocabulary instruction. Unpublished master's thesis, Brigham Young University, 1961.

Olson, A. Phonics and success in beginning reading. *Journal of Developmental Reading*, 1963, *6*, 256–260.

Otterman, L. M. The value of teaching prefixes and root words. *Journal of Educational Research*, 1955, *47*, 611–616.

Perry, Janet. A study of readiness and the most effective methods of word recognition with attention to visual and auditory correlations. Unpublished master's thesis, East Tennessee State College, 1960.

Powell, M., and Parsley, K. The relationships between first grade reading readiness and second grade reading achievement. *Journal of Educational Research*, 1961, *54*, 229–233.

Ramsey, W. An evaluation of a Joplin plan of grouping for reading instruction. *Journal of Educational Research*, 1962, *55*, 567–572.

Rivkind, H. The development of a group technique in teaching word recognition to determine which of four methods is most effective with individual children. Unpublished doctoral dissertation, University of Florida, 1958.

Robeck, Mildred. Effects of prolonged reading disability; a preliminary study. *Perceptual and Motor Skills*, 1964, *19*, 7–12.

Roberts, R., and Coleman, J. An investigation of the role of visual and kinesthetic factors in reading failure. *Journal of Educational Research*, 1958, *51*, 445–451.

Sachs, H. J. The reading method of acquiring vocabulary. *Journal of Educational Research*, 1943, *36*, 457–464.

Sartain, H. Do reading workbooks increase achievement? *Elementary School Journal*, 1961, *62*, 157–162.

Saxton, H. L. An investigation of the value in basal reading materials for superior readers. Publication No. 23. Storrs: University of Connecticut, 1957.

Schneyer, W. Reading achievement of first grade children taught by a linguistic approach and a basal reader approach. *The Reading Teacher*, 1966, *19*, 647–652.

Scott, Mary. A study to determine the effectiveness of teaching reading skills to second-grade children with reading difficulties. Unpublished master's thesis, University of Tennessee, 1959.

Serra, Mary. How to develop concepts and their verbal representations. *Elementary School Journal*, 1953, *53*, 275–285.

Severson, Eileen. The teaching of reading—study skills in biology. *American Biology Teacher*, 1963, *25*, 203–204.

Sheldon, W., and Lashinger, D. Effect of first grade reading instruction using basal readers, modified linguistic materials, and linguistic readers. *The Reading Teacher*, 1966, *19*, 576–579.

Shores, J. H. Reading of science for two separate purposes as perceived by sixth grade students and able adult readers. *Elementary English*, 1960, *37*, 461–468.

Sipay, E. A comparison of standardized reading scores and functional reading levels. *The Reading Teacher*, 1964, *17*, 265–268.

Sochor, Elona. Literal and critical reading in social studies. *Journal of Experimental Education*, 1958, *27*, 49–56.

Sparks, P. E., and Fay, L. C. An evaluation of two methods of teaching reading. *Elementary School Journal*, 1957, *77*, 589–596.

Spencer, Doris. Individualized first grade reading versus a basal reader program in rural communities. *The Reading Teacher*, 1966, *19*, 595–600.

Stauffer R. The effectiveness of language arts and basic reader approaches to first grade reading instruction. *The Reading Teacher*, 1966, *20*, 18–24.

Traxler, A. Improvement of vocabulary through drill. *English Journal*, 1938, *27*, 491–494.

Traxler, A., and Townsend, Agatha. Another five more years of research in reading. Bulletin No. 16. New York: Educational Records Bureau, 1946, 21.

Ungaro, D. The split-vu reading program: a follow-up. *Elementary English*, 1965, *52*, 254–257, 260.

Vanderlinde, L. Does the study of quantitative vocabulary improve problem solving? *Elementary School Journal*, 1964, *65*, 143–152.

Vernon, M. D. The perceptual process in reading. *The Reading Teacher*, 1959, *13*, 2–8.

Vite, Irene W. Individualized reading—the scoreboard on control studies. *Education*, 1961, *81*, 285–290.

Walker, F. Evaluation of three methods of teaching reading, seventh grade. *Journal of Educational Research*, 1961, *54*, 356–358.

Williams, Joan. A comparison of reading test scores and informal reading inventory scores. Unpublished doctoral dissertation, Southern Illinois University, 1963.

Wozencraft, Marian. Word meaning difficulties. *Elementary English*, 1964, *41*, 44–46.

Wyatt, Nita M. The reading achievement of first grade boys versus first grade girls. *The Reading Teacher*, 1966, *19*, 661–665.

Zingle, H., and Hohol, A. E. Predictive validity of the *Metropolitan Readiness Tests*. *Alberta Journal of Educational Research*, 1964, *10*, 99–104.

Piaget and Reading Instruction

RONALD J. RAVEN

RICHARD T. SALZER

The complex process of reading includes many types of skills and abilities, from the making of simple associations to the complex analyses involved in critical thinking and problem solving. Increasingly, in recent years, students of the field of reading instruction have come to the realization that, in order to grasp the fundamental nature of the reading act, investigators must gain an understanding of the individual's perceptual and cognitive skills. Piaget has described in some detail the ontological development of the perceptual and logical operations which the child employs in structuring his universe (Piaget, 1963). It therefore appears advisable that students of reading seek among Piaget's findings for insights and clues which may apply to their problems of theory, research, and practice.

PIAGET'S THEORY
OF INTELLECTUAL DEVELOPMENT

Piaget has convinced many psychologists and educators that it is useful to divide childhood and adolescence into major developmental epochs or

PIAGET AND READING INSTRUCTION by Ronald J. Raven and Richard T. Salzer. From *The Reading Teacher*, 24 (April 1971), pp. 630–39. Reprinted with permission of the International Reading Association and Ronald J. Raven.

periods. One stage is followed naturally by the next, and transition is marked by the presence of well-defined behaviors of the former period and the emerging characteristics of the next.

The sensori-motor period (birth to two years, approximately) Piaget identifies as one in which the infant, at a reflex level in complete self-world totality, moves to the stage where his motor activities in relation to his environment show good organization. The infant carries on countless interactions with the things about him and notions of time-space and matter evolve. Eventually he perceives relationships and formulates primitive ideas of causality. Notions that he develops through these events are based on actions and displacements, but not thought. The complex systems of behavior and changes which occur when these interact with the environment produce representations in the form of well-developed images within the child.

The preoperational period spans the years from approximately two to seven. At this stage the child does not employ logical operations in his interactions with the environment. Rather, he tends to orient his activities on the basis of appearances; he is easily misled by what he sees. The child centers on only one aspect of an object or event at a time, on a single variable when he attempts to solve a problem. The classic Piaget experiments during this stage pose the questions of what happens to the quantity of a liquid when it is poured into a container of a shape different from that which originally held it. The preoperational child, dominated by whatever aspect of the situation has seized his attention, answers in such a way as to indicate the presence of a belief that the quantity of liquid alters when vessels of varied dimensions are used. He cannot coordinate two related ideas, nor can he be expected to focus on attributes because of their relevance rather than their degree of obviousness. When confronted with twenty wooden beads, nearly all of which are red and two or three are yellow, the preoperational child, while he knows that all are wooden, states that there are more red than wood beads. Piaget's interpretation is that the youngster, overwhelmed by what he sees, cannot keep in mind that the beads are possessed of the two attributes at the same time.

It is important to realize that the operations which a child does develop during this stage, i.e., simple sorting by one variable and ordering of a small number of objects, depend on sensori-motor components or representations already developed in the preceding period. Although language may change the mode of the child's thinking, its development does not relieve the dependency of preoperational thought on basic sets of displacements, interactions, and representations which evolve from sensori-motor experience.

The concrete-operational period (7–11 years, approximately) is one in which the child's cognitive activities are much better organized than in the preceding stage. This greater organization has been achieved through the development of what Piaget terms the logical structure of groups. Groups are composed of elements and operations performed on these elements. The elements can be separate objects placed together because of some common attribute, e.g., size, shape, or color. The operations can be those of addition, subtraction, multiplication, division, setting elements into correspondence, or measurement.

The group, that is, the operations and the elements, possesses the properties of compositions, associativity, identity, and reversibility, and the child in this stage engages in corresponding mental operations. Composition enables the child to view the parts and represent them as contained in the whole or set; he puts one and one together figuratively as well as literally. Associativity allows him to arrange and rearrange elements in various ways while remaining secure in the knowledge that the whole has not been permanently affected. The identity operation permits him to maintain a perception of the original state or condition of elements so that, when change takes place, he can perform operations which will return them to that condition. Reversibility enables him to coordinate or compare the transformations made among the elements of a group. While identity allows one to make correspondences between a representation and another set of elements, reversibility permits a comparison of two groups that change in time or change within a group over a period of time.

These four operations enable the child to make multiple classifications, to realize that an object has many properties simultaneously and that any of these can be of greater significance than others at some point. Hierarchical classification, the formation of increasingly inclusive groupings, also becomes possible. Seriation, the placing of elements in order according to one or more criteria, is another ability that the individual comes to possess during this period.

The formal-operational period (beginning at age 11 or 12, approximately) is characterized by the ability of the youngster to control formal logic. While the concrete-operational child reasons only from directly observed data, his older counterpart begins to deal with propositions and hypotheses apart from direct experience.

Four modes of logic enable the child to operate at this level: conjunction, disjunction, negation, and implication. The frequently recurring association of two properties expressed as "this rod is steel and bends" refers to a conjunction. Conjunctions allow the individual to say, "It is this element (x) and that element (y) that exist together" or "cause something."

The disjunction combination presents alternatives. The student can say that he has short rods that bend or short rods that do not bend. There are two possibilities, bend and not bend, and only one of these can occur in the same situation. Thus, the disjunctive operation allows the student to say, "It's got to be this element (x) or this element (y)."

The negation operation states that two variables or attributes do not exist together or are not responsible for an effect. Neither mass alone nor volume alone determines whether an object floats or sinks. In negation, the student states, "Neither element (x) nor element (y) causes this," or, "These two elements (x and y) do not go together."

The last of these four combinations, implication, states that every time one variable appears a particular result occurs. When the string is lengthened, the frequency of the pendulum increases. In an implication operation, "When this element (x) occurs, then this element (y) will be true or occur."

The student in the formal-logic stage can combine these operations in various ways to produce hypotheses and deductive statements. He can determine the relevancy of variables and how these affect one another to produce a specific outcome.

RELATIONSHIP OF PIAGET'S STAGES TO READING INSTRUCTION

Sensori-Motor Period

While it is fashionable in some quarters to consider the possibility of offering infants instruction in reading, an examination of Piaget's theory leads to the conclusion that other activities are much more important for optimal development. Manipulative experience with a wide range of types of objects and materials during this stage appears most important for the development of images and cognitive growth. There is little reason to believe that any precisely described set of experiences should be considered crucial. The child's perceptual and intellectual abilities will develop adequately given almost any collection of artifacts that he and others may manipulate.

Preoperational Period

Piaget divides this period into two stages, preconceptual (age two to four) and intuitive (four to seven). In the preconceptual phase rapid growth of language takes place for most youngsters, and it seems logical to some that reading instruction should accompany this development. This evolving language is based in the motor manipulation of the previous period. The child has, at most, mental images of objects and physical operations to which verbal labels have become attached. These labels are not abstractions in the usual sense of that term, and they certainly may not validly be attached to other labels. Preoperational thought develops through sensori-motor activities—not through language. For the preconceptual-phase child, language cannot be something apart from objects and experience. The name of the thing inheres in the thing itself, the arbitrary nature of language having yet made no impression on the child. A chair must be called "chair"; "rocker" is something else entirely.

Thought processes in the two-to-four-year-old are not sufficiently stabilized to permit him to profit much from practice on conceptual skills of any kind. Every event is new. The child thinks neither deductively nor inductively but "transductively," from point to point, making little or no differentiation concerning the degree of relevance between pairs of observations. Everything is related to about the same degree, which literally means that nothing is specifically related.

Obviously, there is little encouragement here for those who advocate systematic programs of "nursery school reading." The child's thought processes, according to Piaget, simply do not appear sufficiently stable to guarantee anything but frustration for those who would attempt didactic instruction of any kind. In the specific case of reading, there is no basis in Piaget's work for believing that the child from two to four has any interest in written language, except as it may constitute something interesting in the environment that merits whatever attention the individual youngster may desire to give it. As Almy (1967) has pointed out, the important implications for reading instruction of Piaget's work at the preoperational level relate to the necessity of providing many and varied concrete experiences, the sensory and motor activities out of which concepts and complex thinking may develop. Such opportunities will likely influence ultimate reading achievement to a greater extent than specific perceptual discrimination training now offered in many nursery schools and kindergartens.

It is, of course, during the intuitive phase (age four to seven) that most children experience initial reading instruction. The cognitive benchmark is conservation of substance, the dawning realization that substantial change may take place in a system without the alteration of fundamental characteristics. Development of the over-all understanding of conservation of substance at approximately age seven marks, for Piaget, a major change in style of thinking on the part of the child, as he moves from near-total dependence on perception to a greater reliance on thought to check what he sees. It may be that this ability represents what most reading-instruction programs require and that its appearance constitutes "readiness." Almy, *et al.* (1966) have provided evidence of a rather high correlation between conservation ability and beginning-reading achievement.

Of the abilities which contribute to the development of conservation, reversibility and de-centration appear to have substantial significance for initial reading instruction. Reversibility permits the child to conserve by thinking, in the case of liquid, "If the juice is poured back into the first glass, it will come up to the top again." He solves many other problems by "undoing" some operation and coming back to the starting point. This is a mental activity which the preoperational child cannot perform, and the inference might be drawn that he should not be expected to succeed in decoding-emphasis reading programs which require him to convert graphemes to phonemes and then validate his transformations. Almy (1967) comments that the child who has not achieved reversibility "may lack the stability of perception necessary for formal reading instruction."

The characteristic of "centration" in the preoperational child's thinking refers to his inability to consider more than one aspect of a situation at a time; he is so impressed with the height of a column of water that he fails to notice how narrow it is. The beginning reading programs in most wide use continually require the child to deal with words in two almost entirely unrelated ways, however—as line puzzles to be remembered and deciphered and as signifiers of meaning. Piaget's theory leads one to believe that the child under seven cannot ordinarily be expected to engage in such mental gymnastics with facility.

The preoperational, non-conserving child cannot handle altered circumstances very well; a situation somewhat transformed is an entirely new situation. He should not be expected to view a wide variety of events and then identify their common characteristic. In presenting the young reader with upper- and lower-case letters, different type faces, manuscript and cursive writing, variations in the rendering of particular alphabet letters, and all of these in many different combinations and contexts, those responsible for initial reading instruction constantly expose children to transformed situations and expect them to isolate the single common attribute which is the key to solving the problem.

Neither can the preoperational child, since he lacks all but rudimentary classification skills, successfully engage in rule-learning and application. As Downing (1969) has noted, Piaget contends that the individual must create his own rules, assimilating new experiences into his own system and periodically accommodating by revising the system when he sees that it no longer serves adequately. The preoperational child should not be expected to pursue a reading program based on rules of grapheme-phoneme relationships. He may successfully memorize the verbal formulas but will have difficulty classifying situations to which they are appropriate.

Piaget's theory supports what might be thought of as an activity curriculum, a nursery school experience which emphasizes interaction with materials and exploration of the environment; a kindergarten in which reading and books are simply part of the general environment; and a beginning-reading program growing out of the progression through motor and perceptual functioning to symbolic activity. It should also be noted that the preoperational-period child relishes practice on evolving skills. The infant will, over and over again, put the beads into the plastic bottle and empty them out again. The somewhat older child works the same picture puzzle many times in succession. Elkind and Weiss (1967) found children in the beginning-reading period consciously practicing left-to-right progression, even in situations unrelated to reading. Evidently, there is nothing negative with respect to repetition and drill for the child of this age; he seems to enjoy it and actually imposes such activity on himself. To criticize certain methodology or materials for reading because they appear dull or repetitious to adults or to insist that practice should be de-emphasized out of a concern for the child's welfare is, in both cases, to ignore the possible validity of a Piagetian interpretation.

Piaget also emphasizes that cognitive activity should be carried out in social situations where children are working together, sharing information, and learning to take into account another person's point of view. The implications for classroom practice appear self-evident.

Concrete-Operational Period

Piagetian theory holds that by seven years of age the child has reached a point where he has the ability to "reason," but he reasons adequately only about direct experiences, not abstractions. One difficulty at this stage is that the child can think about and discuss matters much in advance of any content which he finds it possible to read for himself. Furth (1970) has argued that acceptance of Piaget's position should lead school people to postpone formal reading instruction for most of the elementary-school years. He stresses that the traditional emphasis on reading and writing in the early grades takes so much time and energy that over-all intellectual development may be significantly interrupted. When emphasis is placed on learning to read, the child finds himself in a position of constantly dealing with content at least five years below what his intellect could handle.

But the concrete-operational child does have the ability to study various aspects of language, including reading. Because he possesses the operations of identity and reversibility the student can view a system, make transformations upon it and, then, since he retains the original perception, return it to its previous condition. He can hold a basic idea in mind and manipulate and expand it in various ways. Specifically, rearrangement of language elements—words, phrases, sentences—becomes possible. The child can determine, through a comparison of the original with subsequent changes, whether or not various modifications of word order or substitutions have altered meaning. The concrete-operational child can make seriations and multiple and hierarchical classifications of objects and concepts close to his own life experience. He knows that objects and events have many attributes and that a word may have different meanings in various contexts. He can group words by their linguistic function and place sentence elements in various relationships with one another.

It is reasonable to infer from the findings of Piaget that reading activities during the concrete-operational period, in terms of content, can vary widely, but it should not be expected that students will reason well about what they have read unless it relates rather closely to direct experience. In any reading program organized along Piagetian lines, reading activities during the concrete-operational period would provide increased emphasis on developing logical operations by including opportunities to combine sentence and word elements, associate elements in different ways, establish correspondence or identity among elements, and would encourage students to transform the order of elements and observe the differences produced.

Formal-Operational Period

Many collections of reading exercises published for use in secondary schools include items which provide practice in the advanced skills of critical and creative reading and problem solving. Piaget's contribution would involve sequencing of materials to provide a correspondence between the logical operations embedded in the content and the reader's likely manner of structuring knowledge or solving a problem. For the attainment by the student of maximum comprehension of all components of a reading unit, the structure of the material should follow the pattern which Piaget has found to characterize the unfolding of the logical operations by means of which the individual manipulates or processes information. The student's pattern of processing information as he attempts to deal with novel and complex situations occurs in the following sequence: (1) classification and seriation; (2) correspondence; (3) logical multiplication; (4) tautologies; (5) implications; and (6) ratio and proportional thinking.

The student first attempts to group variables and attributes in classes and to order the elements within each class by some attribute such as weight or size. After he has produced the seriation of a possibly relevant variable and the seriation of the effect, the student makes correspondences between elements of each group of seriations. For example, he may seriate the length of a pendulum string and the period of a pendulum. He noted that a long period is associated with a long string and a short period with a short string. After making this correspondence, the student who wants to know if a change in length will bring about a change in period performs a logical multiplication. In the initial stage of logical multiplication, the individual knows that he can change the length or not change it, and observe a change in the period or not. What is called for is a two-by-two table with these four elements in the margins:

	Period Change	No Period Change
Length Change	A	B
No Length Change	C	D

After multiplying the row margin element by the column margin elements, the student notes that the products of the logical multiplication in cells A and D are found in reality. He observes a temporal association between length change and period change and between no length change and no period change. In the case of the situations represented by cells B and C, he finds no temporal association between length change and period change. The process of logical multiplication allows the student at the concrete stage to determine if an association exists between a variable and an effect.

In the stage of formal operations logical multiplication is not necessary to isolate the effect of a variable. The individual comes immediately to the four possible outcomes: (1) variable change with effect change; (2) no variable change with effect change; (3) variable change with no effect change; (4) no variable change with no effect change. The observer is simultaneously aware of all possibilities, and the operation which enables him to do this is termed a tautology.

The operations thus far described enable the individual only to determine relevant and irrelevant variables. When he deals with more variables and ones which interact among themselves, additional operations are necessary: negation, in which a change is counteracted by returning the influential variable to its original condition; reciprocity, in which a different variable is manipulated to compensate for the change; the formulation of ratios which summarize the nature of reciprocal relationships between variables; and proportional thinking in which he determines the relationships between ratios. These descriptions of the sequence in appearance of logical operations can be used to structure content in a manner which enables the student to participate actively in the process of determining the effects of variables and the relationships among thase variables and effects. If the sequence is followed, all content needed to understand a given problem will be included. Merely telling the youngster, as most textbook presentations do, that length makes a difference in the period of a pendulum does not suffice; too much information remains to be acquired in some other way, probably outside of class.

The statement to a student that an association exists between a variable and an outcome may lead to correct answers in recitation or on examinations but it fails to provide information for the handling of more complex and novel situations. Inhelder and Piaget (1958) describe the sequence by which content might be so structured that various logical relationships become available to the student for analysis. In following such a pattern a learner can build a total schema which he understands very well, rather than simply learn to repeat verbal formulas. The type of associative verbal chaining found in most textbooks does not lead the learner to analyze logical relationships and thus attain a good level of comprehension.

THE IMPORTANCE OF SEQUENCE

What can be learned from Piaget has more to do with the developmental unfolding of mental operations than the age-level descriptions of cognitive skills. Whether an individual is forty years old or eleven, he still follows Piaget's sequence of logical operations when he confronts novel and complex problems or situations. He will, at these times, exhibit some preoperational-stage thinking, then go through a concrete stage, and finally progress to formal operations. Some individuals will move more rapidly than others through these stages and the progression seems less apparent in some, but it is there, nonetheless. When readers deal with content that is unfamiliar to them, it may be anticipated that their understanding will go not much deeper than the making of a few verbal associations unless steps are taken by the teacher to lead them through a sequence from unorganized focussing on first one element and then another to comprehensive analysis of all relevant relationships.

References

Almy, Millie. Young children's thinking and the teaching of reading. In Frost (Ed.) *Issues and innovations in the teaching of reading.* New York: Scott, Foresman, 1967. Pp. 89–93.

Almy, Millie, Chittenden, E., and Miller, Paula. *Young children's thinking.* New York: Teachers College Press, 1966. Pp. 139–140.

Downing, J. How children think about reading. Distinguished Leader's Address, Annual Convention of the International Reading Association, Kansas City, May, 1969.

Elkind, D., and Weiss, J. Studies in perceptual development III: perceptual exploration. *Child Development,* 1967, *38,* 553–561.

Furth, H. G. *Piaget for teachers.* New York: Prentice-Hall, 1970. P. 4.

Inhelder, Barbel, and Piaget, J. *The growth of logical thinking from childhood to adolescence.* New York: Basic Books, 1953.

Piaget, J. *The psychology of intelligence.* New York: Littlefield, Adams, 1963.

Reading: A Psycholinguistic Guessing Game

KENNETH S. GOODMAN

As scientific understanding develops in any field of study, preexisting, naive, common sense notions must give way. Such outmoded beliefs clutter the literature dealing with the process of reading. They interfere with the application of modern scientific concepts of language and thought to research in reading. They confuse the attempts at application of such concepts to solution of problems involved in the teaching and learning of reading. The very fact that such naive beliefs are based on common sense explains their

READING: A PSYCHOLINGUISTIC GUESSING GAME by Kenneth S. Goodman. From *Journal of the Reading Specialist,* 4 (May 1967), pp. 126–35. Copyright © 1967 by the College Reading Association. Reprinted by permission of the College Reading Association and Kenneth S. Goodman.

persistent and recurrent nature. To the casual and unsophisticated observer they appear to explain, even predict, a net of phenomena in reading. This paper will deal with one such key misconception and offer a more viable scientific alternative.

Simply stated, the common sense notion I seek here to refute is this: "Reading is a precise process. It involves exact, detailed, sequential perception and identification of letters, words, spelling patterns and larger language units."

In phonic-centered approaches to reading, the preoccupation is with precise letter identification. In word-centered approaches, the focus is on word identification. Known words are sight words, precisely named in any setting.

This is not to say that those who have worked diligently in the field of reading are not aware that reading is more than precise, sequential identification. But, the common sense notion, though not adequate, continues to permeate thinking about reading.

Spache presents a word version of this common sense view: "Thus, in its simplest form, reading may be considered a series of word perceptions."[1]

The teacher's manual of the Lippincott *Basic Reading* incorporates a letter-by-letter variant in the justification of its reading approach: "In short, following this program the child learns from the beginning to see words exactly as the most skillful readers see them . . . as whole images of complete words with all their letters."[2]

In place of this misconception, I offer this: "Reading is a selective process. It involves partial use of available minimal language cues selected from perceptual input on the basis of the reader's expectation. As this partial information is processed, tentative decisions are made, to be confirmed, rejected or refined as reading progresses."

More simply stated, reading is a psycholinguistic guessing game. It involves an interaction between thought and language. Efficient reading does not result from precise perception and identification of all elements, but from skill in selecting the fewest, most productive cues necessary to produce guesses which are right the first time. The ability to anticipate that which has not been seen, of course, is vital in reading, just as the ability to anticipate what has not yet been heard is vital in listening.

Consider this actual sample of a relatively proficient child reading orally. The reader is a fourth grade child reading the opening paragraphs of a story from a sixth grade basal reader.[3]

"If it bothers you to think of it as baby sitting," my father said, "then

don't think of it as baby sitting. Think of it as homework. Part of your

education. You just happen to do your studying in the room where ~~your~~ (the) baby brother is sleeping, that's all." He helped my mother with her coat, and then

they were gone.

So education it was! I opened the dictionary and picked out a word
that sounded good. "Philosophical!" I yelled. Might as well study word
meanings first. "Philosophical: showing calmness and courage in the face of
ill fortune." I mean I really yelled it. I guess a fellow has to work off steam

once in a while.

[Reader miscues marked above the text: "hoped . . opened a" above "I opened the"; "s" above "was!"; "Phil/ōso/phi/cal he" and "what" above "Philosophical"; "it means" above; "Phizo . . Phizo/sophicly" above; "his" above "the"; "fort . . future . . futshion" above "fortune"]

He has not seen the story before. It is, by intention, slightly difficult
for him. The insights into his reading process come primarily from his errors,
which I choose to call miscues in order to avoid value implications. His
expected responses mask the process of their attainment, but his unexpected
responses have been achieved through the same process, albeit less successfully
applied. The ways that they deviate from the expected reveal this process.

In the common sense view that I am rejecting, all deviations must be
treated as errors. Furthermore, it must be assumed in this view that an error
either indicates that the reader does not know something or that he has been
"careless" in the application of his knowledge.

For example, his substitution of *the* for *your* in the first paragraph of
the sample must mean that he was careless, since he has already read *your*
and *the* correctly in the very same sentence. The implication is that we must
teach him to be more careful, that is, to be more precise in identifying each
word or letter.

But now let's take the view that I have suggested. What sort of information could have led to tentatively deciding on *the* in this situation and not
rejecting or refining this decision? There obviously is no graphic relationship
between *your* and *the*. It may be, of course, that he picked up *the* in the
periphery of his visual field. But, there is an important non-graphic relationship between *the* and *your*. They both have the same grammatical function:
they are, in my terminology, noun markers. Either the reader anticipated a
noun marker and supplied one, paying no attention to graphic information,
or he used *your* as a grammatical signal, ignoring its graphic shape. Since
the tentative choice *the* disturbs neither the meaning nor the grammar of
the passage, there is no reason to reject and correct it. This explanation
appears to be confirmed by two similar miscues in the next paragraph. *A*
and *his* are both substituted for *the*. Neither are corrected. Though the substitution of *his* changes the meaning, the peculiar idiom used in this dictionary definition, "in the face of ill fortune," apparently has little meaning to
this reader anyway.

The conclusion this time is that he is using noun markers for grammatical, as well as graphic, information in reaching his tentative conclusions. All together in reading this ten-page story, he made twenty noun marker substitutions, six omissions and two insertions. He corrected four of his substitutions and one omission. Similar miscues involved other function words (auxiliary verbs and prepositions, for example). These miscues appear to have little effect on the meaning of what he is reading. In spite of their frequency, their elimination would not substantially improve the child's reading. Insistence on more precise identification of each word might cause this reader to stop seeking grammatical information and use only graphic information.

The substitution of *hoped* for *opened* could again be regarded as careless or imprecise identification of letters. But, if we dig beyond this common sense explanation, we find (a) both are verbs, and (b) the words have *key* graphic similarities. Further, there may be evidence of the reader's bilingual French-Canadian background here, as there is in subsequent miscues (*harms* for *arms, shuckled* for *chuckled, shoose* for *choose, shair* for *chair*). The correction of this miscue may involve an immediate rejection of the tentative choice made on the basis of a review of the graphic stimulus, or it may result from recognizing that it cannot lead to the rest of the sentence, i.e. "I hoped a dictionary . . ." does not make sense. (It isn't decodable.) In any case, the reader has demonstrated the process by which he constantly tests his guesses, or tentative choices, if you prefer.

Sounds is substituted for *sounded,* but the two differ in ending only. Common sense might lead to the conclusion that the child does not pay attention to word endings, slurs the ends, or is otherwise careless. But, there is no consistent similar occurrence in other word endings. Actually, the child has substituted one inflectional ending for another. In doing so he has revealed (a) his ability to separate base and inflectional suffix, and (b) his use of inflectional endings as grammatical signals or markers. Again he has not corrected a miscue that is both grammatically and semantically acceptable.

He for *I* is a pronoun-for-pronoun substitution that results in a meaning change, though the antecedent is a bit vague, and the inconsistency of meaning is not easily apparent.

When we examine what the reader did with the sentence "Might as well study word meanings first," we see how poorly the model of precise sequential identification fits the reading process. Essentially this reader has decoded graphic input for meaning and then encoded meaning in oral output with transformed grammar and changed vocabulary, but with the basic meaning retained. Perhaps as he encoded his output, he was already working at the list word which followed, but the tentative choice was good enough and was not corrected.

There are two examples, in this sample, of the reader working at unknown words. He reveals a fair picture of his strategies and abilities in these miscues, though in neither is he successful. In his several attempts at *philosophical,* his first attempt comes closest. Incidentally, he reveals here that he can use a phonic letter-sound strategy when he wants to. In subsequent attempts he moves away from this sounding out, trying other possibilities, as if trying to find something which at least will sound familiar. Interestingly, here he has a definition of sorts, but no context to work with. *Philosophical* occurs as a list word a number of times in the story. In subsequent attempts, the child tried *physica, physicacol, physical, philosoviqul, phizzlesoviqul, phizzo soriqul, philazophgul.* He appears to move in concentric circles around the phonic information he has, trying deviations and variations. His three unsuccessful attempts at *fortune* illustrate this same process. Both words are apparently unknown to the reader. He can never really identify a word he has not heard. In such cases, unless the context or contexts sufficiently delimit the word's meaning, the reader is not able to get meaning from the words. In some instances, of course, the reader may form a fairly accurate definition of the word, even if he never recognizes it (that is, matches it with a known oral equivalent) or pronounces it correctly. This reader achieved that with the word *typical,* which occurred many times in the story. Throughout his reading he said *topical.* When he finished reading, a check of his comprehension indicated that he knew quite well the meaning of the word. This phenomenon is familiar to any adult reader. Each of us has many well-defined words in our reading vocabulary which we either mispronounce or do not use orally.

I've used the example of this youngster's oral reading not because what he's done is typical of all readers or even of readers his age, but because his miscues suggest how he carries out the psycholinguistic guessing game in reading. The miscues of other readers show similarities and differences, but all point to a selective, tentative, anticipatory process quite unlike the process of precise, sequential identification commonly assumed.

Let's take a closer look now at the components the reader manipulates in this psycholinguistic guessing game.

At any point in time, of course, the reader has available to him and brings to his reading the sum total of his experience and his language and thought development. This self-evident fact needs to be stated because what appears to be intuitive in any guessing is actually the result of knowledge so well learned that the process of its application requires little conscious effort. Most language use has reached this automatic, intuitive level. Most of us are quite unable to describe the use we make of grammar in encoding and decoding speech, yet all language users demonstrate a high degree of skill and mastery over the syntax of language, even in our humblest and most informal uses of speech.

Chomsky[4] has suggested a model of sentence production by speakers of a language (Figure 1) and a model structure of the listener's sentence interpretation (Figure 2).

Thus, in Chomsky's view, encoding of speech reaches a more or less precise level and the signal which results is fully formed. But in decoding, a sampling process aims at approximating the message, and any matching or coded signal which results is a kind of by-product.

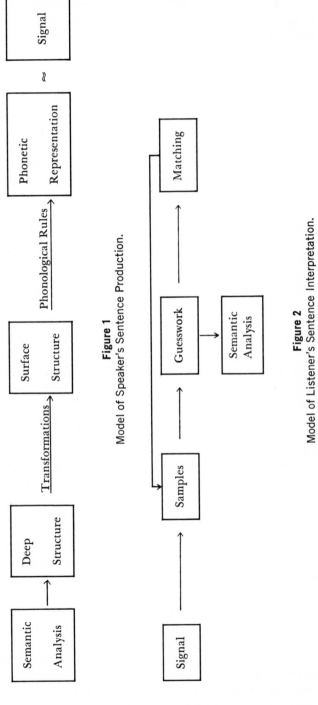

Figure 1
Model of Speaker's Sentence Production.

Figure 2
Model of Listener's Sentence Interpretation.

In oral reading, the reader must perform two tasks at the same time. He must produce an oral language equivalent of the graphic input which is the *signal* in reading, and he must also reconstruct the meaning of what he is reading. The matching in Chomsky's interpretation model is largely what I prefer to call a recoding operation. The reader recodes the coded graphic input as phonological or oral output. Meaning is not normally involved to any extent. This recoding can even be learned by someone who doesn't speak the language at all, for example, the bar mitzvah boy may learn to recode Hebrew script as chanted oral Hebrew with no ability to understand what he is chanting; but when the reader engages in semantic analysis to reconstruct the meaning of the writer, only then he is decoding.

In oral reading there are three logical possible arrangements of these two operations. The reader may recode graphic input as oral language and then decode it. He may recode and decode simultaneously. Or, he may decode first and then encode the meaning as oral output.

On the basis of my research to date, it appears that readers who have achieved some degree of proficiency decode directly from the graphic stimulus in a process similar to Chomsky's sampling model and then encode from the deep structure, as illustrated in Chomsky's model of sentence production. Their oral output is not directly related to the graphic stimulus and may involve transformation in vocabulary and syntax, even if meaning is retained. If their comprehension is inaccurate, they will encode this changed or complete meaning as oral output.

The common misconception is that graphic input is precisely and sequentially recoded as phonological input and then decoded bit by bit. Meaning is cumulative, built up a piece at a time, in this view. This view appears to be supported by studies of visual perception that indicate that only a very narrow span of print on either side of the point of fixation is in sharp focus at any time. We might dub this the "end of the nose" view, since it assumes that input in reading is that which lies in sharp focus in a straight line from the end of the nose. Speed and efficiency are assumed to come from widening the span taken in on either side of the nose, moving the nose more rapidly or avoiding backward movements of the eyes and nose, which of course must cut down on efficiency.

This view cannot possibly explain the speed with which the average adult reads, or a myriad of other constantly occurring phenomena in reading. How can it explain, for example, a highly proficient adult reader reading and rereading a paper he's written and always missing the same misprints. Or how can it explain our fourth grader seeing "Study word meanings first," and saying, "Study what it means"?

No, the "end of the nose" view of reading will not work. The reader is not confined to information he receives from a half inch of print in clear focus. Studies, in fact, indicate that children with severe visual handicaps are able to learn to read as well as normal children. Readers utilize not one, but three kinds of information simultaneously. Certainly without graphic input there would be no reading. But, the reader uses syntactic and semantic information as well. He predicts and anticipates on the basis of this information, sampling from the print just enough to confirm his guess of what's coming, to cue more semantic and syntactic information. Redundancy and sequential constraints in language, which the reader reacts to, make this prediction possible. Even the blurred and shadowy images he picks up in the peripheral area of his visual field may help to trigger or confirm guesses.

Skill in reading involves not greater precision, but more accurate first guesses based on better sampling techniques, greater control over language structure, broadened experiences, and increased conceptual development. As the child develops reading skill and speed, he uses increasingly fewer graphic cues. Silent reading can then become a more rapid and efficient process than oral reading, for two reasons: (1) the reader's attention is not divided between decoding and recoding or encoding as oral output, and (2) his speed is not restricted to the speed of speech production. Reading becomes a more efficient and rapid process than listening, in fact, since listening is normally limited to the speed of the speaker. (Recent studies with speeded up electronic recordings where distortion of pitch is avoided have demonstrated that listening can be made more rapid without impairing comprehension, too.)

Though the beginning reader obviously needs more graphic information in decoding and, therefore, needs to be more precise than skilled readers, evidence from a study of first graders by Yetta Goodman[5] indicates that they begin to sample and draw on syntactic and semantic information almost from the beginning, if they are reading material which is fully formed language.

RIDE IN[6]

STOP AND GO[7]

Jimmy said, "Come here, Sue,

Look at my ~~toy~~ tr̶a̶i̶n̶.

See it go.

Look at my little ~~train~~ (toy) go."

Sue said, "Stop the ~~train~~ (toy).

Stop it ~~here~~ (come), Jimmy."

Jimmy said, "I can stop the ~~train~~ (toy).

See the ~~train~~ (toy) stop."

Sue said, "Look at my ~~toy~~ (too).

It is in the ~~train~~ (toy).

See my little red ~~toy~~ (too), Jimmy.

It can ride in the ~~train~~ (toy)."

Jimmy said, "See the ~~train~~ (toy) go.

Look at it go."

~~Sue~~ (Suzie) said, "Look at my little red ~~toy~~ (too).

See it go for a ~~train~~ (toy) ride."

~~Sue~~ (Suzie) said, "My little red ~~toy~~ (too)!

Jimmy, my ~~toy~~ (too) is (said) not here.

It is not in the ~~train~~ (toy).

Stop the ~~train~~ (toy), Jimmy.

Stop it and look for my ~~toy~~ (too)."

Here are excerpts from two primer stories as they were read by a first grade child at the same session. Ostensibly (and by intent of the authors) the first, from a second pre-primer, should be much easier than the second, from a third pre-primer. Yet she encountered problems to the point of total confusion with the first and was able to handle exactly the same elements in the second.

Note, for example, the confusion of *come* and *here* in "Ride In." This represents a habitual association in evidence in early reading of this child. Both *come* and *here* as graphic shapes are likely to be identified as *come* or *here*. In "Stop and Go" the difficulty does not occur when the words are sequential. She also substitutes *can* for *and* in the first story, but encounters no problem with either later. *Stop* stops her completely in "Ride In," a difficulty that she doesn't seem to know she has when she reads "Stop and Go" a few minutes later. Similarly, she calls [ride] *run* in the first story, but gets it right in the latter one.

Though there are miscues in the second story, there is a very important difference. In the first story she seems to be playing a game of name the word. She is recoding graphic shapes as phonological ones. Each word is apparently a separate problem. But in "Stop and Go" what she says, including her miscues, in almost all instances makes sense and is grammatically acceptable. Notice that as Sue becomes better known she becomes *Suzie* to our now confident reader.

A semantic association exists between *train* and *toy*. Though the child makes the same substitution many times, nothing causes her to reject her guess. It works well each time. Having called [train] *toy,* she calls [toy] *too* (actually it's an airplane in the pictures), not once, but consistently throughout the story. That doesn't seem to make sense. That's what the researcher thought too, until the child spoke of a "little red *too*" later in retelling the story. "What's a 'little red too'?" asked the researcher. "An airplane," she replied calmly. So a train is *toy* and a plane is a *too*. Why not? But, notice that when *toy* occurred preceding *train,* she could attempt nothing for *train*. There appears to be a problem for many first graders when nouns are used as adjectives.

Common sense says go back and drill her on *come, here, can, stop, ride, and;* don't let her go to the next book which she is obviously not ready to read.

But the more advanced story, with its stronger syntax, more fully formed language and increased load of meaning makes it possible for the child to use her graphic cues more effectively and supplement them with semantic and syntactic information. Teaching for more precise perception with lists and phonics charts may actually impede this child's reading development. Please notice, before we leave the passage, the effect of immediate experience on anticipation. Every one of the paragraphs in the sample starts with "Jimmy said" or "Sue said." When the reader comes to a line starting *Jimmy,* she assumes that it will be followed by *said,* and it is not until her expectation is contradicted by subsequent input that she regresses and corrects her miscue.

Since children must learn to play the psycholinguistic guessing game as they develop reading ability, effective methods and materials, used by teachers who understand the rules of the game, must help them to select the most productive cues, to use their knowledge of language structure, to draw on their experiences and concepts. They must be helped to discriminate between more and less useful available information. Fortunately, this parallels the processes they have used in developing the ability to comprehend spoken language.

George Miller has suggested that ". . . psycholinguists should try to formulate performance models that will incorporate . . . hypothetical information storage and information processing components that can simulate the actual behavior of language users."[8]

I'd like to present now my model of this psycholinguistic guessing game we call reading English. Please understand that the steps do not necessarily take place in the sequential or stretched out form they are shown here.

1. The reader scans along a line of print from left to right and down the page, line by line.
2. He fixes at a point to permit eye focus. Some print will be central and in focus, some will be peripheral; perhaps his perceptual field is a flattened circle.
3. Now begins the selection process. He picks up graphic cues, guided by constraints set up through prior choices, his language knowledge, his cognitive styles, and strategies he has learned.
4. He forms a perceptual image using these cues and his anticipated cues. This image then is partly what he sees and partly what he expected to see.
5. Now he searches his memory for related syntactic, semantic, and phonological cues. This may lead to selection of more graphic cues and to reforming the perceptual image.
6. At this point, he makes a guess or tentative choice consistent with graphic cues. Semantic analysis leads to partial decoding as far as possible. This meaning is stored in short-term memory as he proceeds.
7. If no guess is possible, he checks the recalled perceptual input and tries again. If a guess is still not possible, he takes another look at the text to gather more graphic cues.
8. If he can make a decodable choice, he tests it for semantic and grammatical acceptability in the context developed by prior choices and decoding.
9. If the tentative choice is not acceptable semantically or syntactically, then he regresses, scanning from right to left along the line and up the page to locate a point of semantic or syntactic inconsistency. When such a point is found, he starts over at that point. If no inconsistency can be identified, he reads on seeking some cue which will make it possible to reconcile the anomalous situation.
10. If the choice is acceptable, decoding is extended, meaning is assimilated with prior meaning, and prior meaning is accommodated, if necessary. Expectations are formed about input and meaning that lies ahead.
11. Then the cycle continues.

Throughout the process there is constant use of long- and short-term memory.

I offer no apologies for the complexity of this model. Its faults lie, not in its complexity, but in the fact that it is not yet complex enough to fully account for the complex phenomena in the actual behavior of readers. But such is man's destiny in his quest for knowledge. Simplistic folklore must give way to complexity as we come to know.

References

1. George Spache, *Reading in the Elementary School* (Boston: Allyn and Bacon, 1964), p. 12.
2. Glenn McCracken and Charles C. Walcutt, *Basic Reading,* Teacher's Edition for the Pre-Primer and Primer (Philadelphia: B. Lippincott, 1963), p. vii.
3. William D. Hayes, "My Brother is a Genius," in *Adventures Now and Then*, Book 6,

Betts Basic Readers, 3rd ed., Emmett A. Betts and Carolyn M. Welch (New York: American Book Company, 1963), p. 246.
4. Noam Chomsky, lecture at Project Literacy, Cornell University, June 18, 1965.
5. Yetta M. Goodman, College of Education, Wayne State University, Doctoral Study of development of reading in first grade children, in progress.
6. "Ride In," *Time to Play*, Second Pre-Primer, Betts Basic Readers, 3rd ed., Language Arts Series (New York: American Book Company, 1963).
7. Emmett A. Betts and Carolyn M. Welch, "Stop and Go," *All in a Day*, Third Pre-Primer, Betts Basic Readers (New York: American Book Company, 1963).
8. George A. Miller, "Some Preliminaries to Psycholinguistics," *American Psychologist*, Vol. 20 (1965), p. 18.

Nonstandard Language
and Reading

RICHARD L. VENEZKY

INTRODUCTION

The child whose language habits differ markedly from the socially acceptable *patois* of the school system faces both overt and covert discrimination in education. On the inter-personal level he is an odd duckling—his kinder-peers, conservative and conformist (as all children tend to be) view *different* as *inferior,* with no exceptions given to what adults might class as prestige forms of speech; his teacher, as well meaning as she might be, may not comprehend all that he says, and worse, will have difficulty viewing nonstandard as anything except substandard. On the less personal level, the situation is potentially more harmful; the educational process and especially the reading programs are not equipped for him. The articulation and discrimination screening, the readiness tests, the reading materials, and the sacred Teacher's Handbook, with rare exceptions, are designed solely for producers of WASP-speech. For the English of the American Indian, the Mexican-American, the urban Negro, the Appalachian, and others, there is no standard guide which distinguishes normal articulation from aberrant articulation, that lists expected vocabulary or age-graded syntactic development, or that suggests how reading is to be taught where dialect-based problems exist. That such children do not fit comfortably into the existing school

NONSTANDARD LANGUAGE AND READING by Richard L. Venezky. From *Elementary English*, 47 (March 1970), pp. 334–45. Reprinted by permission.

systems has been observed for many years, but what to do about the situation is still in doubt. The purpose of this article is to discuss approaches for teaching reading to speakers of nonstandard English, with special emphasis on the initial reading process and the language or dialect of the reading materials. Relevant literature will be discussed, but these reviews will be, by desire and necessity, selective. Where more extensive reviews exist, they will be cited in the bibliography.

CLARIFICATION OF THE PROBLEM

Available Choices

The problem is, to be more specific, "What language or dialect should a child first encounter in the materials used for teaching reading: his own or some standard form?" Each of these choices carries far-reaching implications. For the nonstandard avenue, it is assumed that *all* materials—testing, readiness, reading—will be adapted to the speech habits of the child and that at some point *after* he acquires literacy in his own form of language he will learn to speak and to read the standard form. This last proviso, an accepted expectation where American Indian languages or Spanish are involved, meets occasional opposition when English dialects are involved. From the standpoint of achieving educational and economic opportunity—which are primary concerns of the public educational system—it is nevertheless an inescapable conclusion.

For the standard language approach, it is required, but often not stated, that the child learn to speak the standard language before he attempts to read it. (Whether or not he ever encounters reading in his native language or dialect is a matter totally divorced from considerations of initial reading and will not be discussed here.) For children who do not speak English, it is both foolish and disastrous to attempt to teach reading in standard English. The result, as verified by the Texas school system where this was the practice until recently, is a first-grade failure rate (for pupils with no pre-first grade experiences) approaching 80 percent.[1] For speakers of nonstandard English dialects, training in the standard language is also required before reading can be attacked. Nevertheless, the amount of such training is considerably less than what is required for non-English speakers.

Types of Differences

Within the bounds just established, two types of deviation from standard English should be distinguished: language differences and dialect differences.

[1] This figure is stated by Anne Stemmler, "An Experimental Approach to the Teaching of Oral Language and Reading," *Harvard Educational Review*, 36 (Winter, 1966), 42–59.

The first is a clear-cut, well-understood situation in which no amount of verbalization, experimentation, or forensics can alter the basic fact that a child who does not speak English well cannot learn to read English.[2] Either the child learns to speak English before he learns to read, or he learns to read in his native language. We no longer take seriously the contention that a child (or any other illiterate) can attempt to learn simultaneously to speak and to read a language with other than debilitating results.

The second situation, that of dialect deviation, requires slightly different considerations, in that verbal communication is not totally impaired. While it is clear that *if* reading is to be taught in the child's dialect then tests for language ability must be altered, it is not so clear that changes in the reading materials are either necessary or desirable. But discussion of this must be withheld until the problem of native literacy versus standard literacy is discussed.

NATIVE LITERACY PROGRAMS

Native literacy programs are based upon the assumption that the most efficient method for teaching literacy in the national (or official) language of a country to non-speakers of that language is to teach literacy first in the native language, then (or simultaneously with the teaching of reading in the first language) teach the national language orally, and finally teach reading in the national language. The first official codification of this view was in a UNESCO report published in 1953.[3] Since that time native literacy programs have begun in a number of countries, including Peru where it is by law part of the educational process. Furthermore, experiments which compare the native literacy approach with the straight standard language approach have been carried out in the Philippines (Orato, 1956), in Mexico (Modiano, 1968), and in San Antonio, Texas (Horn and Arnold, 1967).

The basis for native literacy programs is both theoretically and logically appealing from many standpoints. The teaching of reading to non-speakers of the national language has been uniformly dismal on this earth. By teaching reading in the native language, reading instruction can begin at an earlier age than if the standard language had to be taught first; the child's cultural heritage is honored; and a most difficult task—learning to read—is undertaken in the language that the child will always be most comfortable with—his own.

On the other hand, native literacy programs are expensive; they require

[2] I am defining reading not as the mechanical translation from writing to sound, but as translation from writing to that form of language which the reader already attaches meaning to.

[3] UNESCO, *The Use of Vernacular Languages in Education.* Monographs on Fundamental Education, No. 8. Paris UNESCO, 1953.

not only the development of new reading materials, but the training of special teachers and the design of testing procedures which are valid for the languages concerned. In the United States we are still struggling to develop reading and testing materials that are valid for a single language; to repeat this process for *all* languages spoken natively within the USA would require expenditures in excess of what we can realistically hope for in the coming decade (with or without Vietnam, the Moon, Mars, or the quaintly named layers that lie beneath the seas).[4] There are over one hundred Indian languages spoken in the United States. In some other countries the situation is even more trying; South America has over 500 different languages and Indonesia 200. All of this was pointed out by Bull in a review of the UNESCO document just mentioned (Bull, 1955). Before we dedicate ourselves to the native literacy approach, we would like some assurance that the payoff will be high. But at present the available data on this topic cannot be interpreted so positively. None of the major studies shows unequivocally superior results for the native literacy approach.

Philippines Experiment

In the Philippines experiment, begun in the province of Iloilo in the 1948–49 school year, one group of classes (controls) received all their instruction in the official school language (English), while a second group (the experimental group) received instruction for the first two years in the local vernacular (Hiligaynon) and then switched to English for the remainder of their schooling.

Schools were selected from representative economic levels (poorest, average, and richest) and from urban, agricultural, and fishing village areas. Teachers were equated for experience and for a variety of other factors. In the sixth and final year of the experiment, there was no statistical difference between the groups for reading ability, although the experimental classes were statistically superior in social studies. The experimental classes were slightly, but not statistically, superior in arithmetic and reading, while the controls were better in language abilities. There were, however, undeniable non-scholastic advantages for the vernacular group: interest was reported to be higher, parents became more involved with the schools, and the general

---

[4] Consider, for example, what the complexities of reading instruction would be in Hawaii for the native literacy approach in public schools. English, of course, would be one language of instruction, as would be Hawaiian pidgin—the *lingua franca* of the islands—and Hawaiian, which is still the native language for many families on the outer islands. Then there would be Japanese (there are, according to Aspinwall [1960], 78 Japanese language schools in Hawaii with over 12,000 students), Chinese (over 1000 students on the island of Oahu alone attend Chinese language schools), the Philippine languages Tagalog, Visayan, and Ilocano (12% of the population according to the 1950 census was Filipino), Korean, Portuguese, Spanish (Puerto Rican), and the various languages of the Samoans and Okinawans who have immigrated to Hawaii.

relationship of the school to the community was improved over what it had been.[5]

San Antonio Project

In the San Antonio Language-Bilingual Research Project, four treatments were studied for their effects on reading and other abilities of disadvantaged Mexican-American children:

1. "English"—children receive intensive English instruction using science as the content vehicle.
2. "Spanish"—children receive intensive Spanish language instruction using science as the content vehicle.
3. "Non-Oral"—children receive science instruction without intensive language instruction.
4. "Control"—children receive the standard school district curriculum.

After several years of this program, no increase in reading ability over that resulting from the standard teaching methods has been found.

> The findings of the research thus far support the notion that the experimental language treatments (English and Spanish) have resulted in growth in oral language skills and that the experimental science treatment (non-oral) has resulted in growth in science concepts. . . . Apparently, with the instruments used, growth in reading in the experimental groups was not increased over the control groups. (Horn and Arnold, 1967, 2–3)

It should be pointed out that *language* growth generated by language-oriented instructional programs appears with more statistical significance when the criterion is an *oral language* test rather than a *reading* test (Taylor, 1969). The most telling point that the Taylor study makes is that language programs for linguistically different learners which do *not* include intensive, structured oral language instruction will result in little or no pupil improvement toward achieving a socially unmarked style of oral language.

Further studies are underway, however, comparing bilingual instruction, English as a second language instruction, and the standard curriculum.[6]

[5] The Philippines study, though carefully designed and executed, suffered from the over-enthusiasm of its director for the native literacy approach. For example, the project reported at the end of the fourth year that the control group showed a *slight* advantage in all subjects except social studies. However, an independent evaluation made by the Director of Public Schools in the Philippines at the same time showed *significantly superior* achievements for the control group in all subjects including social studies. (The fourth year was the only year, however, in which the control group was superior in reading, which may have been a temporary result of the introduction of English into the curriculum for the experimental group in the previous year.)

[6] A variety of reports are available on the San Antonio Project, including studies of language, school achievement, and oral-aural instruction. These can be found in the general bibliography under Arnold (1968), Horn and Arnold (1967), Jameson (1967), McDowell (1966), Ott (1967), Pena (1967), Stemmler (1966), and Taylor (1969).

Modiano Study

In a study reported by Modiano (1968), where reading instruction in the vernacular languages in the Highlands of Mexico was claimed to be superior to that in the national language (Spanish), neither the schools nor the teacher backgrounds were equivalent, and were probably more important factors than the teaching methods. This study took place in Cheapas, Mexico, near the Guatemalan border, and involved twenty-six schools, thirteen which taught reading in native languages, and thirteen which taught reading in Spanish only. Unfortunately, the native language schools were all National Indian Institute schools, using teachers recruited from the local population, many of whom were graduates themselves of the Institute schools. The Spanish-only schools, on the other hand, were all federal and state schools; many of the teachers, according to Modiano, "represented the element which had exploited them (the Indian tribes) for decades. . . . Most of the remaining federal and state teachers were recent normal school graduates from other regions of the country; some came with missionary zeal, some were demoralized by the difficult living conditions they found, but none spoke the language of their students" (Modiano, 1968, 38). It would have been startling, to say the least, if the Indian Institute schools did not show the greatest success in teaching reading, regardless of the teaching procedures they employed. Nevertheless, what is surprising is that even in the Indian Institute schools, far less than 50 percent of the students were able to understand what they read in Spanish, according to teacher evaluations.

Peru

In Peru, a program for bilingual schools in various jungle tribes was initiated in 1951, including a teacher training program which teachers attended three months a year for five years (Gudschinsky, 1959). During the first three years of schooling, the 3 R's were taught in the local vernacular and Spanish taught orally. For the next three years, the 3 R's were taught in both Spanish and the local vernacular. As yet, however, there has been no published evaluation of this program.

Conclusions

In summary, one would conclude that the native literacy approach, although possessing obvious cultural advantages over the standard language approach, has yet to be proven scholastically superior. The only logical alternative—intensive oral language instruction in the national language prior to the teaching of reading—has the advantage of teaching a second language at an age when most children acquire new languages rapidly. (The older a child becomes, the more difficult it is to teach him a new language.) It also has the theoretical advantage of allowing every child to learn reading with a well-established teaching method, substantiated by both experimentation and use, and supplemented with diagnostic tests and remedial materials. That no country, with the possible exception of Austria, has approached this ideal should not be taken as proof that it is unattainable. Furthermore, if the teaching of reading is so difficult a task as the last one thousand years (or so) of experience has shown it to be, then it seems that more is to be gained by concentrating on the improvement of teaching for one language, rather than for five, ten, or one-hundred languages, especially since the ultimate goal, at least within the United States, is to teach reading in a single language.

What must be understood here is that developing an efficient reading program for a language, and especially for one that has no prior literacy experience, is not simply a job of developing a few primers. Studies are needed to determine which are the most commonly used words, inflections, and syntactic forms in the language, as well as to ascertain which letters are confusable. Then, sequencing of the letters, sounds, vocabulary, and syntactic forms must be decided upon, textbooks written, reading tests developed, and teachers trained. Although some of these factors are ignored in current native literacy programs, they are all essential for effective teaching.

The drawback to the standard language approach is that where the standard language cannot be taught at the kindergarten level (or before), children will lose up to one year (on the average) of reading experience while they are acquiring the second language. This may not be a serious limitation, however, since the first two school years could be restructured to use the initial non-reading period efficiently. Perhaps the San Antonio project will provide more information on this topic. It should be pointed out, however, that where children do not have the attention span, motor coordination, or cognitive skills necessary for learning to read, no amount of language juggling in the reading texts will produce good readers until these deficits are overcome. As pointed out by Stemmler (1966), for Spanish-Americans such deficits usually accompany nonstandard speech and must be given as much attention as the speech itself.

DIALECT DIFFERENCES

To understand the reading problems of speakers of nonstandard dialects, we must navigate through an immense and confusing sea of research reports, eye-witness accounts, sermons, and prophesies—some objective and informative, some careless and uninteresting, and some the vacuous creakings and groanings that so often misdirect the researcher, as did the voices of the Sirens affect the ancient sailors. If quantity of verbiage and number of experiments reflected knowledge gained, there would be many authorities on this issue, but such has not been our fate. Why so many middle-class, standard speakers do not become adequate readers is still a mystery; hence, it should not be surprising that when nonstandard speech and poverty are added, even the problem itself becomes obscured. What we do know is that speakers of nonstandard English come mostly from the lowest socio-economic levels (almost by definition), that they as a group score lower than the higher socio-economic children on IQ tests, that they tend to fall behind in school work, especially in reading, and that the difference between their performance and that of the upper group widens as the child progresses (an ironic term) through school. This latter phenomenon, called the "cumulative deficit" by Deutsch (1965), has been validated quite clearly by Coleman (1966). But the picture is not totally one of low socio-economic level equals poor performance. According to Coleman's study some disadvantaged groups do not fall irretrievably into this pattern. American Indians, for example, while testing below the national average in verbal skills at the beginning of grade one, are equal to the national average in nonverbal skills at that time.

Nevertheless, a high failure rate for all speakers of nonstandard English persists, regardless of the potential which these children show in test situations, and educators are under extreme pressure to rectify the situation.

Alternatives

What, then, can be said specifically about the teaching of reading to nonstandard English speakers? Should it be done in the child's own dialect? Should it be done in standard English, or what? It is beyond questioning that the differences in the child's speech and standard English are a barrier to learning, but the size and significance of this obstacle are not known. Certainly, any method adopted for teaching reading must include training for the teacher in understanding the child's language patterns. This requires, for teaching reading in the United States, training for at least these dialects:

1. Northern urban Negro
2. Southern Mountain (Appalachian)
3. Spanish-American
4. American Indian
5. Hawaiian pidgin
6. Southern rural (Negro and white)
7. Acadian English

While data exist on all of these (some are not single dialects, but groups of dialects), few teacher training materials are available. (Published accounts of each dialect are listed in the bibliography). A substantial step in this direction, however, can be found in a recent report by Davis *et al.* (1969, 1970), *Language Resource Information for Teachers of the Culturally Disadvantaged.* (Other materials for teaching English to speakers of nonstandard dialects are listed in the bibliography).

For the reading materials themselves, the alternatives that we have to choose from appear to be:

1. Prepare all materials in the dialect of the child.
2. Continue with the standard language materials now available, but teach standard English (and standard culture) before reading instruction begins.
3. Modify the content and vocabulary of standard English materials to better reflect the environment of the child, but do not alter the spelling or syntax, other than to try to avoid those patterns which are markedly different in the nonstandard dialect.

The Dialect Approach

Approach one, which has been tediously and somewhat irrationally promoted recently, has few merits and many liabilities. On the positive side, it is argued, the child will receive "powerful ego-supports" through the credence given to his language (Baratz, 1969), but this would be true only if the child's parents and teachers also felt similarly—and there is considerable doubt that they would. According to Goodman (1965, 858), who has been involved with the teaching of reading to Negro children in the inner city of Detroit, ". . . parents and leaders in the speech community . . . would reject the use of special materials which are based on a non-prestigious dialect. They usually share the view of the general culture that their speech is not the speech of cultivation and literature." In addition to this problem, there are practical matters which make this approach difficult to implement. In integrated classrooms, presumably, each child would have the reading materials which most closely match his language and environment; but this would make group instruction nearly impossible and, worse, render the teacher's task insufferable. Then there is the job of preparing special materials for each dialect group: Southern regional white, Appalachian, Northern urban Negro, American Indian, Hawaiian pidgin, Mexican-American, Cuban derived Spanish-American, Southern Negro, etc., and not just reading materials, but also—according to Baratz (1969)—"transitional readers" that would aid the child in changing from vernacular texts to standard English texts.

If we had any evidence that the dialect approach would yield a significant advance in reading ability, we would not object to the costs and tactics involved, but most of the evidence indicates that dialect differences *per se* are not major barriers for learning to read. Studies by Peisach (1965), Weener (1969) and Eisenberg *et al.* (1968) indicate that lower SES Negro children do not find educated white speech any less intelligible than Negro speech (educated or uneducated). If these results can be accepted, then it is difficult to maintain that the vapid, emasculated language of almost all introductory readers could, by itself, pose a serious reading barrier—assuming that the child is allowed to translate what is written into his own speech, just as

Eastern New Englanders, Southern whites, and all other different but standard speakers do.[7]

The Standard Language Approach

Teaching English as a second dialect as a first step for teaching reading—as opposed to teaching standard English as the *only* dialect—has been advocated for a number of years. McDavid (1964, 208), for example, wrote:

> It is likely that teaching some form of standard English as a second language will be necessary; and it might be easier to start this second language in the kindergarten or earlier, and use this as the vehicle for reading . . .

Recently projects for teaching English as a second language (dialect) were begun (among others) in Tougaloo College, Mississippi; Temple University; Claflin College, North Carolina; and Wakulla County, Florida. (A list of such projects can be found in the bibliography.) Of these projects, one of the most interesting for the present topic is the Wakulla County undertaking, now in its third year of operation.[8] Oral language materials are in use in grades 7–9 of the county's consolidated high school and in grades K through 6 of an elementary school. Teachers are trained to use audio-lingual techniques and are given inservice assistance in their proper application. In teacher training workshops and in meetings during the school year, stress is placed upon the concepts of appropriate and inappropriate speech in an attempt to eliminate the notions of "correct" and "incorrect." In the elementary school, children do not read materials in class that they have not already learned orally. Even though it is too early to evaluate this program in detail, its planning and initial success are encouraging.

The standard language approach to teaching reading is a more practical approach than the first, but still not a completely satisfactory one. If the entire reading situation is to be familiar and comfortable, then not just standard English language but some standard English culture must be taught—and this might delay the teaching of reading for a semester or a year. While it would be desirable under this approach to teach standard English in kindergarten, there are barriers to this at present; some states do not have kindergartens, others would not accept the teaching of a second dialect at this level without considerable persuasion (observe the resistance to reading readiness in some school districts). Furthermore, it has one of the drawbacks

---

[7] If the dialect approach were adopted, the content, syntax, and morphology of the readers would need to be changed, but probably not the orthography. The reasons for this are discussed by Shuy (1969, 122–24).

[8] I am indebted to Mrs. Polly Guilford Caskie for her assistance in obtaining information on this project. Mrs. Caskie, along with Mrs. Ann Burks, directed the project for its first two years. A description of the project by the two directors can be found in *Elementary English,* May, 1969.

of the first approach in that it is difficult (but not impossible) to implement in mixed-dialect classrooms. However, a procedure for overcoming this difficulty is to delay the teaching of reading for all students in a mixed-dialect class until each has acquired the language patterns necessary for handling the reading materials. There is no reason to believe that a delay of a few months in the introduction of reading will seriously impede any child's natural development. Furthermore, if this procedure does improve the teaching of reading to nonstandard speakers, it is a small price to pay for such high gains.

The Common Core Approach

The third approach—developing materials in standard English which minimize dialect and cultural differences—appears from the evidence available to be a practical goal, either by itself or in combination with approach two. One effective means for minimizing cultural differences is to base the content of the reading materials upon a school subject like science (as is being done in the San Antonio project) or civics, which the children learn together as a common experience.

To minimize dialect differences requires careful comparisons of standard English with the major nonstandard dialects, a task that has already been undertaken for Northern Negro speech. Of the syntactic forms which distinguish Northern Negro from white speech, Shuy (1969, 129) lists only three which would require special attention for cross-dialectal materials: negation (*doesn't have* vs. *ain't got no*), past conditional questions (*Mother asked if I ate* vs. *Mother asked did I eat*), and negative + *be* (*When I sing he isn't afraid* vs. *When I sing he don't be afraid*). Of these, only the plain negative is a problem, since the other two can be, and perhaps should be, avoided in beginning readers. It is doubtful, though, that even this construction is a reading barrier for any English speaking child, except for the most extreme of the culturally deprived, for whom almost everything in the reading situation is a problem. What is more important is allowing the child, regardless of his own dialect, to translate from standard written English to his own speech—as pointed out by Goodman and others. To achieve this requires extensive training for teachers on what is natural for the children he will be teaching and why learning a new dialect should not be confused with learning to read.

CONCLUSIONS

It is on this last point that the major research and training efforts should be exerted. At the same time, materials and techniques for teaching standard English need to be developed. Although there is not complete agreement on when these should be introduced in the educational system, there is agreement that they should be introduced at some point. As for the dialect of the reading materials themselves, the available evidence (and it is far from conclusive evidence) indicates that standard English is suitable under the following conditions:

1. Children whose dialects deviate markedly from standard English should be taught the standard brand before they are taught reading, under the explicit assumption that it is a second dialect and not a more correct dialect that is being taught.
2. Reading materials for beginning reading should, in content, vocabulary, and syntax, be as dialect free (and culture free), as possible. Given the inanity of present day materials, this should not be overly difficult to achieve.
3. Children should be allowed to translate from writing to that form of language from which they already obtain meaning; that is, dialect differences should not be considered reading errors.

If all of these provisos can be followed, there may exist a basis upon which good reading programs can be developed. If they cannot be adopted, then we should consider developing separate reading materials for each non-standard dialect. However, under either situation, we should not expect a major improvement in reading ability from the elimination of the dialect mismatch alone. This will come only with the development of better methods for teaching reading than are available now.

Bibliography

Selected References on Specific Dialects

Acadian English
McDavid, Raven I., Jr., "Some Notes on Acadian English," in A. L. Davis *et al.*, 1969, 1970 (see Programs and Materials).

American Indian
Ohannessian, Sirapi, *A Study of the Problems of Teaching English to American Indians: Report and Recommendations.* Washington, D.C.: Center for Applied Linguistics, July, 1967.

Salisbury, Lee H., *Teaching English to Alaska Natives.* Paper delivered at TESOL Conference, New York City, March 17, 1966.

Sizemore, Mamie, *Teaching Reading to the Bilingual Child.* Phoenix: Arizona State Department of Public Instruction, 1963.

Appalachian
Berrey, Lester V., "Southern Mountain Dialect," *American Speech,* XV (1940), 45–54.

Furbee, N. Louanna, "Transcription of Appalachian English," in A. L. Davis *et al.*, 1969, 1970 (see Programs and Materials).

Hawaiian Pidgin
Hormann, Bernhard L., "Hawaii's Linguistic Situation: A Sociological Interpretation in the New Key." *Social Progress in Hawaii,* 24 (1960), 6–31.

Tsuzaki, Stanley M. and John E. Reinecke, "English in Hawaii: An Annotated Bibliography," *Oceanic Linguistics,* Special Publication. No. 1, 1966.

Voegelin, Carl E. and Florence M. Voegelin, "Hawaiian Pidgin and Mother Tongue," *Anthropological Linguistics,* 6 (1964), 20–56.

Negro

Bailey, Beryl, "Toward a New Perspective in Negro English Dialectology," *American Speech,* 40 (1965), 171–77.

Burks, Ann T. and Polly D. Guilford, "Wakulla County Oral Languages Project," *Elementary English,* 5 (1969), 606–11.

Labov, William, "Some Sources of Reading Problems for Negro Speakers of Nonstandard English," in Alexander Frazier (ed.), *New Directions in Elementary English.* Champaign, Ill.: National Council of Teachers of English, 1967.

Loman, Bengt (ed.), *Conversations in a Negro American Dialect.* Washington, D.C.: Center for Applied Linguistics, 1967.

Morris, Emily Pettigrew, "Transcription of Negro Child's English," in A. L. Davis *et al.,* 1969, 1970 (see Programs and Materials).

Politzer, Robert L. and Diana E. Bartley, "Standard English and Nonstandard Dialects: Phonology and Morphology." Research and Development Memorandum No. 46, Stanford Center for Research and Development in Teaching, Stanford University, June, 1969.

Spanish American (Mexican and Puerto Rican)

Jameson, Gloria Ruth, *The Development of a Phonemic Analysis for an Oral English Proficiency Test for Spanish-Speaking School Beginners,* Austin: The University of Texas, 1967.

McDowell, Neil A., *A Study of the Academic Capabilities and Achievements of Three Ethnic Groups: Anglo, Negro and Spanish Surnames, in San Antonio, Texas.* Austin: The University of Texas, 1966.

Ott, Elizabeth H., *A Study of Levels of Fluency and Proficiency in Oral English of Spanish-Speaking School Beginners.* Austin: The University of Texas, 1967.

Pena, Albar A., *A Comparative Study of Selected Syntactical Structures of the Oral Language Status in Spanish and English of Disadvantaged First Grade Spanish-Speaking Children.* Austin: The University of Texas, 1967.

Simpson, Dagna, "Transcription of Puerto Rican English," in A. L. Davis *et al.,* 1969, 1970 (see Programs and Materials).

Programs and Materials

Anderson, Lorena A., "Reading in Appalachia," *The Reading Teacher* (January, 1967), 303–06, 312.

Arnold, Richard D., *1965–66 (Year Two) Findings, San Antonio Language Research Project.* Austin: The University of Texas, 1968.

Burks, Ann T. and Polly D. Guilford, "Wakulla County Oral Language Project," *Elementary English,* 5 (1969), 606–11.

Davis, A. L., *et al., Language Resource Information for Teachers of the Culturally Disadvantaged.* Final Report, USOE Project Number 6-1340 (Chicago, April, 1969); Champaign, Ill.: National Council of Teachers of English, in press.

Corbin, Richard and Muriel Crosby, *Language Programs for the Disadvantaged.* Champaign, Ill.: National Council of Teachers of English, 1965.

Horn, Thomas D. and Richard D. Arnold, "Capsule Description of San Antonio Language-Bilingual Research Project," Austin: The University of Texas, 1967 (mimeograph).

Johnson, Kenneth R., *Teaching Culturally Disadvantaged Pupils.* Chicago: Science Research Associates, 1968.

Lin, San-su C., *Pattern Practice in the Teaching of English to Students with a Nonstandard Dialect,* New York: Bureau of Publications, Teachers College, Columbia University, 1965.

Lin, San-su C., "Experiment in Changing Dialect Patterns: The Chaflin Project," *College English,* 24 (May, 1963), 644–47.

Shuy, Roger W., "A Linguistic Background for Developing Beginning Reading Materials for Black Children," in Joan C. Baratz and Roger W. Shuy (eds.), *Teaching Black Children to Read.* Washington, D.C.: Center for Applied Linguistics, 1969.

Stemmler, Anne, "An Experimental Approach to the Teaching of Oral Language and Reading," *Harvard Educational Review,* 36 (Winter, 1966), 42–59.

Taylor, Thomasine H., *1968–69 (Year Five) Findings: A Comparative Study of the Effects of Oral-Aural Language Training on Gains in English Language for Fourth and Fifth Grade Disadvantaged Mexican-American Children.* Austin: The University of Texas, 1969.

General Bibliography

Aspinwall, Dorothy B., "Languages in Hawaii," *Publications of the Modern Language Association,* 75 (1960), 7–13.

Baratz, Joan C. and Roger W. Shuy, *Teaching Black Children to Read.* Washington, D.C.: Center for Applied Linguistics, 1969.

Berrey, Lester V., "Southern Mountain Dialect," *American Speech,* XV (1940), 45–54.

Booth, Robert E., *et al., Culturally Disadvantaged: A Bibliography and Keyword-out-of-Context (KWOC) Index.* Detroit: Wayne State University Press, 1967.

Bull, William E., Review of: *The Use of Vernacular Languages in Education.* (Monographs on Fundamental Education, No. 8), Paris: UNESCO, 1953. *International Journal of American Linguistics,* 21 (1955), 288–94.

Cazden, C., "Differences in Child Language: an Interdisciplinary View," *Merrill-Palmer Quarterly,* 12 (1966), 185–221.

Cohn, W., "On the Language of Lower-Class Children," in E. T. Keach, R. Fulton, and W. E. Gardner (eds.), *Education and Social Crisis.* New York: Wiley, 1967.

Coleman, James S., *Equality of Educational Opportunity.* Washington, D.C.: U.S. Department of Health, Education, and Welfare, 1966.

Deutsch, Martin, "The Role of Social Class in Language Development and Cognition," *American Journal of Orthopsychiatry,* 35 (1965), 78–88.

Eisenberg, Leon *et al.,* "Class and Race Effects on the Intelligibility of Mono-syllables," *Child Development,* 39 (1968), 1077–89.

Goodman, Kenneth S., "Dialect Barriers to Reading Comprehension," *Elementary English,* 42 (December, 1965), 853–60.

Gudschinsky, Sarah. "Recent Trends in Primer Construction," *Fundamental and Adult Education,* XI (1959), 67–96.

Horman, Bernhard L., "Hawaii's Linguistic Situation: A Sociological Interpretation in the New Key," *Social Progress in Hawaii,* 2 (1960), 6–31.

Knight, Lester N., *1966–67 (Year Three) Findings: A Comparison of the Effectiveness of Intensive Oral-Aural English Instruction, Intensive Oral-Aural Spanish Instruction, and No Oral-Aural Instruction on the Oral Language and Reading Achievement of Spanish-Speaking Second and Third Graders.* Austin: The University of Texas, 1969.

Labov, William, *The Study of Nonstandard English.* Champaign, Ill.: The National Council of Teachers of English, 1970.

Labov, William, "Stages in the Acquisition of Standard English," in Roger W. Shuy (ed.), *Social Dialects and Language Learning.* Champaign, Ill.: National Council of Teachers of English, 1965, 77–103.

Lloyd, D., "Subcultural Patterns Which Affect Language and Reading Development," in

E. T. Keach, R. Fulton, and W. E. Gardner (eds.), *Education and Social Crisis*. New York: Wiley, 1967.

McDavid, Raven I., Jr., "Dialectology and the Teaching of Reading," *The Reading Teacher*, 18 (December, 1964), 206–13.

Modiano, Nancy, "National or Mother Language in Beginning Reading: A Comparative Study," *Research in the Teaching of English*, 1(1968), 32–43.

Orata, Pedro T., "The Iloilo Community School Experiment: The Vernacular as Medium of Instruction," *Fundamental and Adult Education*, VIII (1956), 173–78.

Peisach, E. Cherry, "Children's Comprehension of Teacher and Peer Speech," *Child Development*, 30 (1965), 467–80.

Raph, Jane B., "Language Development in Socially Disadvantaged Children," *Review of Educational Research*, 35 (1965), 389–400.

Shuy, Roger W., "A Selective Bibliography on Social Dialects," *The Linguistic Reporter*, 10 (June, 1968), 1–5.

Shuy, Roger W. (ed.), *Social Dialects and Language Learning: Proceedings of the Bloomington, Indiana Conferences, 1964*. Champaign, Ill.: National Council of Teachers of English, 1965.

Stewart, William A., "Foreign Language Teaching Methods in Quasi Foreign Language Situations," in William A. Stewart (ed.), *Non-standard Speech and the Teaching of English*. Washington, D.C.: Center for Applied Linguistics, 1965.

Stodolsky, Susan S. and Gerald Lesser, "Learning Patterns of the Disadvantaged," *Harvard Educational Review*, 37 (Fall, 1967), 546–89.

UNESCO, *The Use of Vernacular Languages in Education*. Monographs on Fundamental Education, No. 8. Paris: UNESCO, 1953.

Weener, Paul D., "Social Dialect Differences and the Recall of Verbal Messages," *Journal of Educational Psychology*, 60 (1969), 194–99.

Witty, Paul A. (ed.), "Reading and the Underprivileged," *Education*, 85 (April, 1965), 450–506.

Reading:

A New Perspective

RONALD WARDHAUGH

Having looked at the teaching of reading from various points of view, all of them with a deliberate linguistic coloring, we may now attempt a definition of reading. When a person reads a text, he is attempting to discover the meaning of what he is reading by using the visual clues of spelling, his knowledge of probabilities of occurrence, his contextual-pragmatic knowledge, and

READING: A NEW PERSPECTIVE from *Reading: A Linguistic Perspective* by Ronald Wardhaugh, © 1969 by Harcourt Brace Jovanovich, Inc., and reprinted with their permission.

his syntactic and semantic competence to give a meaningful interpretation to the text. Reading is not a passive process, in which a reader takes something out of the text without any effort or merely recognizes what is in the text. Nor does it appear to be a process in which he first recognizes what is on the page and then interprets it, a process in which a stage of decoding precedes a stage of involvement with meaning. There is little reason to suppose that there are two such discrete, non-overlapping stages. Reading is instead an active process, in which the reader must make an active contribution by drawing upon and using concurrently various abilities that he has acquired.

These abilities are of many different kinds. For example, there is the ability to associate certain sounds and certain letters. The reader must be able to react to significant rather than nonsignificant visual clues. He must also be able to use both short- and long-term memories effectively during the processing involved in reading. These abilities are not used automatically in all circumstances, because even the best readers make some mistakes; such mistakes indicate that the processing called for was incompletely or inaccurately carried out. The processing itself is not just processing of visual signals in order to convert these signals into some kind of covert speech. The conversion is not the end point of the process, because semantic and syntactic processing are necessary in addition to the processing of the visual signals.

Semantic and syntactic processing require a knowledge of the language—knowledge in the sense of competence—and they require this knowledge to be used actively. One cannot read a foreign language (except in the sense of barking at print) unless one has some underlying competence in that language, some training in its orthographic principles, and some knowledge of the subject matter, and can bring all these to bear on the task. A child cannot learn to read English unless he has some underlying competence in the English language (though this competence may be added to as a result of reading experiences). He must learn to react to the orthography, and ideally the subject-matter he is asked to read about should touch on something within his experience or be relevant to that experience in some way. Given these conditions, he will find the task of learning to be a meaningful one.

In beginning reading instruction considerable emphasis must be placed on teaching the association of orthography to phonology. This association is not as simple as certain claims have made it out to be, however, nor should it be the only area of concentration. Certain claims too about the relationships of symbols to sounds are open to question. For example, the claims about the importance of "silent" speech or about the mediational role of "internalized" speech, in understanding how people learn to associate symbols with sounds, demand serious consideration but are as yet unsubstantiated. Similarly, statements about what is regular and irregular in English orthography and how and why the irregularities must be controlled in beginning reading texts are sometimes conflicting. There is also conflicting opinion about the need to modify existing English orthography or to use only one type of print or to teach minimal letter and word shapes in contrast with each other, just as one might teach minimal phonological pairs. In the area of sentence types there is discussion about the desirability of restricting the content of readers to some of the simple recurring superficial patterns of the child's spoken language rather than including patterns that are infrequent or complex.

Linguists cannot provide complete answers to many of these problems because the problems are not exclusively linguistic. In every case there are variables other than linguistic ones to be considered. The problems are mainly pedagogical, and while linguists can provide some help in finding solutions, they cannot provide total solutions. There appears to be no more justification for talking about *a linguistic method* or various *linguistic methods* of teaching reading, particularly beginning reading, than for talking about a linguistic method or methods of teaching a foreign language. Linguistic methods are methods that linguists employ in doing linguistic research and possibly in teaching linguistics. Reading is not linguistics. It has a large linguistic content, but it also has content that is nonlinguistic; consequently, methods for teaching reading must draw on other sources in addition to linguistic ones. But such methods should build on sound linguistic knowledge.

It is also apparent that children will learn to read only by being given help with just that task, and that they do not learn to read by being told about the task. They do not learn to read by learning rules about what to do when they are confronted with certain difficulties particularly when these rules are either too sophisticated, complicated, or inconsistent to be applied with a reasonable chance of success. They must learn to relate certain sounds to certain symbols, to distinguish *d* from *b* and **mat** from **mate,** to recognize that left to right direction is important as in **dog** vs. **god** and **top desk** vs. **desk top,** to recognize that the grammatical signals of written language are basically those of spoken language, and to use contextual clues in the decipherment of written texts, as in resolving the ambiguity of **He gave her a bow.** A few very basic rules such as those that apply to the *c* in **city** and **cat,** the *igh* in **fight,** and the *gh* in **enough** may be useful to beginning readers; however, it is doubtful that teaching children long lists of unordered phonic generalizations has any real benefit.

Of course, children do learn something which might be called a set of rules that they use in reading, because they do learn to read with greater or lesser success. Even the mistakes they make show them to be employing inappropriate rules rather than exhibiting randomized behavior. A child learns to read **city** and **cat** correctly as the result of experience with words beginning *ci-* and *ca-* and with his unconscious assimilation of the rule that almost always *c* followed by one group of vowel letters is associated with an [s] sound and by another group withh a [k] sound. He may not be able to verbalize the rule, any more than he could tell you how he ties his shoe laces; but just as he can demonstrate that he knows the rules for tying shoe laces by tying shoe laces, so he can demonstrate his knowledge of the rules for pronouncing *c* by reading *city* and *cat* correctly. His knowledge of the rules is demonstrated by his performance and it is unnecessary for him to learn to verbalize a statement about what he has learned, that is, about what he knows. In studying the linguistic and reading performance of children, it would be well for a teacher to try to arrive at an understanding of what unconscious rules a particular child is applying to his tasks. It would also be wise to see the whole of the child's behavior as rule-governed, so that "mistakes" may be regarded as instances of applying inappropriate rules, rather than as the results of random behavior. In fact, the whole notion of "mistake" and "error" could well be discarded in favor of this kind of approach. Admittedly, not every mistake will be explicable in these terms, but it seems more fruitful to hypothesize that "mistaken result from the application of rules which are different from the rules of mature language users" than to hypothesize that "mistakes are instances of random (or perverse) behavior."

Reading requires certain perceptual skills that are not required for spoken language and, conversely, does not require certain perceptual skills required for spoken language. It has been claimed that when we read we "hear" what we read, that the visual symbol somehow triggers an aural one. While there is some evidence for silent speech (Edfeldt, 1960) and for the claim that speech perception has a motor basis, this evidence is by no means conclusive. It is well known that receptive control of language always exceeds productive control, that silent reading speed often exceeds aural comprehension speed, and that some people learn to read English who cannot or do not speak English for various reasons. While there is in every normal human being the capacity for language acquisition, this capacity can apparently be realized by linguistic stimuli other than aural stimuli, even though the latter are those to which most people actually do respond (or resonate). A normal child reacts naturally to the spoken language around him, and it provides him with all the stimuli he needs to become a speaker of the language. Some of those stimuli apparently come from within the child himself, from his innate propensities to learn a language. A child who is not normal, who is deaf or dumb or both, still has these propensities but must react to different external stimuli. His task may be much more difficult, but it is probably never impossible.

Reading is a different kind of linguistic performance from listening, just as listening is from speaking. The range of understanding in listening is greater than the range of production in speaking, and the range of understanding of written material is usually greater than that of spoken material. The latter is true mainly because one can read and reread, and thereby control the speed of the processing of the content that is being read. The material to be read is often rather different from that met in listening, however, and these differences can create difficulties. In general, written language is more deliberate, more complex, more heavily edited, and less redundant than spoken language, and it offers no opportunity to question the writer in order to seek clarification of his statements.

In both kinds of performance the individual makes a large personal contribution; as often as not, he hears what he wants to hear and reads what he wants to read rather than what was originally said or written. Comprehension is not a passive process. The comprehender must continually make hypotheses about what he is hearing or reading, attempt to match these hypotheses with other data he has available to him, and modify the hypotheses if they are inadequate.

Sometimes, of course, people adopt processing strategies that result in selective listening or reading, strategies that in effect allow them to ignore data that do not conform to their hypotheses. The result is a mishearing or misreading of the original content, a type of "mistake" that is a direct consequence of the contribution of the comprehender to the process of comprehension. For example, we sometimes anticipate words in a conversation or text only to discover ourselves to be wrong, or we do not wait for sentences to be completed because we assume we know what their endings will be, or we miss spelling mistakes because we are more concerned with meaning than with proofreading. Many of the mistakes students make in reading are made because the students have adopted inappropriate strategies in their processing. In the later stages of reading instruction, when reading for implications and reading between the lines become an important part of instruction, the possibilities for adopting inappropriate strategies increase. That errors and mistakes do occur in these circumstances should be expected; indeed it would be well to avoid the use of such terms as "errors" and "mistakes" in discussing such varieties of linguistic performance. As we have seen, these mistakes are generally perfectly explicable, because they are principled, motivated, and rule-governed.

One of the most interesting attempts to explain what happens when children make mistakes in reading has come from Goodman (1967). Goodman has shown that children reading unfamiliar textual material are forced to play what he calls a "psycholinguistic guessing game." The child must draw upon the rules he has internalized to read the novel text. He must try out the knowledge he has acquired of sound-symbol relationships, grammatical patterning, semantic collocations, and the real world in an attempt to impose some kind of order or meaning on the text. He must adopt a strategy that allows him to draw upon these different varieties of knowledge concurrently, and he must be prepared to make hypotheses, more or less educated guesses. Sometimes he will guess incorrectly, so that his responses will not conform to those of a mature reader, but his guesses will rarely be unmotivated; they will be "miscues," in Goodman's terms, rather than mistakes. The miscues can provide a great deal of insight into the particular strategies that the child is using, into the kind of psychological and linguistic—hence psycholinguistic —processes he is using subconsciously. Naturally, one can do no more than infer these processes from the responses, but it is still possible to give a fairly accurate account of the kind of reading competence that underlies the observed reading behavior. A reader's miscues in reading are evidence that his competence in reading varies from that of a mature reader, not that he lacks reading competence.

The competence that a reader uses is not the same competence that interests the linguist attempting to write a grammar for English. The two are not unrelated, however. Both are models of ideal systems. The linguist's model is the ideal system that characterizes the language; the reading researcher's model is the system that the reader has access to in his attempts to comprehend what he is reading. The latter model includes the linguistic competence of the reader that is relevant to his task. But it also includes nonlinguistic content, because the task is a perceptual and cognitive one, involving many competences other than that which interests the linguist. Both models must make allowance for performance characteristics, too: speakers and readers make mistakes, find their memories overburdened, and get confused as they react to inappropriate stimuli. Such phenomena, however, must be clearly distinguished from those that seem directly to manifest competence. People generally know when they have made a mistake, when they cannot remember how a sentence began, and when they are confused. It is important, therefore, that teachers distinguish this kind of knowledge from that kind which leads a reader to read *dog* as *bog* and *He's growing* as *He goin'*, in the belief that he has responded correctly.

One interesting set of performance variables is related to oral reading. There appear to be more performance variables in oral reading than in silent reading, because there is an extra set of production variables involved in the task. This extra set adds new complications to the already complicated task of studying where the process of comprehension may break down. In both silent and oral reading, the reader is required to get the meaning from the print in front of him. To find out whether or not the reader did get the meaning, one can use several methods. The reader can be asked to read the passage aloud, to answer questions, or to do something else—for example, to perform an action. In such ways one may attempt to discover if the process of comprehension has been completed. This process may break down in two critical places. The reader may or may not understand what was written and may or may not communicate that understanding or lack of understanding. He may understand and indicate that he understood; he may not understand and indicate that he did not understand; he may understand but fail to indicate this fact; and he may not understand but seem by his response to have understood. In judging a student's success in reading, we try to safeguard against the third and fourth possibilities, but we are not always successful. For this reason we must be cautious before we say that someone does not comprehend either what we say to him or what we require him to read.

The teaching of reading must be clearly distinguished from the teaching of speaking. Children come to school already speaking a dialect of the language, and it should be possible to teach them to read by drawing upon the language competence they exhibit in that dialect. There is an important distinction between students who have certain kinds of performance limitations, such as memory, perceptual, and motor limitations, and students who speak nonstandard dialects. Students of the first type have congenital or acquired deficiencies for which reading teachers must compensate. Students of the second type may or may not, of course, exhibit some of the same problems and as a group may actually have a greater incidence of such problems because of various deprivations in their background, but they should not be treated in the same way as the first group when they do not have these problems.

A student who says *wif* because he has a physical defect (and the loss of teeth should not be regarded as a physical defect in this sense) should be treated quite differently from one who says *wif* because that pronunciation of *with* is a feature of his dialect. To send both students to the speech therapist for the same "treatment" is a tragic mistake. The same may be true of pronunciations like *wed* for *red, Buce* for *Bruce,* and *fevver* for *feather.* To regard such pronunciations as obstacles in learning to read is extremely unwise. A teacher might be tempted to accept the pathological or maturational *wif* and condemn the dialectal *wif;* again, such a reaction would betray a lack of understanding of language function. It should be remembered that so-called poor articulation and poor enunciation have little to do with reading success and failure or with anything we might consider to be normal language use. No normal person in normal conversation "talks like a book" clearly enunciating every sound. We all know how tiresome it is to converse with people who over-enunciate in situations calling for a relaxed speech style. A pronunciation such as *wif* is at most a symptom of, say, either a minor pathological defect or a dialect difference; and in either case it is the cause that should be treated, not the symptom. Such treatment may be considered worthwhile only if the particular pathological cause can be remedied or if it is considered desirable to make a standard available to the speaker.

The teaching of reading should take place within a total language program in which reading instruction plays an important part. This total program should emphasize the discovery of how language is used, rather than prescribe how language should be used, as most programs do at present. There are at least two good reasons for such a change in emphasis. First, the discovery approach conforms better to good linguistic, psychological, and pedagogical principles than a prescriptive approach. Second, understanding a process is likely to lead to better use of that process, but only if that understanding has been arrived at in a meaningful way rather than by rote. Language in all its diversity of forms and uses is a fascinating subject for study and can provide a wealth of meaningful exploratory experiences for students of all ages. Children are naturally inquisitive, and it is just as valuable for them to explore their linguistic environment as it is to explore the surrounding fields and woods or streets and stores. Such exploration is likely to be

very useful to the child as he begins to understand his linguistic environment, to discover its possibilities, and to use what he finds to further his own
ends.

The actual finding-out process should make use of various types of
experiences and strategies, so that the teaching is eclectic rather than stereotyped. There are all too many gimmicks and panaceas in existence today in
the form of simple solutions to what are essentially complicated problems.
Children are different, teachers are different, language has many different
facets to it. There is no one royal road to learning; more likely there are a
great many paths, few of which are very straight. Children require a variety
of linguistic experiences resulting in a variety of effects according to their
needs and abilities. Language is uniform and consistent only in the abstract
forms described in books by linguists; in real life language is extremely
diverse, just as the people who use it are very different. Students cannot learn
to savor this diversity if the curriculum offers each student exactly the same
linguistic diet.

Some Notes on Strategy
and Content for Elementary
Reading Programs in the '70's

ERNEST HILTON

The decade just ended was clearly a period of sweeping curriculum
review and innovation. It was, inevitably, a time of considerable confusion
about ends and means in education. What will be the main currents in the
new decade? Particularly, how will the teaching of reading in the elementary
school proceed? Some general outlines, with regard both to strategy and content, seem to be discernible.

1. *The teaching of reading will be given top priority in the elementary
   grades.*
   That reading is a top-priority concern hardly requires argument. The

SOME NOTES ON STRATEGY AND CONTENT FOR ELEMENTARY READING PROGRAMS IN THE '70's by
Ernest Hilton. From the *Elementary School Journal,* 71 (April 1971), pp. 384–90. Published
by the University of Chicago Press. © 1971 by The University of Chicago. Reprinted by
permission.

ability to read at least reasonably well is obviously a necessity for effective living—for progress in school, for occupational success and mobility, and for responsible participation in civic affairs. Reading is, in short, a versatile and dependable tool for learning. The times in which we live are so charged with new knowledge and so shaken by change that it seems fair to suggest that only those who have learned to learn can develop the flexibility of response, the adaptiveness, to live effectively. All must learn to read. The ability to read is so important that any child who does not achieve reasonable success in it is severely handicapped in ways that impinge on personality development and on effective living, in the total sense of that term.

So much for a brief restatement of why reading is important. There is nothing particularly new in the argument, unless it is that the pace of life today lends a special urgency to the importance of learning to learn. Why, then, does it seem probable that reading will be given a higher priority in the years just ahead than in the years just past? The obvious answer is that there is widespread dissatisfaction with past performance. In plain language, a great many people believe that the schools have not done a very good job of teaching reading. Reports on what is true and what is not true about reading achievement at different grade or age levels differ in details—some are more hysterical than others—but there is persuasive evidence that the concern about the teaching of reading is a justified concern. All is not well. Thus, the generally approving response to the Nixon administration's proposed "Right To Read" campaign for the 1970's is understandable.

To assert a priority for reading is fairly easy; to act on that priority is more difficult. Any readjustment of priorities involves making some choices. In assigning reading top priority, perhaps the most difficult choices must be made in finding more time for reading. Other concerns—other school subjects, if the term is a plainer one—have crowded into the primary grades over the past several years. As evidence, it may be noted that few textbook series in what we call the content subjects used to include books for Grades 1 and 2. Today almost all series do in science, social studies, mathematics, and English. Indeed, books or workbooks (or programs packaged in other than book format) for kindergarten are common. One must assume that time is budgeted for those subjects. What we used to call the "daily schedule" also allocates time for what are, justly or unjustly, called the "special" subjects. It is not unusual to find a foreign language program beginning in Grade 3.

To do better in reading, a first step—and an important one—is to budget more time for reading; more time for teaching reading and more time for children to practice reading. Doing so should be a significant part of the strategy in the '70's, even though it means taking time from other concerns for each of which persuasive claims can be made. There is no other choice unless more time is made available by lengthening the school day. One of the reasons why more time must be given to reading is that stronger, not weaker, reading programs are needed. We need not only to do better; we need to do more. When more time is allocated for reading, good teachers will find they can adjust the pace for different children, moving more slowly and surely with some, and more rapidly but still surely with others. And, for all, there may be more time to read, an activity that surely has a place in the reading program.

Other choices must be made. The budget for materials reflects a school's priorities. So, too, does the allocation of staff resources, including supervisory services. Fortunately, aides and volunteer workers can fill productive roles in the reading program, and in the next few years a good many schools may explore this way of strengthening the program.

> 2. *There is no one best way to teach reading, and programs in the '70's will continue to use various methods and materials.*

Method is always a central concern in elementary-school curriculum practice, and in no subject is it more centrally a concern than in reading. It therefore is not at all surprising that professionals and non-professionals alike have given an enormous amount of attention to problems of method. The literature—research reports, theoretical discussions, speculation—is so extensive that it seems to defy orderly review. Yet, out of it all has emerged no clear case for the superiority of a given method or a given set of materials, in terms so convincing that one can say, "This, at least, is the way to teach reading."

All this is not to say that all the effort has been unproductive. Indeed, a great deal is known about method. There is persuasive evidence in support of certain points of view. One of the most debated issues has been that of the place of what is commonly called "phonics." If the differences in viewpoint are thought of in terms of extremes, on the one end of the scale is what we may call the "look and say," or "whole word" method; on the other, an approach that insists on "decoding" by knowledge of sound-symbol relationships as the method. Materials on decoding either impose a rigorous control in introducing sound-symbol relationships or use an artificial (augmented) alphabet in reading to achieve "regularity."

The realities of general practice, however, seldom reflect extreme positions. Moreover, as many have said, any general method must accommodate itself to concerns other than decoding, as, for example, the concern that what children are asked to read be expressed, insofar as is practicable, in "natural" language patterns. Another concern, and surely one worthy of serious consideration, is with the content and the quality of what is to be read—in plain terms, concern that what is to be read be worth reading. It is not easy to bring these concerns together. For example, it is difficult, if not impossible, to use "natural" language and at the same time control sound-symbol relationships.

There is a mainstream position in which the several concerns are accommodated—a method that strongly emphasizes the decoding skills and at the same time emphasizes reading for meaning. It seems quite safe to assert that this position will prevail through the '70's.

However, in saying that there is no one best way to teach reading, no one best set of materials, some cautions are in order. For one thing, the importance of the decoding skills is so great that the fact bears repetition. For another, it does not follow that all reading materials are equally good and useful. And, perhaps the most urgent caution is this: although there is no one way to teach reading, it does not follow that what may be called "grab-bag" teaching is good. One may find that it is difficult to defend the superiority of Method A over Method B, but it is nevertheless true that either is better than no "method." For any child—and for any school—the reading program should be a planned program, one in which there is a sensible sequence, one in which there is consistency. Not only teachers, but learners as well, need to know the arrangement of the learning experiences, to know at any point where they have been, where they are, and to have some sense of where they are going.

3. *The quality of the teaching will continue to be the most important factor in reading programs.*

Research supports common sense in identifying the teacher as the critical factor in the reading program. More than semantics is involved, however, in so stating the idea that attention is focused on teaching rather than solely on the teacher. So stated, the proposition allows for the important contributions of supervisor and administrator, and for the influence teachers have on one another as they work together in a program. But, whether the proposition is stated so that the focus is on the teacher or on teaching, it seems quite clear that the general idea it expresses will hold true for the '70's.

There have been, and still are, those who look to advances in educational technology for improvement in curriculum practice. There is a sound basis for such hopes. Certainly anyone who has had opportunities to observe children and a computer at work together in what is called computer-assisted instruction must respect what the computer can do to individualize learning. Yet, at least to date, the role of the computer is limited largely to drill and practice experiences. More significantly, the economics of the situation make it highly unlikely that computer-assisted instruction will be available to many schools in the '70's. One can, it seems, assert that reading will be taught by human teachers through the '70's, without denying that a time may come when computer-assisted instruction will play an important part in reading programs.

If all this is reassuring to teachers, it is probably a good thing. At the same time, it must be said that each teacher carries a sobering responsibility—a responsibility that is, in some measure, a moral responsibility. If there is to be a new element in the '70's, it may be what is suggested by the currently popular word "accountability." Indeed, it seems probable that in the years just ahead there will be a stricter accounting of performance. If so, the development is one that good teachers will welcome.

4. *In most schools, reading programs in the '70's will center on a basal reading series, with increasing use of varied supplementary materials.*

Although there is no one best way to teach reading, no one best set of materials, it remains true that in any school the program must have a structure. What is to be taught must be defined and ordered. The several concerns that come together in what we call "method" must be harmonized in some sensible way. Traditionally, these ends have been served by defining the program around a basal reading series. Recent studies of curriculum practice tell us that this remains true in most schools, probably in something more than 90 per cent of all schools.

All signs indicate this will be true in the '70's. Conditions that in part explain reliance on a basal series can be identified. For one thing, class size remains relatively high. The self-contained classroom remains the basic unit of organization. Teacher turnover continues.

Yet there is widespread awareness that a basal series, however carefully developed, falls short of providing a total program. In the '70's there will be increasing use of supplementary materials of various kinds. Some few schools—but a growing number—will use computer-assisted instruction for drill and practice experience, achieving a larger degree of individualization than is possible with conventional materials. For the most part, however, the supplementary materials will be printed materials. There are signs of what they will be like. Some promising programmed materials are available. Other materials, not programmed in any strict definition of the term, show the influence of the ideas underlying programmed instruction. That is, they proceed in small, clearly defined steps; some are wholly or largely "self-directing" and "self-correcting." There are materials designed for small-group or team-learning experiences.

Moreover, there are some new materials—and likely to be more—that seem to fall somewhere between basal and supplementary. These materials provide sequential learning experiences adequate to full-time programs over a substantial period of time and cover a substantial body of reading skills. Some of these may prove to be particularly useful with children who for one reason and another do not succeed in the basal program and for whom a new start with different materials may be the answer.

5. Reading programs in the middle grades will be strengthened.

The improvement of reading instruction in the middle grades may be one of the most important developments in the years just ahead. There is widespread awareness that for too many pupils present programs in these grades do not result in adequate growth in reading power. Some of that awareness comes from finding that many children cannot deal successfully with their textbooks in the content subjects. In this connection, it may be observed that those textbooks have become more difficult than they used to be. Some of that awareness is rooted in the general complaint of secondary-school teachers that children come to those grades unable to read (or "study") effectively. (And the textbooks there, too, are more difficult than they used to be.) It is no longer good enough to characterize the middle-grade program as "reading to learn." That formula must be revised to "learning to read to learn."

Some changes are in order, and there are signs of change. There is widespread dissatisfaction with the content of traditional middle-grade readers, content perhaps most accurately described as simple narrative material. Too, there is wider readiness to accept the view that vocabulary controls in these grades can and should be greatly relaxed. Several of the newer basal series include substantial blocks of informational-type content, reflecting a view that development of what we may call the "reading-study skills" requires informational content, as appropriate to that purpose.

It has long been popular to urge teachers to teach reading-study skills as they teach the content subjects, and the teaching of reading skills is always a part of good teaching in those subjects. Yet it is unfortunately true that teaching reading skills and teaching content somehow get in each other's way. Reading materials designed to build reading-study skills, with content appropriate to the purpose, provide for direct focus on the objectives sought.

There is, too, the need to teach literature. Here, obviously, the appropriate content is literature—and the term means something more than the simple narrative material of the conventional readers. Moreover, the teaching of literature proceeds to objectives that we may call "understandings." Through literature, children can share in the experiences of all kinds of people—people like themselves and contemporary with them and people removed from them in time and place and circumstance. The study of literature is above all else a humanizing, liberalizing study, one that feeds the growth of values. Thus, it should not be cluttered with skill-building exercises; rather, it should proceed directly toward its intrinsic uses.

To note the importance of experiences with literature is to suggest the importance of the elementary-school library. Certainly one of the improvements to be hoped for in the '70's is substantial extension of library resources and services in the schools. Under present conditions of school finance, the development does not seem a likely one. With libraries or without them, reading programs can and should provide planned programs in the study of literature, integral in the total reading program for the middle grades. Those years are, to use poetic language, the Golden Years for reading literature and for forming the attitudes that lead to lifelong reading pleasure.

There are clear signs that schools will give top priority to reading instruction in the '70's. This will mean, among other things, budgeting time for effective reading programs—time for teachers to teach reading, time for children to practice reading. There is no general agreement on any one best way to teach reading or on any one set of materials as better in all ways than others; consequently, reading programs will make use of varied methods and materials. Yet, in any one school, there must be structure to the program. To say that there is no one best way is not to say that "grab-bag" teaching is good. The quality of instruction will continue to be the most important element in a reading program, and it is likely that teaching performance will be subject to more searching review and evaluation than in the past. Most schools will continue to develop programs around a basal reading series, making effective use of varied supplementary materials that will increasingly be so designed that children can be as self-directing as possible. Middle-grade reading programs will be strengthened; there will be clearer focus on the reading-study skills and on literature, using materials appropriate to the objectives sought.

1   Suggestions for Further Reading

Reviews of summaries and applications of research in reading will be found in the following publications: Mildred A. Dawson (ed.), *Combining Research Results and Good Practice* (International Reading Association, 1967); Helen K. Smith (ed.), *Perception and Reading* (International Reading Association, 1968); Warren Cutts, *Research in Reading for the Middle Grades* (U.S. Government Printing Office, 1963); Doris V. Gunderson, *Research in Reading at the Primary Level* (U.S. Government Printing Office, 1963); James L. Laffey (ed.), *Reading in the Content Areas* (International Reading Association, 1972); N. L. Gage (ed.), *Handbook of Research on Teaching* (Rand McNally, 1963), 865–928; C. W. Harris (ed.), *Encyclopedia of Educational Research,* 4th edition (Macmillan, 1969), 1069–1104.

A succinct interpretation of the contributions of other disciplines to the field of reading is George D. Spache, "Contributions of Allied Fields to the Teaching of Reading," in Helen M. Robinson (ed.), *Innovation and Change in Reading Instruction* (National Society for the Study of Education, 1968) 237–90. Psychological theory and its relation to reading and reading instruction are reviewed by Russell G. Stauffer, *Directing Reading Maturity as a Process* (Harper and Row, 1969), 292–352; and Emerald V. Dechant, *Improving the Teaching of Reading* (Prentice-Hall, 1970), 516–82. A good review of reading theory will be found in Harry Singer and Robert B. Ruddell (eds.), *Theoretical Models and Processes of Reading* (International Reading Association, 1970). For a better understanding of how language and reading development are related, see Frank Smith, *Understanding Reading* (Holt, Rinehart and Winston, 1971); and Doris V. Gunderson (compiler), *Language and Reading: An Interdisciplinary Approach* (Center for Applied Linguistics, 1970).

Some answers to persistent questions about reading that teachers and parents ask will be found in Nila Banton Smith (ed.), *Current Issues in Reading* (International Reading Association, 1969). Good summaries of emerging guidelines for teaching reading appear in Helen M. Robinson (ed.), *Innovation and Change in Reading Instruction* (National Society for the Study of Education, 1968), Chapters 2, 3, 4, and 9.

2

DIAGNOSTIC TEACHING
OF READING

A viable reading program is one that develops the basic skills pupils need in order to read, teaches them how they can use reading as a tool for learning, fosters appreciation of and taste in literature, and develops permanent interest in reading. These become the objectives of instruction and at the same time serve as guidelines for evaluating the progress children make in reading.

Reading is not a simple or a single skill. Rather, it is complex and consists of many different components. Children do not learn to read in a few years just as they do not learn to master any other complex activity in a short time. They learn some reading skills and develop some attitudes toward reading as they move from one stage of development into another. But it takes them a long time to achieve proficiency in reading. What they may be able to accomplish at one point in their reading development will not be good enough at another. This fact explains why some pupils can cope with early reading demands but not with later ones. It also underscores the need for continuous evaluation and for orderly reading experiences based on such evaluation.

The diagnostic teaching of reading is a continuous process. It focuses more on evaluation than on measurement since its intent is to increase learning rather than to grade children's performances. The aim of diagnostic teaching is to identify growth areas in which pupils are progressing satisfactorily as well as to pinpoint others to which greater attention must be given. Teaching plans are based on pupils' reading performances and directed toward specific learning tasks. Some initial appraisal precedes instruction and yields tentative judgments about where pupils are on the reading continuum. Further evaluation accompanies instruction and provides teachers with the data necessary to make their teaching relevant to the needs of the pupils.

Wanda Gale Breedlove expresses the need for diagnostic teaching with the census slogan, "How will we know where we're going if we don't know where we are?" She makes a strong case for diagnostic teaching by pointing out that not only does the learner benefit from knowing how good his performance is, but the teacher benefits as well, for an awareness of the student's capabilities gives direction to the teacher's efforts. The role of the teacher in diagnostic teaching is not only as a model and reactor but also as a learner, since he searches for different ways to approach his pupils and help clarify their understandings. Pupils must analyze their errors to improve their performances, and teachers must analyze their teaching performances to improve their teaching methods.

Breedlove suggests that teachers rely on the materials pupils read to find out where they are, their strengths and weaknesses, and their reading progress. These materials include texts, workbooks, tapes—whatever teachers use for reading instruction—at levels suitable for different groups of pupils. Analysis of pupil responses to word recognition, comprehension, and other skill exercises reveals the directions instruction might take and suggests the strategies to accompany them. Conferences allow teacher and pupils to develop prescriptions for learning and to facilitate the evaluation of progress or lack of it. Pupils are encouraged to participate actively with teachers in trying out procedures, predicting outcomes, and evaluating the results of their efforts.

In "Classroom Diagnosis of Work-Study Skills" Harold L. Herber deplores the amounts of time, energy, and money that are wasted on testing by many schools. He observes that few purposes are served when schools merely give tests and record scores. "Even in these schools where teachers are required to enter in their record books both the ability and achievement scores for students in all of their classes, relatively little attention is paid to that information. . . . If it is not used, then it should not be accumulated." To counter what Herber believes to be too prevailing a practice, he offers justifications for testing: "If [tests] are used to identify the needs and strengths of individual students and if those needs are served and the strengths reinforced as a result of this knowledge, then the testing program is worthwhile and should be continued." This attitude is in harmony with that of Breedlove, who stresses the study of pupil responses in order to develop appropriate instructional plans.

Herber classifies work-study skills into three categories: receptive, reflective, and expressive. He believes that content classes are better vehicles than reading classes for the development of these work-study skills since in content classes teachers need not concern themselves with problems of transfer of learning, and pupils receive immediate reinforcement of their efforts. In the self-contained classroom this means that teachers will focus on these skills as pupils seek to master concepts in science, social studies, mathematics, and other content areas.

Pupils' levels of attainment must be taken into account as teachers seek information about the work-study skills. It is one thing to be able to identify a main idea when it is clearly stated and followed by details, all of which bear upon it. It is quite another when pupils have to *infer* the main idea from related but diverse information. So to speak about competence in any skill implies *degrees* of attainment.

Unlike Breedlove, Herber suggests that the results of standardized tests, when adequately understood and treated, have value for diagnosing pupils' skills. After indicating how classroom teachers might use the test data to assess pupils' needs, he points out the weakness of standardized tests. He gives a number of reasons for preferring to rely more on informal inventories for evaluating work-study skills. He cautions that an inventory that measures general reading skills rather than specific work-study skills will fail to reveal the ability of students to read informational materials. Evaluations must be based on functional reading in order to make diagnosis functional. "Functional diagnosis is not easy, but it is exciting and it is effective. What more return can one ask for an investment of one's energy and time?"

The preparation of informal reading inventories and the interpretation of their results are the subjects of Robert A. McCracken's "The Informal Reading Inventory as a Means of Improving Instruction." After defining terms and offering a rationale for informal evaluations, the author describes in explicit terms what such tests would include and how they would be administered. Oral and silent reading, word meaning, comprehension, reading rates, study skills—all these would be covered in a comprehensive inventory.

Standards for evaluating reading achievement are expressed in fairly precise ways. Teachers are interested in ascertaining the independent, instructional, and frustration reading levels of each pupil, and McCracken offers them guidelines to follow. The percentages of accuracy he suggests for pronunciation and comprehension vary to some extent from those given by others, so teachers should use them with some flexibility. The procedures for preparing and administering informal inventories and interpreting their results also reflect some differences between this author's views and those of other reading specialists.

How teachers can use the results of informal reading inventories to influence instruction and the attitudes of children toward individual differences are the topics covered by the final section of the article. McCracken concludes by referring to a problem created for other learning areas: pupils who understand why reading instruction must be differentiated soon ask why there is no differentiation of instruction in their other subjects. All pupils should be so influenced!

The last article in this chapter describes still another form of informal inventory. This is the cloze test, which John R. Bormuth has worked with for some time and has validated for use in assessing the degree to which instructional materials can be understood by pupils. Bormuth provides the rationale for using cloze procedures to evaluate the difficulty students have in reading materials and contrasts cloze tests with conventional ones. He provides experimental evidence to justify the use of cloze tests as a measure of comprehension ability and as a measure of comprehension difficulty.

Cloze testing involves the deletion of every *nth* word from selected passages. Bormuth suggests the deletion of every fifth word. He says that deletions should not be more frequent, but recognizes that they may be less frequent. Pupils are expected to supply each missing word, and according to the author, "responses that exactly match the deleted words furnish the most valid measures of comprehension." Detailed information about constructing and administering the cloze tests and interpreting their results is given.

Bormuth concludes: "An important way to adjust instruction is to place in each child's hands materials having a level of difficulty that is appropriate to his level of reading skill. The cloze readability procedure provides several devices to help accomplish this objective." What should be added to this statement is the idea that cloze testing offers still another instrument to help us engage in diagnostic teaching.

The Diagnostic Teaching of Reading

WANDA GALE BREEDLOVE

"How will we know where we're going if we don't know where we are?" The census slogan well-known to an estimated two hundred million Americans suggests the importance of evaluation *before* planning. *Evaluation* and *planning* are words common to education but often divorced from each other. Planning is requested at the beginning of instruction and all too commonly evaluation is required only at the bottom of a lesson plan, at the conclusion of a project, or at the end of the term. In contrast, diagnostic teaching is the interrelation of evaluation and planning contiguous with instruction.

Textbooks on the teaching of reading, in particular, emphasize planning and evaluation prior to, during, and after instruction to determine the reading status of pupils, to diagnose specific strengths and weaknesses, and to assess pupil progress (*12*). A most useful strategy for teaching diagnostically often cited and discussed in reading circles is a test-teach-test-teach cycle that is open-end and continuous (*5*).

TEST-TEACH CYCLE

This brand of diagnostic teaching refers to some form of teacher observation and testing that involves an initial "look" at the child on a specific learning task to determine what, if any, of the required skills he does not now know.

Evaluation initiated before teaching gives the teacher direction. It not only assesses where the students now are but also indicates where the students are not—the *are now* being those skills and abilities that the student exhibits under the testing conditions and the *are not now* those skills and abilities that he is unable to perform (*3*).

The teacher can then plan a program intended to assist the child in learning or applying these skills and abilities. A check-up or post-test on the

THE DIAGNOSTIC TEACHING OF READING by Wanda Gale Breedlove. From *Diagnostic View-points in Reading*, ed. Robert E. Liebert (1971), pp. 19–28. Reprinted with permission of the International Reading Association and Wanda Gale Breedlove.

same task assures the child and the teacher of mastery or the necessity to develop an alternative teaching strategy. Mastery necessitates setting up a pretest for the next skill or ability. Lack of mastery presents a problem-solving task to the teacher and the learner. The cycle of test-teach-test-teach is self-perpetuating—continuous. It leads from one test to the next and one plan to an alternative on an individual basis through all skills, methods, and materials. To elaborate on the test-teach pattern, consider the role of the learner and the role of the teacher in diagnostic teaching.

READING: AN EMPIRICAL EXPERIENCE

Reading is an empirical experience. The learner is continually testing his perception of the printed page with his stored past experiences and making predictions. Each response is an experiment—a test run to determine whether what he reads reflects the print on the page. This experimentation is based on the learner's experiences and will be interpreted in light of his peculiar view of himself and the reading act.

Reading, whether interpreted as an act of decoding, encoding, or both, follows a pattern of formulating tests and evaluating results, as do other dimensions of learning—as does teaching! Further, neurophysiological and linguistic theory would appear to reinforce the essential character of testing and evaluation for the diagnostic teaching of reading if, as Miller, Gallanter, and Pribram *(8)* submit, testing and evaluation are integral functions of the brain in processing information and dictating action in the learning process. Testing every operation he performs is the only way a learner can confirm that he is reading c-a-r as *car* or indicate to himself that he needs to modify his information, experience and/or environment, or the way he manipulates the information so that he will be reading c-a-t as *cat* and not *car*.

ROLE OF THE LEARNER

Testing is vital to the learner. The results of the test, correct or incorrect, are important both to the learner and to the teacher. A significant role of the teacher is to supplement a student's inadequacy in testing his own performance. The teacher can temporarily assume a testing facility for the child. Snygg *(10)* considers the implications of the value of error recognition to the student in his cognitive field theory of learning when he suggests, ". . . learning does not take place unless the learner finds that he has made a mistake. . . ." There is no reason for the learner to respond differently unless a response does not work. If a response does not work, then the learner must try to combine his information in other ways, reexamine the environment for more clues, and sort the experiences he has had for similar situations; in short, he must change his way of thinking about the particular problem. An error alerts the student that there is an element in the situation that is different from what he has supposed. Predictions, operations, and evaluation follow.

The reader who corrects his oral reading on the basis of sentence sense is running one such trial when he reads, "Sam is a cool car—I mean, cat." This reader has set an objective—meaning. He proceeds through the material and might well read, "The villagers journeyed west" as "The villagers traveled west" with no oral correction or recognition of miscalling a word. The sentence passed a meaning objective; none for word recognition was in effect. Learners determine their own objectives and run tests accordingly. Sometimes learners agree with those of the teacher; often they do not. It is obvious that objectives based on individual perceptions differ for individuals. Certainly, the more closely the teacher can set objectives with students or take existing student objectives to achieve her own criteria of student performance the more likely specified learning is to occur, especially if learning is the individual *becoming* through his own processes of experiment.

A focus on learning implies change—change on an individual basis and change that develops after some difficulty in meeting a situation. The optimum level of difficulty proposed by emphasis on error recognition would be "one which allows the student to win success after difficulty" (*10*). The ensuing change can and often has been measured in terms of specific behaviors. But in addition there is now measurable evidence that the process is more important than the product. Learning expresses itself experimentally as evidenced by the increased weight of the brain of laboratory animals (*6*). Learning as change is structural and chemical change and is prior to behavioral change. It is change within as well as without.

As the learner formulates and modifies predictions, he learns. Imagine a young child who predicts that *ed* forms the past tense of verbs. He has heard others use *ed* in statements, like "Mommy walk*ed* to the neighbors" and "Brother stay*ed* at Grandma's." The child generates, "I went*ed* with Daddy" by forming a word he has never spoken before. This act cannot be imitation. It is a more important process. He has predicted that if he did something in the past, *ed* will express what he wants to say about it in the present. But this prediction, no matter how dependable, will not always work. Other ways of sorting information and predicting must be found so that the learner can exercise control over his environment. Mother responds, "You *went* with Daddy yesterday." Mother provides a model for what the child wants to be. She "teaches" by example and provides constant feedback for the child, by pointing out incongruities that the child has not had the experience to recognize himself and by expanding his restricted information.

ROLE OF THE TEACHER

Now to refine the *role* of the teacher in the diagnostic teaching process, the teacher can serve much the same role in learning as a parent does in language acquisition. The teacher, too, can serve as model and reactor, but there are unique ways in which she can facilitate learning. A brief review of the learner and the learning process illuminates the diagnostic teacher's role. Learning is becoming. Applied to the teacher, this statement means that a teacher need not have all the answers. She, too, is a learner. Another important consideration is the value of error recognition. The teacher may learn most herself when her usual answers to student learning difficulties are least effective. It is then that she searches for new ideas and alternate ways of presenting information. It gives the teacher an opportunity to increase the weight of her own brain, to work through strategies, to exercise her mental prowess. Teacher activity of this kind is problem solving. Personally and professionally, the teacher in such a scheme is always becoming her best self.

The teacher as learner values student errors as well as her own. Rosenburg makes student errors the primary source of information for adjusting teaching methods *(9)*. If the teacher analyzes the results of tests, she can develop a plan of processes, procedures, and materials to "try out" with each student based on his specific errors or patterns of errors. The teacher's plan might best be thought of as "testing" hypotheses based on a comparison of information collected from student responses during paper and pencil testing and informal observation which how she presented materials and information to other students—a process of making the "best guesses" she can to help her solve the teaching problem of a particular student on a specific skill under specified conditions, unique to any teaching problem she has ever encountered before.

SUGGESTIONS FOR THE CLASSROOM

The teacher may well puzzle, "Diagnostic teaching sounds good, but does it have any practical application for my classroom of thirty students? Is there any way to work it in with basal lessons? Isn't diagnostic teaching something like individualized instruction? What materials can I use? How can I find time? Will it really make any difference in the reading level of my students?"

Frankly and honestly, there are no conclusive answers to these queries. The individual teacher-learner is probably the only one who can attempt an answer. Even then, the answer will only be a tentative one—a working hypothesis until tried with learners, modified, and evaluated by teacher and student.

A response to these questions is, however, possible in terms of the search that teachers have made in their classrooms and research that has been conducted in other learning laboratories. I would like to submit suggestions for the classroom in three areas introduced earlier in this discussion: a student's current reading status, specific strengths and weaknesses, and progress.

Initial testing and evaluation screen general student performance and direct additional testing. In a seventh grade spelling class the teacher assigns Unit 32, "The Consonant Sound *N*." Students work on assignments in the unit during the week, and on Friday the teacher dictates words from the unit. The expedient of giving the same unit test on Monday can eliminate those students who already spell the words in the unit and thereby free them to work on spelling words that they cannot now spell. Those who cannot spell the words on Monday, but by studying in the book can do so by Friday, continue the routine and demonstrate learning-gain success after difficulty. Those students that cannot spell the words on Monday and cannot spell them on Friday, try studying words devised from less difficult lists or from a different way of working with the same words in terms of length of time and alternative exercises. Granted the teacher has not yet located specific ways of working with each student on specific skills; she has begun to place students on instructional levels and through additional evaluation during the course of classroom assignments will locate patterns of errors. This first rough testing in the subject helps the teacher to determine instructional level, much as reading out of a graded basal reader or subject matter textbook in a group informal reading inventory alerts the teacher to groups of children that can proceed in the materials at their grade level, as well as to groups of children that require testing in graded books at lower levels of difficulty, and to others that can perform reading tasks far above grade level.

MATERIALS, PROCEDURES, PROCESSES

As the teacher tests students in multigraded texts, she discovers one student has no way of attacking words, another can sound out letters in words but is unable to blend them, a number of students can answer comprehension questions when the teacher reads a selection to them but cannot answer questions from their own reading, or that many of her students cannot answer questions requiring reorganization of ideas. Evaluation of this kind alerts the teacher to areas of instruction appropriate for individuals, small groups, and the whole class.

The search begins for materials on the reading levels of some pupils, word analysis work sheets, tapes of phonic blending exercises, and reading paragraphs that ask for reordering sequence of events. Some of these materials will serve as further tests on particular student problems, and the teacher will predict other ways of working from these additional pupil responses. A student may not respond to a piece of material at all. This lack of response may lead the teacher to choose other reading selections or to assist the pupil in developing his own materials.

As the teacher views pupils more closely for specific strengths and weaknesses, she is looking for an every-pupil-response. Essentially the teacher directs each individual to materials and with methods that result from predictions made from individual responses. If in a classroom of thirty pupils students are to respond to different items, the teacher must incorporate into the program some form of self-checking material. Items on teacher-developed reading kits require individual pupil responses and self-checking. Teachers organize workbook exercises, stories, and pictures into kits corresponding to the order of skills presenting in basal materials or on scope and sequence charts coded at a number of difficulty levels. In his book, *Materials for Remedial Reading*, Gilliland (4) offers suggestions for arranging these materials to include varied presentations of skills from many different texts. The workbook sheets serve as initial tests of skills. Students proceed to easier or more difficult exercises or to another skill altogether on the basis of their responses. Answer keys mounted to the back of these materials encourage self-correction. Plastic film placed over the pages and marked with a grease pencil or crayon that can be wiped clean render the materials reusable. The teacher can collect and with the assistance of her pupils construct extensive files of readily available exercises on every conceivable skill at all levels of difficulty.

In addition to the representative materials cited certain teaching procedures expand the usefulness of testing-teaching patterns in the classroom. One of these techniques, the construction of instructional objectives, assists the teacher in formulating teaching goals with built-in tests and established levels of mastery. To clarify this relationship, examine the following objective stated in behavioral terms: "The learner will be able to name the letters of the alphabet when presented in random order with 95% accuracy." Teachers of beginning reading might well want children to recognize the letters of the alphabet. The behavioral objective emphasizes the test for learning, observation of the learner, and evaluation of the product. Evaluation is built into teaching in the planning stage of instruction (7).

Numbers of objectives are operating in the classroom for groups and individuals simultaneously. Checklists are an effective way of cataloging objectives for easy access. Structural analysis skills, visual symptoms, reading interests, and language patterns are a few of an infinite variety of observations that are possible. During instruction constant checks can be conducted for each pupil on a variety of skills and abilities. A favorite format is one that includes the names of all pupils on the same sheet to aid in the comparison and contrast of pupils that exhibit similar patterns for grouping purposes and team learning or highly individual responses for special attention.

As evaluation continues in the teaching strategy, more and more instruction will be directed for individual pupils because unique characteristics of pupils once recorded will dictate the formulation of widely differing hypotheses about the approaches and rates and materials in each experimental process. An individual conference provides an appropriate setting for guiding individual study. A brief discussion with each student to develop learning prescriptions is central to testing student and teacher predictions for their mutual evaluation of the learning process. Process, after all, is the chief concern—a problem-saving attitude developed by solving problems.

A problem to solve is one that the learner recognizes. He compares *what is* with his conception of *what ought* to be and solves the problem by "filling in the gap." Filling in the gap may be accomplished by one of a number of heuristic devices, such as relating the unknown to the known, restating the problem in other words, solving a related problem, decomposing the problem into simpler problems, working backward, or omitting certain details.

The teacher translates her objectives into student tasks. She offers feedback that confirms a match or mismatch. Based on a comparison of his response with what is expected, she tests heuristic prescriptions in the form of oral discussion questions or written exercises to lead the student to a learning experiment. Teacher preinstruction for the experiment consists of organizing items and stimuli in order to direct student "tests."

Given the previously stated objective of naming the letters of the alphabet, a learning experiment develops. The learner predicts that the symbol *j* on the first flashcard presented represents the oral "jay." As he continues naming the letters and confirming his "educated guesses," the teacher notes a pattern of misnamed letters, *b, p,* and *d* on a checklist. She hypothesizes that an important element in this pattern of errors may be an inability to distinguish these symbols visually. The teacher decomposes the original problem into simpler problems. She selects a paragraph and asks the pupil, along with another who is misnaming *q* and *p,* to circle *p* with a red crayon each time it occurs in a paragraph. She gives each pupil a sample of the letter. She then asks both pupils to complete the same activity for another troublesome letter with a blue crayon. When completed, each student tests his associations with those of the other. One of the students is unable to distinguish between the various forms of the letters *q* and *p* visually. The teacher reevaluates and directs the student to cut out *p*'s from a magazine. The student that completed the visual task requires a different prediction. "Say the name of the letter I say after me," requests the teacher. She flashes the symbol *b* and says "bee." The student responds, "bee." He predicts "bee" when *p* is shown as well. Predictions and tests continue using various auditory materials and questions until the student organizes the auditory information in these related problems into a scheme for naming the letters in random order.

Student hypothesis testing and mutual evaluation in small groups is equally practicable for developing comprehension skills. In a most intriguing discussion of *Teaching Critical Reading at the Primary Level*, Stauffer *(11)* encourages students to predict story endings, test their predictions one with another, and to change predictions as the story unfolds. It is this willingness to make "best guesses" and to continually evaluate ideals and attempt other responses in the light of a problem that best characterizes the student under the influence of the diagnostic teacher. Listening to students discuss their own problems and how they attempt to solve them gives clues about the individual thinking-testing process and affords the teacher unusual opportunities for observing current mental operations and suggesting others (*8, 12*).

For the teacher interested in developing diagnostic teaching abilities, teacher-training materials are available. One, a test of problem-solving facility, gives practice in evaluating pupils and predicting instructional tactics (*1*). Simulation exercises produced by Della-Piana and associates (*2*) involve comparing student reading responses with possible teaching strategies to formulate instructional hypotheses.

The foregoing discussion calls for a diagnostic search of the total learning field for materials, techniques, and processes. It asserts the need for an experimental attitude in teacher and learner to constantly evaluate change and the tentative answers that change brings. From the variations of the print on the page to the firing of electrical impulses in the brain, the learning payoff is the potential for the learner and the teacher-learner to be engaged in the process of evaluating, predicting, acting, and becoming more able to learn in the process.

References

1. Burnett, R. W. "The Diagnostic Proficiency of Teachers of Reading," *Reading Teacher,* 16 (January 1963), 229–239.
2. Della-Piana, Gabriel, Betty Jo Jensen, and Everett Murdock. "New Directions for Informal Reading Assessment," in William K. Durr (Ed.), *Reading Difficulties: Diagnosis, Correction, and Remediation.* Newark, Delaware: International Reading Association, 1970, 127–132.
3. Freidman, Miles, et al. "Readiness and Instruction: Individual Diagnosis and Treatment," in Edith Grothberg (Ed.), *Critical Issues in Research Related to Disadvantaged Children.* New Jersey: Educational Testing Service, 1969.
4. Gilliland, Hap. *Materials for Remedial Reading and Their Use.* Billings: Montana Reading Clinic, 1968, 97–104.
5. Harris, Albert J. *How to Increase Reading Ability.* New York: David McKay, 1968.
6. Hilgard, Ernest R., and Gordon H. Bower. *Theories of Learning.* New York: Appleton-Century-Crofts, 1966.
7. Mager, Robert F. *Preparing Instructional Objectives.* Palo Alto, California: Fearon Publishers, 1962.
8. Miller, George A., Eugene Galanter, and Karl H. Pribram. *Plans and the Structure of Behavior.* New York: Holt, Rinehart and Winston, 1960.
9. Rosenburg, Marshall B. *Diagnostic Teaching.* Seattle: Special Child Publications, 1968.
10. Snygg, Donald. "A Cognitive Field Theory of Learning," *Association of Supervision and Curriculum Development Yearbook,* 1966.
11. Stauffer, Russell G., and Ronald Cramer. *Teaching Critical Reading at the Primary Level,* Reading Aids Series. Newark, Delaware: International Reading Association, 1968.
12. Strang, Ruth. *Reading Diagnosis and Remediation,* ERIC/CRIER/IRA Reading Review Series. Newark, Delaware: International Reading Association, 1968.

Classroom Diagnosis
of Work-Study Skills

HAROLD L. HERBER

Taking into consideration the time, energy, and money that are expended on testing in schools throughout the United States, diagnosis is one of the least profitable activities in education. At specified times throughout the year millions of students are tested with innumerable devices. Millions of dollars are spent on these tests which measure the variables of human ability, aptitude, and achievement.

Most of the tests are designed either to predict the future or assess the past. Some tests are used to determine students' native ability and to measure their aptitude for certain types of academic endeavor. Students' futures are determined in large part on how well they perform on these tests. If they do well, they are encouraged to pursue more sophisticated studies in the areas of their strength; if they do poorly, they are consigned to involvement in less rigorous intellectual pursuits. In this way, the tests are predicting and determining the future.

Tests also assess the past. Achievement tests determine how well students have learned the content of different subject areas and the proficiency they have developed with skills required for independent pursuit of the curriculum. How well students have progressed is used as an index of the quality of the instruction they have received.

Tests which measure current achievement of students during the course of a year's study in a given subject are rarely standardized. They frequently are constructed by teachers merely to measure the amount of information acquired and retained in a content area. Frequently they exclude the work-study skills needed for independent acquisition and application of ideas. All learning stops when these tests are administered because they measure primarily what one already knows rather than the power to acquire additional information and to use it correctly.

But let us continue consideration of value received for money spent in the area of diagnosis. This testing produces mounds of papers to be corrected, with scores to be computed and recorded and analyzed by frustrated teachers. Scores for these millions of students are entered on well-wrought

CLASSROOM DIAGNOSIS OF WORK-STUDY SKILLS by Harold L. Herber. From *Progress and Promise in Reading Instruction*, A Report of the 22nd Annual Conference and Course on Reading, University of Pittsburgh, 1966, ed. Donald L. Cleland, pp. 64–75. Reprinted by permission.

records (in many cases not even this is done). Over the years the information is accumulated dutifully until seniors are identified by fat folders in the guidance office. To this accumulation is added, each year, the latest information from the most recent tests, entered by tired teachers, concerned counselors, or suspicious secretaries.

This ritual is performed each year throughout the country and millions of dollars are spent in the effort. Unfortunately after the feverish activity of administering the tests and scoring and recording the marks on cumulative records has been completed, one finds that comparatively little is done with the information other than to compute grade and/or class medians to indicate growth or lack of it.

It has been my sad experience to observe that in many schools with elaborate testing programs, teachers are comparatively ignorant of their students' academic and intellectual needs. Even in these schools where teachers are required to enter in their record books both the ability and achievement scores for students in all of their classes, relatively little attention is paid to that information. If this information is worth accumulating, it should be used. If it is not used, then it should not be accumulated. Little is accomplished if the only purpose in administering tests and recording scores is to compute grade and class medians.

The factor for determining if a test should be administered is an affirmative answer to the question: "Will it benefit the student in his pursuit of quality education?" If tests are used only to indicate that courses of study are accomplishing something for the mass of students then they have little value. If they are used to identify the needs and strengths of individual students and if those needs are served and the strengths reinforced as a result of this knowledge, then the testing program is worthwhile and should be continued.

It is in light of this latter purpose for testing that I would like to pursue our topic: "Classroom Diagnosis of Work-Study Skills in Secondary Schools."

WORK-STUDY SKILLS

Before we consider their diagnosis, it is important to consider what is meant by work-study skills. In order to establish a context for my paper on diagnosis it is necessary to enlarge on the identification of work-study skills.

In a publication from the International Reading Association it is suggested that study skills can be divided into three categories: the *receptive,* the *reflective,* and the *expressive.* (1) The *receptive* category embraces those skills which are needed to gain information from the printed page. Word analysis, word recognition, and word meaning skills are involved at this level. Basic comprehension skills such as reading for main ideas and details, also are exercised at this level. Locational skills are important here and students with competence establish purposes for reading and will select correct and needed information according to those purposes.

The second category of study skills is the *reflective*. When students have acquired the information from the text, they must manipulate it and reflect on its meaning. At this level students apply interpretive skills to determine the author's meaning. Students perceive cause and effect relationships, distinguish between fact and opinion, detect bias or assumption, perceive implications. They observe the organizational pattern of what is read, and this aids retention and recall.

Also at this level students manipulate the details which are acquired at the receptive level and through this manipulation begin to see relationships emerge. From these relationships they form concepts, generalizations, which they apply to previously learned information or to present experience.

The third category into which study skills can be grouped is labeled the *expressive*. When operating efficiently within this category students are able to transfer the meaning of what they have read to other situations. They are able to draw conclusions by seeing relationships among the many details they have received and reflected upon. They are also able to suspend judgment or wait on their conclusions until they have acquired sufficient evidence to warrant the formulation of a conclusion. In his article "Organization Produced," Courtney[2] suggests that after the students have acquired the information and reflected upon its meaning they are able to report or give expression to the ideas. They can follow the same organizational pattern which appears in the reading selection or develop a new pattern to give expression to the ideas they have developed. Through the organization they produce, students give evidence that they perceive relationships among ideas that have been acquired through the study processes. They are able to make use of the information so as to extend their knowledge.

IN THE CLASSROOM

The context in which work-study skills are developed, that is, the classroom—determines the nature of the skills being produced. Work-study skills can be acquired through reading classes. Not only the skills which might be classified as receptive, but also those which would be considered within the reflective and expressive categories can be taught and reinforced in reading classes at all grade levels in secondary schools. When taught in *reading classes,* the skills in each of these categories are of a general nature—applicable to many types of material. Consequently, the skills still require adaptation when transfered to other subject areas to be applied to the study of content materials.

When *content classes* are the context for the development of work-study skills, one finds that here, also, skills in all of the classifications can be taught and reinforced:—*receptive, reflective,* and *expressive.* The skills encompassed in each of these categories are taught as they appear in the materials peculiar to various content areas. When instruction of this type is provided in each of the content areas there is no need to be concerned about transfer. Each skill is taught as it is needed in order to read the content materials under consideration. Students experience immediate reinforcement as they apply the skills to required reading material.

In summary, then, "Classroom Diagnosis of Work-Study Skills" suggests that we are concerned with skills which students must employ to acquire or receive, retain or reflect upon, and to use or give expression to ideas which are present in the required reading matter in all subject areas. It is with this understanding that we pursue our topic in detail.

OBJECTIVES

What is the purpose for diagnosing work-study skills? Obviously it is to determine students' relative strengths and weaknesses in the use of skills which have been identified as essential to satisfactory achievement in any given subject areas. But the question that is of vital importance is, "To What End?"

If one is engaged in diagnosis, one should be essentially concerned with the needs and potential of *individuals.* There is ample evidence that diagnosis is conducted by people concerned solely with the performance of the *total group.* However even these people cannot ignore scores of individuals since the total group performance is determined only by compiling the scores for each individual. Therefore any diagnosis, group or individual, necessarily must take into account the performance of individuals. And it is to this end that one should engage in diagnosis: so that he might serve needs of individual students. In this manner, Smith and Dechant say:

> . . . the child (may) be helped to grow from dependence to independence in his learning. The major goal of effective teaching is that the child become independent through acquisition of effective work and study habits and the techniques for self-directed learning. Accomplishment of such a goal demands that not only teachers of reading but all teachers employ methods that will help their students learn and learn how to learn. Of course motivation for learning is exceedingly important also, but motivation without direction rarely results in optimum learning.[3]

Intellectually, teachers are committed to the principle that the needs of individuals must be discovered and be well-served so independence can be achieved. And this is the basis for diagnosis.

However, one finds a peculiar phenomenon here. *Diagnosis* should be based on one purpose, service to individuals. Yet because teaching is frequently conducted according to an opposing practice—service to the entire class rather than the individual—diagnosis frequently follows suit. Diagnosis is geared to finding needs of the class, and the needs of individuals are not given careful consideration.

If diagnosis is to provide information on individual students and if this information is to make possible instruction geared to the needs of individual students, several factors need to be taken into account as one selects instruments for the diagnosis. As already has been discussed, study skills can be grouped into several categories: *receptive, reflective,* and *expressive.* This alone injects complexity into the diagnosing procedures. However, there is the added factor that the skills which are found in these classifications can be employed at many levels of sophistication. For example, the skill of reading for main ideas is listed in the *receptive* classification. This skill can be applied at a very elementary level wherein students perceive the main idea of an expository paragraph which has a clearly stated topic sentence followed by several supporting statements. Students might well be helped to discover the main idea by being given several alternatives from which they select the best. This is reading for "main idea" at a simple level. Contrast the more sophisticated level where students determine a subtly implied main idea couched in abstract exposition with complex terminology and sentence structure. Both processes are identified by the same label—"main idea"—but a wide gap of sophistication separates the application in each instance. One finds comparable levels of sophistication for each component skill within the three classifications of study skills given above. Therefore, if the needs of individuals are to be served, one must know if a student is functioning principally in the receptive, the reflective, or the expressive classifications and one also must know the level of sophistication which characterized the student's application of given skills within each of these classifications.

Let us add to the complexity. Even as skills have degrees of difficulty, it is true that expository and narrative materials have layers of meaning. One might read a given account, whether it be expository or narrative, and read it either at the literal level of comprehension, the interpretive level of comprehension, or the applied level of comprehension. In the first instance a student would perceive the straightforward meaning that is conveyed, discerning what the words *say.* In the second instance, the interpretive level, the student would determine the meaning of what was said—interpreting its meaning according to certain criteria. At the applied level the student would apply his interpretations to his previous knowledge. These levels of comprehension reflect layers of meaning in the material and also correspond to the classifications of study skills identified above.

Again, if we are to serve the needs of individual students it is necessary for us to know both the degrees of sophistication with which they are able to handle given study skills and the layers of meaning or—if you will—the levels of comprehension at which they are able to function in reference to given expository or narrative material. This knowledge is the object of diagnosis in the classroom.

CLASSROOM DIAGNOSIS

I would like to limit my discussion to diagnosis in content classrooms because, I believe, little is done in these areas and also because relatively little direction is available in the literature. As related to content areas, there are two *kinds* of diagnosis in terms of attack: *direct diagnosis* and *functional diagnosis*. According to media employed, diagnosis can be classified into three categories: standardized tests; informal inventories; response to instruction. I will discuss these media for diagnosis in terms of their relative value. My comments on these media will be organized under the kinds of attack possible in diagnosing skills needs: direct or functional.

Direct Diagnosis

The most readily available means for classroom diagnosis of work-study skills is the standardized test. Tests are available for every grade level and for many combinations of reading and study skills. I would refer you to Simmon's and Rosenbloom's *Reading Improvement Handbook*[4] for a good list of such tests.

The convenience of a standardized test is apparent to anyone who has ever administered one, particularly when contrasted with the complexities encountered when structuring and administering and interpreting one's own test. One needs only to follow directions accurately in order to obtain the desired results. Standardized tests have been administered nationally and national norms established; so one is able to compare the performance of his own students with that of other students across country.

In addition to the factor of convenience, standardized tests also have value in that they provide a general index of students' performance in reading. From this index one can infer what achievement might be if the general skills were to be converted to the related work-study skills which are required in various subject areas.

Even this general index alone can be of value. It can contribute to the diagnosis of students' skills if the scores are plotted on a scattergram. One axis represents ability and the other represents reading achievement. One may plot the ability—reading achievement correlation of his students in a given class and see how their scores are distributed on the scattergram. This plotting makes visible the range of differences among students in a given class and makes clear the need for individualizing instruction. Since one axis represents general reading achievement one may infer that a similar distribution would occur for the same students if work-study skills were to be plotted rather than general reading skills.

Other things can be done with data from standardized tests. These procedures ensure more value received for the amount of time, energy, and money expended. For example, one can make an item analysis to determine the reading processes students must employ in order to perform successfully on each test item. With this information one can make sets of answer keys in which only those spaces which correspond to items requiring a given skill are punched out. These keys are placed on the answer sheets, one at a time, one for each type of skill. Thus, at a glance, one is able to determine relative strength and weakness in the application of given skills. This analysis compensates for one of the weaknesses in standardized tests which is that they provide an index of only general reading performance—a rather general application of general skills. But through this item analysis one is able to determine relative strengths and weaknesses in skills which are appropriate to the reading of various content area materials. Thus standardized tests can contribute to classroom diagnosis of work-study if one analyzes the data beyond the general index scores.

Still another bit of information can be secured and this has significance for work-study skills. We know that as they study, students have different rates of learning; they pace themselves differently. This has significance for performance on standardized reading tests. We have found that when we examine the *accuracy score* of a student on a given test we learn a good deal about his work habits. Some students work rapidly and are relatively inaccurate, but because they react to more items they are likely to achieve a higher score. Other students work at a very slow pace but achieve 100% accuracy. However, since they cover only relatively few items, they achieve a lower score. The question is, which one is the better student; which one is the better reader? Information of this type gives us a clue as to how to work with these two types of students in content areas. Since our goal is to serve the needs of individual students, then simply through this kind of analysis of performance on standardized tests we are able to determine, to a degree, the work habits of individuals. Standardized tests can contribute to a diagnosis of work-study skills.

In any of these ways standardized tests are rendered more valuable and can contribute to diagnosis of work-study skills. However, there are certain drawbacks that should be pointed out. Because of these factors I consider standardized tests as the least valuable for classroom diagnosis.

First, standardized reading tests do not take into account the fact that given skills can be applied at various levels of abstraction and there are levels of comprehension at which students can perform. Some tests measure skills in reading for main idea, for example. Because a student has not achieved the level of sophistication in the use of that skill which is required by a particular test, he does not score correctly. The examiner—analyzing the test—assumes the student lacks this skill completely. Yet we often find that the student does have the ability to perceive main ideas but at a more elementary level than the test required. We need this information in order to serve his learning needs, to know where to begin instruction. If he has absolutely no concept of what a main idea is, we do one thing; if he has a minimal awareness, we do another. Standardized tests do not provide this kind of information.

There is another weakness in standardized tests and that is in reference to what I call the transformation of skills. As students apply a given reading skill first in one subject, then in another, and then another, they must learn how to transform that skill to meet the demands of the different kinds of materials being read. Cause and effect relationship is applied to science material in one fashion, to social studies material in another, and to mathematics in still another. A student must know how to make this transformation or adjustment as he moves from one type of reading to another. Standardized reading tests do not measure this ability to transfer skills. Generally these tests measure the use of a given skill with either narrative or expository material and not too much consideration is given to the content area to which the material is related. Hence no consideration is given to assessment of students' ability to transform skills even though such information is crucial when planning a program for improving reading in content areas. It is for this reason, as well as others cited above, that I place standardized tests at the lower end of the value scale for instruments useful in determining strengths and weaknesses in work-study skills.

Another type of direct analysis is provided through informal inventories. Skills are identified and a direct analysis is made of students' competence in their application. Informal inventories are more helpful than standardized tests for diagnosing work-study skills because they can be designed for specific purpose in a local situation. There need not be a great deal of concern about standardization. Generally inventories are assigned around the material that is to be used by students in the subject areas for which the analysis is being made or, at least, in material of similar nature and quality.

Generally the procedure is for teachers to identify the kinds of work-study skills essential to satisfactory performance in a given subject area. Items are designed which will cause the students to react to content material in a manner which indicates their facility with specific skills. One must be careful lest he develop an inventory which measures *general* reading skills rather than the *specific work-study skills* peculiar to the kind of material being read.

These tests can be valuable if carefully designed. Through these instruments one is able to determine the relative competence of students in their ability to acquire, retain, and use information in subject content material. These tests determine students' familiarity with the kinds of materials required in the courses and their ability to transform skills to suit the demands of the text material. They provide a beginning point for instruction, having assessed the levels of need for each student. Again, if individual needs are to be served, the needs of all individuals must be ascertained.

One may enlarge the informal inventory to embrace not only skills but also awareness of content to determine background information and understanding of concepts as well as appreciation of purposes for studying concepts. One must be certain, however, that he has determined his purpose for the test before he includes items of this nature.

Functional Diagnosis

It is frequently said that the best testing is actually good teaching. It is true that the manner in which the students respond to good instruction reveals much about their ability and achievement levels. If one wishes to identify how well students perform with given work-study then it seems to me most efficient to provide instruction in the application of those skills to material normally required of them in a given course. As one observes students' response to this instruction, one is able to adjust the levels of instruction to meet the needs which are revealed.

For example, we have pointed out that students read at various levels of comprehension. We also have suggested that any given skill can be applied with varying degrees of sophistication. Based on our knowledge of our students' general performance level—which may be based on intuition or on standardized test scores—we determine that certain of them should react to an assigned reading selection at given levels of comprehension: some at the literal, some at the interpretive, some at the applied. We provide guidance at these levels, helping students to apply the skills at these levels. We are able to observe students' response to this instruction. If they respond well we can be certain that we are on the right track, and that we are meeting their needs and that we can begin raising the level of sophistication of skills applied to improve their competence in work-study skills. If the task is too easy for them, we are certain that we are not challenging them and that we are not giving them assistance at the level at which they need it. Where it is too difficult, obviously we will lower the level of required performance.

This functional diagnosis of work-study in the classroom can be accomplished only when there is conscious effort to serve individual differences. Only when one serves the individual needs of students can one determine the levels at which they are performing and the levels at which they need help in developing and applying work-study skills.

How one engages in this functional teaching, how one organizes his course, how one prepares his materials, and how one plans the development of content in this functional approach to diagnosis, is not within the purview of this paper. We do have evidence, however, that when students are given proper direction for reading the required text and are guided in reacting at the levels at which they are capable, they develop proficiency in work-study skills and this proficiency can grow in terms of sophistication and abstraction, at the pace at which the students are capable of progressing. When this kind of instruction takes place one does not need to rely upon standardized reading tests for complete diagnosis. Indeed one does not need to administer standardized reading tests frequently. In the same manner one does not have to become heavily involved in informal inventories because one can accomplish the same objective as he observes how students react within the framework of the regular assignment providing, again, that he has made an effort to differentiate levels of reaction to the material.

Functional classroom diagnosis of work-study skills also has another advantage and that is one does not become bogged down in record keeping. I am considerably concerned with the fact that we often spend so much time diagnosing students and recording information that we do not have sufficient time left to teach—and after all, this is our main purpose in being. Again, through functional diagnosis one is able to test as he teaches, economizing the time of both the teacher and the students.

"Classroom diagnosis of work-study skills" says to me that as I teach students what I want them to learn, I simultaneously, assess their response to my instruction. This assessment tells me how to adjust my instruction to meet their capabilities for reacting to it. My adjustment is such that I guide their reaction to the material, using skills inherent in that material, so they have a conscious experience in the use of appropriate work-study skills. How well they respond to that instruction is my diagnosis and determines the levels of abstraction at which subsequent lessons will be geared.

Functional diagnosis is not easy, but it is exciting and it is effective. What more return can one ask for an investment of one's energy and time?

Bibliography

1. Herber, Harold L. (ed.) *Developing Study Skills in Secondary Schools,* Newark, Delaware: International Reading Association, 1965.
2. Courtney, Brother Leonard. "Organization Produced," *Developing Study Skills in Secondary Schools,* Newark, Delaware: International Reading Association, 1965.
3. Smith, Henry P. and Emerald Dechant, *Psychology in Teaching Reading,* Englewood Cliffs, New Jersey: Prentice Hall, 1961.
4. Simmons, John S. and Helen O'Hara Rosenbloom, *The Reading Improvement Handbook,* Pullman, Washington: Reading Improvement, 1965.

The Informal Reading Inventory
as a Means of Improving Instruction

ROBERT A. McCRACKEN

Teachers give informal reading inventories every time they make a reading assignment, every time they give a test, every time they discuss with children what has been read. The informal reading inventory can lead to improved instruction, but using an informal reading inventory does not automatically improve instruction. For an informal reading inventory to affect improvement in teaching, a teacher must know what an informal reading inventory is; how to administer, record and evaluate the results; and how to use the results.

This paper is organized into two sections. The first section defines an informal reading inventory, tells how to administer it, and presents objective standards for evaluating the results. The second section concerns the use of informal reading inventory results in the classroom.

WHAT IS INFORMAL READING TESTING?

An informal reading test or inventory is a nonstandardized reading test. A child's abilities in reading are tested using excerpts from a graded set of books or a single text. The child reads these excerpts orally and/or silently and the teacher obtains samples of the child's reading performance at each book level. The child's reading performance is evaluated against predetermined standards.

One basic purpose in informal testing is to determine if a text which the teacher wishes to use is too hard to read, about right in reading difficulty, or too easy for a given child. (A book which is rated as too easy in reading difficulty may be used because its content is important, but it would not be used as a text from which to teach a student to read.) A second basic purpose of an informal reading test is to determine the book level or levels at which each child can be instructed in reading. These two purposes are not in conflict. This second purpose, however, usually requires more time and more testing.

THE INFORMAL READING INVENTORY AS A MEANS OF IMPROVING INSTRUCTION by Robert A. McCracken. From *The Evaluation of Children's Reading Achievement,* ed. *Thomas C.* Barrett, Perspectives in Reading 8 (1967), pp. 79–96. Reprinted with permission of the International Reading Association and Robert A. McCracken.

The word *informal* may be misleading. The testing procedures and standards are set and fairly formal. *Informal* means that the testing is non-standardized in the technical sense of test construction and administration. *Informal* does not mean relaxed or subjective.

Informal reading testing presumes that reading achievement reflects a developmental growth pattern similar to growth in physical weight, height, shoe, or shirt size. One does not need to know the size of a shirt to determine if it fits a child. One puts the shirt on the child and observes if the shoulders are too broad or too small, if the sleeves are a reasonable length, if the neck can be buttoned, etc. One can judge if a shirt size is proper because one knows how a shirt should fit. As a matter of convenience (perhaps necessity in our society) shirt sizes have been given numbers and manufacturers use the same standards for marking shirt sizes. However, one rarely measures the length of a child's arm or the size of his neck to determine his shirt size. One uses the shirt as the measuring stick. If a size fourteen shirt is too tight in the neck, one tries on a size fifteen, etc. When a size fourteen shirt becomes too small because a child is growing, the next larger size is bought. This approach is informal testing of shirt size, and the procedures used are fairly regular. One accepts and uses these fitting procedures because they work.

Informal reading testing does the same thing with books; it helps a teacher decide whether or not a book is the right size for a child, and it determines which book sizes are acceptable for instruction in reading. In informal reading testing one tries on a book for size.

Figure 1 presents this concept diagrammatically. Note that in this example the child can wear a size 12, 13, or 14 shirt even though size 13 is the best fit. Note that the child needs instruction in reading from book sizes 6, 7, 8, and 9. With instructional help he can read from all these levels. The best book for instruction is book 7, but books are not too easy until book 5 level and below nor too hard until book 10 level and above. A child's instructional level in reading usually is more than a single book level although we sometimes say that a student's instructional level is the midpoint of his instructional reading range or the level from which he can be instructed best.

HOW IS AN INFORMAL READING TEST ADMINISTERED?

Betts *(1)*, Cooper *(3)*, Durrell *(4)*, Harris *(5)*, Johnson and Kress *(6)*, Russell *(7)*, Sheldon *(8)*, and others have described informal reading inventories. Basically the method used in administering an informal reading inventory is as follows:

1. The child is asked to read both orally and silently from a graded series of books, usually a basal reading series. The child begins at a

Figure 1
Shirt Size and Book Size Measurements

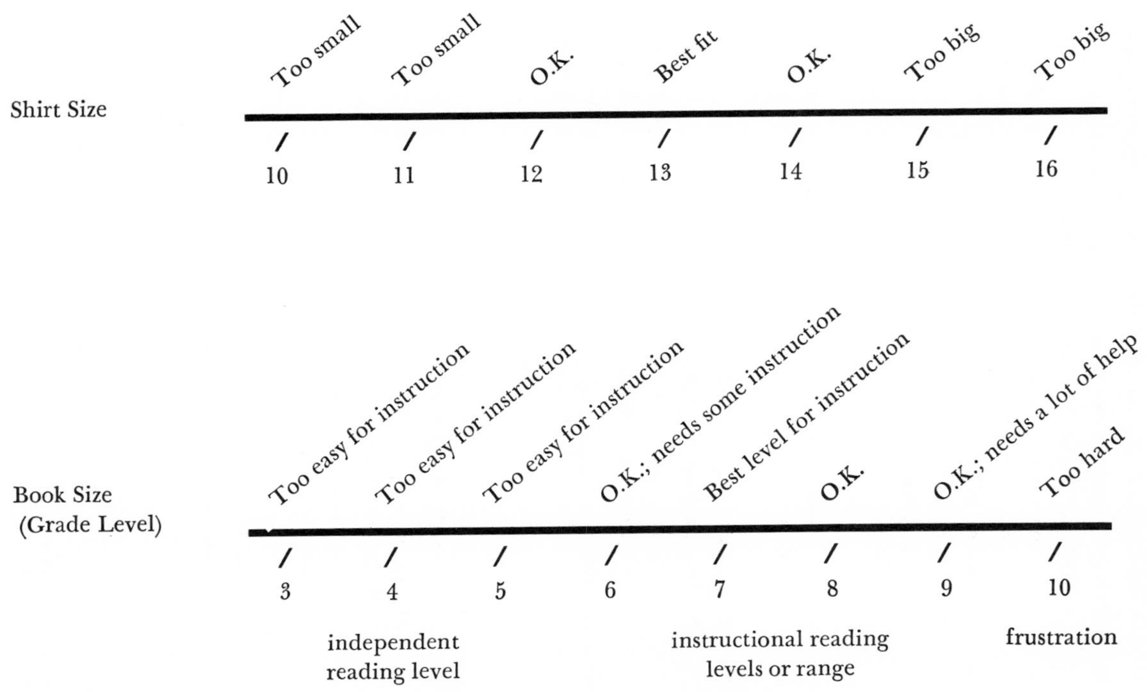

Shirt Size

10	11	12	13	14	15	16
Too small	Too small	O.K.	Best fit	O.K.	Too big	Too big

Book Size
(Grade Level)

3	4	5	6	7	8	9	10
Too easy for instruction	Too easy for instruction	Too easy for instruction	O.K.: needs some instruction	Best level for instruction	O.K.	O.K.: needs a lot of help	Too hard

independent
reading level

instructional reading
levels or range

frustration

level which is easy and the testing proceeds upward until the material is too difficult for him to read. Usually one selection is read orally and one silently at each book level.

2. As the child reads orally, the manner in which he reads is recorded. Almost any deviation from completely fluent reading is counted as an oral reading error.

3. After reading each selection, the child's comprehension is checked by having the child retell the story, by asking the child questions, or both.

A comprehensive informal reading inventory would include tests for the following abilities:

(a) to read orally without error
(b) to pronounce vocabulary in context (this is the percentage of words which a child recognizes when he is reading orally)
(c) to pronounce words in isolation, usually from word lists of *new* or *difficult* words introduced at a given book level
(d) to demonstrate comprehension of material read orally and material read silently (oral responses, written responses, responses to questions, and free responses)
(e) to define words in context, a part of comprehension which is frequently overlooked
(f) to answer questions which require going beyond recall, a part of comprehension which is frequently overlooked
(g) to record speed of oral reading
(h) to record speed of silent reading
(i) to reread orally or silently to find the answer to a question missed in a comprehension check
(j) to skim new material to find the answer to a question
(k) to skim material which has already been read to find proof of an answer
(l) to apply appropriate study skills to text material, such as locating information using an index, using a glossary to determine word meaning, etc.

STANDARDS FOR EVALUATING
AN INFORMAL READING TEST

The reading achievement of the child at each book level is evaluated as being *independent reading level, instructional reading level,* and *frustration level.* The terms are almost self-explanatory.

The *independent reading level* is the highest book level at which a child can read without assistance. His comprehension is excellent, his reading is fluent, and he is completely comfortable when reading.

Figure 2

Standards for Evaluating Achievement on an Informal Reading Inventory

Skill	Frustration Level	Instructional Level		Independent Level
		(questionable)	(definite)	
vocabulary (pronouncing in isolation)		below 50%	50% to 89%	90% to 100%
(pronouncing in context)*	94% or less	95% to 96%	97% to 98%	99% to 100%
errors**	1/10 or less	1/11 to 1/19	1/20 to 1/39	1/40 or better
comprehension and defining vocabulary in context	50% or less	51% to 69%	70% to 89%	90% to 100%
Speed	Silent reading speed definitely slower than oral (15 or more words per minute)	Any speed less than the listed minimums, or when oral and silent reading speeds are about the same.	Speed exceeds suggested minimums and silent speed exceeds oral speed by 15 or more words per minute.	Speed exceeds suggested minimums and silent speed is double oral speed.

*Percentage of words known when reading a paragraph or story. *Unknown words* are generally those which the examiner has to pronounce for the child.

**This is an error ratio—the number of errors: the number of words read; e.g., three errors in reading 96 words yields a ratio of 1/32 (instructional level), seven errors in 96 words yields a ratio of 1/13 (instructional level), twelve errors in 96 words yields a ratio of 1/8 (frustration level).

The *instructional reading level* is the book level (usually levels) at which the child can profit from and needs instruction from a teacher. A child's instructional reading level is almost always two or three book levels and sometimes six or seven.

Frustration level is the lowest book level at which the child cannot be expected to learn to read even with excellent instruction.

Figure 2 lists the standards for evaluating a child's achievement on an informal reading inventory. These standards are suggested as ones a teacher should use in learning how to use an informal reading inventory. The standards are based upon those found in the literature but are more detailed and more objective. For example, 75 to 90 percent is a common standard of comprehension for instructional level and 50 percent and below, for frustration. The literature is not clear about what to do with comprehension between 50 and 75 percent. A teacher who is experienced in the administration of an informal reading inventory should make subjective judgments when determining a child's reading levels. However, a teacher who is not experienced in administering an informal reading inventory should not make subjective judgments. Subjective judgments made by a teacher inexperienced with an informal reading inventory usually rate the child too high, placing him in frustration level for instruction.

The following rules are applied in evaluating a child's reading performance in using the standards in Figures 2 and 3. These are applied at each book level or to each book which is checked.

1. To rate a child's reading as independent, *EVERY* test score must rate as independent level. If seven scores rate as independent and one rates as instructional, the performance is rated as instructional. This classification means that the child is almost, but not quite, at the cutting point for independence. (Note the continuum in Figure 1.)
2. If *ONE* test score rates as frustration, the child's reading is rated as frustration regardless of the quality of the other scores.

Figure 3
Suggested Minimum Speeds of Reading in Basal Readers

	Words per minute	
Book Level	*Oral*	*Silent*
Primer—1^2	60	60
2^1 & 2^2	70	70
3^1 & 3^2	90	120
4	120	150
5	120	170
6	150	245
7	150	300

3. If one-half or more of the scores fall under the questionable half of instructional level, the performance is rated as frustration level.
4. If a child makes a better score when reading from a higher book level, the higher score is accepted as valid and the lower score is disregarded. For example, if after silent reading a child comprehends 95 percent of the material read at sixth reader level, but only 60 percent at the fourth or fifth reader level, one would have to conclude that the 60 percent score was invalid.

COUNTING ORAL READING ERRORS

There is some disagreement in the professional literature in the enumerating and the counting of oral reading errors. There is some disagreement about which errors are important enough to be counted. There are two considerations in determining what to count: (a) the error counting should be objective so that examiners can agree, and (b) the error counting should be easy enough to learn so that lengthy or highly specialized training or skill is not necessary. The following lists the oral errors to be noted in scoring an informal reading inventory. This list is based upon experience in training classroom teachers to administer informal reading inventories.

1. repetition—the repeating of a word or phrase
2. substitution—saying one word instead of the one in print
3. addition—inserting word or words or adding an affix
4. pronunciation—the examiner pronounces an unknown word for the child
5. omission—omitting a word, a phrase, or an affix
6. mispronunciation—saying a word in a manner which is definitely incorrect and not a result of defective speech or colloquial pronunciation
7. punctuation—phrasing in which the punctuation is definitely misread or added. Ignoring punctuation is not an error.

It was found one could get reliable counting of errors if one eliminated *hesitations* as an error category. Hesitations were not scored reliably; classroom teachers could not agree whether the hesitations had occurred.

One found that classroom teachers could not always agree on the classification of some types of errors. One did not seem able to teach which errors were significant and which were not—indicating that a criterion for errors which just counted the number of errors was best.

It was also found that the error pattern seemed related to level of difficulty and not to the type of difficulty the child might be having. For example, a good reader in sixth grade will make no errors when reading orally from a second or third reader. He begins to make repetitions as the difficulty of the material increases to fourth and fifth grade levels.

In the sixth and seventh grade level selections, the good reader begins to make substitutions and additions, but he will correct these errors. At the eighth and ninth grade levels, he begins to meet unknown words, to make omissions, and to mispronounce words without correcting these errors. Finally, he waits for assistance in pronouncing words in tenth grade level material and in materials above this level.

As the level of difficulty increases, the beginning errors persist; but proportionately they are less. This finding seemed also to indicate that the counting of the number of errors is more important than is the classification.

It has been argued that self-corrected errors should not be counted. However, a child who makes numerous errors and self-corrects all of them soon becomes frustrated through lack of success and through the slowness of intake of ideas. Self-correction cuts down reading rate. Slow reading rates are associated with frustration, with students *not* reading, and with students *not* doing assignments even though they seem able to do so.

Each type of error is counted equally; a repetition is counted as one error, an omission is counted as one error, or a word which has to be pronounced by the teacher is counted as one error. The type of error may have significance in determining what the student needs to be taught; but in determining instructional reading level the number of errors, not the kinds, is what is important. (The author suggests that diagnostic analysis of error pattern is valid only within the instructional range.)

To make error counting objective and precise, six rules are used:

1. Count only one error at any one place in the reading. Many times a student will make more than one type of error at one point in the story. For example, a student may omit a difficult word, reread (repetition) and mispronounce the omitted word, reread again (another repetition) and pronounce the word correctly. All of this would be counted as one error.
2. Count as one error if a student corrects an error, with or without repeating other words.
3. Count as one error the omission of more than one word of consecutive print.
4. Count as one error the addition of two or more words consecutively.
5. Count as one error if the child makes a second error caused by his forcing grammatical agreement. For example, a child who substitutes *he* for *they* will probably add an *s* to the verb, reading *he wants* for *they want*. The same thing happens when a male proper name is read as female. Later, the pronoun *he* is sometimes read as *she,* or *him* as *her.*
6. Count as one error the mispronouncing of a proper name or difficult word if the word appears more than once in a 100 to 150 word selection and is mispronounced two or more times. For example, students will sometimes read *Bill* as *Billy* consistently. Count as one error if a

proper name has two or more words in it and both are mispronounced. Count errors on simple words each time they occur. For example, if *a* is substituted for *the* three times, count three errors.

NOTE ON FRUSTRATION LEVEL

When a book or story is at frustration level for a student, this means that the book or story is so hard that the student cannot learn to read from the book even with help; it means that he will not read from the book if assigned to work alone in it; it means that if he is forced to try to read, he will fail and be frustrated in his attempts. A student does not have to exhibit all of the characteristics or symptoms of frustration to have reached frustration. One inability or several partial inabilities are sufficient to cause frustration. Frustration level usually is considerably higher than independent level; that is, a child meets frustration in books which are much harder in reading level than the level of the books which he can read independently.

Adults can experience frustration level by reading a technical text in a discipline in which they are ignorant, reading a simple fairy tale in a foreign language in which they have only a minimum competence, or by reading a mature novel or adult text while holding the book upside down. It is sometimes necessary to read for five minutes or more to become frustrated. It is very hard to be frustrated in thirty to sixty seconds even though all the characteristics of frustration may be evident. When reading from the technical text in an unknown discipline, the frustration will probably come from inability to understand the material. When reading from a simple story in a foreign language, the frustration will probably come from inability or uncertainty in how to pronounce the words. When reading from the adult story while holding the material upside down, the frustration will probably come from making and correcting numerous mistakes. Each one of these inabilities or difficulties is sufficient to cause personal frustration and an unwillingness to read if the reading is carried on for half an hour or more. The author strongly recommends that all beginning reading teachers force themselves to experience frustration in reading by trying all or at least one of these.

Note that frustration is not a matter of averaging. A perfect comprehension score does not offset inability to read orally; the ability to read fluently orally does not offset 30 to 40 percent comprehension. It is perfectly reasonable to expect perfect comprehension of a fairy tale printed in a foreign language, but the inability to "read" is frustration.

NOTE ON RELIABILITY AND VALIDITY
OF INFORMAL TESTING

Does informal testing give a fair sample of how a student will perform in a whole book? One of the beauties of informal testing is that it can be repeated using different pages when a teacher is in doubt. If a teacher is uncertain about error recording, if a teacher is uncertain whether a particular paragraph is typical of the book in which it is found, she can select another section and repeat the testing. For most students the following guides will ensure valid testing:

1. Select paragraphs or passages which are 100 to 200 words in length. Longer passages do not seem to be necessary, and they add to the testing time. A total of 100 words is ample for oral reading.
2. Select passages which can be comprehended without special knowledge of what has preceded or what comes next. Select passages which have something to be comprehended. Some 100 word samples convey little meaning.
3. Thirty seconds of elapsed time usually are sufficient for oral reading although this period may not cover 100 words. If a child is struggling through a passage of 150 words and is less than halfway through in thirty seconds, there is no need to continue to prove that he is frustrated. If a child is frustrated on the first three or four sentences of a story, he will remain frustrated. A teacher should stop the testing and shift to a lower level.
4. Be careful in selecting stories or passages from the first unit of a basal reading book since the first unit sometimes is a review of the previous level.

With short passages it is improbable that any student will be frustrated when asked to read (provided the teacher pronounces the unknown words). Since testing is sampling of the student's reading achievement, one must remember that the amount of frustration encountered in reading for one or two minutes of testing will be multiplied when a student is expected to read from a text for 15 minutes or more. A little bit of frustration, the small signs, encountered during testing should be accepted as indicative of frustration.

In the same way, the small amount of instruction apparently needed in short passages near a student's independent reading level should not be ignored. These small instructional needs are also multipled as the amount to be read is increased. If a student needs help in pronouncing or understanding one word in 50 running words in a story, a teacher would have 40 words to teach in a 2000 word story. Teaching 40 words before or while a story is being read would be an impossible teaching task.

NOTE ON SPEED

Informal testing can be conducted without measuring speed of reading. Speed of reading, however, seems to be a highly sensitive measure of the difficulty a child is encountering while reading. Speed of reading is measured in words per minute. Words per minute may be a misnomer. A better name might be *ideas perceived per minute.* The number of ideas in a paragraph seems to be related to the number of words so that measures of speed of reading may be measures of ideas perceived per minute.

A child will not read for any length of time if his intake of ideas is so small per minute that he is bored or frustrated by lack of progress. The use of speed seems justified when selecting library books for free reading or textbooks for daily instruction, particularly for those children who can read but don't or won't. Speed is a good predictor of frustration of longer passages and a good predictor of which children are able to do their homework assignments fast enough to bother doing them regularly. Failure to meet the suggested minimum standards predicts that a child will not do an assignment or read a book; surpassing predicts that he will, if he measures at least at instructional level otherwise. Knowing whether a child will read a book or do an assignment is probably as important as knowing if the child can.

Speed testing is the easiest of the informal testing measures to make objectively. Examiners may disagree concerning error count or comprehension percentage, but there is little disagreement about rate if a stopwatch is used.

To evaluate speed it is usually necessary to have measures of both oral and silent reading speeds. The difference between oral speed and silent speed determines the evaluation as much as the speeds themselves. The measurement of silent speed should be accompanied by a measurement of comprehension because a high silent speed without comprehension is meaningless. The frustration caused by low comprehension takes care of this disparity.

Note that speed, by itself, cannot cause a child's reading to be rated as frustration level unless the child's silent speed is significantly less (15 words per minute or more) than his oral speed at the same level. This circumstance occurs rarely. Speed can contribute to a frustration rating since speeds below the minimum standards are scored under the questionable part of instructional level. Oral and silent speed are counted as separate scores when determining if half or more of the child's scores fall under the questionable part of instructional level.

The standards for speed in Figure 3 are minimum standards, not average speeds. Average speeds are well above these minimum standards. The standards are for use at traditional basal reader levels. A teacher may use these with science, social studies, or trade books; but she should be cautious in determining the "basal reader level" of such books. The use of the levels yielded by the Botel Predicting Readability Levels (2) is a good technique. The speed standards are by book level regardless of the child's grade placement. A child reading at a given book level either exceeds or does not exceed the minimum speed standard. He does not pass or fail. His words per minute *must not* be read as a grade level by moving left in the chart from the speed to a book level. The comparisons for oral and silent speed, however, can be used without regard to level.

USING AN INFORMAL READING
INVENTORY TO AFFECT INSTRUCTION

In one third grade in a traditional school, basal reading was the adopted program. It was September. Mrs. Smith was the teacher. She had taught fifteen years but she was new to teaching third grade. She asked the reading consultant for help because the children in her reading groups were not responding well. She had inherited three reading groups from the second grade and had shifted one child.

Her top group had six children reading from a 3–2 level basal reader and doing the accompanying workbook exercises. The children were a joy but always finished their reading seat-work before the teacher had another activity ready. Her middle group had fourteen children reading from a 3–1 level and doing a good job. Her bottom group had eight children trying to read from a 3–1 level basal reader. They could not work independently even after instruction. They had trouble with silent reading, needed constant help when reading orally around the circle, and rarely got better than 50 percent the first time they did their workbook exercises. The teacher was using the same techniques with each group, techniques which seemed to work only with the middle group.

The reading consultant administered an informal reading inventory. The reason for Mrs. Smith's difficulties was apparent from the results. All six pupils in the top group were independent at level 3–2. All fourteen pupils in the middle group needed instruction at third reader level. All eight pupils in the bottom group were frustrated with 3–1 level material. Mrs. Smith and the second grade teacher had recognized individual differences, knew how to conduct informal testing without realizing it, but did not know how to record or evaluate the results.

Mrs. Smith saw the implications, but she was worried. The children would not like to be treated differently. The low group would be embarrassed by an easy book. They had read the 2–2 book last year!

The reading consultant made a chart, reproduced in Table 1. Each child took off his shoe and read his shoe size.

Each child was asked, "Why do you wear that particular shoe size?"
Pupils answered consistently, "Because it fits."

"Why don't you wear a bigger shoe? Don't you want your foot to grow faster?"

"That's crazy," a pupil said. "If my shoe didn't fit, it would hurt my foot or fall off when I run."

The reading consultant and the children talked about shoe sizes and the sequence of numerals indicating sizes. They talked about the impossibility of feet growing to be size 6 without having first been size 5 or size 4. They agreed that feet grow gradually from size 1 to 2, from 2 to 3 to 4, etc., not suddenly. They talked about book size and developed the concept that the numerals on basal readers are sizes, not grade level. They developed the

Table 1
Shoe Size of 28 Third Grade Children in September

Size		Number of Pupils
7–8		1
5–6		5
4		4
3		5
2		6
1		6
12		1

Table 2
Book Size of 28 Third Grade Children in September

Book Size		Number of Pupils
6 and above		2
5		2
4		2
3^2		6
3^1		8
2		5
1		3

concept that children learn to read book 2 after mastering book 1, book 3 after mastering book 2, etc.

The reading consultant made another chart, reproduced in Table 2. He told the children that he had measured their book sizes just as a shoe salesman might measure their foot sizes. He asked the pupils what their book sizes meant. From the top group came responses such as, "I need a harder book. Our reader is too easy. I've got a big book size." From the bottom group came responses such as, "I knew that book was too hard. I need an easy book. No wonder reading is hard."

Mrs. Smith told the children that many of them were going to shift into different books for reading instruction, that they would work in these books for one week, and that she would then ask them if their books fit. She explained that after the shoe salesman fits the shoe to your foot, he asks you to walk around a bit to see how it feels. After a week's instruction Mrs. Smith was going to ask, "How does your book fit?"

For a week the top group worked in book 4 and was assigned to choose library books for independent reading. The middle group continued reading from 3–1 level. The bottom group worked from a reader for bridging 1–2 and 2–1 levels. The methods of instruction shifted slightly during this first week primarily because the children in the bottom group did not need constant attention.

At the end of the week one boy asked to change. He was the poorest reader in the middle group. He wanted to work in the bottom group. Two of the top group children said that book 4 was, "Awful easy, but better than 3–2."

Some things stand out in this story:

1. *Children recognize and accept individual differences.* Teachers project adult fears when thinking that children are embarrassed by our recognizing that they are *poor* readers. The use of the word *poor* reflects this attitude. No one speaks of a *poor* shoe size. Children frequently are relieved when the teacher recognizes their difficulties. In the same way, adults are relieved when a doctor says, "You have *mal-and-sic-itis*. It will take awhile but we can cure it." Compare reactions to this statement and to one in which the doctors says, "I don't think there is anything wrong with you. Just try a little harder to think that you're well."

2. *Children can understand the need for grouping and individual attention.* They accept book size as a concept, and they accept instruction whenever they can succeed. *Poor* readers do not object to *easy, baby* reading books if they are successful in them. *Poor* readers don't want to fail in *easy* materials. If they are going to fail, they want to fail something respectable. Failure at grade level is respectable. It is this reaction to failure in *easy* books which has led teachers to conclude that pupils reject *easy* materials.

3. *A low reading group can work independently much of the time*. The material has to be at their instructional level.

Mrs. Smith had a worry. Won't the children in group one miss the skill program? Obviously not. The children already had mastery of the skill program. Mrs. Smith had another worry. Won't the low reading group be retarded by the lack of challenge? One can infer the answer by observing the top group. The top group came to third grade with mastery of the third grade reading program without ever having been taught from a reader harder than 2–2. Perhaps these children would have been more advanced had they had instruction at higher levels. But one cannot, on the basis of observations of top reading groups, conclude that *challenging* children makes them successful. Our most successful groups are those which have never been challenged much by reading group work. Working at an easy level with high success seems more important than challenge.

This story does not end with three groups in basal readers. The top group expanded into individualized reading without the teacher's being aware of it. Much of the reading instruction shifted to social studies and science. The success of the top group in self-selection led to the middle and bottom groups' having the same privilege. The classroom library was greatly expanded with plenty of easy picture books.

The informal testing led to a closer analysis of individual needs. Mrs. Smith assumed responsibility for continuous diagnostic observation. When a child had difficulty at instructional level, Mrs. Smith could see the difficulty because it was not shrouded with the maze of troubles which abound at frustration level. The able readers moved into projects which occasionally frustrated them, but more often just highlighted instructional needs; inefficient study skills and inefficient, ineffective note-taking stood out.

Mrs. Smith developed a sensitivity to standards of performance so that her instruction took its cue from pupils' performances, not from grade level expectancies. The stumbling of the poor reader group no longer sounded right because that was the way the poor reading groups always sounded. The fluency of the top reading group no longer sounded right when it reflected complete independence with the material. Both Mrs. Smith and the pupils were affected by the use of the informal reading inventory, and so was the teacher of grade four the following year when the pupils did not want to be in the same book and told the teacher why. But that is another story.

The description of another class, a fifth grade with 37 pupils, follows. Mr. Baron wanted to improve his social studies teaching. He had 40 copies of one text, as mandated by the district curriculum. He was doing the best job he could, but found that discipline sometimes was a problem. When discipline was not a problem, the children were apathetic and he had trouble covering the work. Mr. Baron knew about informal testing, although he had never really used it much. With 37 pupils he said he didn't have time to test each child. He already had the grades for the first six weeks of work in social studies: 5 A's, 11 B's, 15 C's, 4 D's, and 2 F's. Mr. Baron said they had tried projects and grouping but it didn't work. He had reverted to reading the text around the room. "At least I know that they have covered the material that way," he said.

Mr. Baron sounds like a teacher you and I don't want in our school. But he is not a poor teacher. He is frustrated. This is the classic syndrome of frustration in reading; the child and the teacher are equally frustrated.

The reading consultant visited Mr. Baron's social studies class for one day and listened to the reading circle. He noted the names of the pupils who were obviously frustrated, those who found the material to be at their independent level, and those who read with instructional competence. The consultant compared his results with Mr. Baron's grades. Much to Mr. Baron's surprise the reading consultant had identified the D and F pupils as frustrated and identified the A students as independent. The reading consultant had rated five others very close to frustration. Mr. Baron admitted that they were really D pupils but he had too many already. Mr. Baron had done his informal testing, although he did not realize it. But what to do?

Space does not permit describing the intervening steps. They are apparent from the results. The informal reading inventory, however, was discussed in a manner similar to that in Mrs. Smith's class.

Two months later Mr. Baron still had 40 basic social studies texts. Mr. Baron worked with his whole class to set purpose. He then read this basic text quickly, precisely, with added but not overwhelming explanation to those students who wanted to listen while 22 other pupils worked with 46 other books and two sets of encyclopedias. Most of the 46 other books were social studies texts. There were only single copies of 35 of them. Each book had been numbered to tell the book size. Each of the 22 children used the index or table of contents, working out page references which augmented the content of the *basic text*.

Two days later the pupils were all reading. The former F students were looking at pictures and reading captions and were reading some of the material from a social studies book labelled with a numeral one. Some A pupils were working in an adult encyclopedia, some with junior and senior high texts, and one pupil was tackling a college text. The pupils were fitting themselves to book levels. Study guides were developed jointly with Mr. Baron from the basic text material. For two days to two weeks pupils read, discussed in groups, collated and wrote, and finally summarized and tested.

Again some things stand out:

1. Pupils willingly accept individual differences and individual treatment.
2. A teacher was unaware that he had even given an I.R.I. and he was therefore unaware of the implications.
3. Poor readers can read independently in content areas.

One problem developed in both of these classes. The pupils soon asked, "Why do we all have the same spelling list? Why are we all at the same place in our arithmetic book?" But these are the problems which teachers know how to solve.

References

1. Betts, Emmett A. *Foundations of Reading Instruction*. New York: American Book Company, 1950.
2. Botel, Morton. *Botel Predicting Readability Levels*. Chicago: Follett Publishing Company, 1962.
3. Cooper, J. Louis. "Criteria for Determining Reading Levels and Suitability of Reading Materials," (mimeographed bulletin). Storrs, Conn.: The Reading Study Center, University of Connecticut (undated).
4. Durrell, Donald D. *Improving Reading Instruction*. New York: World Book Company, 1956.
5. Harris, Albert. *How to Increase Reading Ability*. New York: Longmans, Green and Company, 1956, 1961.
6. Johnson, Marjorie Seddon, and Roy Kress. *Informal Reading Inventories*. Newark, Del.: International Reading Association, 1965.
7. Russell, David, *et al. The Ginn Basic Readers*, Teachers' Manuals. New York: Ginn and Company, 1960, 1961.
8. Sheldon, William D., *et al. The Sheldon Basic Readers*, Teachers' Manuals. Boston: Allyn and Bacon, Inc., 1957, 1958, and 1963.

JOHN R. BORMUTH

Educators must have a valid method of finding out whether instructional materials are understandable to their students, for students must acquire much of their knowledge by reading written instructional materials. The conceptual or aesthetic merits of a set of materials is a primary consideration in the selection of materials. But materials can have little educational value if they are written in language that is so complex and obscure children cannot understand the contents. The readability formulas presently available are too inaccurate to provide educators with much help in this matter. And,

THE CLOZE READABILITY PROCEDURE by John R. Bormuth. From *Elementary English,* 45 (April 1968), pp. 429–36. Reprinted by permission.

while it is now possible to construct highly valid readability formulas (6), such formulas are still in the development stages.

This paper will describe ways in which teachers can use the cloze readability procedure to determine if instructional materials are understandable to children. A somewhat oversimplified description of the cloze readability procedure includes these steps: (a) passages are selected from the material whose difficulty is being evaluated, (b) every fifth word in the passages is deleted and replaced by underlined blanks of a standard length, (c) the tests are duplicated and given, without time limits, to students who have *not* read the passages from which the tests were made, (d) the students are instructed to write in each blank the word they think was deleted, (e) responses are scored correct when they exactly match (disregarding minor misspellings) the words deleted. When the tests have been made properly, a student's score can be interpreted as a measure of how well he understands the materials from which the tests were made.

The first section of this paper will discuss the validity of the cloze readability procedure. The second section will describe how the cloze readability procedure may be used to place a child in materials that are graded in difficulty, and to select materials that are understandable for a group.

VALIDITY OF THE CLOZE READABILITY PROCEDURE

Logical or Face Validity

Similarity to Conventional Tests. At first glance a cloze readability test appears to be a completely different kind of test and some authors have made much of this fact, attempting to construct all sorts of mystical theories about cloze tests. Some have professed to see a similarity between the processes involved in responding to a cloze test and the clozure phenomenon observed in the perception of geometric figures. Indeed, it was from just this kind of conjecture that cloze procedure got its name.

On closer inspection it can be seen that many of the items in cloze readability tests are identical to those found in reading comprehension tests made by conventional methods and that the processes required to fill cloze blanks are probably not different from those required to answer conventionally made items.

Conventional completion test items are made by simply deleting a word or phrase from a sentence. For example, given the sentence *The boys rode horses,* it is possible to make the completion questions,- - - -*rode horses, The boys- - - -, The boys- - - -horses,* and *The boys rode- - - .* The familiar wh- questions are made in much the same manner. A word or phrase is deleted, a wh- phrase is inserted in its place, and the sentence is transformed so that it begins with the wh- phrase. This gives the questions. *Who rode horses? What did the boys do? What did the boys do to the horses?* and *What did the boys ride?* As in cloze tests, the correct answers to these questions are the words or phrases deleted.

Contrasts with Conventional Tests.   But items made by cloze and conventional test making procedures differ in several important respects. First, in a cloze readability test, only one word is deleted at a time while in conventional tests, whole phrases and clauses may also be deleted. Further, in cloze readability tests, structural words may be deleted. (Structural words consist of classes such as articles, prepositions, conjunctions, modal and auxiliary verbs, *etc.*) But in conventional tests, only lexical words (consisting roughly of verbs, nouns, adjectives, and adverbs) may be deleted by themselves.

A second major difference is the fact that cloze readability tests are made only from the sentences in the text while conventional test items may be made either from sentences in the text or from the sentences that can be derived from the text (5). A sentence may be derived by any, or all, of three processes. The simplest type of derived sentence is obtained by transforming the sentence. For example, the sentence *The boys rode the horses* can be transformed into *Horses were ridden by the boys* and then transformed again into questions such as *By whom were the horses ridden?* Sentences can also be derived by substituting synonomous words or phrases for the words or phrases in the sentence in the text. Finally, derived sentences may be obtained by explicating the statements implied by the fact that two sentences are contiguous. Consider the sentence, *The boys got home first* followed by *They rode horses*. The contiguity of these sentences implies the sentence *Riding the horses caused the boys to get home first*. Only conventional test items can be made from sentences derived from but not actually in a text.

The third major contrast is the fact that cloze readability tests are taken by students who have not read the undeleted version of the passage.

Probably too much has been made of these contrasts between cloze and conventional tests. The student has eighty percent of the text on which to base his responses, so his responses very much depend on his ability to understand the text. Also, the fact that he has not read the original text may require that he uses processes similar to those required to answer questions made from derived sentences plus a sensitivity to the author's style and the tone of the passage. However, the contrasts do exist and so the question must be referred to the researcher, the final arbiter of such disputes.

Concurrent Validity

There have been many studies in which the objectives were to determine if scores on cloze readability tests correlate with scores on conventionally made comprehension tests and if the cloze difficulties of passages correlate with the difficulties of the passages as determined by conventional tests. By now, this literature has grown too large to review in detail in this paper. Since extensive analyses of this research are available in Rankin (13) and Bormuth (5) only a few of the most decisive studies will be mentioned here. In general, these studies seem to show that cloze and conventional tests measure the same processes.

Validity as a Measure of Comprehension Ability.   Cloze tests seem to measure a wide variety of comprehension responses. Wilson Taylor (18), the originator of the cloze procedure, found a correlation of .76 between scores on a cloze readability test and scores on a multiple choice test made from the same passage. Bormuth (3) constructed tests to measure the comprehension of vocabulary, explicitly stated fatcs, sequences of events, inferences, causal relationships, main idea, and author's motive in each of nine passages. He gave these and the cloze readability tests to elementary school students. The correlations between the cloze and conventional tests over each passage ranged from .73 to .84. When the correlations were corrected for the unreliabilities of the tests, the correlations approached 1.00. When the conventional tests were scored to obtain scores for each type of item, and then factor analyzed along with the cloze test scores, only one factor emerged. Kohler (11) performed a somewhat similar factor analysis study using tenth-grade students and obtained similar results.

To determine if cloze readability tests measure some of the subtler responses to language, Bormuth and Hook (9) studied the correlations between cloze readability tests and tests of ability to recognize an author's style. Two tests of ability to recognize authors' styles were made by selecting short passages from several of the works by an author, works that the students in the experiment had not read. The passages were then mixed with passages from works by other authors and given to college students who had just studied two books by each of the authors. Scores based on ability to correctly identify the passages by an author had significant correlations with scores on cloze tests made from passages taken from works of the author.

Validity as a Measure of Comprehension Difficulty.   The mean percent of items a group answers correctly on a cloze readability test seems to provide an accurate measure of the difficulty of the passage, almost regardless of how difficulty is measured. Sukeyori (16) found a correlation of .83 between the cloze readabilities of passages and the combined subjective ratings of the passages by three judges. Bormuth (8) found a correlation of .92 between the cloze readabilities of passages and the difficulties of the same passages as measured by multiple choice tests. Subsequently, Bormuth (2) used each of the four forms of the Gray Oral Reading Paragraphs. He found correlations ranging from .90 to .95 between the cloze and word recognition difficulties of the paragraphs and correlations ranging from .91 to .96 between the cloze and the comprehension difficulties of the paragraphs.

Experimental Validity

One study (8) approached the problem of cloze readability test validity experimentally. Passages were varied systematically in language complexity and subject matter. Both cloze and multiple choice tests were made over each passage and given to students at three different grade levels. Each factor and the interaction between language complexity and subject matter produced significant effects on both kinds of test scores. The effects were approximately proportional on the two kinds of test scores.

Validity of the Procedure Itself

A cloze test can be made, administered, scored, and interpreted in a number of ways. The particular set of alternative procedures actually used in the cloze readability procedure represent what researchers have found are the best procedures when validity, economy, and convenience are considered simultaneously.

Test Construction. The practice of deleting every fifth word is followed because it is simple and economical to use and because it provides the greatest number of items possible for a given passage and thereby provides the most reliable measure of passage difficulty. While deletions may be less frequent than every fifth word, MacGinitie (12) has shown that when a deletion system leaves less than four words of context between items, a student's ability to answer an item begins to depend heavily upon whether he was able to answer correctly the adjacent items. When this occurs, the scores become difficult to interpret in any meaningful way.

Administration. Cloze tests may be administered either with or without the student reading the passage from which the test was made. Research shows that the two methods are about equally valid. Taylor (17) found that scores on cloze tests administered after students had read the passage had slightly higher correlations with scores on comprehension tests. Rankin's (14) studies showed the same results. But the data in both studies showed that this effect probably was the result of scores being somewhat more variable than when the students had not read the passage, an effect that is more economically and easily obtained by simply adding a few items to a test. Therefore, because of the savings in testing time and preparation of materials and because results which are just as valid can be obtained, it is the most desirable procedure to give the tests to students who have not read the passages from which the tests are made.

Scoring. A student's response can differ from the deleted word in semantic meaning, grammatical inflection, and spelling. Users of the cloze readability procedure have settled on the practice of scoring correct just those responses which exactly match the deleted word, but minor misspellings are disregarded. This practice is based on findings by Taylor (18) Rankin (14) and Ruddell (15) that including synonyms as correct responses slightly increases the correlations between cloze scores and scores on comprehension tests. But their data show that it does so simply by increasing the variability of the scores, an effect that is far more easily obtained by adding a few items to the test.

Bormuth (7) classified responses into three categories depending on whether root forms of the responses were identical to, synonomous with, or semantically unrelated to the word deleted and then further classified the responses in each category according to whether they were grammatically correct or not. Only the grammatically correct responses had significant correlations with a comprehension test. When the scores based on the responses exactly matching the deleted words were held constant, all the other correlations dropped to zero. Hence, responses that exactly match the deleted words furnish the most valid measures of comprehension.

Interpretation.   There is some value in knowing that one passage is more difficult for students than another. But a cloze readability score has little value unless a teacher can say that the score does or does not represent a satisfactory level of performance on the materials from which the test was made. A standard has long been accepted (19) for conventional comprehension tests and this standard is widely used in practice (1;10). It asserts that materials are suitable for use in a child's instruction when he is able to answer correctly 75 percent of the questions asked him about the materials. The materials are said to be suitable for his independent study when he can answer 90 percent of the items. Bormuth (2;4) found that a score of 75 percent on conventional comprehension tests is comparable to a score of 44 percent on a cloze readability test made from the same passage and that answering 57 percent of the cloze items is comparable to answering 90 percent of the items on conventional comprehension tests.

Summary

In general, the studies of the validity of tests made by the cloze procedure seem to justify four assertions. First, cloze readability tests provide a valid measure of a student's reading comprehension ability. Second, the cloze readability procedure provides a valid method of measuring the comprehension difficulties of passages. Third, the procedure itself seems to incorporate both the most valid and the most economical of the possible alternatives for designing a cloze readability procedure. Finally, cloze readability scores can be used to judge the suitability of materials.

APPLICATIONS

Perhaps the most important advantage of the cloze readability procedure is that it requires little training in testing technology of the person who wishes to use the procedure in many of its important applications in schools. This section will describe two of the most important types of applications.

Placing Students in Graded Materials

One of the most critical tasks a teacher must perform in reading instruction is to place the students in basal or other practice reading materials that have the appropriate level of difficulty. The materials must present enough difficulty to permit practice of reading skills but not so much difficulty that the student develops faulty reading habits and feelings of frustration. The method of testing materials that is presently advocated calls for the teacher to have the student read orally a sample passage from each level of materials and then answer questions about what he just read. The teacher notes the adequacy of both the child's word recognition and comprehension. This method has undeniable advantages, but because it requires much time to administer and a relatively high degree of training on the part of the teacher, it is seldom used.

The cloze readability procedure can be used to make a set of tests which permit the rapid and accurate assignment of students to materials having an appropriate level of difficulty. The basic steps of this procedure consist of making a cloze test over each of the texts in the series, administering them to the students, scoring the tests, and placing the students in the materials on which their cloze readability score fell into the appropriate range.

The most critical part of this procedure is to select a test that best represents the difficulty of a text. This is done by initially making several tests from passages randomly selected from the book, finding the mean difficulty of the entire set of tests, and then discarding all but the test having a difficulty closest to the mean difficulty of all the tests.

A step by step description of this process includes these steps. (a) Select several passages from a book, say from six to twelve, using some random method for selecting the passages. Each passage should begin at the normal beginning of a paragraph and each should be at least 250 words in length. The test, for reasons of both convenience and test reliability, should contain exactly 50 items. (b) The tests are then given to students at the grade level at which the text is most commonly used, 25 to 30 students are usually enough to obtain reliable results. (c) The mean score on each test is calculated and then the mean of the mean scores is calculated. (d) Finally, the test whose mean score is closest to the mean of the entire set of tests is selected and the rest of the tests are discarded. (e) When a test has been selected for each of the texts a teacher is likely to use, the tests can be mimeographed and compiled into booklets which can be administered as group tests. When a student's score falls between 44 and 57 percent on one of these tests, the materials are at the level of difficulty thought to be suitable for use in his supervised instruction. Materials on which a student's score is above 57 percent are suitable for use in his indepentdent study.

The reliability of this procedure depends upon four factors. First, if longer tests are used, the students' scores will be more accurate, but the tests will also require more time to administer. Second, if a larger number of tests are made when selecting the test to represent the materials, the test selected will more accurately reflect the difficulty of the materials. If the tests are to be used frequently, it is probably worthwhile to select the test from a larger number of tests. Third, some materials vary unevenly in difficulty as they proceed. These materials are poorly constructed and their use should, if possible, be avoided. Fourth, the procedures outlined for constructing, administering, and scoring the cloze tests must be followed exactly or the results will be meaningless.

Selecting Materials for a Group

When materials are being considered for adoption by a school, one of the important questions that must be considered is whether the materials are understandable to students. While the quality of the conceptual content of materials is of paramount importance, that content has little likelihood of being learned unless it is presented in an understandable manner. The cloze readability procedure can be used for evaluating the suitability of materials for a group.

Criteria for Evaluation.   When the same text is to be used with all the students in a group, two criteria must be used in judging the suitability of the text. First, the materials whose difficulty is most appropriate are those on which the largest number of students can demonstrate a satisfactory level of performance. Second, the best materials are those in which the level of difficulty is fairly uniform throughout the materials. Either all sections of the book should exhibit about the same level of difficulty or the sections should gradually become more difficult as the student proceeds through the book.

Designing the Tests.   From the point of view of accuracy in evaluating materials, it would be ideal if a cloze readability test were made over the entire book. But practical necessity demands that testing time and materials preparation be kept at a minimum. Consequently, a procedure for sampling passages is usually required. If done carefully, sampling techniques will lead to accurate results.

The best plan is to divide the book into sections, select two or more sample passages from each section, and use those passages to make the cloze tests. The passages should be selected by some random process. For example, the paragraphs in a section might be numbered, the numbers written on slips of paper, the slips shuffled, and two or more slips drawn with the restriction that no two passages should contain the same material. The passages may be as short as a paragraph or as long as seems to make a convenient test. (A 250 to 300 word test fits nicely on one sheet of paper.) But each sample should be a length of continuous text, and it should begin at the beginning of a paragraph. The samples need not be of exactly identical length since the evaluator will be working with percentage scores.

Selecting the Students.   The students to whom the tests are given should be either the entire population who will use the book or a sample of students who are truly representative of that population. A good sample of students can be obtained by randomly drawing one or more students from every classroom in which the book will be used or by numbering the students in the population and randomly drawing the required number of students.

Administering the Tests.   For practical reasons, it is seldom desirable to give all the tests to every student. It is perfectly permissible to break the group up into subgroups and administer a fraction of the tests to each subgroup. But the selection of subgroups should be done by a random method to avoid biasing the means of the individual tests.

Analyzing the Results.   The analysis of students' scores begins by converting each score on each passage separately into a percentage score. A useful analysis is to determine what proportion of the scores were 44 percent or larger. This provides a measure of the proportion of students from whom the book, as a whole, is or is not suitable. Another analysis is to calculate this proportion of scores but to calculate it separately for each passage and for each section. When a frequency distribution is made of these proportions or when their standard deviation is calculated, the evaluator obtains a measure of how variable the different sections of the book are in difficulty. The evaluator can also plot a graph of the section difficulties to determine how the difficulty changes across sections, but for this purpose it is best to calculate the means and plot them.

Comparing Alternative Texts.   If the evaluator has some training in statistics or has access to a consultant who is competent in these matters, it is possible to compare texts and even compare two or more textbook series. Using an analysis of variance and a carefully designed procedure for selecting the sample passages from each text or series it is possible to find out if texts differ in difficulty, if the texts differ in the variability of their difficulty, and if the texts increase systematically in difficulty as they proceed from section to section and text to text.

Assigning a Grade Placement to a Text.   Often it is not possible to administer the cloze readability test to a representative sample of the students who will use it. And even if it is possible to do so within one school system, the results are seldom generalizable to other school systems. Consequently, it may be desirable to express the text's difficulty in a more generally useful form, as a grade placement. When a grade placement number is attached to a book, it can be interpreted as the average level of reading achievemnt attained by children who are able to read the book at the minimum level of comprehension.

The method is fairly simple, but it requires having a reading achievement grade placement score on each student and it requires some amount of calculation. The grade placement score is first correlated with the student's cloze readability percentage score. Then, using the common regression prediction formula, the evaluator calculates the reading grade placement score that is comparable to a score of 44 percent on the cloze readability test. This is the number assigned as the grade placement of the material. It can be calculated either for each passage in the text or for the text as a whole. The grade placement number is then useful to teachers in other schools, who, if they use the same reading achievement test, can calculate the proportion of their students who will be able to understand the text at a minimum level of competence by counting the number of students who have reading achievement scores falling above the grade placement number assigned to the text.

CONCLUDING REMARKS

Educators have long felt the need to adapt instruction to the individual differences among their students but their efforts to do so have often been hampered by the absence of practical procedures for attaining this objective. An important way to adjust instruction is to place in each child's hands materials having a level of difficulty that is appropriate to his level of reading skill. The cloze readability procedure provides several devices to help accomplish this objective.

Bibliography

1. Betts, E. A., *Foundations of Reading Instruction.* New York. American Book Company, 1946.
2. Bormuth, J. R., "Cloze Test Readability: Criterion Reference Scores," *Journal of Educational Measurement,* (1967). (in press)
3. Bormuth, J. R., "Factor Validity of Cloze Tests as Measures of Reading Comprehension Ability." Paper read at the American Educational Research Association in February, 1967.
4. Bormuth, J. R., "Comparable Cloze and Multiple Choice Comprehension Test Scores," *Journal of Reading,* 10 (February, 1967) 291–299.
5. Bormuth, J. R., *The Implications and Use of Cloze Procedure in the Evaluation of*

Instructional Programs. Center for the Study of Evaluation of Instructional Programs, University of California, Los Angeles, Report No. 3, 1967.

6. Bormuth, J. R., "Readability: A New Approach," *Reading Research Quarterly*, 1 (1966) 79–132.
7. Bormuth, J. R., "Validities of Grammatical and Semantic Classifications of Cloze Test Scores," *Proceedings of the International Reading Association*, 10 (1965) 283–286.
8. Bormuth, J. R., *Cloze Tests as Measures of Readability.* Unpublished doctoral dissertation, Indiana University, 1962.
9. Bormuth, J. R. and Ora M. Hook, "Cloze Tests as a Measure of Ability to Detect an Author's Style," *Proceedings of the International Reading Association*, 10 (1965) 287–290.
10. Harris, A. J., *Effective Teaching of Reading.* New York: David McKay Company, 1962.
11. Kohler, E. T., "A Factor Structure Study of Cloze Tests." Paper read at the annual meeting of the National Council on Measurement in Education, New York, 1967.
12. MacGinitie, W. H., "Contextual Constraint in English Prose Paragraphs," *Journal of Psychology*, 51 (1961) 121–130.
13. Rankin, E. J., Jr., "Cloze Procedure—A Survey of Research," *Yearbook of the South West Reading Conference*, 14 (1965) 133–148.
14. Rankin, E. J., Jr., *An Evaluation of the Cloze Procedure as a Technique for Measuring Reading Comprehension.* Unpublished doctoral dissertation, University of Michigan, 1957.
15. Ruddell, R. B., *An Investigation of the Effect of the Similarity of Oral and Written Patterns of Language Structure on Reading Comprehension.* Unpublished doctoral dissertation, Indiana University, 1963.
16. Sukeyori, S., "A Study of Readability Measurement—Application of Cloze Procedure to Japanese Language" (English Abstract), *Japanese Journal of Psychology*, 28 (1957) 135.
17. Taylor, W. L., "Recent Developments in the Use of 'Cloze Procedure,'" *Journalism Quarterly*, 33 (1956) 42–48.
18. Taylor, W. L., "'Cloze Procedure': A New Tool for Measuring Readability," *Journalism Quarterly*, 30 (1953) 415–433.
19. Thorndike, E. L., "Reading and Reasoning: A Study of Mistakes in Paragraph Reading," *Journal of Educational Psychology*, 8 (1917) 323–332.

2   Suggestions for Further Reading

Lucid examinations of the rationale for diagnostic teaching in all areas of learning are offered by Jack C. Merwin, "Historical Review of Changing Concepts of Evaluation," and Benjamin S. Bloom, "Some Theoretical Issues Relating to Educational Evaluation," in Ralph W. Tyler (ed.), *Educational Evaluation: New Roles, New Means* (National Society for the Study of Education, 1969), 6–25, 26–50. In the same volume, C. M. Lindvall and Richard C. Cox discuss "The Role of Evaluation in Programs for Individualized Instruction," 156–88.

A challenge is aimed at reading teachers by Richard W. Burnett, "The Classroom Teacher as a Diagnostician," in Dorothy L. DeBoer (ed.), *Reading Diagnosis and Evaluation* (International Reading Association, 1979), 1–10. In the same volume, Guy L. Bond makes a strong case for "Diagnostic Teaching [of Reading] in the Classroom," 126–38.

Detailed descriptions of methods of reading appraisal and evaluation through the use of standardized and/or informal instruments are found in Ruth Strang, *Diagnostic Teaching of Reading*, 2nd Edition, (McGraw-Hill, 1969); Robert E. Liebert (ed.), *Diagnostic Viewpoints in Reading* (International Reading Association, 1971); Thomas C. Barrett (ed.), *The Evaluation of Children's Reading Achievement* (International Reading Association, 1967); Mary C. Austin, Clifford L. Bush, and Mildred H. Huebner, *Reading Evaluation: Appraisal Techniques for School and Classroom* (Ronald Press, 1961).

For descriptions and evaluations of standardized reading tests see Oscar K. Buros, *Reading Tests and Reviews* (Gryphon, 1968).

3

READINESS FOR READING

Learning to read is a continuous process during which one reading experience provides readiness for the acquisition of more reading experiences. Thus readiness is a concern of all teachers who seek to encourage growth in reading. While it is known that readiness for beginning reading is an important stage in the development of reading, the importance of readiness at each level of development has yet to be fully recognized. Readiness might be considered as part of the total evaluation process as teachers strive to discover how effective their teaching has been and whether or not children are prepared to proceed to the next stage with its incumbent problems. Since the stages of reading development do not fall into neat compartments or into a series of discrete steps, it is a mistake to look at readiness as a task which recurs periodically, something to be concerned about, to be tested, and then to be dropped until the next recurrence. From the teacher's standpoint, whether he is responsible for kindergartners or sixth graders, readiness activities should represent an attitude of continuous questing to discover what children are ready for—how far up the hill toward reading maturity they have climbed.

To continue the analogy, this hill toward reading maturity is not always a slow, gradual ascent. The incline becomes steep at times; at other times there are rocks, even boulders, in the path of the children. The teacher's role requires that he know where each child is, that he encourage him to try harder tasks as he succeeds with easier ones, that he smooth the way where possible. This facilitation of movement toward reading achievement is what the concept of readiness is all about.

In an article published some time ago but which expresses principles that are still relevant today, Elona Sochor reviews the elements that teachers should include in appraising pupils' readiness to read, regardless of level: background of knowledge, oral language facility, achievement in reading, purpose for reading, and desire to satisfy the stated purpose by reading. Particularly at higher levels, comprehension is dependent on the reader's background of information and experiences as well as his ability to deal with

121

complex language structures, which in print seem to become greater obstacles to understanding than when they appear in oral speech. Failure at any reading level can lead only to more failure at the succeeding level; therefore, reading activities that ensure successful learning experiences bring about the readiness that enables pupils to cope with new learning. Readiness through identification of purpose establishes the set for reading and contributes along with all other factors to the children's acceptance of reading and feeling of assurance that they can fulfill the purpose for reading.

Problems reside not only in the reader but also in the materials for reading. Sochor says that "readiness has to be present to deal with the concise, all-inclusive, expository style, and the sentences filled with unfamiliar, difficult concepts and terminology." Failure to help pupils cope with these difficulties can only produce readers who verbalize but do not comprehend.

In their articles, James L. Hymes, Jr., and Dolores Durkin limit consideration of the readiness concept to beginning reading. Hymes maintains that the notion of "teaching reading readiness" to children before they are six years old is "gobbledegook," and that the "reading readiness absurdity has led to exercises . . . which have been no friend to the field of reading." He favors a child development stance to support the teaching of reading to children under the age of six: teach reading in a way that fits the child, that fits reading, that fits the goals of general education.

In line with Piaget, Hymes believes that all children at a given age possess similar characteristics, but that at the same time they are different in maturation, interest, need, background, and ability. Teaching must reflect an awareness of these differences. Hymes emphasizes the complexity of learning to read and urges that we keep its wide scope in mind and limit the burden of learning technical skills. He believes that our goal "is not to produce a reader but to help build a better human because now the child reads." He does not object to teaching reading to the young child. What he does object to are the rigid, narrow, impersonal, irrelevant programs that he sees all too frequently in his classroom visits. It is difficult to take issue with Hymes if what he observes is the norm for "under-six" reading programs, or for that matter, reading programs intended for any age.

Durkin seems to follow a tougher line on the question of reading readiness, although in many ways she is not unmindful of the pitfalls Hymes underscores. One of the main points she makes is that there is a relational aspect of readiness, that success in beginning reading depends not only on what the child is capable of achieving but also on the kind and quality of instruction he is exposed to. She further says that "we should be thinking in terms of readinesses in the sense that one collection of abilities makes a child ready for one kind of instruction, while a somewhat different collection might make him ready to cope with another."

Durkin points out another flaw in the thinking of many about reading readiness: the failure to recognize that to be successful in beginning reading the child does not have to be ready to learn everything there is to know about reading. Therefore, he needs only enough "readiness" to enable him to take the first step. Mastering the first step will prepare him to take the next one.

Durkin traces the history of the reading readiness concept by examining the validity of psychological beliefs and research findings as they relate to reading readiness. She raises a number of questions about both that cast some doubts on their applicability. Durkin believes that to ask, "Is the child ready?" is the wrong kind of question. "What is he ready for?" is a much more meaningful question but also a more difficult one to answer.

Readiness and the Development of Reading Ability at All School Levels

ELONA SOCHOR

The concept of readiness for learning, with its implications for teaching, has long been recognized in education. Without a state of readiness among learners, most of what may have been developed or taught in a classroom is forfeited.

A state of readiness at any particular time has a highly complex nature. It is a composite of a pupil's physical, social, emotional, intellectual, and language development. It reflects his past environments, his conditioning, his training, and his knowledge.

Moreover, any one of these factors cannot be isolated in reality. They are all highly interrelated in any one child, and the state of relationships may vary in different situations. In any group of children, there will be ranges in differences for each of the factors.

No pupil enters a school building devoid of any readiness. On the other hand, no two learners are alike in their states of readiness. Due to the multiplicity of factors, the ranges of differences increase as pupils grow older.

The existence of readiness for learning cannot be assumed. It must be assured, first, by appraisal and, then, by development. Being fundamental to all instruction, readiness for learning is a basic concern of all teachers at all times and at all school levels.

One important element in any instructional program is the mastery and use of reading ability. Since reading is a learned process, readiness is a factor which must be considered for any activity involving reading. To limit appraisal and development of readiness to beginning reading is to ignore the fact that developing reading ability is a continuous process extending in some respects into college instruction. Insuring readiness for reading must of necessity be a continuous process.

Considerations in readiness for reading then, may be classified into two categories for purposes of discussion: those basic to any learning process; and those that apply more specifically to reading.

READINESS AND THE DEVELOPMENT OF READING ABILITY AT ALL SCHOOL LEVELS by Elona Sochor. Reprinted from the May, 1954, issue of *Education*, by permission of The Bobbs-Merrill Company, Inc.

READINESS FOR LEARNING

Basic considerations in readiness for any kind of learning include (1) physical status, (2) mental capacity, and (3) emotional-social maturity and adjustment. In reading, "A mental, emotional, and physical readiness for sustained reading activities possesses as much significance in a modern secondary school as it does in a modern primary school." (1, p. 104)

Physical Status

Much is known about the importance of physical factors. The need for recognizing physical disability is obvious. A child who is unable to see the printing on a page cannot perceive the words. The child with a hearing loss will not profit from much of the typical activity in auditory discrimination. The malnourished or ill child will be unable to put forth the sustained attention necessary in reading. Such children are not ready for the tasks demanded.

Less commonly accepted, above the "first grade," are differences in physical maturation and make-up. For example, some children do not have the visual skills necessary for reading until they reach seven years of age. Others lack the physical coordination needed for easy and fluent writing until they are nine or ten years old. Nor can all children attain the same proficiency in any one physical activity. Regardless of the level, setting up requirements which demand physical development beyond that which exists merely creates problems in attitudes and habits. Such requirements are not taking into account physical readiness.

Mental Capacity

Mental capacity is significant in learning in that it helps to determine the quality and abstractness of thinking possible. Although the reliability and validity of any intelligence quotient may be questioned, the fact remains that a range in capacity does exist. All children in the ninth grade, for example, are not capable of understanding materials designed for the "average" ninth grader. There is no method, technique, or formula to make such readiness possible. In contrast, some ninth graders will have the ability to do college-level work.

Range in intelligence has other implications for readiness. If pupils cannot grasp certain abstractions, placing them regularly in situations which demand such thinking results only in failure. If differences in capacity have not been cared for in previous teaching, those children with intelligence indices at the lower end of the scale may not have learned as much as they could have. Since those with lower capacity learn more slowly and less than those with higher, an increasingly greater range in readiness as children grow older is to be expected.

Emotional-Social Factors

Emotional maturity and social adjustment are potent factors in readiness for learning. The pupil who is overly insecure, anxious, or fearful cannot attend to learning activities without his personal problems interfering. The one who lacks self-confidence, who is too dependent on others, who cannot accept responsibility may be defeated before he enters a classroom. Inability to respond to a teacher or to classmates without hostility and resentment, to share in the normal give-and-take in a classroom frequently results in aggression or withdrawal. Ignoring such children's lack of readiness produces frustrated unachievers with unhealthy attitudes toward themselves, others, and learning.

READINESS FOR READING

Readiness for an activity involving reading has two aspects: those in the reader and those in the material to be read. Since materials are selected for children, evaluations of reading readiness begin with the child.

Among the factors which must be considered in appraising a pupil's readiness to read, regardless of the level are: (1) a background of knowledge, (2) oral language facility, (3) achievement in reading, (4) a purpose for reading, and (5) a desire to satisfy the stated purpose by reading.

Background

A rich and varied background of information and experience is imperative for reading if a reader is to comprehend. Particularly is this true at the intermediate and secondary school levels where materials to be read are many and diversified.

A background of knowledge which includes well-organized concepts is basic to any reading, for there is not meaning inherent in printed symbols themselves. The reader attaches meaning, or concepts, to them from the background he possesses. When he has no appropriate concepts for a particular symbol, the symbol remains meaningless.

If, in attempting to read a selection, the reader lacks the knowledge he should have to understand the selection, he cannot read it successfully. Moreover, encouraging him to persist with little or no comprehension merely fosters verbalism. Without information, experiences, and concepts to take to reading, a pupil is not ready to read.

On the other hand, this aspect of readiness, in helping to guarantee comprehension, results in new knowledge acquired through the reading. By using and manipulating the information and concepts he has in reconstructing an author's ideas, the reader adds to what he knows by reorganizing his concepts, generalizing, and applying what he has learned.

Insuring adequate background cannot be relegated to a particular time of the year. It is a daily process. Even when a pupil has the basis for new learning, the appropriate knowledge must be called to mind by the teacher or the pupil himself, if he knows how.

Oral Language

Reading is a language process. In the normal sequence of language development, control of the spoken symbol precedes control of the printed symbol. Thinking precedes both. Insuring oral language facility as one element in readiness for reading has two advantages.

First, the thinking process that is basic to language can best be appraised and developed through speaking. Oral expression that is precise, logical, and concise indicates the ideas have been understood and organized. The problem of interpreting and evaluating an author's ideas is far more complex than thinking about and conveying clearly one's own. If thinking does not precede speaking, it will not precede reading; and reading demands thinking.

Second, a reader must have control over the concepts, the vocabulary, and the complexity of language orally at a particular level of difficulty before he can successfully interpret printed language at the same level. He must be familiar with unusual words or expressions before he begins to read. Otherwise he may read, as one child did, "to horse" as "two horses" with resulting confusion in comprehension. Adequate oral language facility is a prerequisite to reading comprehension.

Achievement

Readiness for reading a selection assumes a particular level of achievement. "Each new learning depends upon previous learning." (2, p. 110) What a child has learned about the reading process in a second reader, he will need in the third reader. What a pupil has learned about these United States in the intermediate grades is basic to what he will learn in the junior high school.

Achievement at any level of difficulty in reading includes the two factors already discussed, i.e., a background of knowledge and oral language facility, plus the body of understandings, abilities, and skills necessary to reading for meaning. The latter is commonly organized into three categories: word perception, comprehension, and application. Basic to all of these categories is the realization that words stand for concrete objects, for ideas, and for feelings.

Word Perception. [This] has two aspects: meaning and word form. Appropriate knowledge, previously discussed, results in the first. Ability to associate meaning to the symbol, which is basic to reading, and skills in recognizing and analyzing word forms are necessary for the second. Both aspects must exist to a suitable degree before a reader is ready to comprehend at a given level of difficulty.

The need for developing concepts has already been discussed. The ability to pronounce words correctly does not insure comprehension. Betty could say "fathoms," but she had no concept for the word. Since this was a key word, she was unable to understand the sentence. The meaning aspect of word perception is basic. Moreover, too many unknown concepts in material indicates lack of readiness for reading that material.

Ability to recognize or attack the word form itself is an index to readiness for reading a selection. Even the substitution of *a* for *the* affects meaning: "Give me a ball" is not synonomous with "Give me the ball."

Moreover, word recognition and word attack skills are developed sequentially. There is a state of readiness for the development of each one. When a child cannot hear the difference between consonant sounds, he is likely to have difficulty in (1) associating the correct sound with the visual symbol, the letter, and (2) using the consonant sound in attacking words. If he can't distinguish between long and short vowel sounds, he won't be able to apply the "final *e*" principle in reading or writing. Common is the case of the pupil who persistently omits syllables in words. Upon analysis, it becomes evident that the learner cannot identify the number of syllables heard and frequently even omits them in speech. The student who is unable to use the dictionary may lack many of the background skills that are assumed mastered before he begins to learn how to use it. In each case, the learner is not ready for the advanced skill because he lacks one or more of the basic skills.

Comprehension. Readiness to comprehend necessitates all of the factors discussed in this paper. Particularly significant are the thinking processes, the necessary concepts, and the ability to see relationships between words in context.

Thinking is basic to comprehension, and the ability to think must be established before a pupil is ready to read. Likewise, a reader must have concepts with which to think if he is to comprehend.

A student must also grasp the meaning of groups of words such as are found in phrases and sentences. He must see the relationships between sentences in a paragraph and between paragraphs in a selection.

Nor is it enough that learners be ready to grasp just the stated facts in material read. They must also be ready to draw conclusions and generalizations, to contrast and evaluate, to sense tone, mood, and intent. These comprehension skills and abilities necessitate higher levels of thinking, or critical thinking. Readers must be able to think critically before they are ready to comprehend critically.

Application. Before a pupil is ready to use or apply what he has gained from reading, he must have a great degree of understanding, he must see relationships, and he must have control over the necessary skills and abilities. For example, in outlining from several sources read, he must first understand what was stated and implied in the sources. He must see how the ideas fit together. He must be able to identify the main topics and the related, significant details. Finally, he must know how to set down these ideas in outline form. Until a pupil has the necessary understandings, abilities, and skills to do all these, he is not ready to outline from several sources independently.

Purpose

One element in readiness for reading is the identification of needs that can be satisfied through reading. These needs are the purposes for reading. Such motivation is intrinsic to the extent that the needs are actually learner needs, understood and accepted by the learner. Moreover the needs are recognized and stated prior to the reading.

Identifying a purpose for reading contributes further to readiness. It helps to insure reading for meaning in its fullest sense. It indicates whether the reading is to be a source of pleasure or of information. It dictates the depth of comprehension required and influences the rate of reading. In brief, the purpose establishes readiness by (1) identifying the "why" for the reading and (2) indicating the "how."

Interest

A desire to satisfy felt needs by reading is actually a product of all the foregoing factors. If a well-adjusted learner has a need that to him is worth solving, if he knows it can be solved by reading, and if his past experiences with reading have been successful, he will want to solve that need by reading. Needless to say, until this point is reached, he is not ready to read it.

MATERIALS

Thus far in this discussion of readiness for reading, the child has been the primary consideration. Some attention must be given to materials for reading.

Reading materials are selected in terms of the state of readiness of a learner. If a fifth grader cannot read successfully a third level basal reader, he will be unable to read a fifth reader. If a ninth grader is frustrated by a social studies text designed for and read well by the "average" seventh grader, he will be more frustrated by a textbook designed for the ninth "grade" level. When a high school senior sees no need to read a physics text, he is not ready to do so.

The difficulty of materials depends largely on: (1) the number, difficulty, and strangeness of facts, (2) the vocabulary, terminology, or symbols representing those facts, and (3) the context, or language setting, of the facts.

Materials in the content fields frequently pose problems for readers. Readiness has to be present to deal with the concise, all-inclusive, expository style, and the sentences filled with unfamiliar, difficult concepts and terminology.

The fact that such readiness is assumed to be present has contributed greatly to the problem of verbalism in the schools, i.e., to the number of students who "read" with little or no comprehension.

If all materials to be read were evaluated in terms of pupil readiness before they were used with learners, the many problems that exist in reading ability today could be reduced substantially.

CONCLUSIONS

From the foregoing discussion, the following conclusions may be drawn:

1. Reading readiness functions at all levels and in all learning activities.
2. Readiness for any reading activity is complex, made up of many interrelated factors.
3. Ranges of individual differences must be recognized and considered in readiness.
4. Readiness for reading must be insured for each student (1) if learning is to take place in a healthy situation, (2) if desirable attitudes are to be created toward reading, and (3) if adequate and efficient reading ability is to be developed.

Bibliography

1. Betts, Emmett A. *Foundations of Reading Instruction.* New York: American Book Company, Revised 1954.
2. Bond, G. L. and Wagner, E. B. *Teaching the Child to Read.* Part II and Chapter XIII. New York: The MacMillan Company, 1950.
3. Harrison, M. Lucile. *Reading Readiness,* Part II. Boston: Houghton Mifflin Company, 1939.
4. McKee, Paul. *The Teaching of Reading in the Elementary School,* Part I. Boston: Houghton Mifflin Company, 1948.
5. Robinson, Helen M. *Why Pupils Fail in Reading.* Chicago: University of Chicago Press, 1946.
6. Saul, Leon J. *Emotional Maturity.* Philadelphia: J. B. Lippincott Company, 1947.

Teaching Reading

to the Under-Six Age:

A Child Development Point of View

JAMES L. HYMES, JR.

The question of how much emphasis there should be on teaching the child under six to read print has long been a bothersome one: a source of anxiety to parents, an argumentative question among educators. The old difficulties associated with the question are being heightened today as we move steadily toward the extension of public education downward. Once it could almost tacitly have been assumed that by "the under-six age" one of course meant the kindergarten child. Age five was as far down as schools dipped. Today, however, many public schools are serving four-year-olds in Head Start and Title I programs and in other programs of compensatory education. And as conservative a group as the New York State Board of Regents has gone on record as advocating public education for *all* children from at least three years of age on up. Startling as this may seem to some, even this bold statement must be put against the background of today's Parent and Child Centers of Head Start, serving children under age three, down to infancy, and their parents. The day may come when not only will our public schools serve three-year-olds, but the Three may look like an "old-timer"! It is against this background of the inevitable extension of education downward that one must philosophically and psychologically today consider the question of teaching reading to the "under-six age." Today we have to think about the whole under-six age, not simply its topmost level of Five.

One answer has long been given to Fives that, if it has any worth, could probably apply as appropriately to Fours or Threes or Twos or any young age: We don't teach reading to the under-six age, *we teach reading readiness.* I have long found this a most unsatisfactory, unhelpful response, for Fives or any age. Teaching *reading* readiness? Does this mean that the nursery school and kindergarten also teach science readiness? And art readiness? And music readiness? Social studies readiness? Health readiness? The absurdity is self-apparent. The talk of teaching *reading* readiness, as the special approach to the under-six age, is gobbledegook. We either teach reading or we don't. We either teach science and math and the social sciences and art and music

TEACHING READING TO THE UNDER-SIX AGE: A CHILD DEVELOPMENT POINT OF VIEW by James L. Hymes, Jr. From the *34th Claremont Reading Conference Yearbook,* ed. Malcolm P. Douglas (1970), pp. 79–83. Published by the Claremont Reading Conference. Reprinted by permission.

and language, or we don't. The reading readiness absurdity has led to exercises and drills and workbooks and seatwork which have been no friend to the field of reading, and certainly no friend to young children.

If we rule out "teaching reading readiness" as a possibility, what then? Our title today says: "A child development point of view." From the vantage point of one who tries to watch children, to stay close to children, to study children, to know a little of how they feel and how they think and how they see the world, the answer has to be: *Yes*. Of course! One has to teach reading to the under-six child. To the under-six five-year-old. To whatever under-six age we may have in school, or have in our homes. A child development point of view cannot lead one to say: No, don't teach . . . postpone. It has to say: Teach, and teach as much as each child is comfortably, naturally, easily, rightfully ready for.

This answer of "Yes" underlies the whole nursery school movement in this country, now more than fifty years old. It underlies the whole kindergarten movement here, now more than a century old. Both are grounded in the observation that comes through so clearly as one watches young children: They are ready to learn. Parents seeking nursery schools for fours and threes have used different words: "He's into everything" . . . "We've run out of things to do." But however one says it, wherever one sees it, the fact is that the young child is a bundle of qualities which makes teaching him—reading (and science and math and philosophy and psychology and everything under the sun)—an inevitability.

This is a child full of curiosity, driven to touch and look and taste and ask. This is the child new to our world, smitten each moment by its wonders. This is the child dominated by one overpowering drive: to grow, to be big, to move from dependence to independence. This is the child who shows such gleeful bright pride in each new skill:"I can tie my shoes" . . . "I can climb to the top" . . . "I can write my name." With all this in his nature one *has* to teach as one lives with young children.

We come, then, to what is the central question: *How?* Too often, sadly, if the answer comes through, "Yes, teach the child under six," it is as if one had been given *carte blanche*. Anything goes! Here the smallness and newness and dependency of the young child militate against him. He cannot protect himself; he has to try to go along. And if "anything goes," he can be taken to queer places. The awareness of the young child's readiness, yea eagerness to learn, has to put parents and teachers into a stance of thoughtfulness and sensitivity. At least three considerations certainly must be kept in mind:

1) Yes, teach the under-six age to read *but teach it in a way that fits the child.*

We are talking about a special age. We have to keep reminding ourselves of that. These are five-year-olds (or fours or threes or twos). These are not eight-year-olds or twelves. There are qualities that stamp this age, in Head Start group or affluent suburb, at five or three, experienced, inexperienced, urban, rural—it is the age that counts.

These are all active children. They are moving. On the go. They are not good sitters, not good waiters. They are ready to learn to read any number of things but we have to have a way of teaching them that doesn't depend on their sitting down and shutting up.

These are all very egocentric children, every one of them, simply because they all are new, all just discovering themselves. They talk and think of "I" and "my." Our way of teaching them has to be built on *their* lives, *their* concerns, *their* experiences. This is still where they live most keenly, in their own personal, private world. We will never touch all the eagerness they have to bring if our way of teaching is general, far-off, removed. This age, even more than their much discussed older brothers and sisters, craves relevancy.

This age craves the personal touch, too. Threes, fours, and fives are old enough and ready to go to school and to be in groups. But once they get in school, a good school, they find warmth. Intimacy. Closeness. The best teaching of this age is done eyeball to eyeball, face to face, person to person. We have to have a way of proceeding that does not depend on their always being in a group.

These examples are perhaps sufficient to make the generalization clear: The way we teach has to fit the child. This is not the time or place to try to delineate all the special characteristics that mark this age, except to say: They are there. We have to look for them. We have to respect them and take them into account. We cannot simply plunge ahead, as if the nature of the child was of no importance.

But even this disclaimer makes it important to add one more characteristic of the age (albeit a characteristic not peculiar to this age). The way we teach has to fit *the* child. Each child. The spread of individual differences—in maturation, interest, need, background, ability . . .—is more impressive and more significant in this rapidly changing under-six age than at other stages in development. We speak of "Fives"—we have to for simplicity and speed. We speak of "Head Start groups"—we do for our convenience. We speak of "Fours." But we have to make ourselves remember: You cannot lump them. They always stay individual. And our way of teaching has to reflect this clear awareness.

2) Yes, teach reading to the under-six age *but teach it in a way that fits reading.*

Many of you, better than I, can say what is involved in this area of human experience. But let me suggest a few components that I suspect we would all agree to and accept.

Learning to read is a long, continuous story. It has slow beginnings. It has its peaks. But most of all it goes on and on. It doesn't begin in some one grade, it doesn't end in some one grade. Our approach to young children, as we teach reading to them, has to keep this time-perspective in mind. There *is* time. There has to be time. We must not panic or pressure as if time was running out.

Learning to read print is a complicated process involving many different aspects: memory, discrimination, language, attention-span, solid knowledge of reality. The list could be quite extensive. Our approach to young children must keep this wide scope in mind. Their hearing stories, for example, is a part of it. Their language, as they play, is a part of their learning to read. Their knowledge, as they take trips for example, becomes a part of their learning to read. We must not let the fact that we are teaching young children mislead us into thinking that learning to read print involves only a few, limited kinds of experiences.

Learning to read implies a variety of goals. We seek to build the technical skills so the activity is not a burdensome chore. We seek to build capacities for comprehension and for critical response so the activity is not a mechanical, meaningless performance. We seek to build a love of reading so that one not only can but one does! We must not let the fact that the children are young trap us into acting as if only the teachnical skills mattered. We must be pleased with gains in the direction of any of the goals. And if ever we have to choose, with the young and with the beginner, it would seem to make sense to be most sensitive to the feelings involved and the attitudes. A little love deepened may be immeasurably more significant than a little skill learned.

3) Yes, teach reading to the under-six age *but teach it in a way that fits the goals of general education.*

Our target—under-six and over-six—is not to produce a reader but to help build a better human because now the child reads. Our way of proceeding ought to have as its end result a reader of print, yes, but also: a prouder person, a freer man. A more creative human. Less docile, less hostile. A reader but a deeper-caring soul, someone more broadly aware, more open. . . . The fact that we are teaching young children to read must not make us callous to what liberal or general or humane education is all about.

A program that teaches reading to the under-six age in a way that fits the child, that does justice to the process of reading itself, and that is in tune with what education seeks can be a rich program. It can be a program full of choice, a program of freedom and of excitement. For the sake of teaching reading it can be a program of trips, of jobs and activities, of animals, of visitors, of creative experiences, of play.

Candor compels me to say, however: Almost always something goes wrong. In so many of the classrooms I visit, if the statement is "Yes, we do teach reading to the under-six age," I see a program that is narrow, not broader. I see a program where the children talk less, not more. I see a sitting, quiet program and not one where the youngsters are active. I see a program with store-bought materials, not a program growing out of the children's own activities and experiences, not one I would call relevant to them. I see almost always children brought together in groups and so seldom see the individualized and personalized teaching that I think is called for. I too often see programs where the pressure comes from the teacher, not the children. There is little evidence of love and joy and thrill on the children's part; there is much evidence of control and management on the teacher's part. It seems so often as if one had to produce followers or cows or sheep in order to produce readers.

It shouldn't work out this way but so often seemingly it does. When we consciously teach reading to the under-six child we forget to make our teaching fit the child and fit the field and fit our overall, long-range goals. It may be—one can hope!—that the admission of younger and younger children to our schools may force us to stop and think: Who is here? And what are we really trying to do?

What Does Research Say About the Time to Begin Reading Instruction?

DOLORES DURKIN

Questions about the time to begin reading instruction are invariably bound up with the concept "reading readiness." Consequently, how they are answered directly reflects how this concept is interpreted.

When the term "reading readiness" was first used in the 1920's, the common interpretation was that readiness is the product of maturation; more specifically, of a certain stage in the child's development which equips him with the requirements for success in learning to read. Because this interpretation was generally accepted over four decades and, secondly, because it directly affected the readiness research that was done during the same 40 years, an understanding of why it was both proposed and accepted is important.

Although proposed in the 1920's, the initially assigned meaning stemmed from psychological ideas that were popular at the start of the century. One way to describe them is to describe some of the beliefs of G. Stanley Hall, for it was his teachings that dominated the psychological world at that time.

One teaching was that genetic factors determine the characteristics and

WHAT DOES RESEARCH SAY ABOUT THE TIME TO BEGIN READING INSTRUCTION? by Dolores Durkin. From the *Journal of Educational Research*, 64 (October 1970), pages 52–56. Reprinted by permission.

abilities of each individual. With this as the accepted assumption, it was natural for the early years of the century to give attention to hereditary rather than environmental factors, and to the maturation process rather than to learning and practice.

Another of Hall's influential beliefs was rooted in his acceptance of the doctrine of recapitulation, a doctrine defined briefly but clearly by Hall himself in a 1904 publication:

> The most general formulation of all the facts of development that we yet possess is contained in the law of recapitulation. This law declares that the individual, in his development, passes through stages similar [*to those*] through which the race has passed, and in the same order (14:8).

Hall's acceptance of the recapitulation theory led him to support this view of man: (a) Each individual, as he grows and develops, passes through certain stages, and (b) these stages follow each other in an inevitable, predetermined order. Because the learning process was being assigned only secondary importance, progress through these "inevitable stages" was explained with a reference to maturation.

Later, the special importance assigned to maturation was continued in the writings of Arnold Gesell, a student of Hall's who gave sustained support to his teacher's beliefs. As Gesell offered his explanation of development, he referred to processes like "intrinsic growth," "neural ripening," and "unfolding behavior" (9, 10, 11). Whatever the language, however, the contention was the same: growth and development proceed in stages; progress from one to another is dependent upon spontaneous maturation or, put more simply, the passing of time. Such a contention met with little criticism during the 1920's, and, as a result, during this time "reading readiness" first entered the educator's professional vocabulary. This accounts not only for the original interpretation but also for the quickness with which it was accepted.

Why "reading readiness" became part of the educator's vocabulary in the 1920's can be explained with a reference to the Measurement and Testing Movement, which permeated both education and psychology by 1920 (22). Among other things, its concern for objective measurement led to an abundance of national surveys designed to uncover what and how much children were learning in school. Common among the findings was that the rate of non-promotion for first graders was considerably higher than for children at other levels and, secondly, that inadequate achievement in reading generally was the cause of retentions (5, 6, 20). What subsequently became as frequent as the reports of the two findings was the question: *Why* are first graders not succeeding with reading?

It would seem, at least in retrospect, that a multifactor explanation would be offered that might reasonably include problems related to—too large classes, too few materials, inadequate teacher preparation, wrong methodology, unmotivated children, and so on. This, however, was not the case. Because the 1920's were permeated by the ideas of Hall and Gesell, the *one* explanation that was both proposed and accepted placed the blame on the children's lack of readiness when reading instruction began. Or, in Hall-Gesell terminology, the children were having difficulty because at the time instruction was initiated, they had not yet reached that stage of development which would allow them to be successful. The solution? Within the Hall-Gesell framework, the obvious one was to have the schools postpone instruction until the children matured and became ready for it.

MENTAL AGE DESCRIPTION

Once the "doctrine of postponement" was accepted, efforts were made to define that stage of development which equips children with the prerequisites for success in reading, and to define it in such a way that it could be measured and thus identified. Because of the new availability of group intelligence tests—another product of the Measurement and Testing Movement—the earliest of these efforts sought out a mental-age level that might define it. While other researchers were involved, the one whose findings were to be quoted for an unusually long amount of time was Carleton Washburne, a well-known leader in the then popular Progressive Education Movement. In a research report written by himself and Mabel Morphett in 1931, it was proposed that a child is ready to read when he has a mental age of 6.5 years, and it is only then that he should be introduced to reading (19).

Of interest is the fact that just a few years later Arthur Gates and his associates published a series of research articles in which the reported data went contrary to the Morphett-Washburne proposal. The findings of one study, for instance, led Gates to observe:

> Reading is begun by very different materials, methods, and general procedures, some of which a pupil can master at the mental age of five with reasonable ease, others of which would give him difficulty at the mental age of seven (7:508).

Because conflicting findings were being reported, it was only natural to wonder why the Morphett-Washburne data from a study of one teaching method in one school system (Winnetka, Illinois) were so readily accepted as being applicable to all children. I believe a combination of factors suggests an answer. For one thing, the Morphett-Washburne proposal fit in perfectly with the temper of the times in which it was made. It gave support to the doctrine of postponement because most children entering first grade have not yet reached the mental age of 6.5 years. It also supported the notion that development proceeds in stages, and it honored the Measurement and Testing Movement by being precise and objective. Finally, any attempt to explain the unusual influence of the mental-age concept of readiness must take into account the prominence of Carleton Washburne. He was not only superintendent of the Winnetka schools—widely admired and copied in the 1930's—

but also one of the most prestigious leaders of the Progressive Education Movement. As a result, what Washburne said was listened to—and not only in reading. Even earlier than 1931, for instance, he had made very specific proposals about what was to be taught in arithmetic and at which mental-age level (23).

With all these facts in mind, neither his mental-age description of reading readiness nor the influence it wielded should come as any great surprise. In fact, they simply demonstrate what still continues to be true of research: the quality and general applicability of a study are not always what determine the influence of its findings.

READING READINESS TESTS

While some researchers were pursuing a mental-age description of readiness, others were initiating studies designed to measure combinations of abilities which might also add up to readiness. These attempts to construct and evaluate reading readiness tests began in the late 1920's and have been continued right up to the present (2, 18).

Early forms of the tests, like many currently in use, typically included subtests said to evaluate vocabulary development and auditory and visual discrimination abilities. The most noticeable difference, when earlier editions are compared with the most current ones, lies in the visual discrimination subtest. Now the trend is to use letters and words; earlier, simple pictures and geometrical forms were the usual stimuli. It was, in fact, this use of stimuli other than letters and words that often resulted in low coefficients of correlation for readiness test scores and subsequent achievement in reading. Gates, this time in 1939, was one of the first to make this point when he reported on a very comprehensive study of readiness scores as predictors of success with reading (8). The general conclusion of that report was phrased this way:

> It should be noted that among the tests of little or no predictive value are many tests and ratings widely recommended in books and articles on reading readiness testing and teaching (8:54).

Once again, Gates and other researchers who also found a reason in their data to question the predictive value of readiness tests were generally ignored. In fact, during the 1930's, the 1940's, and even into the 1950's, the typical school practice was to use composite readiness scores, sometimes along with MA data, for making decisions about when to start teaching reading. Such a practice, it must be noted, in no way violated either the doctrine of postponement or the high esteem accorded the maturation process. Still assumed was that entering first graders are too immature to learn to read and would start the year by participating in a readiness program. It was only after such participation that administrators and teachers would begin to consider, with the help of readiness test scores, when reading instruction should begin.

THE 1960'S

Certainly there is no need now to explain with any detail why the 1960's are referred to as a revolutionary period for early childhood education. Suffice it to say that these years became an era in which unprecedented attention went to the young child; in particular, to the unique importance of the early years for his eventual intellectual development (3, 16). It was also an era in which the productivity of learning opportunities was stressed, with very little explicit attention going to the maturation process. Thus, at least for early childhood education, it was a time that contrasted sharply with the four prior decades.

Wih the sharp changes it was only natural to have questions raised about the traditional interpretation and use of the readiness concept. After all, an era which assigns critical importance to learning opportunities during the pre-first-grade period is not likely to be patient with school practices that postpone reading instruction beyond the start of the first-grade year and assume the passing of time will insure a readiness for it.

As the years have shown, the typical response to the impatience was neither complicated nor imaginative. For the most part, schools simply altered the timing of traditional practices. Readiness tests were administered earlier, often in kindergarten where readiness workbooks could be found too. In first grade, reading instruction usually was started sooner than was typical for the earlier decades—although readiness programs still could be found in some first-grade classrooms, especially in school districts that had no kindergartens. In a few places the change in timing was more radical: they introduced reading in kindergarten. In other areas, however, opposition to this was as great and vocal as it had been in years gone by.

With such changes as these occurring in the 1960's, what was learned about readiness, and thus about the optimum time to begin reading instruction? Not much, and for a variety of reasons.

To begin with, the decade gave very little attention to the basic nature of readiness. In fact, some who were urging that reading be started even before the kindergarten year seemed either to ignore the factor of readiness or to take it for granted that all children are ready before the ages of 5 and 6. Those who did deal with the concept merely stressed that many aspects of readiness are learned and therefore can be taught.

Some of the learned and thus teachable aspects were like what was being evaluated in readiness tests; so, with some alterations, they continued to be used in great quantities throughout the 1960's. As was mentioned earlier, one common change in the visual discrimination subtests was the use of letters and words in place of pictures and geometrical forms. A change of more recent origin is the inclusion of a letter-naming subtest. Although this change has been explained with a reference to studies that show a significant correlation between letter-naming ability and later achievement in reading (4), it does not take into account the likelihood that the pre-reader's ability to name letters was the result of much more than something that might be labeled "readiness." More specifically, to assume that a young child's letter-naming ability in and of itself leads to success in reading is to overlook the strong likelihood that the research referred to measured an ability that was one product of an out-of-school environment that will always be contributing to the child's success in school.

This particular use of research is singled out here because it helps to underscore what has always been a serious flaw in readiness research. Here I refer to its unfortunate tendency over the years to present correlation data as if they indicated cause-effect relationships and, secondly, to omit attention to possible reasons for the reported correlations. In fact, the customary procedure has been one in which researchers collect readiness scores at one point in time and reading scores at another. Correlation coefficients for the two sets of data are then reported—and that is it.

Although, in more recent years, this type of research has decreased, it has been replaced only by equally nonproductive studies. For example, it is now common to find reports in which the researcher simply takes for granted the validity of some readiness test as he uses it to assess the value of the variable under study for preparing children to be successful with reading. Thus, in recent years readiness test scores have been used as the criterion measure for evaluating such things as the use of teacher aides, special science materials, a pre-first-grade summer program, Frostig workbooks, and Delacato's crawling prescriptions (1, 13, 17, 21, 25). At other times they have been used to establish the relative value of attending kindergarten and not attending, of having mothers involved in a program and not having them, of one type of maternal behavior *vs* some other type, and so on (12, 15, 24). Underlying all the reports is the implicit assumption that readiness scores really do tell how well or poorly a child will perform when reading instruction gets underway.

While one can understand the desire of researchers to use instruments that will yield "objective" data that can be statistically analyzed—how else can one get "significant" findings?—one cannot help but be disappointed with their failure to point out the possible flaws in an instrument. In fact, if researchers continue to act as if the validity of readiness tests is unquestionable, then we can hardly expect school personnel to rise above traditional practices which should have been seriously questioned right from the start. Because the most important reason for questioning both the practices and the research on which they are based still exists, it will be dealt with now in some detail.

WRONG QUESTION

For as long as the reading readiness concept has been with us—and this is true whether maturation or learning or some combination of the two is given credit for readiness—the assessment question posed by both educators and researchers has been, "Is the child ready?" Unfortunately, such a question is the wrong one to ask because it is incomplete. It focuses only on the child, thus omitting attention to an equally important variable; namely, the reading instruction that will be available.

Another way of making this same point is to say that the traditional way of asking the question neglects the *relational* aspect of readiness. It fails to recognize that whether or not a child is ready—that is, whether or not he will be successful in learning to read—depends not only on his own abilities but also on the kind and quality of instruction that is offered. Realistically, this means that a child might be very ready if one type of instruction can be made available, but unready if another is offered.

Since different kinds of instruction make different demands of the learner, this relational dimension also points out that readiness should not be equated with a single collection of abilities, as has been the traditional practice. Instead, we should be thinking in terms of readiness*es* in the sense that one collection of abilities makes a child ready for one kind of instruction, while a somewhat different collection might make him ready to cope with another.

A SECOND MAJOR FLAW

Still another flaw exists in the kind of thinking and questioning that have been typical when readiness is the concern. This is the failure to realize that the process of learning to read does not require children to be ready to learn everything at once. All of the pieces that comprise "reading ability" are not taught at once; therefore, they need not be learned all at once. Yet, as questions about a child's readiness to read have been considered in the past, answers seem to assume that he must be able to do everything—and right away. Such an assumption needs to be replaced by one which recognizes that a child learns to read, a step at a time; and that the important readiness requirement is that he is able to learn the first step. Fortunately, success with that first step often prepares him to be ready for the second.

IMPLICATIONS FOR FUTURE RESEARCH

If the two flaws which have been mentioned are valid criticisms of the way educators and researchers have traditionally thought about readiness, then certain implications follow.

For example, if readiness is dependent both on the child's abilities and, as Ausubel has phrased it on *"the demands of the learning task,"* then future research efforts ought to go in the direction of (a) assessing more successfully than has been done up to now the relevant abilities of each child; (b) identifying the possible methodologies for reading as well as the learning demands of each; and (c) helping teachers match children in terms of their abilities, with methodology in terms of what it requires of the learner. It must also be emphasized that, once these basic tasks have been done, it is only *longitudinal* studies that will be able to pass judgment on their success.

If, in what seems like a staggering task, it is also kept in mind that a child does not learn to read "all at once," then what will also come to the forefront is the realization that those who make decisions related to readiness need only be concerned with the question, "Is this child ready to read, given the fact that such-and-such will be the first learning requirement?"

Admittedly, the suggestion of a more complicated picture of readiness than has been traditionally inferred in the question, "Is the child ready?" also suggests the need for more complex research than has been undertaken up to now. However, to let a wrong question guide research is to inevitably end up with wrong and meaningless answers. And, we have enough of them already.

References

1. Ayers, Jerry B.; Mason, George E., "Differential Effects of *Science: A Process Approach* upon Change in *Metropolitan Readiness Test Scores* Among Kindergarten Children," *Reading Teacher,* 22:435–439, February, 1969.
2. Berry, Francis M., "The Baltimore Reading Readiness Test," *Childhood Education,* 3:222–223, January, 1927.
3. Bloom, Benjamin S., *Stability and Change in Human Characteristics,* John Wiley and Sons, New York, 1964.
4. Chall, Jeanne, *Learning to Read: The Great Debate,* McGraw-Hill Book Company, New York, 1967.
5. Dickson, Virgil E., *Mental Tests and the Classroom Teacher,* World Book Company, New York, 1923.
6. Editorial, "Educational News and Editorial Comment," *Elementary School Journal,* 33: 641–655, May, 1933.
7. Gates, Arthur I., "The Necessary Mental Age for Beginning Reading," *Elementary School Journal,* 37:497–508, March, 1937.
8. Gates, Arthur I.; Bond, G. L.; Russell, D. H., *Methods of Determining Reading Readiness,* Bureau of Publications, Teachers College, Columbia University, New York, 1939.
9. Gesell, Arnold L., *The Mental Growth of the Preschool Child,* The Macmillan Company, New York, 1925.
10. Gesell, Arnold L., *Infancy and Human Growth,* The Macmillan Company, New York, 1928.
11. Gesell, Arnold L., *The First Five Years of Life,* Harper and Brothers, New York, 1940.
12. Gil, Mohindra, "Relationship Between Junior Kindergarten Experience and Readiness," *Ontario Journal of Educational Research,* 10:57–66, Autumn, 1967.
13. Goralski, Patricia J.; Kerl, Joyce M., "Kindergarten Teacher Aides and Reading Readiness," *Journal of Experimental Education,* 37:34–38, Winter, 1968.
14. Hall, G. Stanley, *The Psychology of Adolescence,* D. Appleton and Company, New York, 1904.
15. Hess, Robert, "Maternal Behavior and the Development of Reading Readiness in Urban Negro Children," Self and Society, *Yearbook of the Claremont Reading Conference,* 32: 83–99, 1968.
16. Hunt, J. McVicker, *Intelligence and Experience,* The Ronald Press Company, New York, 1961.
17. Jacobs, James N.; Wirthlin, Lenore D.; Miller, Charles B., "A Follow-Up Evaluation of the Frostig Visual-Perceptual Training Program," *Educational Leadership,* 26:169–175, November, 1968.

18. Johnson, Roger E., "The Validity of the Clymer-Barrett Prereading Battery," *Reading Teacher*, 22:609–614, April, 1969.
19. Morphett, M. V.; Washburne, C., "When Should Children Begin to Read?" *Elementary School Journal*, 31:496–508, March, 1931.
20. Reed, Mary M., *An Investigation of Practices in First Grade Admission and Promotion*, Bureau of Publications, Teachers College, Columbia University, New York, 1927.
21. Stone, Mark; Pielstick, N. L., "Effectiveness of Delacato Treatment with Kindergarten Children," *Psychology in the Schools*, 6:63–68, January, 1969.
22. Thorndike, Robert L.; Hagen, Elizabeth, *Measurement and Evaluation in Psychology and Education*, John Wiley and Sons, New York, 1969.
23. Washburne, Carleton, "The Work of the Committee of Seven on Grade-Placement in Arithmetic," *Child Development and the Curriculum*, Chapter 16, Thirty-Eighth Yearbook of the National Society for the Study of Education, Part I, Public School Publishing Company, Bloomington, Illinois, 1939.
24. Willmon, Betty, "Parent Participation as a Factor in the Effectiveness of Head Start Programs," *Journal of Educational Research*, 62:406–410, May–June, 1969.
25. Wingert, Roger C., "Evaluation of a Readiness Training Program," *Reading Teacher*, 22:325–328, January, 1969.

3   Suggestions for Further Reading

The developmental point of view and its relation to readiness for learning are explained clearly in Ernest B. Hilgard and Richard C. Atkinson, *Introduction to Psychology*, 4th edition (Harcourt Brace Jovanovich, 1967), 60–90. The application of this viewpoint to readiness for undertaking beginning reading is well treated by Frances Ilg, "The Child from 3 to 8, with Implications for Reading," and Millie C. Almy, "Young Children's Thinking and the Teaching of Reading," in Warren G. Cutts (ed.), *Teaching Young Children to Read* (U.S. Government Printing Office, 1964), 21–30, 97–102. A detailed statement that raises some significant questions about conclusions that have been drawn about child development concepts and beginning reading instruction is Dolores Durkin, "When Should Children Begin to Read?" in Helen M. Robinson (ed.), *Innovation and Change in Reading Instruction* (National Society for the Study of Education, 1968), 30–71.

A number of articles explore the relationship between specified factors and reading success: James T. Fleming, "Promoting Language Skills in Preschool Programs," and Helen M. Robinson, "Perceptual Training—Does It Result in Reading Improvement?" in Robert C. Aukerman (ed.), *Some Persistent Questions in Beginning Reading* (International Reading Association, 1972), 13–19, 135–50; Robert Dykstra, "Auditory Discrimination Abilities and Beginning Reading Achievement," *Reading Research Quarterly*, 1 (Spring 1966), 5–34; Thomas C. Barrett, "The Relationships Between Measures of Pre-Reading Visual Discrimination and First Grade Reading Achievement," *Reading Research Quarterly*, 1 (Fall 1965), 51–76.

Some useful suggestions for developing attitudes and skills that are believed to have an influence on success in beginning reading will be found in Emerald V. Dechant, *Improving the Teaching of Reading*, 2nd edition (Prentice-Hall, 1970), 162–201; and Margaret G. McKim and Helen Caskey, *Guiding Growth in Reading*, 2nd edition (Macmillan, 1963), 64–97.

4

DEVELOPMENTAL READING

A developmental reading program gives recognition to the sequential development of reading skills from the lowest grades through high school and possibly into college. With this concept it is no longer assumed that a child learns to read in grades one, two, and three, but that he learns a kind of reading at each succeeding level. We would like to think that the reader is developing his reading skills and abilities along a continuum, with each step of his progress leading to a logical next step. At no time can all the steps be completed. For by the very nature of the reading process, to complete a step on the continuum is to make another step possible. It is a continuous process of growth. Moreover, it is possible for everyone to improve his reading, no matter how well he now reads.

A developmental reading program works on the assumption that reading achievement can be increased through adequately directed efforts. In the past these efforts have meant intensive instruction during the primary years with less concern for reading in the middle grades. Now it has been shown that if reading achievement is to parallel other academic achievements, instructional programs designed to meet increasingly complex reading requirements must be undertaken.

The success of any program is measured, in part, by the degree to which pupils read to the full extent of their capacities. This, however, is not the same as expecting all children to read on a level equal to their grade placement. The criterion should not be grade placement but individual ability. Children grow and learn at different rates, and instruction must recognize this fact. A valid developmental reading program in which such recognition is inherent will go far in removing the need for elaborate remedial programs.

There are three fairly discrete reading systems, each of which could meet some or most of the requirements of a developmental reading program. These are basal reading, language-experience reading, and individualized reading. The degree to which any one of these systems may fulfill the requirements depends in large measure on the teacher's ability to operate within it. Those who favor one program over another do so on the grounds that it is more "developmental" in terms of the learner and learning. It is becoming increasingly apparent, however, that none of them has a monopoly on validity and that each one can make a contribution to the reading development of all children. Hence, many offer the possibility of adopting the systems in combination, drawing from each one the best that it possesses.

In the first selection in this section, Virgil E. Herrick gives the *Dictionary of Education's* definition of basal reading: "reading aimed at the systematic development of reading ability by means of a series of books or other materials especially suitable for each successive stage of reading development." Proceeding on the assumption that there is a general consensus on the identification of reading skills and methods to help develop them, Herrick points out that while a series of reading textbooks is generally associated with basal reading, "any reading materials used appropriately to help a child achieve a desired reading skill is basal reading material."

Reading textbooks of basal reading programs provide the materials needed to promote the development of specified reading skills. At least this is the claim of publishers who promote their sale and use. How close they actually come to achieving this objective varies from series to series. Publishers revise their reading textbooks periodically to improve them and to include new materials and suggestions for their use. Herrick claims that these textbooks cannot include everything that pupils require for their reading development and that to depend on them exclusively is unwise. A combination of relying on them to offer necessary resources for giving scope and sequence to skill development and relying on teachers for selecting and using materials seems to be a more fruitful plan to follow. Naturally, greater dependence on the teacher to devise his own system to produce adequate reading achievement in children assumes that he is prepared to accept the responsibility. Herrick believes that basal reading materials are no better than what the teacher makes them and that in the end the teacher is the crucial element in any reading system.

Language-experience reading operates on somewhat different assumptions from basal reading. Unlike basal reading programs, which offer specially prepared materials that teachers use to promote reading growth, the language experience system uses the thinking and experiences of children to produce materials for skill development. Thus, one group of children will be developing materials that are quite different from those of another group, since each draws ideas from its own set of experiences and states these ideas in unique ways. Language experiences—productive and receptive—become the vehicles for generating thinking that leads to the creation of stories, which at first teachers transcribe for pupils. Sentence structures that follow children's natural oral language patterns are hallmarks of materials in the language experience system.

R. V. Allen, an advocate of language-experience reading, believes that this system serves the main purposes of a comprehensive reading program: "developing a basic sight vocabulary and competence in using a variety of work recognition skills, providing a wide variety of reading materials or integrating the various communication skills, and developing a genuine desire to read." He believes that language-experience reading offers materials that enable children to learn word skills in a natural setting, that these materials are of real interest to the children, and that children can manage them readily.

It would appear that teachers should be highly competent to function in such a teaching-learning climate. Whether or not all teachers can or wish to are questions that have to be considered. Also, there are real doubts that language-experience reading can offer all the components that are required for the promotion of reading achievement. Its usefulness in primary reading is beyond question; its comprehensiveness for total reading leaves something to be desired.

Individualized reading is a system in which each pupil reads narrative and expository materials of his own choice, meets with the teacher individually to discuss his reading, and receives both individual and group instruction in reading. Although individual instruction receives preference over group activities, children are brought together for reading experiences when they meet common requirements. Individualized reading obviously cannot be introduced until children have acquired adequate reading ability. This does not mean that children have to reach some given level of attainment or that they must wait for others to undertake individualized reading. They will be ready as soon as they are able to read the materials available to them with little direction from the teacher. Thus, some first graders will be able to participate in the program before the year is out; others will not be ready until much later.

W. Paul Blakely and Beverly McKay describe individualized reading programs in their report of the results of a questionnaire study undertaken to determine the means used to supplement a basal reading program with individualized instruction in grades four, five, and six. These grades are the ones in which individualized reading usually appears, although as noted earlier, there is no reason to delay its introduction until then. It is interesting to note that the authors assume that individualized reading cannot stand by itself. Adherents of this program would strongly dispute this assumption.

The overwhelming majority of schools around the country rely on commercially prepared materials to develop reading ability in pupils. Robert Karlin examines those materials that are typically available and offers his assessment of several types. He evaluates the strengths and weaknesses of basal readers and concludes that until a better system is devised, authors should strive to improve basal readers. "But no matter how attractive they do become, the ways in which they are used will determine their effectiveness."

Workbooks next come under scrutiny. Karlin says that "there is nothing wrong with workbooks that we can't correct." He goes on to indicate their weaknesses and suggests how workbooks may be used with greater confidence and efficiency. He explains why most instructional materials packaged in boxes are not self-instructional and how teachers can use these packaged materials. Karlin objects to the indiscriminate use of audio-visual and mechanical aids and shows how more meaningful use can be made of them. The only conclusion he can reach about any reading materials is that they are no better than the teachers who rely on them.

Basal Instructional Materials in Reading

VIRGIL E. HERRICK

with the assistance of

DAN ANDERSON and LOLA PIERSTORFF

The reading act always involves printed or written material to be read for a recognized purpose. In this sense, any material used in the act of reading is basic to that act. To give unique meaning to this chapter, therefore, one must find a special meaning of *basic* as it applies either to the unique way in which the materials are used in the act of reading or to the specialized nature of the selected content.

Examination of statements received by the author of this chapter from a representative group[1] of specialists in reading and related problems reveals the following:

1. As a useful working statement of the meaning of *basal reading*, there is a willingness to accept the definition of the *Dictionary of Education*, namely, "reading aimed at the systematic development of reading ability by means of a series of books or other materials especially suitable for each successive stage of reading development."[2]

2. There is general agreement that it is possible to distinguish among (*a*) categories of skills and habits of reading; (*b*) the varieties of reading materials designed to achieve reading skills; and (*c*) the instructional methods used to develop reading skills.

3. There is general agreement among the respondents mentioned that basal reading materials should help foster continuity in reading development, insure that no gaps exist in necessary reading experi-

---

[1] This group included the following persons: A. Sterl Artley, Emmett A. Betts, Guy Bond, Donald D. Durrell, William S. Gray, Albert J. Harris, Theodore L. Harris, Gertrude Hildreth, Constance McCullough, Margaret McKim, Robert C. Pooley, Helen M. Robinson, David H. Russell, William Sheldon, Ruth Strang, Ruth Strickland, Gertrude Whipple, and Paul A. Witty.

[2] *Dictionary of Education*, p. 443. Edited by Carter V. Good. New York: McGraw-Hill Book Co., 1959.

BASAL INSTRUCTIONAL MATERIALS IN READING by Virgil Herrick, with the assistance of Dan Anderson and Lola Pierstorff. From *Development in and Through Reading*, 60th Yearbook of the National Society for the Study of Education, ed. Nelson B. Henry (1961), Part 1, pp. 165–75. Reprinted by permission.

ence, and provide suitable plans for the organization of reading experiences for all children of school age. Frequently this is called "systematic" development of the reading program.

4. There are differences of opinion among the respondents as to the propriety of using a given set or sets of basal textbooks to serve as the sole source of instructional materials.

5. There is general agreement on the proposal that it is necessary (*a*) to provide for interest areas of reading; (*b*) to provide content necessary to meet varied educational needs; (*c*) to "trigger" reading in different kinds of materials for the full range of purposes for which a child might read; and (*d*) to adapt the level and rate of reading development to the wide range of differences that exist among children.

DIFFERENT CONCEPTS OF BASAL READING MATERIALS

Examination of the different ideas of what makes reading materials basic reveals a number of concepts.[3] The most common point of view would seem to regard basal materials as a basal series of textbooks. In the minds of many, basal reading has become synonymous with a "series of books especially suitable for each successive stage of reading development," or, in other words, with the various programs of materials and books published as basal readers.

The logic of this relationship is simple and direct. Basal reading instruction is that instruction which is concerned with all the fundamental habits, attitudes, and skills which are essential to effective silent and oral reading. Basal reading materials are, therefore, by definition those materials designed to develop these habits and skills. This definition rests on two assumptions: first, that a set of "essential or fundamental" habits and skills is generally known; second, that these habits and skills are of such a nature that a series of books and materials specially prepared are essential to their development. These and other assumptions are examined in the next section.

MAJOR CATEGORIES OF READING SKILLS

Major categories of reading skills are known, but they are not restricted to a given type of material. The first assumption may be accepted with con-

---

[3] For example, see William C. Bagley, "The Textbook and Methods of Teaching," in *The Textbook in American Education*, pp. 7–26. (Thirtieth Yearbook of the National Society for the Study of Education, Part II. Chicago: University of Chicago Press, 1931); American Textbook Publishers Institute, *Textbook in Education* (New York: Lakeside Press, 1949); *Text Materials in Modern Education* (Edited by Lee J. Cronbach, Urbana, Illinois: University of Illinois Press, 1955); Gerald A. Yoakum, *The Place of Textbooks in Children's Reading*, pp. 65–75 (Report of the Fourth Annual Conference on Reading, University of Pittsburgh, June 28–July 9, 1948); and *Materials for Reading* (Supplementary Educational Monographs, No. 86. Edited by Helen M. Robinson. Chicago: University of Chicago Press, 1957).

siderable confidence when these skills are described in such general terms as perception skills, comprehension skills, skills in the use of materials, and the like. Unfortunately, the specific set of independent skill variables which produces the desired reading behavior most economically is in large part unknown.[4]

The most important point in this connection, however, is that, irrespective of the degree to which specific sets of skills have been identified, these skills are more comprehensive than any specific set of reading materials. In a sense, some of these skills lie outside the materials and are found only in the reading behavior of individuals who read.

From this point of view, any reading materials used appropriately to help a child achieve a desired reading skill is basal reading material. Thus, when a social-studies text is used to help groups of students who are reading social-studies material, that text inevitably becomes basal reading material. Similar cases can be made for the classroom newspaper, trade books, and film strips. The key problem of this chapter becomes, therefore, how reading materials are selected, organized, and used to develop essential reading competencies. On one end of a continuum of opinion regarding how this is done is the publisher's complete basal program of materials, with the teacher selecting, adapting, and extending the use of materials within the framework of a particular reading program. On the other end of this continuum is the teacher, developing reading materials which grow out of the experiences of her pupils as well as helping them identify and use appropriate reading materials to deal with their reading needs. Such materials include experience charts, basal text materials, trade books, text materials found in content areas, reference materials, and especially prepared materials of suitable content.

SPECIALLY PREPARED MATERIALS
FOR SPECIFIED PURPOSES

The second assumption is that essential reading skills are such that specially prepared materials are necessary for the development of adequate skills. Also, this assumption implies that some materials are especially suitable for use in the development of reading skills. This means (*a*) that instructional materials can be devised or selected to achieve specific educational objectives more effectively than materials not so designed; and (*b*) that there are recognizable stages in the development of reading skills which require appropriate variations in instructional materials to deal adequately with the needs of pupils at particular stages of progress toward skill in reading. Basal instructional materials in reading, then, are basal in a *second* sense—they are specially designed or selected to achieve certain educational goals more effectively than do other kinds of materials. Their suitability as materials derives not only from the fact that they provide reading experiences or practice in

[4] Donald D. Durrell, *Improving Reading Instruction,* p. 2. New York: World Book Co., 1956.

reading skills but that they are "especially" suitable because of their capacity to provide for greater efficiency in learning these skills than is possible through other similar materials.

The first meaning of *suitable* is essential to all learning and instructional procedures. All programs of formal education are based on the assumption that instructional activities and materials can be identified or devised which will enable students to achieve educational objectives more effectively than is possible with other kinds of activities and materials. It would be hard to deny that certain reading materials are more basic than others in the special sense that they are more suitable to achieve reading goals.

The second idea of *suitability*—that there are certain levels or stages in reading development which demand suitable adaptations in reading materials —is one long accepted by curriculum and reading specialists. This is the essential notion of growth so necessary in all learning. Without it we are limited to a concept of education based on learning specific, unrelated particulars.

The critical point in the decision relating to suitability, so defined, is the judgment that a particular piece of reading material is more suitable (basic) than another to achieve a particular set of reading skills. Anyone making this decision needs to consider two referents: (*a*) the relevancy of the material to the desired reading skills; and (*b*) its relevancy to the reading maturities of children in general or of a particular group. It seems that it would be possible for reading materials to be developed by a single source for all children on the basis of their special relevancy to desired reading goals; there is a question as to the ability of a single source to determine their special relevancy to particular groups of children. It seems that this latter decision must be the special province of the teacher or the pupil.[5]

BASAL MATERIALS DEFINE LIMIT IN READING

An examination has just been made of the meaning of basal reading materials in the sense that they are especially suitable to achieve a set of reading skills and habits. It is necessary now to examine the idea that a series of reading materials may be basic by reason of the overall instructional plan used.

Any given set of basic reading skills can be achieved through the use

[5] It is recognized that this question can be argued from the point of view that a given system of materials can provide for all kinds of degrees of reading skill; then the only choice left to the teacher and student is the one of locating where he is on this continuum of materials. Where the ability of any system of basal materials to encompass this task is questioned, the responsibility of the teacher and student to consider a broader range of appropriate reading materials is correspondingly increased. Acceptance or rejection of this assumption determines the direction and nature of efforts to improve reading instruction and materials.

of different sets of instructional materials and through the employment of different sets of instructional procedures. There is no unique set of materials which has a one-to-one relationship to a given array of reading skills any more than there is a single teaching procedure by which the good life is attained through reading. There may be basic reading skills, but few would accept the premise that there is an equated set of basic instructional methods.

Many will argue also that any set of instructional materials which clothes an over-all program of reading instruction with reality is equally basic. Granted that a reading-program design is fundamental, it cannot be equated with an instructional material any more than it can be equated with a child or an instructional method. Each of these components must reflect and contribute its necessary part to the design; no one part, however, is the design.

Much of the confusion here has grown out of failure to make clear two meanings of the word *basic*. In one sense, all of the necessary components of the instructional act in reading are basic. In the second sense a certain referent is used to give the quality of "basicness" to important instructional decisions. In this second sense, the objectives of reading skills and the learner have greater priority as a basis for decision-making in an instructional program than does a reading material or an instructional method. Similarly, a reading material has priority over instructional method in the sense that the nature of the reading material helps determine method.

This does not mean that the development of such a plan is the sole prerogative of publishers of reading texts and that the desired plan can be adequately assured of success by merely selecting a set of basal readers any more than it can be the sole prerogative of a single teacher and that it can be adequately assured of success by what she does in her classroom. In the first case, many of the necessary components of a program of reading instruction are not available to the publishing company; in the second case, many of the other components of an adequate program are not available to a teacher. The task is to get all components together in a plan which permits each to do the part it can do best.

BASAL MATERIALS PROVIDE
FOR SYSTEMATIC INSTRUCTION

It is proposed that "systematic" instruction be designed to include three objectives: (*a*) the identification of the different things to be accomplished; (*b*) program-planning to insure completeness of coverage in point of time; and (*c*) the organization of functional relationships which ought to prevail among these parts. Thus, instruction is systematic if it concerns itself with all necessary aspects, with all critical relationships, and with the full range of possible development. A distinction should be made between systematic in the sense of regularity in time and systematic in the sense of expectancy of dealing with important aspects of the reading task. We tend to assume the second from the first, primarily because books and time schedules are more commonplace in the sight of administrators and parents.

The Idea of Scope

There are three kinds of things considered in dealing with the question of adequate scope in a reading program: (*a*) the range and validity of the reading skills; (*b*) the range and validity of the nature and form of the reading materials with which the child has to cope (textbooks, trade books, newspapers, dictionaries, pictures); and (*c*) the range and validity of the nature and form of the content read, the ideas important in school, family, and community living, and the variety of literary, poetic, dramatic, and rhetorical forms through which they are expressed. Any adequate reading program would want to consider and make appropriate definitions regarding all three of these scope characteristics.

Again, among our respondents there is obvious evidence that any teacher using a basal text series will want to introduce her pupils to different forms of reading materials which would range more widely than do the content materials of a basal reading series. Practically every publisher's program of materials in reading recognizes this problem of adequate scope in the second and third dimensions and tries to provide for it through both supplementary materials and reading books which contain a varied array of materials drawn from many areas of experience.

It should be recognized that these three aspects of scope can be best defined and developed through the experience of the learner rather than through a range of reading skills, forms of reading materials, and the areas of man's experience. In this way, the learner's needs and purposes for reading would define the skills, the nature of the materials, and the content to be considered. The purpose of instruction would be to stimulate the learner to evaluate his reading experience in light of his growing skill and his need for reading material calculated to satisfy the educational and personal purposes he hopes to achieve through reading.

Both of these approaches would deal with the same problems of scope, and the two would be equally systematic; one approach would place major responsibility on an educational publisher and his resources for such planning and development, and the other approach would place major responsibility for such planning on the shoulders of a teacher and a learner.

The Idea of Sequence

Much is made of the importance of sequential development in reading processes and in reading materials. Each stage in development should always grow out of the preceding stage; each new step should permit a child to succeed in some degree; and the sequence in materials should lead the child continuously toward greater maturity and skill in all the necessary aspects of reading development.

Two very difficult problems confront anyone attempting to develop defensible sequences in educational programs and materials. The first is to know the order in which components of a reading program ought to be introduced; the second is to know the speed at which the development should take place. Yet, there is no disagreement as to the critical importance of these two kinds of decisions in any reading program. In the first approach to this problem, the program of sequence is found in the materials and programs of instruction of the reading series, and children are distributed along this continuum of development. The pattern of development tends to be the same for all children; individual differences are cared for by varying the speed of use and the level of difficulty. In the second approach, the pattern of sequence is found in the child and his reading experiences, reading materials being related to this pattern. Here the learner assumes increasing responsibility for determining the continuity of his learning and for the relating of reading materials to his own development and purposes. There is an increasing body of knowledge about the ability of the child in self-selection at the early periods of his education.[6] Of course, as he grows older, any adequate program of reading instruction should help the child increase his ability to select and use his reading materials so as to achieve his reading purposes.

It appears that the strengths of the over-all planning of the sequence of a program of reading development through reading materials may prove to be weaknesses in programs where teachers and children carry major responsibility for making these decisions. Similarly, the strengths of the individual approach are sometimes regarded as the weaknesses of the publisher's program. To the authors, this suggests that a program which would utilize the strengths of both, with the major focus on children and their reading development, would be better than either one alone.

The Idea of Organization

The third major idea underlying the concept of "systematic" is the one involving organization. The concept of organization builds on the contribution of decisions regarding scope and sequence and devotes itself essentially to the problem of coherency among all the parts in order to achieve some over-all unity. Here the question of the necessary relationships that must exist between skills to be achieved, children to learn, reading materials to be used, and instructional method to be applied are considered. It is conceivable that the patterns of relationship among the important skills and the nature of reading materials would shift as different uses and purposes for reading

[6] Willard C. Olson, *Child Development,* chap. xii. New York: D. C. Heath & Co., 1949.

are met and resolved by the reader. This would cause corresponding shifts in the teaching and instructional methods used.

Again, the critical significance of the organization or the design of the relationship among all the necessary parts of an adequate reading program is not denied by any responsible person in the field of reading or curriculum. The only difference of opinion among individuals is related to how this organization is best achieved.

Some insist that the essential organization and development of reading ability takes place in the internalized perceptions, understandings, and behavior of the learner. The second critical agent in this enterprise is the teacher and her role in assisting the learner to organize and give direction to his reading development. The third important resource would be the array of available reading materials and the knowledge about the reading process possessed by the staff and teacher and used in the development of an adequate program of reading.

Others merely reverse this pyramid of relationships and say there should be a meaningful design in an over-all program of reading materials, reading skills, and instructional procedures ranging over the total program of common education. This is beyond the ability of any single teacher or school system to plan.

The key difference here is not in the need for "systematic development," or for planning, or for bringing the most expert advice and knowledge to this process, but in the determination of the architects of such a system and in the determination of the nature and range of reading materials necessary to produce adequate reading development in children.

Preconceived organizations and systems of basal readers can be useful only within specified limits. If the reading program is to achieve its ultimate purpose, the teacher and student must assume some responsibility for relating materials to purpose; for relating children to variations in materials; for rearranging materials and skills to meet varying reading goals; and for revising and supplementing materials, content areas, and kinds of content comprehension.

There needs to be systematic attention paid to the development of reading skill. To say that one kind of planning is no planning or to say that one form of organization or one time schedule represents no organization are assertions which are obviously unfair and do not lead to the development of reading materials and instructional programs nor to the research that is needed to insure a continuance of the significant development in reading that has taken place during the past half-century. It is much more constructive to regard basal reading programs, individualized reading, different time schedules, and different approaches to organization merely as different means for providing direct, systematic, and planned instruction in reading. We need to examine the relative effectiveness of the means for direct, systematic, and planned instruction rather than merely to say that the teacher's use of time in a science class to relate reading and thinking skills to science reading materials and desired levels of comprehension is unplanned, unsystematic, and indirect instruction.

If such instruction is related to the educational purpose and reading development of the learner, it is systematic instruction, the more so because it takes place in this context. This is not to say that instruction in a formal reading class for a definite period of time and using common basal reading materials might not be highly informal, almost totally unsystematic, and completely unplanned. Of course, the long-advanced argument is that the presence of basal reading materials is some assurance that someone has thought about and planned for the development of reading skills.

In summary, the foregoing discussion has revealed the following:

1. Professional authors and designers of reading programs tend to agree that a series of books or other materials especially adapted to systematic development of reading abilities may be considered basal reading materials. The key terms here are *reading abilities, systematic development,* and especially *suitable materials.*
2. Distinctive definitions can be formulated for basal reading skills, reading materials, and an instructional program. Each of these necessary aspects of reading instruction has implications for what constitutes basal reading materials.
3. Much of the argument about basal instructional materials in reading grows out of the relative effectiveness of a self-contained set of reading materials and reading programs on the one end of a continuum of practice and an individual teacher and a group of students on the other.
4. It is clear that there are only two ways of determining continuity in reading development and instruction: (*a*) to consider an array of instructional reading materials as a referent and then relate children to it; or (*b*) to consider the learner and his background of experience and learning as a major referent and to relate reading materials and instructional procedure to it. Adaptations, naturally, can be made in either approach, but at some point, one or the other of these referents will have to be used for the final decision.
5. Basal reading materials are as good as the instructional methods and program-planning of the teacher making them. Improvements in the teaching of reading are more likely to result in the future from improvements in teaching-learning methodology and over-all program-planning than from improvements in basal reading materials themselves.

The Language-Experience Approach

R. V. ALLEN

What I can think about, I can talk about.
What I can say, I can write—or someone can write for me.
What I can write, I can read.
I can read what I can write and what other people can write
for me to read.

This is the language-experience approach in reading as it is conceptualized by each child. It is the formula that is basic to the implementation of the program as it has been described and developed in San Diego, Calif., and elsewhere. Everything else that is said here and everything that is written about it is an elaboration of this very simple foundation.

HOW DID THE LANGUAGE-EXPERIENCE APPROACH IN READING DEVELOP?

As we began the development of the design for depth research, we became aware that most so-called research in reading dealt with the same basic ideas and that variables tended to be only new embroidery on the same old cloth. No one seemed to reject the basic structure of most present-day reading programs. There was really no opportunity for us to engage in significant research until programs which were significantly different had been established long enough to furnish some areas of contrast to the researcher.

It was during a period of rejecting well-established ideas about reading that we formulated some questions which needed new and imaginative answers. This searching for questions as well as answers led to the description of what is now called the language-experience approach in reading. The approach as we describe it was first tested along with other approaches in the Reading Study Project of San Diego County.

It became apparent to the working committees in our study that the real issue for studies in reading instruction was not one of analyzing two or more approaches to determine which one was *better* than the other, but rather to determine what each procedure might contribute to pupil development. We

THE LANGUAGE-EXPERIENCE APPROACH by R. V. Allen. From *Teaching Young Children to Read,* ed. Warren G. Cutts (1964), pp. 59–67. Published by the U.S. Department of Health, Education, and Welfare.

felt that we should include reading problems which related to the diversity of our school population and to our increased information concerning human growth and development. This meant that we studied and considered many possible ways of teaching reading—especially the beginnings of reading.

As the research team investigated various "approaches to teaching reading," it selected three for detailed study: The *basic reader* approach, the *individualized* approach, and the *language-experience* approach.

The three approaches were tested in many classrooms—not to compare one against another, but to give a team of observers an opportunity to analyze the use of each approach over a period of time. It was during this period of observation, careful reporting, and systematic analysis of data that the research team confirmed the hypothesis: *There are numerous effective ways to teach reading in our schools.*

In the years which have followed the formal study, it is the language-experience approach in reading that has continued to be of interest to educators across the Nation, and in San Diego County it has offered a major breakthrough in opening up reading instruction for inspection without the handicap of vested interests in materials and methods.

WHAT IS THE LANGUAGE-EXPERIENCE APPROACH?

Briefly stated, the language-experience approach is one which brings reading and the other communication skills together in the instructional program. In this approach there is no way, nor any need, to distinguish between the reading program and the development of listening, speaking, and writing skills. The "togetherness" of skill development makes possible the continuing use of each child's own experience background and thinking as he grows toward reading maturity.

More than other approaches which have been described at the classroom operational level, the language-experience approach uses the thinking of individual children in the development of materials which promote skill development. It is called the language-experience approach because teachers use as a major guide a listing of language experiences which were selected during our study as ones which must be developed as much as possible in order to assure effective communication in a democratic society—a society which values divergent thinking and creativity.

The language experiences which have been selected for the basic framework of the program are ones which, when implemented at the classroom level, require the selection of learning experiences which generate productive thinking, allow freedom of expression, stimulate individuality, value ingenuity, satisfy curiosity, and promote personal satisfaction to the extent that learning to read becomes a lifelong experience which requires ever-maturing and more complex skills and knowledge. These language experiences may be described as follows:

1. *Sharing experiences*—The ability to tell or illustrate something on a purely personal basis.
2. *Discussion experiences*—The ability to interact with what other people say and write.
3. *Listening to stories*—The ability to hear what others have to say and relate it to their own experiences.
4. *Telling stories*—The ability to organize one's thinking so that it can be shared orally or through dictation in a clear and interesting manner.
5. *Dictating*—The ability to choose, from all that might be said, the most important part for someone else to write and read.
6. *Developing speaking, writing, and reading relationships*—The ability to conceptualize reading as speech that has been written.
7. *Making and reading books*—The ability to organize one's ideas into a form that others can use and the ability to use the ideas which others have shared through books.
8. *Developing awareness of common vocabulary*—The ability to recognize that our language contains many common words and patterns of expression.
9. *Expanding vocabulary*—The ability to expand one's vocabulary through listening and speaking, followed by writing and reading.
10. *Writing independently*—The ability to write one's own ideas and present them in a form for others to read.
11. *Reading whole books*—The ability to read books for information, recreation, and improvement of reading skills on an individualized and personalized basis.
12. *Improving style and form*—The ability to profit from listening to and reading well-written materials.
13. *Using a variety of resources*—The ability to recognize and use many resources in expanding vocabulary, improving oral and written expression, and sharing.
14. *Reading a variety of symbols*—The ability to read symbols—the clock, calendar, radio dial, and thermometer—in their total environment.
15. *Studying words*—The ability to find the correct pronunciation and meaning of words and to spell the words in writing activities.
16. *Improving comprehension*—The ability, through oral and written activities, to gain skill in following directions, understanding words in the context of sentences and paragraphs, reproducing the thought in a passage, and reading for general significance.
17. *Outlining*—The ability to use various methods of briefly restating ideas in the order in which they were written or spoken.
18. *Summarizing*—The ability to get the main impression, outstanding ideas, or the details of what has been read or spoken.

19. *Integrating and assimilating ideas*—The ability to use reading and listening for specific purposes of a personal nature.
20. *Reading critically*—The ability to determine the validity and reliability of statements.

These language experiences become the major framework within which children learn to read. It is obvious that the ones at the top of the list require less maturity on the part of the learner and less background of experience than those at the end of the list. It should be equally obvious that this program is not conceptualized as a "reading period" during the day; rather, it might be described as the glue that holds the program together. As the program develops, it gives depth of meaning to art and construction activities; it is the vehicle for conveying meanings of social studies emphases; it encourages exploration and discovery in science and mathematics; it builds spirit and understanding into singing of songs and playing of games. It places the "creative thinking process" at the heart of the instructional program.

WHAT CONCEPTS DOES THE TEACHER HOLD?

The language-experience approach is dependent on the evolvement of a conceptual framework more than on the practice of certain methods or the use of certain materials. Teachers and supervisors working in the program establish a pattern of thinking which guides them in the selection of activities, experiences, materials, and evaluation. This conceptual framework helps teachers establish goals for teaching which interrelate reading instruction with instruction in the other communication skills. Some of the concepts which a teacher must hold in order to work within the spirit of the language-experience approach were identified as follows by teachers participating in the San Diego County Reading Study Project:

1. As a basis for reading, the child should gain the feeling that his own ideas are worthy of expression and his own language is a vehicle for written communication.
2. The basis of children's oral and written expression is their sensitivity to their environment both within the classroom and in the world at large.
3. Freedom in self-expression, oral and written, leads to self-confidence in all language usage which includes reading skills.
4. Children's oral expression may be stimulated and strengthened through paintings, drawings, and other graphic art or sound symbols.
5. The child's own thoughts may be used as the main basis for development of reading materials in the initial stages.

6. There is a natural flow of language development in children. This flow proceeds in the following steps:
   a. The child's oral expression is stimulated and strengthened through art expression.
   b. The child's written expression flows easily from his oral expression.
   c. Motivation for reading follows easily from the child's seeing his own language in written form.
   d. After reading his own language in written form, the child moves naturally into reading the written language of other children and adults.
7. Numerous activities, experiences, and devices are used to provide for interaction of children, such as those included above.
8. Utilization of the child's language as a basis of reading instruction results in a high degree of independence in writing and reading.

WHAT ARE SOME OF THE GOALS?

When the teacher is using the language-experience approach, there are three major goals in achieving a balanced reading program: Developing a basic sight vocabulary and competence in using a variety of word recognition skills, providing a wide variety of reading materials or integrating the various communication skills, and developing a genuine desire to read.

Developing a Basic Sight Vocabulary and Word Recognition Skills

A common goal of all plans or approaches is to help each child develop a basic sight vocabulary. In most plans the selection of the vocabulary to be developed is on a basis of high frequency in our language. Material is developed which repeats each word a sufficient number of times for most children to recognize it at sight.

In the language-experience approach, the idea of the highly controlled vocabulary for beginning readers is rejected as invalid. The development of a basic sight vocabulary is deemed to be an individual matter and is governed to a great extent by the *oral expression* of the learner. From oral expression the next step is *writing,* or recording the oral language. This is done by the teacher or the child according to maturity and ability. *Recall,* or reconstruction of the written language (reading), is a third step in the sequence of developing basic sight vocabulary.

Early recognition of words of high frequency in our language is a natural result of repetition which cannot be avoided in an environment of language production. Each child gradually gains a sight vocabulary which is functional to him and which reaches far beyond the words which are selected for other reading programs. Ceilings are lifted for all children.

Among the word recognition skills which are developed in all successful reading approaches but treated differently in the language-experience approach is phonetic analysis. Phonics instruction is a necessary and natural part of the language-experience approach, but it is developed from a "say it" to "see it" sequence rather than from the "see it" to "say it" sequence of other approaches.

The direct teaching program for phonics and other word recognition skills is more closely related to the writing and spelling activities where children are dealing with the language letter by letter, syllable by syllable, and word by word. The application is necessary and immediate. The desire to create stories and do independent writing provides a powerful motivation to acquire skills necessary for selecting the correct symbols to represent the sounds of oral language. The phonics learnings take place in their natural setting and have immediate application. They are applied to the real language experiences of each child, including skills of listening, speaking, word recognition, and spelling.

Providing Materials for Reading

The problem of providing appropriate reading material for each child in a given classroom has been and is a source of real concern for a teacher or administrator who knows anything of learning processes. Within a given classroom there may be the son of an English professor and one of a migrant farmworker. Both have good ideas; both have information; and both have self-motivation to share their ideas and information with others. But the information shared will probably be quite different and the quality of oral language might be poles apart. Between these two children of extreme contrast in experience and language development there is in every classroom a wide range of differences among the other children.

What materials will the teacher use to help each child conceptualize reading as a record of oral language? What material can be selected which will be of interest to the wide range of individuals? How can a teacher have enough materials which are not too difficult for some and too easy for others?

Professional books, as well as teacher's manuals, stress that the materials for successful reading instruction must meet several criteria. They must be related to oral expression, they must be interesting to children, and they must be easy for children to read.

Maybe you have tried using materials which have been developed with an extremely limited vocabulary. They are easy for some, but are ridiculous in terms of their relationship to oral expression and interests of children. This is especially true at the beginning levels where the concocted materials are devoid of any real meaning or interest. There is no story, no message from an author, absolutely no similarity to the oral language of the children who are learning to recognize the words.

The language-experience approach features children as authors with unique language abilities, with wide interests, and with individual vocabulary control built in. In the process of dictating and writing their own ideas, children learn to recognize enough words that they can read what other people have written, both within the classroom and in the world of books.

Some people might say that oral language of children is so far advanced by the time they start to learn to recognize the symbolic forms of words that anything they would dictate or write would be too difficult. But analysis of materials on the difficulty of reading selections shows little evidence of any attention to the question, "What makes a sentence easy or difficult for a child to read?" It is quite possible that for many children the choppy, unnatural sentences of present-day preprimers and primers are more difficult to read than more natural sentences might be. The experience of teachers who have emphasized authorship in their classrooms bears this out.

To the extent that children perceive themselves as authors—producers of reading materials—they are interested in interacting with the products of other authors. First, they are interested in knowing what other authors in their class have produced; later, their interests expand to encompass the whole world of authorship. Their interest in a book is not based on the fact that they can learn *how* to read it, but that the author has something to say. Reading of whole books becomes a natural desire and a natural language experience for children. They assume responsibility for selecting their own material; in fact, self-selection of materials is mandatory in the language-experience approach. Many books must be in the environment—books that have been produced by the children, books purchased and brought into the classroom, books from the public libraries, and books from home. Books must be selected with a wide range of difficulty, a wide range of interest and information, and a wide range of literary forms. The success of the language-experience approach depends on the production of a balanced program of reading materials and the use of increasingly varied reading materials.

Developing Motivation for Reading

Motivation for reading is stimulated through the child's realization that his oral language expression, based upon his own experiences and thought, can be written and read, and that he can read the thoughts and ideas of others. This is quite different from approaches where children are motivated to read by being helped to see the relationship of their own experiences to the story selection to be read. It assures active participation in a developmental reading program at an earlier age—at any age that a child is interested—in dictating and observing his own language being made into reading. It has built-in success from the beginning and for every child. There is no need to ask a child to reconstruct his language (read it) until he gives evidence of a desire to do so. Success, immediate reinforcement, involvement of self, and interaction with others are forces which are ever present. The power in the program is self-generated.

HOW CAN THE CLASSROOM BE ORGANIZED?

Classroom organization must be adapted to serve an approach which does not require require regular reading periods and follow-up activities each day for every child. Organization, materials, and facilities must be provided for a strong emphasis on production of materials. Such a program does not require the kind of information which is supposedly collected by the use of readiness tests and achievement tests. Ability grouping within the classroom for direct reading instruction is considered to be not only unnecessary, but highly undesirable. Grouping processes are used to facilitate the work of production. They do not dominate the program to the extent that they build into children self-perceptions which are damaging to them in their language development.

To accompany the emphasis on production, there must be plenty of writing materials and a plan for their distribution. A variety of reading materials for information, recreation, and skill development is essential. The program is incomplete until there is provision of sharing, discussing, and interacting of ideas, thoughts, and concerns of children in the class with the ideas, thoughts, and concerns of good adult authors. Usually this requires that the teacher read some good literature to the children each day.

HOW CAN PUPIL PROGRESS BE EVALUATED?

A program based on the gradual maturing of language experiences of children must be evaluated on a broader base than that offered by standardized tests of reading achievement. This base rests on the following understandings:

1. Ability to express personal ideas in oral and written form is a continuing expectancy.
2. Development of a positive attitude toward reading of many types and for many purposes is a measure of growth.
3. Evidence is sought that students are gaining in self-confidence, in valuing their ability to communicate their own ideas, and in their interest in the ideas of other people.
4. Choosing reading for information, for recreation, and for the im-

provement of skills is considered just as significant as evidence that one has the ability to read.

5. Interpretation of content of reading is expected along with simple comprehension.

6. Clarity of ideas, quality of expression, and correctness of language are expected as well as ability to use word recognition skills for oral and silent reading of prepared materials.

The teacher has multiple clues of progress in skill development and creative thinking which are not present in reading programs where children are always working with and reworking other people's language. When there is a balance in the classroom between producing and using language, there are signs of development which do not appear when children deal daily with the task of trying to fit someone else's answers to someone else's questions.

WHAT IS AHEAD?

We are not sure of what lies ahead, but we welcome the opportunity to stand at the edge of mystery in such fascinating work—the teaching of young children.

Individualized Reading as Part
of an Eclectic Reading Program

W. PAUL BLAKELY

BEVERLY McKAY

Although some of the more partisan advocates of Individualized Reading have presented it as an all-or-nothing program, there have been expressed authoritative opinions that it may contribute rewardingly, along with elements of other recognized types of reading instruction, to an eclectic reading program. Witty wrote,

INDIVIDUALIZED READING AS PART OF AN ECLECTIC READING PROGRAM by W. Paul Blakely and Beverly McKay. From *Elementary English*, 43 (March 1966), pp. 214–19. Copyright © 1966 by the National Council of Teachers of English. Reprinted by permission of the publisher and W. Paul Blakely and Beverly McKay.

It seems that a defensible program in reading will combine the best features of both individual and group instruction in reading. . . . A defensible reading program . . . recognizes the value of systematic instruction, utilization of interests, fulfillment of developmental needs, and the articulation of reading experience with other types of worthwhile activities.[1]

Likewise, Strang raised the question whether it is necessary to choose between individualized and basal reader approaches, and identified the effective teacher as one who, whatever the major approach used, introduces all the necessary features of a successful reading program.[2] Artley, Robinson, and Barbe are among the other specialists who could be cited to the same effect.[3, 4, 5]

To give further substantiation to these opinions, and to provide a source of guidelines for schools and teachers wishing to use individualized reading in an eclectic reading program, the authors undertook the following investigation during the school year 1962–63. It was the purpose of the investigation to discover what means are being used to supplement a basal reader program with individualized instruction in grades four, five, and six.

The investigation was carried out by means of a questionnaire which was constructed for the purpose and sent in the quantity of five copies each to the elementary supervisors or comparable officials in fifty Iowa school systems. The school systems were selected arbitrarily and subjectively, with geographic distribution within the state and elimination of very small systems being given consideration. Each of the fifty officials was requested to distribute the five questionnaires to teachers of grades four, five and/or six whom he believed to be using individualized reading procedures along with a basal reader program.

A return of 124 questionnaires of the 250 thus distributed, was received. The return percentage of 49.6 should be interpreted bearing in mind that some officials may have had no teachers in their systems eligible to receive the questionnaires under the terms specified, and others may have had fewer than the five for whom questionnaires were supplied.

Of the 124 questionnaires returned, eleven answered negatively the first question, "Do you use individualized reading as part of your reading program, *along with a basal reading series?*" (This happened in spite of the stipulation in the accompanying letter to the elementary supervisor or

[1] Paul Witty, "Individualized Reading—a Summary and Evaluation," *Elementary English,* 36 (October, 1959) 450.

[2] Ruth Strang, "Controversial Programs and Procedures in Reading," *The School Review,* 69 (Winter, 1961) 420–21.

[3] A. Sterl Artley, "An Eclectic Approach to Reading," *Elementary English,* 38 (May, 1961) 326.

[4] Helen M. Robinson, "News and Comment: Individualized Reading," *The Elementary School Journal,* 60 (May, 1960) 411–20.

[5] Walter B. Barbe, *Educator's Guile to Personalized Reading Instruction.* Englewood Cliffs, New Jersey: Prentice-Hall, Inc., 1961, pp. 223–24.

other official which was intended to prevent it.) This comparison of eleven with 113 (total, 124) in no way represents the prevalence or scarcity of the practice being investigated, of course.

Individualized reading was identified in the first question as follows:

> Individualized reading is not new! It refers to the procedures involved when reading time is spent by children reading materials which they themselves select, with teacher guidance when necessary, and the activities associated with such reading: pupil record-keeping, individual teacher-pupil conferences, and individual or group instruction in reading skills when need arises.

Two respondents of the 124 described a program which was more or less strictly individualized reading rather than a use of it in combination with the basal reader program. This left a population of 111 respondents who indicated that they did use individualized reading along with a basal reading series, and on whose answers the following analysis is based.

THE ROLE OF INDIVIDUALIZED READING IN THE ECLECTIC PROGRAM

In the questionnaire, the respondent was offered four possible procedures among which to indicate the one she was using; or, in case none of the four was appropriate, a fifth choice, "Other." An examination of Table 1 shows that the use indicated most frequently was that of a supplement to the basal reader, used regularly regardless of whether or not the basal reader has been completed. Other uses indicated with considerably less frequency were (in descending order) a special approach for retarded readers,

Table 1

Method of Incorporating Individualized Reading
into the Reading Program Selected Iowa Schools, 1963

Method	Teachers Indicating	Percent of Total
To fill out a year or semester for only the superior group	11	10
To fill out a year or semester for any group which finishes basal readers	24	22
As a special approach for retarded readers	30	27
As a supplement to the basal reader, used regularly even though the basal reader has not been completed	88	79
Other	19	17

to fill out a year or semester for any group which finishes basal readers, miscellaneous "other" uses, and to fill out a year or semester for only the superior group. (The percentages in the tables do not necessarily total 100. A respondent might indicate more than one response to most questions.) Among the "other" practices reported were use of individualized reading in a program of interclass grouping ("Joplin Plan"), use of the Science Research Associates Reading Laboratories, use of individualized reading for twelve weeks followed by the basal reader program, and use of individualized reading as a special approach for both the retarded and the superior readers. One teacher reported an individualized reading group which children might join when they demonstrated that they had acquired certain skills.

BASIS OF STUDENTS' BOOK SELECTIONS

Respondents were asked, "How do students select books?" An analysis of the responses, which were not structured on the questionnaire, is shown in Table 2. The basis mentioned most frequently was interest, while teacher guidance, selection from a group which the teacher has selected as being at his level and suitable, and selection on the basis of relation to reading and other subject units being studied were mentioned less frequently. Miscellaneous other bases, mentioned from one to eight times each, were availability, appearance and physical characteristics, recommendations of friends, guidance of librarians, individual ability, and selection from books and stories suggested in the basal reader.

Table 2

Basis of Students' Book Selections in Reading Programs
Selected Iowa Schools, 1963

Method	Teachers Indicating	Percent of Total
Interest	77	69
With teacher guidance	25	23
From group teacher has selected as being at his level and suitable	25	23
Relation to reading and other subject units being studied	20	18
From books and stories suggested in basal reader	8	7
Individual ability	8	7
Guidance of librarian	6	5
Recommendations of friends	4	4
Appearance, physical characteristics	2	2
Availability	1	1

SOURCES OF BOOKS AVAILABLE
TO CHILDREN

Ranking high as sources of books used by children in individualized reading, as mentioned by the 111 respondents, were the school central library, the public library, and the classroom library. Less frequently mentioned were the county library (in Iowa, usually associated with the Office of the County Superintendent of Schools) and the children's homes. Other sources, mentioned by a few respondents, were book clubs, the teacher, the S.R.A. Laboratory (a misinterpretation of the question), and the library service of the Iowa State Education Association (a sales, not a lending, agency). The information concerning sources of books is presented in detail in Table 3.

Table 3

Sources of Books Available to Children Selected Iowa Schools, 1963

Source	Teachers Indicating	Percent of Total
School central library	82	73
Public library	73	65
Classroom library	67	60
County library	24	22
Home	22	19
Book clubs	7	6
Teacher	6	5
S.R.A. Reading Laboratory	4	4
I.S.E.A. Library Service	1	1

TYPES OF MATERIALS USED

Table 4 shows that the most frequently mentioned types of materials used in the individualized reading part of the eclectic reading program were fiction trade books, non-fiction trade books, various basal readers, periodicals, and content texts. The S.R.A. Reading Laboratory was mentioned by five percent of the respondents, while newspaper and comic materials were mentioned in three responses. It should be noted that fiction and non-fiction trade books were both mentioned by a large majority of the respondents.

METHODS OF KEEPING RECORDS
OF CHILDREN'S READING

The variety of methods of keeping records of children's reading associated with individualized reading is shown in Table 5. Mentioned most

Table 4

Types of Materials used in Reading Programs
Selected Iowa Schools, 1963

Type	Teachers Indicating	Percent of Total
Fiction trade books	102	92
Non-fiction trade books	99	88
Various basal readers	83	75
Periodicals	73	66
Content texts	67	60
S.R.A. Laboratory	5	5
Newspapers	1	1
School newspapers	1	1
Comic-type	1	1

frequently were filing cards, student notebooks, charts, and written reports. Thirteen percent of the respondents said that no records were kept. Mentioned once or no more than four times were the S.R.A. record-keeping procedure, graphs, check sheets, cumulative folders, and questionnaires.

Of the teachers reporting no record keeping procedure, one said, "I do not keep a chart or file. I believe if a child will read for enjoyment and not because of a star or a check, he is on the way to a life of reading, and not just a year or twelve years."

Table 5

Methods of Keeping Records of Children's Reading
Selected Iowa Schools, 1963

Method	Teachers Indicating	Percent of Total
Filing cards	33	30
Student notebooks	29	26
Charts	28	25
Written reports	22	20
No records	14	13
S.R.A. procedure	4	4
Graphs	3	3
Check sheets	3	3
Cumulative folders	2	2
Questionnaires	1	1

TYPES OF TEACHER-PUPIL CONFERENCES

One of the elements that usually distinguishes individualized reading from simple "free reading" is the provision for definite individual discussion and instruction involving the teacher and the pupil. Table 6 shows that only twenty-five percent of the respondents indicated the use of individual conferences, while twenty-four percent indicated the use of small group conferences, and thirty-five percent, a combination. Twenty percent indicated that they held no conferences.

Table 6

Types of Teacher-Pupil Conferences in Reading Programs
Selected Iowa Schools, 1963

Type	Teachers Indicating	Percent of Total
Individual	28	25
Small group	27	24
Combination of above	35	31
No conferences	21	20

ACTIVITIES THAT TAKE PLACE DURING TEACHER-PUPIL CONFERENCES

Table 7 indicates that the activity taking place most frequently in the individualized reading conferences in the respondents' classrooms was the child's telling the story in his own words. Oral reading and question-answer sessions were mentioned by fifty-one and forty-one percent of the respondents respectively; while fewer mentioned checking for comprehension and vocabulary and helping in correcting difficulties, and discussion of story, characters, incidents, *etc.* Activities mentioned by one to six percent of the respondents were discussion of book to be read next, discussion of written report, pupil evaluation of his own achievement, taping of oral reading or reporting, and dramatization. Three respondents said they varied the activities to meet the needs of the children. The fact that a large number of the respondents mentioned several activities indicates that many teachers follow this practice, which is, of course, necessary for true individualization of reading instruction.

OCCASIONS FOR GROUP INSTRUCTION

The inclusion in Table 8 of thirteen categories derived from answers to the question, "What occasions, if any, are used for *group* instruction specifically related to the individualized reading part of the program?" indicates the wide variety of such occasions. Those mentioned most frequently

Table 7

Activities Which Take Place During Teacher-Pupil Conferences
in Reading Programs Selected Iowa Schools, 1963

Activity	*Teachers Indicating*	*Percent of Total*
Child telling story in own words	68	63
Oral reading	56	51
Question-answer session	45	41
Check for comprehension, vocabu-lary, *etc.* and help in correcting difficulties	13	12
Discussion of story, characters, incidents, *etc.*	12	11
Dramatization	6	6
Taping of oral reading or reporting	3	3
Activities varied to meet needs of children	3	3
Pupil evaluation of own achievement	2	2
Discussion of written report	1	1
Discussion of book to be read next	1	1

were need of the group for help with a particular skill, opportunity for individual ideas or discoveries with the class, opportunity for oral book reviews, need to prepare the class to select and evaluate books, a number of students' having chosen the same or related material, need for the whole

Table 8

Occasions for Group Instruction Specifically Related
to the Individualized Reading Part of Programs Selected Iowa Schools, 1963

Occasion	*Teachers Indicating*	*Percent of Total*
Group needs help with a particular skill	19	17
Sharing individual ideas or discoveries with class	18	16
Oral book reviews	9	8
Preparation of class to select and evaluate books	9	8
Number of students choose same or related materials	8	7
Planning by whole class for a particular activity	6	5
Introduction of new concepts	5	5
Stressing reading skills in teaching the content areas	5	5
Follow-up activities	3	3
Wide interest shown in some phase of work	2	2
Oral reading to class	2	2
Panel discussions	1	1
Word building and analysis	1	1
None	27	24

class to plan for a particular activity, need to introduce new concepts, and need to stress reading skills in teaching the content areas.

Group instruction or sharing provides an opportunity for interaction among students and the bringing together of ideas, opinions, and concepts gained from their independent reading experiences. Instruction provided in groups, where common need or readiness warrants it, is also more economical of teacher time than individual instruction and thus more efficient.

GOALS OF THE INDIVIDUALIZED READING PART OF THE PROGRAM

As shown in Table 9, and as might be expected because of the nature of individualized reading, the most frequently mentioned goals of the individualized reading part of the eclectic reading program were love of reading

Table 9

Goals of Individualized Reading Part of Programs
Selected Iowa Schools, 1963

Goal	Teachers Indicating	Percent of Total
Love of reading	37	33
Broadened interests	36	32
Increased comprehension	22	20
Increased knowledge	20	18
Enriched vocabulary	19	16
Greater independence in work	14	13
Mastery of skills	13	12
Adoption of reading as a leisure activity	11	10
Development of literary appreciation and taste	10	9
Improved fluency	10	9
Increased speed	10	9
Increased amount of reading	8	7
Reading of wider variety of materials	8	7
Improved self-expression	8	7
Improved research skills	7	6
Independent application of word attack skills in context	7	6
Broadened background	5	5
Development of ability to select materials wisely	4	4

and broadening interests. It is significant, however, that four of the next five items in rank have to do with skills of reading: increased comprehension, enriched vocabulary, greater independence in work, and mastery of skills. Skills areas mentioned less frequently are improved fluency and speed, improved self-expression, improved research skills, independent application of word attack skills in context, and development of ability to select materials wisely. Mention by several respondents of increased knowledge and broadened background indicates another potential contribution of individualized reading.

TEACHER OPINION OF THE VALUE OF INDIVIDUALIZED READING AS PART OF THE READING PROGRAM

It is probably not surprising, in view of the selection process used in getting respondents in this investigation, that 108 of the 111 were favorable toward the use of individualized reading in conjunction with the basal reader program. Individual comments included the following: "Interest has been established within the slower group to stimulate their seeking the help needed." "In my opinion, the basic text does not provide very much challenge to the better readers and by individualizing the program you can make these people stretch their minds." "I feel that each child is progressing at his own rate and developing interests." "Individualized reading is essential! It is a self-motivator for application of skills taught. It removes the temptations of poor work-study habits, dawdling, and mischief. It provides for repetition of skill teaching. Its content leads children into joyful experiences with reading."

CONCLUSION

The results of the investigation reported here, based on questionnaire responses of 111 middle-grade teachers, give credibility and meaning to the assertion that individualized reading procedures may enrich and strengthen an eclectic reading program, offering contributions that complement the basal reader series.

Reading Materials:
Rationale and Review

ROBERT KARLIN

Instructional Materials are big business! Witness the association of industrial corporations with publishers and the purchase of educational publishing organizations by their cousins who had limited their activities to other areas. Although huge sums of money have been spent for instructional materials, the market has expanded as a result of new monies available to some school districts for the first time. We who have not spent much time in sections other than metropolitan will find hard to believe the fact that tens of thousands of children actually do not have enough materials from which to learn. I am thinking of not only the economically depressed sections of the country but also so many of our rural areas where either tax money, know-how or concern is lacking. The Federal Government through different titles now is making it possible for school districts to strengthen their programs by providing funds for all sorts of materials. For some this means breaking new ground; for others freeing funds for other things. The net result is larger sums of money for the purchase of materials, and materials for teaching reading will not be slighted.

Competition among publishers of reading materials is keen. Each desires to corner as much of the market as possible. In order to consummate a sale amounting to several millions one company had to demonstrate the superiority of its materials over the competition. This demonstration brings up the question of how we determine the superiority of one set of reading materials over another. Do we do this on the basis of research findings, universally accepted criteria, judgments based upon personal prejudices, or what? Perhaps a little of each, and in some instances, no real judgments at all.

Although there has been some research involving the use of reading materials, such as studies in which readiness or upper level workbooks were used with one group and not another, or in which outcomes of instructional programs were compared, the total amount is limited. For example, one reviewer found "no major studies of the evaluation of materials of their usefulness"[1] over a three-year period. Another, three years later, summarized but

READING MATERIALS: RATIONALE AND REVIEW by Robert Karlin. Adapted from a paper presented at the Ninth Annual Meeting of the College Reading Association, Jersey City State College, April 2, 1966. Copyright © 1966 by the College Reading Association. Reprinted by permission of the College Reading Association and Robert Karlin.

two studies of the types mentioned earlier.[2] As recently as 1965 a third compiler mentioned one study that compared the use of a mechanical device "with regular methods of teaching reading."[3] We have few if any studies which sought to determine the superiority of one set of materials over another. Perhaps from a research point of view what we are asking for cannot be done; that is, separating materials from programs. But I can envision a study in which a given skill is taught and then materials used to determine their effectiveness in strengthening its development. And self-teaching materials offer other opportunities also to ascertain superiority.

Universally accepted criteria for reading materials? No such things. Specialists in children's literature have suggested guidelines we might follow, but what guidelines are there for choosing one set of instructional materials over another? I suppose if we were to establish any, we would be concerned about such factors as content, interest, format. Of course, the most important factor might be the extent to which our purposes are met by materials.

I would settle for the latter, but experience tells me no such thing. Too many reading materials are chosen on the basis of what we are told about them. Publisher's promotions and claims are powerful influences in determining school sales. I would concede that selection on this basis is no worse than that emanating from ignorance.

Since we don't have much evidence about the worth of instructional materials intended to promote reading development, I will have to rely on my own experiences to assess them. Perhaps some of your own are similar to mine.

BASAL READER

How do we rate basal readers? Let us consider the old guard first and then evaluate the newcomers. We are all familiar with the typical basal reader with its paper-back pre-primers and one or more hardbacks for each grade level. What are their features? According to the publishers and advocates, these materials deal with activities familiar to many children and based upon their common interests. The selections are graded in difficulty by controlling vocabulary load, density and difficulty of ideas, sentence length, and so on. The content includes narrative and expository selections, fiction and poetry and is presented in an attractive format to hold children's attention and promote the development of reading ability.

We are told these features are necessary and desirable. But criticisms have been leveled against these books: the content is unexciting to children, particularly boys, and does not sustain their interest; writing styles with their repetitious and limited vocabularies are of poor literary quality; the selections do not reflect the cross section of American life with its diverse peoples, values and environments; there is a limited amount of subject-matter content with which to develop reading and study skills associated with it.

There is no doubt that some of these criticisms are valid, perhaps not wholly but certainly in part, but my guess is that we apply some of our adult common sense to these materials and draw conclusions that we support strongly with the help of authority. In so far as the unexciting content is concerned: certainly at the earliest stages, if we accept the readers' approach to word identification, there can't be much of any story, let alone exciting ones. Of course, as time goes on and children develop some basic skills, selections can contain more "meat" as well as deal with activities of a less sedentary nature. I am all for appealing to more boys, but I am not so sure the action which some critics want is the diet young children should have. Certainly it shouldn't be the sole fare.

What about poor literary quality? I don't know of anyone who would defend most basal readers on literary grounds. The first books in the series rely on limited vocabulary; such a condition can put a crimp in anyone's writing, Dr. Seuss notwithstanding! But once children have developed adequate word-attack skills, they need not be tied down to uninspired writing. With some modifications the writings of our better trade book authors could find their way into the readers. We are beginning to see some changes in this direction already occurring.

Most publishers of basal readers would plead guilty to the charge that these books reflect American middle class attitudes, white ones at that, and do not truly represent American diversity. You are all familiar with the claim that large numbers of children cannot and do not identify with the basal readers' characters and surroundings which are totally foreign to them; that they reject these and as a result are doomed to almost certain failure. Although I personally might prefer to include selections which more closely portray life as many people know it, I am not so sure for example, that it is necessary to give economically and culturally disadvantaged children heavy doses of what they know all too well, or that heroes they read about have to be exclusively of their own kind. I would agree that we need diversity and balance. Here is one area which research might well explore. Some publishers, in reply to this criticism, color a face here and there. What this means to children I do not know. More about this later.

It seems to me that criticism of most readers for their failure to deal with content systematically is valid. With conditions as they are, it is unrealistic to assume that teachers will offer this instruction as children study textbooks and other materials. I would recommend the inclusion of material which is representative of the types of reading we expect our pupils to do. Surely instruction in reading content is basic.

A number of new basic series have introduced significant changes in orthography, word patterns, and story settings. The materials through which a new orthography is introduced are quite similar to those with which we are familiar. One basic series that attempts to control sound patterns reads much like its counterparts of the "look, look" variety. A few others could also qualify for criticism on similar grounds. They are not literary or exciting by any stretch of the imagination. But all their worth must be assessed against standards that measure how well children learn to read and how much they desire to read.

Two sets of readers depart from the usual in that one stresses city living and the other the Negro. I would reject any set of materials which delimits a reader's perspective. Of what significance are ideas that are always comfortingly familiar? That we need some does not deny the need for others which are quite different. Do we expect the city child not to know or care about his cousins in the suburbs and rural communities? Do we assume he is a cliff dweller for all times? And a poor one at that? This brings me to the readers which are intended essentially for young Negro children. How are they different? Unlike the series which color an occasional face brown, these books deal with lives of Negro families. Although these families do not own private homes as pretentious as their white counterparts in other series, they do have their plots of grass and cars and do enjoy life in the suburbs. To the children for whom these materials are intended, this kind of life is quite foreign. How different, then, are they from the usual? In color. Will these materials help to produce better readers? My guess is that they won't, but I am prepared to look at outcomes dispassionately.

Some of my comments have been seconded by people in the field. Undoubtedly exceptions to them will be taken by others who feel strongly about basal readers. Until we can devise a better mousetrap I would suggest we strive to improve them. I would take issue with those who say that basal readers have inherent weaknesses which can't be overcome. No matter how attractive they do become, the ways in which they are used will determine their effectiveness. I can foresee a time when it might be possible to dispense with basal readers, when computer retrieval systems make available to us what we want and when we want it and when teachers know what they want and what to do with it when they have it.

WORKBOOKS

Workbooks may be divided into two classes: those which are designed to be used with a reading series and others that are independent. Whether the workbooks parallel reading programs or go their own way, they contain practice exercises in one or more of the following: readiness, word identification, comprehension, study skills. Independent workbooks tend to stress individual skills (such as phonic workbooks or those intended for upper grades) [rather] than cover the wide range found in series workbooks.

One of the problems associated with workbooks is the failure of many teachers to recognize to what purposes they might be put. As I see them, workbooks contain exercises which offer **practice**: in interpreting pictures, in matching letters with sounds, in discriminating between similar words, in using context clues and recognizing word endings, in dividing words into syllables, in reading for details and main ideas, in developing vocabulary, in summarizing and outlining, in drawing conclusions, and so on. Few, if any, offer **instruction** in skill development. Pupils require practice after instruction, some more and others less, and it is possible that a discriminating teacher will find exercises in workbooks that he can use for such purposes.

Teachers as a group prefer to use workbooks rather than prepare their own materials. They argue that they provide for individual differences, save time and effort, contain exercises superior to those which they might devise, free teachers to work with children who need extra help. The critics point to their cut-and-dried format, isolated exercises, mechanical responses, limited content. It would not be difficult to find samples to support each viewpoint.

What position do many of us take? There is nothing wrong with workbooks that we can't correct. I suspect we have been taken in by the claims some people have made for workbooks and then complain that they are not doing the job. Let's first recognize that no amount of time pupils spend with these materials will do them any good if they are unable to perform the tasks required of them. If children are weak in auditory discrimination of consonant blends and the practice exercise requires them to match these blends with pictures, what usefulness will the exercise have for them? Or if a group of children are weak in recognizing the central thought of a paragraph, will an exercise that requires them to perform this task enable them to do so? Recognize workbooks for what they are. Teach first and assign those exercises which give practice in doing what you've taught.

This brings us to weaknesses of many workbooks. On a given page you might find a number of different components, to some of which, perhaps, your pupils are not ready to respond. Or there is an inadequate amount of practice material to which they can respond. You can overcome these weaknesses by removing the pages of different workbooks, cutting some into smaller parts and bringing together sections containing exercises covering given skills. These might be mounted and placed in envelopes for use when needed.

Another suggestion. You can obtain added mileage from some workbooks by taking ideas from their better exercises and applying them to the materials which your pupils are reading. Such practice will be of help to the busy teacher (and to one who needs ideas) as well as tie more closely skills practice to reading activity.

There is another point about workbooks I need to make. Generally, each page or exercise has a stated purpose. A careful examination of some reveals that the exercise does not fulfill the stated purpose. Once again, indiscriminate assignments will lull the user into believing pupils are engaging in and profiting from an activity when in reality no such things are happening. We must know our craft sufficiently well so that we recognize weakness wherever it occurs.

Let's take a quick look into the future. You have just taught a skill lesson to a group of children (to vary routines) who are reading on different levels. You have been working on clues for drawing conclusions. Now you need some practice material. You go to your console, push some buttons, wheels whir, and out of the units that are part of each desk come materials that are just right for each child. As soon as the child finishes the page he inserts it into the machine which indicates the correctness of his responses. If you are seeking oral responses the child's screen lights up, material suitable for him appears and he responds. Each correct response is confirmed; incorrect responses are noted, fresh material provided with oral explanations, followed by new practice exercises. Automatic workbooks of the future!

PACKAGED MIXES AND PROGRAMMED MATERIALS

There are a group of instructional materials which are packaged in boxes. Some contain materials intended for primary grade use; others provide materials for the middle grades, junior and senior high schools. One covers basic word identification, comprehension skills, and rate; another study skills, and so on. The features that promoters of these materials stress are their different levels of difficulty covered and minimal teacher attention required. At the higher levels they are supposed to free the teacher for other tasks.

None of these materials is truly programmed although some publishers describe them as though they were. This fact, however, does not make them self-instructional. What does it mean? Can you take one of these boxes, set your class loose and assume you have an on-going program? From my point of view, no! If you desire your pupils to practice what they have learned, these boxes will help you achieve this purpose. They will not assume the responsibility of providing instruction. They might make your task easier by offering ready-tailored practice materials.

There are a few instructional materials which use programmed techniques, more or less. Two sets of these materials have been written for beginning readers. I find them quite dull in content and design; however, they might appeal to beginners. In so far as their work is concerned, results in producing competent readers as well as eager ones have yet to be established. We should not be prepared to accept data from vested interests until they have been verified. I do know of a tryout in which one of them was found wanting.

There are a few additional materials that follow the programmed design. It seems to me that highly creative efforts might produce instructional materials for teaching some reading skills, if not many of them. Some people feel that many of the higher-level comprehension skills require "talking out" which programming lacks. Provision for audio as well as visual treatments could fill the gaps and surround the learner with "give and take" not presently offered by successive frames of printed explanations, questions and answers. You may be familiar with the experimental program which taught a poem by helping the reader to analyze it. Perhaps more of this type of experimentation will give us insights into how we can get the job done in a meaningful and efficient way. There is still the problem of overcoming impersonal treatment with which programmers have not been concerned but learners are.

AUDIO-VISUAL AIDS

Charts, flash cards, games, word wheels, film strips, records, these and more can help you get the job done and make learning interesting providing they are not used indiscriminately and for their own sake. You must ask yourself this question whenever you are tempted by them: Will they help my pupils learn what they don't know? If the answer is in the affirmative the second question should follow: Under what circumstances might I use them? To illustrate what I mean: here is a word game which you know children enjoy playing. What is the relationship between the words in the game and those with which a group of children have difficulty in the reading they do? If none, then that game is unsuitable. You might pattern your own game after it and substitute the troublesome words. But the game is introduced as part of a total lesson, using context, phonic and structural clues to recognize the words, developing rapid recognition of them, and dealing with them again in context. Under these circumstances playing the game is a meaningful, purposeful learning experience as well as an enjoyable one. It is not an end in itself. These comments also apply to the other kinds of instructional materials mentioned earlier.

MECHANICAL AIDS

Pacers, flashmeters, films. These are used more at the higher levels than at the lower ones since most are intended to promote rapid reading. Unlike the other materials, investigations into their validity have been conducted with elementary, secondary, and college students as well as adults. The evidence we have is fairly clear: flashmeters seem to be of least value; films aren't much better; pacers, if used properly, might be helpful if only to motivate. In a summary of the research the conclusion that any gains achieved with mechanical devices might be duplicated or surpassed through natural means was reached. Gadgets are appealing, but we tire of them if they fail to meet our expectations.

There are some new developments in gadgetry which might be promising. One is an instrument which reads words that are typed on tape. Thus a child can see words on cards at the same time he hears them. The other is a viewing device which provides reading instruction through visual and auditory programs. Both might be useful in a skills program of a knowledge-able teacher.

SUMMARY

We have intimated, if we haven't said, that materials are no better than the teachers who use them, just as our physical plants are as good as the staffs who make them. With the exception of materials that actually free us of teaching responsibilities, how useful instructional materials are depends on how well we understand their strengths and limitations. Some of the most simple kinds of instructional materials can be profitably employed to promote reading; on the other hand, elaborate designs, though impressive, won't help us very much. I have learned to be skeptical of claims; in a world of many marvels and much money we need more educators who say: "I'm from Missouri."

Bibliographical Footnotes

1. Theodore Clymer and Helen Robinson: "Reading" in *Language Arts and Fine Arts*. Review of Educational Research: Vol. XXXI: No. 2: April 1961: 133.
2. Jack A. Holmes and Harry Singer: "Theoretical Models and Trends Toward More Basic Research in Reading" in *Language Arts and Fine Arts:* Review of Educational Research: Vol. XXXIV: No. 2: April 1964: 148.
3. Helen Robinson: "Summary of Investigations Relating to Reading, July 1, 1963 to June 30, 1964." *The Reading Teacher:* Vol. 18: No. 5: February 1965: 396.

4   Suggestions for Further Reading

The characteristics of developmental reading instruction are discussed by David H. Russell, "Continuity in the Reading Program," in Nelson B. Henry (ed.), *Development in and through Reading* (National Society for the Study of Education, 1961), 226–53; Constance M. McCullough, "Balanced Reading Development," in *Innovation and Change in Reading Instruction* (National Society for the Study of Education, 1968), 320–56; and David L. Shepherd (ed.), *Reading and the Elementary School Curriculum* (International Reading Association, 1969).

There are a number of detailed descriptions and evaluations of beginning reading programs: Mildred Letton Wittick, "Innovations in Reading Instruction: For Beginners," in *Innovation and Change in Reading Instruction* (National Society for the Study of Education, 1968), 72–125; George D. Spache and Evelyn B. Spache, *Reading in the Elementary School,* (Allyn and Bacon, 1969), 76–186; Robert C. Aukerman, *Approaches to Beginning Reading* (Wiley, 1971); Jeanne Chall, *Learning to Read: The Great Debate** (McGraw-Hill, 1967), 187–262; Nila Banton Smith (ed.), *Current Issues in Reading* (International Reading Association, 1969), 224–307, 328–56; Elaine C. Vilscek, *A Decade of Innovations: Approaches to Beginning Reading* (International Reading Association, 1968); Robert C. Aukerman (ed.), *Some Persistent Questions on Beginning Reading* (International Reading Association, 1972).

For treatments of specialized reading programs see Doris M. Lee and R. V. Allen, *Learning to Read Through Experience,* 2nd edition (Appleton-Century-Crofts, 1963); Russell G. Stauffer, *The Language-Experience Approach to the Teaching of Reading** (Harper and Row, 1970); Lyman C. Hunt, *The Individualized Reading Program: A Guide for Classroom Teaching* (International Reading Association, 1967); and Jeanette Veatch, *Reading in the Elementary School* (Ronald Press, 1966).

* Available in paperback

5

TEACHING WORD
RECOGNITION

If there is any consensus among the majority of specialists of reading, it is in the recognition that no aspect of learning to read is more important than the ability to perceive words readily and that systematic plans to insure mastery over word recognition skills must be drawn. Several years ago, a group of professional educators with disparate views came together to determine if they could accept some policy statements about the teaching of reading. Virtually the only substantive issue on which they were in complete agreement dealt with word recognition and the requirement that schools must offer the most carefully planned and expertly guided program in order to teach children the word recognition skills, and that the success of such a program depends on teachers who are knowledgeable about reading and learning.

There is also agreement among specialists on the complement of skills that should be included in any word recognition program. There is somewhat less agreement on the priority that each of the skills deserves. And many part company on sequences and methodology. Unfortunately, teachers cannot with full confidence turn to research for the resolution of these differences, for the data yielded by research are limited and inconclusive. Instead, they must rely heavily on theory and demonstration to provide rationales to support instructional programs in word recognition.

In a comprehensive summary of research done mainly on the teaching of letter-sound relationships, Jeanne Chall explores the contributions made by the structural and transformational linguists to our understanding of these relationships, and she discusses some implications for teaching them to children. She cites findings that raise doubts about the structuralists' contention that it is not necessary to offer direct instruction in letter-sound correspondences when spelling patterns in words are controlled. Citing the work of transformationalists and other linguists, she offers some hypotheses regarding the emphasis on whole words, the recognition of more sophisticated relationships between spellings and sounds, and the influence of syntactic and

semantic clues in recognizing words. All these could have an impact on beginning reading instruction.

Chall explores the issue of nonstandard English and its relation to success in beginning reading. It is possible that speakers of nonstandard dialects
would be better off in beginning reading programs that did not stress phonics
as much as other programs. It is also possible that there are other factors that
help to explain the difficulties these children experience in learning to read.
Chall considers these factors and proposes instructional strategies that might
work for culturally different children.

Nothing in Chall's review of research indicates what methods teachers
should adopt in teaching word recognition skills. However, her review does
offer some perspectives that teachers need to be aware of as they plan the
content and strategies for their programs. It also suggests balance in teaching
children how to unlock unknown words.

This last point is echoed by James F. Kerfoot, who believes that all too
frequently multiple approaches to word recognition have been limited to
the question of analytic phonics versus synthetic phonics with some recommending that both be incorporated into a program. In his judgment such
a composite approach is much too narrow for as complex a process as learning
to recognize words.

After identifying the objectives of word recognition, Kerfoot describes
the content of skills and knowledges. Skills include context and sounding;
knowledges cover the meanings, pronunciations, and elements of words. He
uses these terms in a much broader sense than is ordinarily done. Kerfoot
considers four elements in developing the word program: selection of content,
specific versus generic attitudes, sequence, and method of multiple impression.
The last consists of multiple setting and multiple response, both of which
are frameworks into which teaching strategies can fit. Multiple setting involves
the discrimination of words in different fields and forms; multiple response
involves multisensory learning. Kerfoot would maximize the number of
experiences, the variety of settings, and variety of responses in teaching word
recognition skills. He would also apply the well-established principle of using
what children know to teach them what they do not know—in this case using
previously taught words and elements to develop skill in recognizing other
words.

The importance of context clues in reading cannot be overestimated,
according to Robert Emans. In word recognition they serve the following
purposes: they help in remembering words that have been identified earlier
but have been forgotten; they can be combined with phonic and structural
analysis to check the accuracy of tentatively identified words; they help in
the correct identification of words whose pronunciation is determined by their
usage. From the knowledge teachers have about the background of experience
and oral language usages children bring to reading, they can understand how
context clues work in word recognition and can develop some techniques
for teaching children how to use them.

Emans divides context clues for use in word recognition into three main categories: meaning bearing clues, language bearing clues, and organization clues. He recognizes that these classes do not encompass all types of context clues (typographical, for example) but offers these three as being fairly complete. He goes on to suggest what the nature of materials to be used for teaching children how to use context clues should be and offers a sequence of exercises for developing the ability to interpret them.

Harry W. Sartain lists twelve criteria derived from generally accepted principles of learning and reading that teachers might follow in assessing the usefulness of commercial materials designed to teach vocabulary and word recognition skills. Since there is an abundance of these materials, teachers must learn to be discriminating in selecting appropriate ones for work with their pupils.

Research in Linguistics and Reading Instruction: Implications for Further Research and Practice

JEANNE CHALL

Linguists are relative newcomers to reading instruction. Not that they didn't have something to offer us earlier, but, somehow, we were not ready to listen to them. When we did listen, it was to the structural linguists—particularly to Bloomfield and Fries—who addressed themselves primarily to problems of beginning reading, and more specifically to problems of word recognition.

We started to take linguistics seriously after Flesch (*18*) cited the earlier works of Bloomfield (*7*) in his call for a return to phonics as *the way* to start, although Bloomfield himself was just as opposed to phonic methods as he was to the prevailing look-say methods. It is significant to note, however, that Bloomfield's beginning reading program, coauthored by Clarence Barnhart, was not published until 1961, although it had been used experimentally in some schools since the 1930's. Also, Fries' *Linguistics and Reading* did not appear until 1962, and his reading program was not published until 1965.

Bloomfield and Fries shared certain views about reading and its relation to spoken language. Both subscribed to the primacy of spoken over written language; the written form being essentially a visual representation of the spoken form. In alphabetic languages, the letters stand for speech sounds. Thus, for the native speaking child who already has considerable command of the vocabulary and syntax of his language, learning to read is primarily learning the code—or the alphabetic principle—i.e., which letters represent which sounds.

Alphabetic languages, however, are more or less regular; there is a greater or lesser consistency between their distinctive speech sounds (phonemes) and the letters used to represent them (graphemes). Italian, for ex-

RESEARCH IN LINGUISTICS AND READING INSTRUCTION: IMPLICATIONS FOR FURTHER RESEARCH AND PRACTICE by Jeanne Chall. From *Reading and Realism,* Proceedings of the 13th Annual Convention of the International Reading Association, 1969, ed. J. Allen Figurel, Volume 13, Part 1, pp. 560–71. Reprinted with permission of the International Reading Association and Jeanne Chall.

ample, is quite regular while English is comparatively irregular. Thus, according to these linguists, to read English presents an additional hurdle to the beginner. This hurdle becomes even greater, they postulated, when the beginning reading materials use high frequency words that contain different spellings for the same sounds and different sounds for the same spellings, and when the major focus in teaching is on directing the child's attention to the content of what is read.

To simplify the process of learning to read, each believed that the linguist's contribution lay in identifying the basic speech sounds of English and establishing the relationships between these sounds and the letters that are most commonly used to represent them. With his information, it would then be possible to program the first steps in order to facilitate the learning of the alphabetic principle.

Now the crucial question for reading instruction is how these linguistic data are to be used. Knowing that certain sounds are more often spelled in certain ways, and knowing that certain sound-letter correspondences are more frequent than others does not automatically lead to decisions regarding programing and teaching procedures—i.e., *when* they are to be taught and *how* they are to be taught. As we know from the reading programs produced by Bloomfield [Bloomfield and Barnhart (*8, 9*)] and later by Fries (*21*), they chose to teach the most frequent and most regular correspondences first. They also assumed that the best way to teach them was in words carefully selected to permit the learner to discover for himself the relations between the letters and sounds. They were opposed to isolating sounds, to giving direct instruction in letter-sound relations, and to the teaching of rules. They were also opposed to the use of pictures and to encouraging the child's use of context clues, since they might distract the beginner from the major task—paying close attention to the letters. They also believed that the words used in the connected reading matter for the beginner should be selected on the basis of the correspondences previously taught. Only gradually, as each "spelling pattern" is mastered by reading orally words containing a pattern, is another introduced.

There are some minor differences between the Bloomfield and Fries beginning reading programs. Essentially, however, they are similar when compared to the most widely used beginning reading programs of the 1950's and 1960's as represented by the conventional basal readers (*12*). The Fries program puts more emphasis on comprehension (or reading for meanings) than does the Bloomfield, but it contains the same kind of connected reading matter. In the Bloomfield first reader, "Nan had a fat cat" (p. 45), while in the Fries Reader 1, "Dan can pat the cat" (p. 36).

Other linguists or writers who based their programs on "linguistic principles" drew somewhat different implications from these linguistic data for reading instruction. Although they agreed that beginning reading is essentially mastering a code, some gave direct instruction in the sound-letter relations in addition to controlling vocabulary or spelling regularity. Some also used pictures and introduced common, "irregularly" spelled words earlier.

The choice of *what, when,* and *how* to program materials for the optimal learning of sound-letter relations (or phoneme-grapheme correspondences) is not based solely on linguistic principles, even though the choice may have been made by a linguist. Other linguists have come up with different ways of relating spelling to spoken language. But even if we accept the Bloomfield or Fries schemes for relating sound to spelling, the validity of their programing cannot be established solely by linguistic data or theory, but must be tested ultimately by psychological and educational experimentation.

What is the experimental evidence so far? Levin's laboratory experiments *(28)* suggest that the Bloomfield type of programing of one sound for one spelling pattern may not be optimal; i.e., mastering *can, fan, Dan,* then moving to *cat, fat, rat.* Although Levin found that it takes longer to learn two sounds for one letter (e.g., to learn that *g* is pronounced as in both *go* and *gem*) than to learn one association at a time, dual-association learning had greater transfer value. Thus, systems that teach single associations may be easier for initial learning, but their transfer value for reading of English— where more than one sound for one letter or letter combination occurs—may be limited.

There is also some older evidence that direct teaching of letter-sound correspondences helps most pupils even when words are controlled on spelling regularity [Winch *(34)*]. A more recent laboratory experiment by Bishop *(6)* which simulated a beginning reading situation using adult subjects, also found that direct teaching of letter-sound correspondences helps in learning regularly spelled words. She did find, however, that about half of the group who did not receive direct letter-sound instruction were able to make the inferences themselves, and their performance was as good as those who received direct instruction in letter-sound relations. Thus, direct teaching of sound-letter correspondences (phonics) had more transfer value, but word training did produce some transfer.

What about the linguists' view of beginning reading as primarily a decoding process? My interpretation of the experimental, clinical, and correlational studies from 1912 to 1965 [Chall *(12)*] tended to confirm this view. While there were too few experimental comparisons of the Bloomfield and Fries type programs with others, I hypothesized that they would probably produce better results than basal systems (with no control of sound-letter relations), but not necessarily better results than systematic phonics programs which also put greater stress on teaching sound-letter correspondences.

To a certain extent I was not too far off. In his summary of the USOE cooperative first and second grade studies, Dykstra *(16)* reported that at the end of Grades 1 and 2, the linguistic programs, when compared to basal programs, tended to produce better results in word recognition and spelling, although no significant differences were found in comprehension.

However, a phonic/linguistic approach (one that taught sound-letter correspondences directly and used illustrations as well as words controlled on spelling regularity), when compared to basal programs, tended to produce better results in word recognition, spelling, and reading comprehension at the end of Grades 1 and 2.

Admittedly, such large scale methods comparisons are not the best way to determine the effectiveness of the application of linguistic data to reading instruction, since other variables may have possibly contributed to producing the differences found. Viewed over the long run, however, it appears that some concern for the programing of sound-letter correspondences is important, at least for beginning reading instruction. I quote from Dykstra (16: 161): "Control of vocabulary, either by means of a transitional alphabet (ITA) or by means of introducing initially only regularly represented words, appears to facilitate acquisition of skill in unlocking words and in spelling. Some control of vocabulary according to phoneme-grapheme correspondences is likely to be helpful in the teaching of primary reading and spelling."

More recent analyses of English words by linguists go considerably beyond the simpler correspondences postulated by Bloomfield. Hockett postulated an implicit inner level of representation involved in the acquisition of literacy, since English written words are not a simple and direct representation of spoken words (there are too many cases in which the spelling is not predictable from the pronunciation), and English spoken words are not a simple direct representation of written words (there are too many cases in which the pronunciation is not predictable from the spelling).

Indeed, the computer-based data reported by Hanna et al., (24) on sound-to-spelling correspondences, and by Venezky and Weir (32) on spelling-to-sound correspondence patterns indicate that the relationships are more complex than once thought from the analysis of Bloomfield and Fries.

Recent work by Chomsky and Halle (14) may lead to even more complex and powerful rules for the relations between written and spoken words. According to their theoretical analysis, there is a deeper phonological explanation for the relations between the sounds and spelling of English than is found by comparing phonemes with graphemes. Indeed, Chomsky claims that when understood from the standpoint of this deeper phonological level, English spelling makes more sense than we have been led to believe by the descriptive linguists, since it gives the native speaker considerable syntactic and semantic information. Thus when analyzed on a deeper level, retaining the "silent" g in sign and the silent b in bomb makes sense when we come to the derivatives signal and bombardier. He also believes the written language has a life of its own—at a certain point it is not a direct representation of the spoken language, but an even better carrier of semantic and syntactic information for speakers of various dialects.

When the Chomsky-Halle analysis is completed, what will it mean for reading instruction? Carton suggested earlier today that it may bring back a whole word or sight approach as the first step in learning to read. In other words, we need not concern ourselves with teaching or programing sound-letter correspondences. It could, however, mean a different and perhaps more powerful kind of vocabulary control or phonic teaching; it could mean that the value of long and short vowel sounds can be taught more effectively in syntactic environments such as *sign-signal, hide-hidden, bath-bathe* than in the traditional *pin-pine, cap-cape* contrasts which have no syntactic connection. Since it may prove difficult to find enough examples of the *bath-bathe* paradigm (many are of the type *explain-explanatory*), the question arises whether it would be better to delay such instruction until more relevant examples are in the child's spoken vocabulary, or perhaps even to develop the spoken vocabulary in this direction.

The broader implication of the work of Hockett, and particularly of Chomsky, is to ask if the phonics or the simple sound-letter correspondences now taught in the present "linguistic" type programs are general enough? Or would Chomsky's more sophisticated information about the relationships between spelling and sounds lead to more effective sets of phonic principles and sequencing? It may be that Chomsky's deeper phonological rules will be more useful at later stages of reading and spelling instruction, while the simpler, more naive ones now taught are quite suitable for the beginner.

THE INFLUENCE OF CONTEXT
ON WORD RECOGNITION

The Chomsky-Halle scheme suggests that the spelling of a word gives the reader more than a clue to the sound of the word, that it can also give the native speaker syntactic and semantic clues.

Recent research on the oral reading errors made by first graders suggests that in the reading of connected material, syntax and meaning do, in fact, play an important role in word recognition.

In a recent study, Rose-Marie Weber (*33*: 29), a linguist with Project Literacy at Cornell, summarized the past research on oral reading errors: "In all of reading research the interest shown in words as visual displays stands in contrast to the neglect of written words as linguistic units represented graphically. That the reader's knowledge of the grammatical structure of his language comes into play during reading hardly enters into any discussion of reading errors." This is somewhat surprising, as most programs since the 1920's have put so much stock in context as a clue to word recognition.

Her own analysis of the errors made by 21 first graders who were taught by a regular basal reading program (Scott, Foresman) considered various linguistic levels: (a) the word's match with the stimulus as a graphic display, (b) its morphological structure relative to that of the stimulus, (c) its syntactic function in a phrase as indicated by its part of speech, (d) its syntactic acceptability in the sentence, (e) its semantic appropriateness to the sentence, and (f) its appropriateness to the meaning of the entire passage. Full stops (nonrecognitions), hesitations, and repetitions were not counted as errors.

She found that substitutions of one word for another comprised 80 percent of the total errors made by these first graders. Omissions and insertions constituted 10 percent and reversals and scrambles of words, less than 3 percent.

When substitution errors were further classified on an index of graphic similarity (e.g., identical letters, position of identical letters, length), she found that the high group had a higher index of graphic similarity than the low group. Comparing errors over time, both high and low groups showed an increase in the degree to which their substitutions approached the graphic similarity of the stimulus words.

No particular part of speech was more susceptible to error than any other, when compared to frequency in the text read. However, parts of speech that expanded the sentence (i.e., noun modifiers, adverbs, and some function words) were most often omitted or inserted.

Grammatical constraints were also a factor in the substitution errors, with 91 percent of the errors judged grammatical in terms of the preceding context, and 64 percent judged grammatical in terms of the entire sentence.

For sentences that remained grammatically intact in spite of the error, 93 percent were found semantically appropriate up to the point of the error, and 68 percent semantically appropriate in terms of the entire selection.

She also found an interaction between the use of graphic cues and contextual cues (syntactical and semantic). The higher the graphic similarity of the error, the lower its contextual appropriateness. Also, grammatical acceptability and semantic appropriateness tended to decrease with time, reflecting, no doubt, the increasing ability of the children to respond to the words in terms of sound-letter correspondences.

Her conclusions (*33*: 102) with regard to the strategies used by first graders were as follows: "This analysis of errors on the syntactic and semantic levels suggests that even early readers can successfully make use of preceding verbal context; it is clear that they do not depend solely on graphic representation to make a response. Reading instruction might well incorporate guidance on the optimal balance in the use of correspondences between sounds and letters and the expectations transferred from verbal experience. *However, this description leaves us far from discerning what the optimal balance might be*" (emphasis mine).

In a similar study of oral reading errors among first graders who also learned to read in a basal reading program, Biemiller (*5*) found (although he counted nonrecognitions as errors) a "fairly regular" progression in the types of errors made at the beginning to the end of the first grade. He divided these into three major phases, the first phase being characterized by a preponderance of substitution errors that showed heavy reliance on context. Some children remained at this phase all year. Most moved, however, to a second phase when the majority of their errors were "non-responses." It was the better readers who reached this second phase earlier, and they were the most able readers by the end of the year, "while those children who never adopted a non-responding strategy (and continued using context predominantly) were almost without exception the poorest readers at the end of the year" [Biemiller (4)].

The third phase was characterized by greater flexibility in strategies used to identify words. When reading relatively easy material (overall error rate less than 5 to 10 percent of words read), most errors indicated the use of context information. In addition, however, some errors also showed evidence of paying attention to graphic details. On difficult materials (overall error rate higher than 10 percent), less context information and more graphic information was used.

Biemiller noted that all children seemed to go through these three phases—the better readers at a faster pace, the poorer readers at a slower pace.

The implications for research of the Weber and Biemiller error studies are extremely suggestive. The most obvious question that arises is whether the same kinds of errors, and particularly the developmental phases described by Biemiller, would be found among first graders taught by other than basal reader programs? Is it possible that the particular methods and materials by which these children were taught (with their use of illustrations, their emphasis on reading for meaning, the learning of a limited number of sight words first with a slow introduction of phonics and the relatively limited vocabulary load) influenced the strategies they used to recognize words? Or are the strategies part of a general developmental sequence in learning to read, irrespective of the methods and materials used?

Biemiller (5) also analyzed the errors of first graders who were taught by a modified basal plan where "less constrained books were used," along with a somewhat heavier phonics program. He found no important differences in the kinds of errors made by children of comparable ability on materials of comparable difficulty as compared with those taught by a regular basal program.

Since neither programs controlled words used in the connected reading matter for spelling regularity and, in fact, encouraged the use of contextual constraints, we still do not know whether those programs that discourage guessing, e.g., highly systematic phonics programs as well as the "Bloomfield type" linguistic programs produce similar or different kinds of strategies. Also, do they ultimately produce the kind of flexibility in strategy in the third stage found by Biemiller at about the same time?

An earlier less systematic study by MacKinnon (30) suggests that the materials (particularly the sentences, and types of illustrations) make a difference in pupils' ability to recognize new words. He found that comparable groups using the Gibson-Richards materials (21) which carefully control sentence patterns and use stick figures that help trigger the meaning of the sentence were more successful in recognizing untaught words than those using regular basal readers.

It seems to me that longitudinal studies of oral reading errors carried out on the same children over a number of years may be one of the best ways to study *how* children learn to read. This kind of careful analysis may lead to more definitive answers on the recurring debates over *which* methods and materials are better or worse and, indeed, whether methods make any difference at all.

Analyses of oral reading errors of children strong or weak on different "readiness" factors, of children taught by different methods and materials, might well be a welcome relief from the too common experimental design of comparing Method A with Method B, where pupils are tested only at the beginning and at the end of each school year. With these designs, too much valuable data is lost, and it becomes very difficult to disentangle the significant factors that make for any of the differences found.

The implications of these kinds of error data for understanding the beginning reading process and for the diagnosis and teaching based on individuals needs are enormous. We may find that the same kinds of errors may be signs of progress for certain kinds of pupils, at certain times, while they may be signs of problems for others. Biemiller *(4)*, in fact, suggests that the beginning context phase, which he found among first graders using basal reader types of programs, should be skipped or deemphasized—that the beginner should be discouraged from obvious guessing. At a later point, after he has passed the "non-response" phase, guessing should be encouraged since the child now has more command of the sound-letter correspondences to make a good guess. Indeed, he found the poorest readers at the end of Grade 1 never went beyond the first context phase. It was only when they went through the "stop" or nonrecognition phase that they were able to proceed to the third phase—the one of flexible strategies—relying on context when reading relatively easy materials, and relying more on graphic cues when reading more difficult materials.

The possibility of this type of research is quite exciting. Such studies can help give us a picture of the developmental process of learning to read as it relates to ways pupils are taught, the materials on which they practice, and their own strengths, weaknesses, and styles of learning. For example, do children with poor visual memory and good intelligence stay too long in the early context phase when taught by a basal approach? Does a heavier decoding emphasis program (whether a Bloomfield type, a strong phonics type, or i.t.a.) help them skip the early context phase, but keep them too long on the nonrecognition phase? Or does it keep them too long on a graphic similarity phase, with little flexibility in using syntactic and semantic cues?

It seems to me that a linguistic analysis of oral reading errors, similar to those of Weber and Biemiller, would be especially helpful in studying the kinds of reading problems found among children with nonstandard speech, and then, perhaps to clues as to the methods and materials most suitable for them. At least such studies could give us some idea as to where their greatest difficulties lie—whether in the use of context, or in the ability to use sound-letter correspondences. Would an early emphasis on phonics help or hinder their acquisition of early reading skill? Or would the phonological differences between their own dialects and those of standard English make for more problems?

Labov's extensive analyses of Negro speech suggests that some phonics teaching would indeed help—but the teacher must be especially sensitive in teaching it. He found large-scale phonological differences among Negro speakers of nonstandard English that coincide with important grammatical differences. The result is a large number of homonyms in the speech of Negro children which are different from the set of homonyms in the speech of their teachers. Some of the phonological differences and their grammatical consequences found by Labov are:

1. l-lessness resulting in such homonyms as tool = too; help = hep; all = awe.
2. Simplification of consonant clusters at end of words, e.g., passed = pass; mend = men; hold = hole.
3. Other phonological variables, such as no distinction between short *i* and short *e* before nasals so that pin = pen; tin = ten, and since = cents.

Such phonological differences, according to Labov, make it difficult for Negro children to recognize many words in standard spelling. They may look up words in a dictionary under the wrong spelling, and may be unable to distinguish words which are plainly different for the teacher. If neither the teacher nor the children are aware of the great differences in their set of homonyms, confusion may occur.

What is even more serious for reading, according to Labov, is that the various final consonants affected by phonological differences represent the principal English inflections, coinciding with grammatical differences. Thus, with the loss of /l/, the colloquial future is identified with the colloquial present, e.g., you'll = you, and they'll = they. The past tense may also be affected since the -ed is often omitted by phonological processes. Through the use of an ingenious series of tests, particularly the oral reading of sentences designed to determine the grammatical significance of -ed, e.g., "When I liked a story, I read every word" the proper reading of the homograph *read* indicates whether or not the reader interpreted the -ed suffix as a past tense signal, Labov found that -ed was interpreted correctly less than half of the time, less often, in fact, than the -ed was pronounced.

The implications of such dialect differences for the teaching of reading, according to Labov, are:

1. In the analysis and correction of oral reading, teachers must distinguish between errors in word recognition and differences in pronunciation from standard phonology because of dialect differences. [It is

interesting to note that W. S. Gray made the same point in his instructions to the examiner for his Standardized Oral Reading Paragraphs Test (23)]. Information on the dialect patterns of Negro children should be helpful in making such distinctions.

2. In the early stages of teaching reading and spelling, it may be necessary to spend more time on the grammatical function of certain inflections, e.g., -ed. The child may say *pass* for *passed,* but if he knows that it means the past tense, no fuss should be made. Also, it may be necessary to treat the final elements of certain clusters with the special attention given to silent letters such as the *b* in *lamb.*

3. A certain amount of perception training in the first few years of school may be helpful in teaching children to hear and make standard English distinctions.

The key to the situation, according to Labov, is for the teacher as well as the writer of instructional materials to know the system of homonyms of nonstandard English and to know the grammatical differences that separate her own speech from that of the child. She should accept his system of homonyms, but not his grammatical differences.

Would Labov's suggestions help the teacher? Can materials be produced that give special attention to the nonstandard phonological and grammatical differences? And would such materials help those teachers who may not be sensitive to phonological and grammatical differences?

It seems to me that a linguistic analysis of the oral reading errors of Negro children taught by different methods and materials would be extremely useful, especially if such analyses were combined with measures of understanding of sentences and selections. Such studies may reveal that programs which emphasize phonics or spelling patterns may be more confusing, especially if the teacher is not aware of dialect differences and insists on standard English pronunciation. Or, they may reveal, as some authors of phonics programs claim, that an early and heavy phonic and spelling emphasis is beneficial not only for reading and spelling, but for the development of accurate and distinct speech. Indeed, if this is the case, it may be less threatening and condescending to teach standard English phonology and grammar through reading instruction than through more direct practice in speech.

We are still left, however, with an important question. Why the cumulative deficits found in reading achievement among disadvantaged children? Why the increasing retardation, compared to national norms, found among lower class children, particularly lower class Negro children, as they advance through school? Can this be explained by the dialect differences found by Labov, and can they be corrected by better beginning reading instruction? Or are more fundamental differences in language involved? If reading is the psycholinguistic guessing game that Goodman (22) suggests, then I believe we must look for more than dialect differences. According to Goodman, "Skill in reading involves not greater precision, but more accurate first guesses based on better sampling techniques, greater control over language structure, broadened experiences, and increased conceptual development. As the child develops reading skill and speed, he uses increasingly fewer graphic cues" (p. 7). If Goodman is correct, then it seems to me we might find a more powerful hypothesis for the cumulative deficit phenomenon in Basil Bernstein's theory of the different "codes" of lower and middle class speakers. According to Bernstein (3), language depends on the social relationships that exist between speakers. If the relationships are close, if much is shared in the environment, then a restricted code is used. In a restricted code there is heavy dependence on gesture and facial expression; sentences are short, with few logical connectives, since everyone "knows" what you mean. When the relationships are not close, more is put in the verbal messages; sentences are longer, more modifiers and clauses are used. According to Bernstein, the middle class child is exposed at home to *both codes* while the lower class child is exposed only to a restricted code.

From my work in readability measurement [Chall (*11*), 1958], it seems to me that the restricted and elaborated codes of Bernstein are essentially simpler or more complex forms of language—in fact, they would easily be classified as easier or harder to read and understand by any standard readability formula. If so, we may then hypothesize that it is probably at about fourth grade level, when the language of the reading materials and textbooks approaches the "elaborated code" stage—when the language becomes more abstract, more removed from the here and now, etc.—that the lower class child begins to experience still other difficulties in reading, difficulties over and above any dialect differences that may interfere in his early reading.

We need to test these hypotheses. More specifically, we need to compare the oral language performance of lower class children—in terms of complexity of syntax, breadth of vocabulary, level of concept—with this reading ability on material of equal complexity. We need to make the same kind of comparisons among children of the same age from middle class homes. Thus we may determine where the essential problems lie.

When such data are obtained, it may be possible to devise and test different instructional strategies for the teaching of reading to lower class children. At least two major strategies seem appropriate even at our present state of uncertainty. One would emphasize language, enrichment of experience, and concept development right from the first grade or even earlier, with no major change in the teaching of reading, since the improved language should help the lower class child deal with the elaborated code of the more advanced reading material he meets in later grades. The other strategy is to put an early and heavy stress on reading. Perhaps, through early independence in reading, he may develop an earlier understanding of the elaborated code, which may, in turn, influence his own use of it in speech and writing. Other strategies may be various combinations of the previous two. Indeed, many of the existing programs may be thus classified.

READING AT THE HIGHER LEVELS

Although most of my paper was devoted to implications of the work of linguists to problems of beginning reading instruction, I believe the real promise of linguistics and perhaps its greatest contributions to reading instruction will ultimately come in its application to the understanding of the comprehension process.

Much of the exciting work in linguistics, particularly Noam Chomsky's transformational grammar (*13, 14*), has resulted in a series of studies in the reading and understanding of sentences and in readability measurement [Bormuth (*10*)], that confirm the importance of syntax in the comprehension process.

Many studies [see for example Levin and Turner (*29*)] indicate that the reader supplies his knowledge of grammar in reading to a greater extent than previously supposed. However, there does not seem to be any simple relationship between transformational grammar and the performance of the reader. The reader employs his knowledge of grammar, but not in an obvious way.

The study of Bever and Bower (*3*) suggests that the best readers among able college students do not read sentences in a linear fashion, but in terms of their deep syntactic structure in Chomsky's sense. Since only 8 percent of the best readers did so, and were self-taught, it suggests the possibility that others can be taught to do so.

Considerable research has been carried on within the past few years on the relation between syntactic structure and the comprehension of written text—mostly sentences. Audrey Toan Edwards (*17*), in a review of such studies (most of them carried out with adults and college students and far from conclusive), suggests that statements are easier than questions, positive statements easier than negative ones, and positive statements containing verbs easier than those containing nominalizations.

Even if we know more definitely than we now know what syntactic structures make sentences easier or harder, the implications of such knowledge for reading instruction are by no means obvious and are open questions for the researcher in reading.

According to Edwards, it *could* mean that the best way to program instructional materials would be to introduce sentence types in order of increasing difficulty. On the other hand, one can make a point for introducing together such corresponding forms as statements and questions in order to make clear their relationship. The findings of the Levin-Turner eye-voice span studies (*29*) suggest that marking phrase boundaries by large spaces, gradually fading them out, and gradually elaborating phrases, as suggested by Allen (*1*), might have validity as a training device.

It might also suggest programing instructional materials by including sentences containing adverbs and prepositional phrases which can appear in several positions. The child would then read all the possible sentence permutations, or read a sentence and then write prescribed transformations, so as to gain insight into the permutability of language [Hansen (25)]. Mellon (31) found this effective for improving writing, i.e., the writing became more complex in sentence structure. A tenable hypothesis is that such practice in writing may improve reading ability as well.

The Bever and Bower (3) study referred to earlier suggests the possibility of using typographical devices to focus the reader's attention on the deep structure rather than on the linear order of words.

In conclusion, reading comprehension has so far remained a mystery. While the battles have raged over the beginning reading process and the best possible procedures for teaching the beginner, it is at the higher levels of reading where we really need to know what is happening and why. Hopefully, when we know this, with the help of some of the newer linguistic and psycholinguistic research, we may be able to design instructional and remedial methods and materials that will work better than the ones we use today.

References

1. Allen, Robert L. "Better Reading Through the Recognition of Grammatical Relations," *Reading Teacher*, 18, 194–198.
2. Bernstein, Basil, "Language and Social Class," *British Journal of Sociology*, 11, 1960, 271–276.
3. Bever, Thomas, and Thomas Bower. "How to Read without Listening," Project Literacy Reports, No. 6, Cornell University, Ithaca, N.Y., January 1966.
4. Biemiller, Andrew J. "A Guide to Oral Reading Errors as Indicators of Progress in Learning to Read—With Some Teaching Suggestions," unpublished paper, Project Literacy, Cornell University, Ithaca, N.Y., March 1968. (See also unpublished doctoral dissertation "Changes in the Use of Graphic Information and Contextual Information during the Acquisition of Reading." Cornell University, Ithaca, N.Y.)
5. Biemiller, Andrew J. "Patterns of Change in Oral Reading Errors During the First Grades," unpublished paper, Cornell University, Ithaca, N.Y., 1968.
6. Bishop, Carol. "Transfer of Word and Letter Training in Reading," unpublished master's thesis, Cornell University, Ithaca, N.Y., 1962. (Cited in Eleanor J. Gibson, "Analysis of the Reading Process as Perceptual Learning," paper presented at the Conference on Perceptual and Linguistic Aspects of Reading, Center for the Advanced Study in the Behavioral Sciences, Stanford, Calif., October 31–November 2, 1963.)
7. Bloomfield, Leonard, "Linguistics and Reading," *Elementary English Review*, 19, 1942, 125–130, 183–186.
8. Bloomfield, Leonard, and Clarence L. Barnhart. *Let's Read.* Detroit: Wayne State University Press, 1961.
9. Bloomfield, Leonard, and Clarence L. Barnhart. *Let's Read,* Clarence L. Barnhart, Inc., Box 359, Bronxville, N.Y., 1963, 1964, 1965, 1966.
10. Bormuth, John R. "New Measures of Grammatical Complexity," paper read at symposium on Reading as Psycholinguistic Process, Wayne State University, 1965.
11. Chall, Jeanne. *Readability: An Appraisal of Research and Application.* Bureau of Educational Research, Ohio State University, Columbus, Ohio, 1958.
12. Chall, Jeanne. *Learning to Read: The Great Debate.* New York: McGraw-Hill, 1967.
13. Chomsky, Noam. *Syntactic Structures.* The Hague: Mouton, 1957.
14. Chomsky, Noam. "Comments for Project Literacy Meeting," Project Literacy Reports, Cornell University, Ithaca, N.Y. September 1964. (See also Chomsky, Noam and Morris Hall, *Sound Pattern of English,* New York: Harper & Row, 1968.)

15. Chomsky, Noam. *Aspects of the Theory of Syntax.* Cambridge, Mass.: M.I.T. Press, 1965.
16. Dykstra, Robert. *Continuation of the Coordinating Center for First-Grade Reading Instruction Programs.* Final Report, Project No.: 6-1951, U.S. Department of Health, Education, and Welfare, Office of Education, Bureau of Research, 1967.
17. Edwards, Audrey Toan. "Syntactic Structure and Comprehension of Written Text: A Review of the Literature," qualifying paper, Harvard Graduate School of Education, July 1967.
18. Flesch, Rudolf. *Why Johnny Can't Read.* New York: Harper and Brothers, 1955.
19. Fries, Charles C. *Linguistics and Reading.* New York: Holt, Rinehart and Winston, 1962.
20. Fries, Charles C., et al. *A Basic Reading Series Developed upon Linguistic Principles.* Columbus, Ohio: Charles E. Merrill Books, 1965.
21. Gibson, Christine M., and Ivar A. Richards. *Language Through Pictures Series.* New York: Washington Square Press, Pocket Books, 1963.
22. Goodman, Kenneth S. "Reading: A Psycholinguistic Guessing Game," paper presented at the American Educational Research Association, New York, February 16, 1967.
23. Gray, William S. *Standardized Oral Reading Paragraphs.* Public School Publishing Co., 1916. (See also *Directions for Scoring Test Papers,* 1955 edition. Indianapolis, Ind.: Bobbs-Merrill.)
24. Hanna, Paul R., et al. *Phoneme-Grapheme Correspondences as Cues to Spelling Improvement.* U.S. Gov't Printing Office, U.S. Department of Health, Education, and Welfare. U.S. Office of Education, 1966.
25. Hansen, Duncan N. "Progress Report: A Reading Curriculum for a Computer Assisted Instructional System," The Stanford Project, Institute of Mathematical Studies in the Social Sciences, Stanford University, 1966.
26. Hockett, Charles F. "Relationships between Written and Spoken English," in Project Literacy Reports, No. 5, Cornell University, Ithaca, N.Y.: November 1965.
27. Labov, William. "Some Sources of Reading Problems for Negro Speakers of Non-Standard English," in Alexander Frazier (Ed.), *New Directions in Elementary English.* Champaign, Ill.: NCTE, 1967.
28. Levin, Harry. "Reading and the Learning of Grapheme-to-Phoneme Correspondences," paper presented at the Conference on Perceptual and Linguistic Aspects of Reading, Center for Advanced Study in the Behavioral Sciences, Stanford, Calif. October 31–November 2, 1963.
29. Levin, Harry. and Elizabeth Ann Turner. "Sentence Structure and the Eye-Voice Span," Project Literacy Reports, No. 7, Cornell University, Ithaca, N.Y., September 1966.
30. MacKinnon, A. R. *How Do Children Learn to Read: An Experimental Investigation of Children's Early Growth in Awareness of the Meanings of Printed Symbols.* Toronto, Can.: Capp. Clark Publishing Co., 1959.
31. Mellon, John: "Transformational Sentence-Combining: A Method for Enhancing the Development of Syntatic Fluency in English Composition," doctoral thesis, Harvard Graduate School of Educational, 1967.
32. Venezky, Richard L., and Ruth H. Weir. *A Study of Selected Spelling to Sound Correspondence Patterns.* Cooperative Research Project, Stanford University, 1966.
33. Weber, Rose-Marie. *A Linguistic Analysis of First-Grade Reading Errors,* preliminary draft of research supported by a grant from the Cooperative Research Branch of the U.S. Office of Education. Cornell University, Ithaca, N.Y., 1967.
34. Winch, W. H. "Teaching Beginners to Read in England: Its Methods, Results and Psychological Bases," *Journal of Educational Research Monographs,* No. 8. Bloomington, Ill.: Public School Publishing Co., 1925.

A Multiple Approach
to Word Recognition

JAMES F. KERFOOT

Multiple approaches are not new to our thinking about reading methods. Composite or eclectic approaches are widely understood and almost universally applied today. But emphasis has been markedly different from program to program. The composite ingredients are present in most current reading programs, but in greatly different proportions. The ingredients of an eclectic reading program might include specific word recognition training in combination with experience charts, topical units, oral reading, comprehension development, recreational reading and great variety of basal and skill-text materials for specific purposes. It may also include the use of the newer media such as film strips to accompany basal readers, programmed material for independent skill development and the use of reading rate controllers in the elementary classrooms. Such a program generally comes to mind when we hear the terms "composite" or "multiple" method.

The idea of a multiple method for the word recognition component of such a program however has been fairly limited to the question of analytic versus synthetic phonics with some authors abandoning the dichotomy and recommending a "dual" approach. The objectives of a sound word recognition program suggest great complexity of process and demand a still broader perspective in its development.

OBJECTIVES OF WORD RECOGNITION

The objectives of word recognition are variously classified but may be represented by the following five characteristics of an effective word recognizer. He has:

1. *An attitude of independence.* Such a child expects that he will be able to solve the problem posed by an unfamiliar word. He is confident that he can be successful.

A MULTIPLE APPROACH TO WORD RECOGNITION by James F. Kerfoot. From *Education for Tomorrow—Reading,* Joint Proceedings of the 26th Reading Conference and the 2nd Intensive Summer Workshop, 1965, ed. Arthur Heilman, Volume 2. Reprinted by permission.

2. *Sensitivity to phonic and structural elements in words.* He is aware of the values of element cues, and he seeks familiarity among them.
3. *A variety of skills and knowledges.* He has the range of tools necessary to identify the words in his own language universe.
4. *Flexibility in their use.* He is able to select the most appropriate skills for a given word to maximize his efficiency in word recognition.
5. *Ability to use them in combination.* He is able to select from his range of skills and knowledges the most efficient ones and make them operate together bringing maturity of attack to his independence.

THE CONTENT OF WORD RECOGNITION

Skill and knowledge are two essential ingredients in word recognition where skill may be defined as the effective use of knowledge.

The Skills

The skills of word recognition include context and sounding. Context makes use of *word* knowledge to identify an unfamiliar word and in a larger sense, context is *reading*. It is the skill of linking word meanings into the larger structures that carry the author's ideas. It is the blending of words into ideas that capture the reader and carry him to successful identification of the unfamiliar words which the ideas predict or which the reader *expects*.

Thus, word recognition leads to thought patterns which in turn facilitate further word recognition. It is a stimulus-response chain which cannot begin without initial word or word element knowledge.

Exercises, oral and written, give experience with the use of context as a word recognition tool, and the use of continuous material in basal readers and recreational reading develops the meaningful contextual blending of word knowledge which we call reading.

Sounding is a skill which uses *element* knowledge to identify an unfamiliar word. Sounding involves: the skill of analysis, the knowledge of elements, and the skill of blending. The word is dissected, the elements identified, and the word reconstructed, i.e. we take it apart, identify familiar elements, and put it back together again. Analysis requires left to right selection of syllables, small words within, polygrams, structural elements or letter sounds. While analysis, blending and context are important word recognition skills, they represent a generalized growth in the ability to deal with the far more important aspect of word recognition, word and element knowledge.

The Knowledges

The knowledges of reading include the meanings and pronunciations of the words and the elements of words. Meaning is both an aid and an end in word recognition as it aids learning, results from sounding, and in addition can derive from other meaning or context. It therefore plays a powerful role in developing word recognition ability at all levels; but it seems reasonable that in developing word recognition skill, particularly in the primary grades, we will be greatly concerned with pronunciation. Mounting evidence continues to indicate that the child has a considerable meaning vocabulary when he comes to school. Estimates range as high as 24,000 words for an average first grader. (7)

One of the major goals of reading instruction and one of the chief characteristics of the effective reader is a large and growing stock of sight words and elements. Let us borrow a term used by Betts (5) and refer to this stock of words and elements as the reader's word and element "bank." In a subject considered by many to be contentless, we may legitimately think of these pronunciation and meaning banks made up of words and elements as the "content" of the word recognition program.

TEACHING THE CONTENT

The teacher's role in developing the content of reading or word and element knowledge involves four responsibilities:

Selection of Content

The first responsibility is the selection of words and elements for instructional emphasis. The child will be given many opportunities to expand his vocabulary along whatever dimensions his personal unstructured reading sends him. As pointed out by Gates, (4) the size of a child's reading vocabulary is considerably in excess of the words included in basal readers. Range of vocabulary is developed largely through recreational and supplementary reading. The words in basal readers however provide *basic* vocabulary training and a setting of familiarity for the development of word analysis skills. Teachers must accept the important principle of probability or frequency as a basis for fluency in reading and word analysis. Since fluency is a function of familiarity, we must select for instructional emphasis those words and elements with which familiarity is most important or which occur most often in a child's reading material.

Many lists are available for the selection of basic vocabulary and high frequency elements. The criterion for a basic word or element bank should be the proportion of words or elements represented by that bank in the material which the child will read. Consideration must therefore be given to the source as well as the frequency of the content selected.

Word lists provide information on the frequency of words in speaking, listening, writing and reading vocabularies of children and adults. The utility of these lists varies with the purposes for which they are used. For example, the type of list selected as a referent in the development of materials will depend upon the author's philosophy and the nature of the group for whom the materials are designed. Word lists make possible the comparison of oral and reading vocabularies which lends support to the emphasis placed on pronunciation in the primary grades.

For the selection of reading content we will necessarily be most concerned with *reading* vocabulary lists. It should be pointed out however that there is much similarity in the number of words in writing and reading lists which make up a particular proportion of the respective usages. Horn, (6) recording the frequency of words in *adult* writing, was remarkably in agreement with Rinsland in number of words and per cent of the list represented, although Rinsland (2) investigated word frequency in the written work of *children*. Both found that 2000 words represented 95% of the words used. Dolch (1) estimated that the same number of words represented 95% of the words to be read in all school books.

One of the most important tools for teachers of reading in the primary grades is the Dolch list of 220 basic sight words. These few words are estimated to represent: 75% of all primer words, 65% of first and second reader words and 50% of all words in elementary school books.

Lists of high frequency elements may also be obtained to aid the teacher in giving experiences with those elements most essential to word recognition fluency. For example, Thorndike (9) has a list of common suffixes, Stauffer (8) has a list of common prefixes, and Hildreth (5) discusses lists of common syllables. Little use is made of such lists today primarily because they are closely associated with the meaningless, synthetic, blab school methods by which they were taught. It must be clear however that, whatever methods are being used, there are word parts to which a child must respond quickly in the sounding process. In other words, they must become *sight* elements whether deliberately taught in some methods or incidentally learned in others. In the reaction against fractionating methods, many teachers have lost sight of the importance of the fractions. We do not wish the child to be continuously aware of word elements as he reads, but it is unfortunate when teachers are not.

Specific vs. Generic Attitudes

We are charged then with a second responsibility, the development of appropriate attitudes toward word recognition which will provide a clearer perspective on the role of word and element knowledge in the reading process. Two attitudes are essential if we are to achieve instructional focus in "teaching" word recognition.

First, there must be an attitude of *commitment*. Teachers must raise and demand a clear answer to the question "teach what"! We must be committed to a particular stock of words and elements as the essential or *basic* instructional content of reading and develop the necessary reading skills in connection with growth in these basic knowledges.

Once we are firmly committed to a particular word and element bank as the minimum instructional content of reading, a second attitude is needed. The words and elements in our basic lists must be thought of as *individuals*. If we commit ourselves to a 2000 word pool to give the child 95% mastery in his reading, then each word must be taught and each word must be learned. We can no longer think of the methods of teaching sight vocabulary in general, we must weigh methods for teaching each specific word. The task becomes clearer. We do not teach *"words."* This *particular* word is to be taught! We have been generalists too long. There is a basic content to be learned. Is it any wonder that even the most sophisticated diagnosticians will report, for example, that "the child is having difficulty with initial blends," when in fact he cannot pronounce the blend "GR" but can recognize "BR" and "DR" and "TR." Or he may note that the child is weak in sight words. But *which* sight words? The point is that the number of basic elements and words is *not* overwhelming, and it is high time for us to get specific.

Sequence

A third responsibility is determining sequence. The two major criteria which we use to establish a sequence of instruction are frequency and regularity. (Regularity refers to the consistency of grapheme-phoneme correspondence.) Words may be introduced in the order of decreasing frequency or in the order of decreasing regularity, and both criteria are valid. However, frequency and regularity are related since the regularity of the word is a function of the frequency of its elements, and the frequency of a word adds to the regularity of its parts. There are, of course, high frequency irregular words and regular words of low frequency.

Much of the conflict between those who put their eggs in the frequency or in the regularity basket could be resolved if the criteria were combined and those words which were both common and regular were taught in the beginning stages of reading instruction.

Other criteria for word sequence include utility related to the interest value of stories created from basic vocabulary and the criterion of minimal contrast among words as they are introduced. The coordination of such criteria in the development of reading material is a problem currently facing the authors of basal readers and is perhaps a refinement beyond the concern of the classroom teacher. High frequency regular words are the best choices for initial emphasis in developing the word and element banks. A high frequency regular word is of value by itself and is a better vehicle for learning high frequency elements than is a high frequency irregular word.

Method of Multiple Impression

The method by which a word is best learned will vary from word to word but a general approach may be discussed. The method may be termed "Multiple Impression."

Multiple Impression views the problem of mastering a word as a problem involving the ability to discriminate configuration properties from the field and form variations in which a word may be found, and to generalize response, i.e. respond singly to the stimulus variations for a specific word. The two components of Multiple Impression are multiple setting and multiple response.

Multiple setting is concerned with the need to discriminate a commonality of configuration from the other properties of the setting in which the word is presented. Why does the child read "stop" on a stop sign and not recognize it in a book? He has responded to the total field of the stop sign, to the color red, to the eight sides of the sign and to the word stop. When he has learned to respond to the word stop in a different field he will begin to conceptualize the configuration. Great variation may be observed in the settings in which a child must accurately respond if he is to have truly mastered a word. Consider some of the different fields in which the word "stop" might occur and the variations in form to which a child might respond.

Multiple Setting

Field	*Form*
Stop Sign	Separated
Flash Card	Whole
Chalk Board (isolation or context)	Small
Pocket Chart (isolation or context)	Large
Book	Printed Upper Case
Experience Chart	Printed Lower Case
Letter	Type Set
Multi-color Background	Hand Painted (teacher or child)
Other Words Present Exercise	Different Color
Word List	Felt or Flannel
Ditto Material	Blocks
Lotto Chart	Cursive
Bulletin or Flannel Board	
With Pictures	
Tachistoscope Projection	

Multiple response is concerned with the variations in response to a word presented in a particular setting. Multi-sensory learning is more effective than a single-sensory approach to a word. Therefore, a variety of response types should be elicited to provide for multi-sensory associations. Multiple response involves the following:

Multiple Response

Seeing	Syllabicating
Hearing	Thinking
Saying	Sounding
Writing	Spelling
Tracing	Combination

Which of these combinations shall we use? Any and Many! If we are committed to teaching the word "stop," Multiple Impression directs us to maximize the variety of settings and responses and to give many experiences with a word until it becomes a rapidly identified sight word wherever it is found. Such a method gives new value to many abandoned methods as they become part of a larger picture and contribute to the multiple impressions necessary to assure sight word or element permanence.

Individual differences in words suggest certain patterns of experience rather than others. We should be aware of these differences and structure experiences accordingly. For example, nouns lend themselves to some concrete associations with pictures and objects which are not possible with more abstract words. Verbs and adjectives sometimes may be dramatized. Abstract words such as "where" are best left in context and are more difficult to learn than the more concrete words. As the importance of each word becomes evident to us, greater effort will be directed toward providing the multiple impressions suggested by the special characteristics of that word.

PHASES OF INSTRUCTION

The development of word recognition ability involves three phases of instruction:

Focus Phase

The focus phase emphasizes the *teacher* who provides appropriate stimulus controls and focuses attention on a specific word or element such as a syllable, a large phonogram, a small word within the large word, or an affix.

Interaction Phase

The interaction phase divides emphasis on *teacher and pupils* as they interact on sight-sound correspondences; comparing, contrasting and multiply responding; noting striking characteristics; suggesting the most useful parts; developing analysis skill as attention is focused on useful analytic divisions; and evolving generalizations.

Generalization Phase

The generalization phase emphasizes the *pupils* as they test and generalize their knowledge by attacking unfamiliar words.

EVALUATION

Several devices for appraisal are available to every teacher. Evaluation of the word and element banks can be done with 20–25 word samples of the vocabulary from the backs of the basal readers, with word lists, and with phonogram lists. Oral reading can be used effectively to appraise word pronunciation and meaning as well as contextual skill. Standardized tests are useful but give general appraisal of skills and a sampling of knowledges. The emphasis must be on *specific* appraisal, and we must not be discouraged when a child does not learn. Some children according to Gates (3) require as many as 40 repetitions to learn a word. We must therefore adjust the method to the group and cloak ourselves in the patience and persistence which accompany commitment.

SUMMARY OF THE METHOD

The method of Multiple Impression can be summarized in the following four points:

1. Maximize the number of experiences.
2. Maximize the variety of settings.
3. Maximize the variety of responses.
4. Regress to previously taught words and elements in addition to giving experiences with new ones in a developing *spiral* approach to teaching the basic content of reading.

References

1. Dolch, E. W., *Better Spelling*, Champaign, Ill.: Garrard Press, 1942.
2. Folger, S., "The Case for a Basic Written Vocabulary," *Elementary School Journal*, 1946, 47, 43–47.
3. Gates, A. I., *The Improvement of Reading*, New York: The Macmillan Company, 1958.
4. Gates, A. I., "The Teaching of Reading—Objective Evidence Versus Opinion," *Phi Delta Kappan*, 1962, 43, 197–205.
5. Hildreth, G., *Teaching Reading*, New York: Holt, Rinehart and Winston, 1961.
6. Horn, Ernest, "The Curriculum for the Gifted; Some Principles and an Illustration," *Twenty-third Yearbook of the National Society for the Study of Education, Part I*, Bloomington, Ill.: Public School Publishing Company, 1924.
7. Smith, Mary K., "Measurement of the Size of General English Vocabulary through the Elementary Grades and High School," *Genetic Psychology Monographs*, 1941, 24, 311–345.

8. Stauffer, R. G., "A Study of Prefixes in the Thorndike List to Establish a List of Prefixes That Should Be Taught in the Elementary School," *Journal of Educational Research,* 1942, 35, 453–458.
9. Thorndike, E. L., "The Teaching of English Suffixes," *Teachers College Contributions to Education,* 1941, No. 847.

Use of Context Clues

ROBERT EMANS

> *Mary had a little lamb,*
> *Its fleece was white as* _____.

Few four-year-old children would be unable to complete the sentence with *snow*. Likewise, "Becky and her mother wanted to go shopping. They climbed into the _____ to go to the store." Few children, even before entering school, would have difficulty with supplying any one of several words which would make sense: *car, automobile, bus, streetcar.* Children use context in their oral language, easily and naturally. Children, and adults too, use context clues to aid them in their reading.

It is easy to find testimonials to the importance of context clues in reading. Open almost any textbook on the subject and there are such statements as:

> It would be difficult to overestimate the value of the context in children's word perception in reading (7:16).
> Contextual clues provide one of the most important aids to word identification and interpretation (6:84).
> Context clues are perhaps the most important single aid to word perception (*11*:25).
> The person who has not developed skill in the use of verbal context has not become a mature reader (22:23).
> It is important to know, however, that many children who are thought to be in difficulty in reading because of limited skill in analytical techniques or because they have insufficient knowledge of phonetic, structural, or visual elements are usually in difficulty because they are not using context clues well (*4*:321).

USE OF CONTEXT CLUES by Robert Emans. From *Reading and Realism,* Proceedings of the 13th Annual Convention of the International Reading Association, 1969, ed. J. Allen Figurel, Volume 13, Part 1, pp. 76–82. Reprinted with permission of the International Reading Association and Robert Emans.

Obviously, statements praising the worth of context clues are easily found. Much has been written about how the use of context helps the reader develop the meaning of words. As important as it may be this topic is not the concern of this paper. Rather, the purpose is to attack the more elusive problem and explore what aid the use of context clues gives the reader in respect to word recognition.

There are at least four uses of context clues in word recognition. These can be summarized as follows:

1. Context clues can help children remember words they have identified earlier, but forgotten. Most teachers can cite examples of a child's having difficulty with a partially known word and then recognizing the word in a new setting after being told that the word is a familiar one and that it makes sense. For example, if a child reads "Bill was a cow" for "Bill saw a cow," asking him if what he reads makes sense will often enable him to correct himself.

2. Context clues may be combined with other word-analysis clues (phonic and structural analysis) to check on the accuracy of words tentatively identified by the use of other clues. Bond and Wagner state that context clues serve as "checks on the accuracy of all the other techniques that are used" (5:172).

3. Context clues help in the rapid recognition of words for all readers by helping one anticipate what a word might be. The ability to draw an accurate inference to what a word is can serve as a time-saver. It is a faster technique than other word recognition aids such as phonics. It enables the reader to use only those phonic and other analytical techniques which are necessary to distinguish one word from another. For example, instead of having to sound out a word, the efficient reader uses only enough phonic clues to recognize the word quickly when combined with the meaning clues.

4. Context clues are required for the correct identification of some words. Gray states, "The pronunciation of many words (*permit*, for example) depends upon their meaning in a given context" (*11*:148). Other words which require the use of context clues are *lead* in a pencil or *lead* the way, *wind* a ball of string or the *wind* blew, *tear* a piece of paper or a *tear* flowed down her cheek, and piggy *bank* or a *bank* to fish from.

HOW DO CONTEXT CLUES WORK IN WORD RECOGNITION?

Following the importance of context clues and some of the uses of context clues in word recognition, one should ask how context clues work? By answering this question, one can gain a better idea as to how to teach the use of context clues.

To understand how context clues work it must be recalled that the child brings to reading a background of experience and oral language. Likewise, the child must bring to the reading situation a habit of demanding meaning from his reading. A child must combine his experience, his oral language, and the meaning he gets from his reading if he is to use successfully context clues in recognizing words. When he meets a word which he cannot recognize, he uses his experiences, oral language, and the meaning of the words, phrases, sentences, and paragraphs surrounding the word to anticipate what the word might be. Bond and Wagner state, "Instead of having to recognize the word from the total of words in the English language, the use of context clues limits the choice of words to the few that would fit the meaning of the passage being read" (5:172). By also using the other word recognition skills the child has at his disposal, he tentatively identifies the word and checks to see if the word makes sense. For example, if a child reads the sentence, "Jenny picked up her _____ to draw," he can, from his experience, limit the words to such possibilities as *pen, crayon, pencil,* or *chalk.* He would not have to select the word from the 800,000 or so possible words in the English language. By combining this information with various phonic clues, the child could recognize the exact word more quickly than by using only phonics.

With respect to the point that context clues may be used in conjunction with other word recognition techniques, Bond and Tinker state, "Meaning clues alone are not enough for good reading at any level. They must be accompanied by the use of a flexible set of word recognition skills. It is the interaction of all the word-study skills that forms the foundation on which a competent reader builds his reading structure" (4:322). DeBoer and Dallmann state, "Context clues are most effective when they are employed along with other methods of word attack" (8:111). In actual reading, the use of context clues is probably so closely tied in with other word recognition techniques that neither can be separated. Context clues alone are seldom adequate because they provide only one aid to word recognition. They may suggest one of several possible words but seldom point to the specific word. For example, in the sentence. "The mouse nibbled a piece of _____," any number of possible words could fit the meaning. However, by combining the sense of the sentence with the phonic clue that the word begins with a *ch* sound, the reader can readily supply the word *cheese.* Children should probably be discouraged from using context clues alone. By combining them with other word recognition techniques a child would be discouraged from wild guessing. Therefore, in relation to the discussion that follows, it should be remembered that whenever context clues are taught, they should probably be combined with other word recognition aids.

Some people might regard the use of context clues as untutored or guessing; and in a sense it is. However, it is probably more accurately described as inferential reasoning which must be developed, guided, and used in many areas of life. Nila Banton Smith states, "Surely this process of examining meanings, reasoning, and deducing an unrecognized word is not just a matter of chance guessing" (20:186). Kolson and Kolinger state, "Guessing is the mainstay of the contextual clue skill and should be encouraged, but wild guessing is a symptom of a disability in contextual clue use" (14:65). The sophisticated use of context clues, therefore, should probably be developed along with reasoning and the use of other word recognition skills.

THE CLASSIFICATION OF CONTEXT CLUES

Various attempts have been made to classify the wide variety of context clues. Although these classification schemes may be closely related to those for developing word meanings, they also have relevance for the use of context clues in word recognition. Artley (3) identified ten types of contextual aids the reader might find in printed matter: typographical (e.g., quotation marks, parenthesis), structural (e.g., appositives, nonrestrictive clauses), substitute words (synonyms, antonyms), word elements (roots, suffixes, prefixes), figures of speech (similes, metaphors), pictorial representation (e.g., pictures, diagrams, charts), inference, direct explanation, background of experience of the reader, and subjective clues (e.g., tone, mood, intent). Likewise, McCullough (15) identified two general classes of clues, idea and presentation. Idea clues included pictorial illustration, verbal, experience, comparison and contrast, synonym, summary, mood, definition, and familiar expression. The presentation clues included the position of words, the sequence of a sentence or paragraph, and the general organization of a selection. From a study of 500,000 running words Deighton (9) identified four *key words* classes (definition, examples, modifiers, and restatement) and *inferential clues* for which the reader has no direct clue except his ability to draw inferences. In his dissertation, for which he won the IRA research award, Ames (1) found fourteen clues from his case studies of mature readers using a variety of contextual situations:

1. Clues derived from language experience or familiar expressions
2. Clues utilizing modifying phrases or clauses
3. Clues utilizing definition or description
4. Clues provided through words connected or in series
5. Comparison or contrast clues
6. Synonym clues
7. Clues provided by the tone, setting, and mood of a selection
8. Referral clues
9. Association clues
10. Clues derived from the main idea and supporting details pattern of paragraph organization
11. Clues provided through the question-and-answer pattern of paragraph organization
12. Preposition clues
13. Clues utilizing nonrestrictive clauses or appositive phrases

14. Clues derived from cause and effect pattern of paragraph and sentence organization

Concerning the Artley and McCullough classifications, Russell states, "these are often too technical for systematic use in the elementary school. . . ." (*19*:300–301). Likewise, Ames states in respect to his own study that "It must be stressed that much more research is necessary and one would be ill-advised to try to develop elaborate instructional procedures based on the present classification scheme" (2:81). An appropriate task regarding the implementation of context clues in word recognition would appear to be the development of a simplified scheme for classifying the numerous kinds of context clues identified. The next few paragraphs will suggest such a possible scheme.

Most context clues for use in word recognition seem to fall into one of three main categories: meaning bearing clues, language bearing clues, and organization clues. The meaning bearing clues use the sense of the sentence or sentences surrounding the unrecognized word. The category includes such clues for recognizing unknown words as familiar expressions and idioms, definitions, descriptions, examples, synonyms, antonyms included in the text, as well as comparisons and contrasts, and the tone, mood, and setting of what is being read.

The language bearing clues use knowledge of syntax, the structure of sentences, as aids in word recognition. Hildreth states, "The use of context clues has its roots in linguistics" (*13*:156). There are a number of examples of language bearing clues. One such aid is the noting of phrases which may serve as a clue in recognition of modified unknown words. Another such aid is the recognition of unknown words through referral signal words, such as *these* and *same,* which refer to what has been stated previously. The associating of known words of one part of speech with closely related unknown words of another part of speech (such as nouns and verbs or adjectives and nouns) may serve as another clue. For example, birds fly and fish swim; grass is green, and old ladies usually have gray hair. Finally the recognition of the relationship of nonrestrictive clauses, appositive phrases, or prepositional phrases to other parts of a sentence may serve as another language clue.

Another group of clues involves how sentences or paragraphs are organized. Within this group are such aids as the realization that an unknown word is part of a series of words and an appreciation of the relatedness of main idea to details, of questions to answers, and of cause to effect within sentences or paragraphs.

Therefore, it would appear that many context clues fall within one of these three classifications: meaning bearing, language bearing, and organization. The scheme is not all inclusive. For example, the scheme does not include contextual aids from pictures or the typography. However, it seems to simplify the complex classification schemes previously suggested.

Possibly to date, sufficient emphasis has not been placed on the role that context clues play in word recognition because the classification schemes have appeared to be too complex. The preceding simplified, yet comprehensive, scheme for the classification of context clues is proposed in the hope that it will foster further investigation in this area. Because of the simplification, teachers may feel encouraged to teach the use of context clues as knowledge of the structure and implications for teaching context clues is more attainable.

TEACHING CONTEXT CLUES

Although the teaching of context clues seems complex, there is evidence that teachers should attempt to do so. McCullough (15) concluded that adults fail to use context clues because they were never taught how to use them. In a study by McKee, children were found to use context clues effectively in only about one third of the opportunities presented (17:73), while Porter (21:316) found that third grade children could give an appropriate meaning of a word left out of context in about 80 percent of the cases. Since children may not develop the skill of using context clues without specific training, they should be given help in its development. Hester states, "Systematic guidance is necessary to help him learn this important technique for recognizing words" (12:138).

The goal of instruction for the use of context clues in word recognition is probably to develop such skill that context clues are used easily and automatically. If a child makes as many errors in contextual reading as he does in reading a list of words, he is probably failing to make extensive use of context clues. The problem becomes one of developing instructional procedures.

There is little evidence that children will use context clues more effectively if they have knowledge of sentence patterns. McKee states, such knowledge "contributes little if anything to the pupils' comprehension of the sentences" (18:185). However, children will probably benefit from knowing that (1) a word makes sense within a sentence; (2) readers can use sentence meaning to help recognize an unrecognized word; and (3) more than one word may fit the meaning of a sentence and, therefore, structure and phonic clues are often necessary.

In preparing to teach the use of context clues, materials should be carefully scrutinized to determine if the content gives adequate clues to words which children have not yet learned to recognize in their reading' but possess in their speaking-listening vocabularies. Only a few such words should be presented at any one time, as too many unknown words make using the context difficult and might encourage wild guessing. The exact ratio of unknown words to known words probably depends on the children's intelligence, maturity, and background, although Bond and Tinker suggest that about one word in every forty running words should be unknown (4:321). Nevertheless, the materials used should be easy enough for children to recognize the unknown word without too much difficulty.

The materials should reflect the language patterns of the child whenever possible, be at a concept level appropriate to the children, and have the unknown words evenly distributed throughout the text.

After the materials have been selected, provisions need to be made, as in any reading activity, to assure that children have the background to read the materials through prior direct and vicarious experiences, including discussions, explanations, demonstrations, and field trips. The children need then to be given direct guidance in reading [and] using context clues. Such guidance may include talking about the idea so that knowing the meaning of a sentence or paragraph will help in recognizing unknown words; encouraging children to read the entire sentence before deciding on an unknown word, showing how context clues can be combined with other word recognition techniques, such as phonics; reading the exercises orally to the children and having the children supply the unknown word; covering a few lines in a story and having the children anticipate what will come; asking which part of a sentence or paragraph gives a clue to an unknown word; and showing that some words must be recognized in context, such as, *wound* the clock and *wound* a deer.

Pictures may be used in the lower grades to develop an orientation toward the use of context clues. Hildreth states, "The use of picture clues is similar to the use of context clues for deriving the meaning of new or forgotten words" (13:156). In the lower grades much of the content is carried by pictures in the readers. However, Weintraub found that children do not make as much [use] of illustrations as they might (23). Therefore, children may be taught to look at pictures to get clues for unknown words since pictures are a part of the total context and since they may be helpful in demonstrating to children the concept of using context clues. Picture-word cards, picture dictionaries, and introducing new words in advance of reading with the aid of pictures can be helpful in getting children to use pictures as aids in word recognition.

As soon as children have developed enough sight words to read sentences, pictures become less [important] and sentences become more important for developing the use of context clues. Sentences, paragraphs, riddles, and stories with parts of words omitted may be given to children. Emans (10) found the following hierarchy of exercises, easiest to most difficult, to be signified at the .001 level of confidence for children from grades three to ten:

1. No clue given other than context
2. Beginning letter given
3. Length of word given
4. Beginning and ending letters given
5. Four word choices given
6. Consonants given

Teachers can probably think of variations to the exercises. For example, in the multiple-choice type of exercise, words with the same sounds or words with similar configurations may be used.

In summary, this paper shows the importance of helping children develop skills in the use of context clues in word recognition and makes suggestions as to how to teach these skills.

References

1. Ames, W. S. "A Study of the Process by Which Readers Determine Word Meaning Through the Use of Verbal Context," unpublished doctoral dissertation, University of Missouri, 1965.
2. Ames, W. S. "The Development of a Classification Scheme of Contextual Aids," *Reading Research Quarterly,* 2 (1966), 57–82.
3. Artley, A. S. "Teaching Word-Meaning through Context," *Elementary English Review,* 20 (1943), 68–74.
4. Bond, G. L., and M. A. Tinker. *Reading Difficulties: Their Diagnosis and Correction.* New York: Appleton-Century-Crofts, 1967.
5. Bond, G. L., and Eva B. Wagner. *Teaching the Child to Read* (3rd ed.). New York: Macmillan, 1960.
6. Carter, H. L. J., and Dorothy J. McGinnis. *Teaching Individuals to Read.* Boston: D. C. Heath, 1962.
7. Cordts, Anna D. *Phonics for the Reading Teacher.* New York: Holt, Rinehart and Winston, 1965.
8. De Boer, John J., and Martha Dallmann. *The Teaching of Reading.* New York: Holt, Rinehart and Winston, 1964.
9. Deighton, L. *Vocabulary Development in the Classroom.* New York: Teacher's College, Bureau of Publications, 1959.
10. Emans, R., and Gladys Mary Fisher. "Teaching the Use of Context Clues," *Elementary English,* 44 (1967), 243–246.
11. Gray, W. S. *On Their Own in Reading.* Glenview, Illinois: Scott, Foresman, 1960.
12. Hester, Kathleen B. *Teaching Every Child to Read.* New York: Harper & Row, 1964.
13. Hildreth, Gertrude. *Teaching Reading: A Guide to Basic Principles and Modern Practices.* New York: Holt, Rinehart and Winston, 1958.
14. Kolson, C. J., and G. Koluger. *Clinical Aspects of Remedial Reading.* Springfield, Illinois: Charles C. Thomas, 1963.
15. McCullough, Constance, M. "Learning to Use Context Clues," *Elementary English Review,* 20 (1943), 140–143.
16. McCullough, Constance M. "The Recognition of Context Clues in Reading," *Elementary English Review,* 22 (1945), 1–5.
17. McKee, P. *The Teaching of Reading.* Boston: Houghton Mifflin, 1948.
18. McKee, P. *Reading: A Program of Instruction for the Elementary School,* Boston: Houghton Mifflin, 1966.
19. Russell, D. H. *Children Learn to Read* (2nd ed.). Boston: Ginn, 1961.
20. Smith, Nila Banton. *Reading Instruction for Today's Children.* Englewood Cliffs, New Jersey: Prentice-Hall, 1963.
21. Spache, G. D. *Reading in the Elementary School.* Boston: Allyn and Bacon, 1964.
22. Tinker, M. A. *Bases for Effective Reading.* Minneapolis: University of Minnesota Press, 1965.
23. Weintraub, S. "The Effect of Pictures on the Comprehension of a Second-Grade Basal Reader," unpublished doctoral dissertation, University of Illinois, 1960.

Materials for Developing Reading Vocabulary and Word-Attack Skills

HARRY W. SARTAIN

There is no serious shortage of materials for teaching word-attack skills. The last fifteen or twenty years have seen a vigorously renewed interest in word-analysis instruction, and this trend has been given impetus by the recent loud criticisms aimed at modern education.

The publishers have hastened to meet the requests for instructional aids voiced by parents, teachers, and school administrators. The mountains of materials from which teachers may choose today can be classified roughly into eight categories:

1. Manuals and workbooks that accompany basic reader series.
2. Independent sets of graded textbooks and workbooks.
3. Miscellaneous books and workbooks.
4. Commercial duplicator sets.
5. Chart and card materials.
6. Materials to develop vocabulary through spelling.
7. Materials and experiences planned in the classroom.
8. Professional guides and references for the teacher.

Frequently these materials reflect strong differences of opinion on how word-attack skills are most effectively developed. Some are based on the limited amount of scientific research that has been done, while others ignore research and psychology in favor of Early-American myth and long-standing legend. Some materials have been planned with care and thoroughness, while others resemble a hastily tossed salad of wilted word drills and over-ripe rules camouflaged with an indigestible Flesch-phonics dressing.

Too often the teacher has been forced to use certain materials because of public pressure on the administrator rather than for the reason of having any professional conviction about the worth of these devices. Such situations confound the teacher, confuse the children, and result in eventual deterioration of the reading program.

MATERIALS FOR DEVELOPING READING VOCABULARY AND WORD-ATTACK SKILLS by Harry W. Sartain. From *University of Pittsburgh Conference Proceedings*, ed. Donald Cleland, No. 8 (1962), pp. 107–19. Reprinted by permission.

In order to select materials for teaching reading vocabulary and word-attack skills intelligently, it is essential that a set of criteria or standards be agreed upon. The following list is offered as a guide to further discussion.

STANDARDS FOR SELECTING THE MATERIALS TO TEACH READING VOCABULARY AND WORD-ATTACK SKILLS

1. *The materials should clearly reveal that word-attack skills are tools in the process of gleaning meaning through reading rather than ends in themselves.*

All recognized reading authorities agree that reading is more than verbalizing the sounds that are symbolized in print. The child is not *reading* when he mouths sounds that convey no thought to his mind; he is only performing automatically like the well-trained parakeet. If the word-attack program emphasizes the unlocking of strange words like solving mechanical puzzles, there is grave danger that the child will fail to develop the habit of demanding meaning constantly as his eyes move over the printed page.

2. *The materials should present the skills in situations where the child is motivated to learn and practice them in order to read interesting content.*

A skill is learned more readily if the child anticipates a need for its immediate use than if its use is delayed until sometime in the distant future.

3. *The materials should provide for extensive practice of the skills in normal reading situations.*

A skill is learned only through frequent use. Materials that attempt to teach skills without providing for their functional application are likely to fail in producing good readers. Also, if children learn skills from abnormal materials, there is no guarantee that they can transfer the skills to normal reading.

4. *The materials should harmonize with, rather than conflict with, the basic reading program that is employed.*

Reading is a highly complex process and learning to read is one of the most difficult tasks that the human being ever undertakes. If the average young child is to succeed in this endeavor, he must be helped by a simple straight-forward presentation of skills. Word-attack workbooks that present the usual second-year skills while the child is still learning first-year skills in the basic materials can lead to discouragement and defeat for many children.

5. *The materials should NOT make the child overly dependent upon a single approach to word recognition, but should present several,*

among which are meaning clues, configuration clues, phonic clues, and structural clues.

Written English has developed from such a varied heritage that it refuses to submit to analysis by any single, simple set of rules. Therefore the skillful reader cannot depend upon any one technique for recognizing new words. He must know several, and he must know how to try out different techniques until he finds the one that succeeds against the problem he faces at the moment.

6. *The materials should develop the ability to select the most efficient word recognition technique that can be applied in any specific situation.*

The skillful reader has learned to recognize most words immediately through configuration or context clues without stopping to analyze them. Therefore instantaneous recognition of the whole word or phrase is the final aim. If the efficient reader finds that he does not know such a word as "unforgettable," he does not begin to sound it out letter-by-letter. The analysis of a thirteen-letter word by this process would be too time-consuming. Instead he looks first for larger elements that he already knows—roots, suffixes, prefixes, and syllables. As a *last resort* he applies the letter sounding technique to any unknown syllable within the word. The materials should lead the child to apply the most efficient techniques of analysis first, to alter his approach when needed, and to test the final result by context clues.

7. *The materials should introduce the skills at the developmental levels when the children can learn them most efficiently.*

Children's hearing capability seems to develop in advance of near-point visual efficiency. Thus auditory discrimination of sounds should precede visual discrimination of word elements.

Skills development must fit the mental growth rate as well as the physiological rate. The phonetic analysis skills are too often introduced before children have the mental ability to learn them in the usual class situation. The phonics generalizations tend to be abstract and complex. The research reveals, consequently, that most children must have a mental age of six or seven years to learn phonics. Many do not attain this capacity until they are in second, third, or fourth grade.

Because they stand for known concepts, whole words are more easily learned by very young children than abstract meaningless word elements. Clearly some meaning and structural clues can be learned very early, while others must be delayed until the child has adequate ability to understand them.

8. *The materials should be conducive to differentiation of instruction in accordance with individual needs.*

Since the mental age range in first grade classes is more than four years, and the mental age range in sixth grade classes is more than seven years, it is obvious that all of these children cannot be expected to succeed equally well in the same programs at any given chronological age.

The accounts of early reading instruction in this country tell of the frustration and despair felt by children who were drilled endlessly on word elements before they began to use them in whole words and meaningful context. Some of our critics are intent upon forcing us back into this antediluvian age of education.

9. *The materials should build inductively from known words and facts toward new skills and understandings.*

Most psychologists believe that human beings understand the separate parts of any body of knowledge better if they first see these parts together as a whole body. Therefore word analysis begins with whole words that are known and proceeds with the child's discovering each element and stating the rule for using it.

10. *The materials should provide for skills development in a logical sequence of complexity.*

One example of the application of this principle is the teaching of consonant sounds before vowel sounds. Because each vowel letter represents a number of sounds, it is easier for the small child to learn the more stable consonant sounds before the vowels.

11. *The materials should provide for the development of new skills in a meaningful context.*

The pronunciation of a word element often changes when the element appears in different words. The meaning and pronunciation of a word also depends upon the context in which it is used. Therefore the sounds of letters should not be taught separately from words, and the recognition of words should not be taught separately from the phrases in which they appear.

12. *The materials should NOT build habits which handicap a child at a later stage of development.*

Any word-attack skill that is taught should continue to function as well or better when needed in later years as it does at the time it is introduced. Also, the skills of word recognition should support rather than interfere with comprehension abilities, work study skills, speed adaptation habits, and development of literary tastes.

With these criteria in mind the study and selection of useful materials become much easier than one might think when confronted with the whole array of items that are available.

In summary, it can be stated that the market is flooded with materials for teaching reading vocabulary and word-attack skills, but the materials vary greatly in quality and usefulness. A list of criteria can be helpful in evaluating these materials intelligently. One must be especially alert to avoid being sold a set of materials that does an excellent job of presenting one type of word-attack skills, but handicaps the child through lack of a complete well-balanced program. The "fanatic phonics" books are the ones which are most often guilty of this.

In selecting materials one must have in mind the exact purpose or purposes for which they are needed. Then there are a number of good books, workbooks, charts, and devices which can contribute to successful teaching. The basic reader materials still seem to provide the most well-rounded programs,[1] but other good materials are readily available for supplementary and corrective teaching.

Selected References

1. Ibeling, Frederick W. "The Value of Supplementary Phonics Instruction," *Elementary School Journal*, LXII (December, 1961), 152–156.
2. Sartain, Harry W. "Do Reading Workbooks Increase Achievement?" *Elementary School Journal*, LXII (December, 1961), 157–162.

5   Suggestions for Further Reading

Although published several years ago, William S. Gray, *On Their Own in Reading*, revised edition (Scott, Foresman, 1960) is still the single most comprehensive treatment of word recognition. Theoretical considerations and practical applications in word recognition are presented in a large collection of articles by Mildred A. Dawson (compiler), *Teaching Word Recognition Skills* (International Reading Association, 1971).

Anna D. Cordts, *Phonics for the Reading Teacher* (Holt, Rinehart and Winston, 1965) provides background in the science of phonetics and shows how it affects the teaching of phonics. Other publications that treat phonic instruction in word recognition programs include Dolores Durkin, *Phonics and the Teaching of Reading* (Bureau of Publications, Teachers College, 1964); Roman Gans, *Fact and Fiction About Phonics* (Bobbs-Merrill, 1964); and Arthur W. Heilman, *Phonics in Proper Perspective* (Charles E. Merrill, 1964).

Information about methods and materials for developing word recognition skills will be found in most professional textbooks on the teaching of reading: Nila Banton Smith, *Reading Instruction for Today's Children* (Prentice-Hall, 1963), 167–253; Albert J. Harris, *How to Increase Reading Ability*, 5th edition (David McKay, 1970), 315–89; Paul McKee, *Reading: A Program of Instruction for the Elementary School* (Houghton Mifflin, 1966), 45–136; Dolores Durkin, *Teaching Them to Read* (Allyn and Bacon, 1970), 233–321; and John J. DeBoer and Martha Dallmann, *The Teaching of Reading*, 3rd edition (Holt, Rinehart and Winston, 1970), 96–171.

6

READING FOR MEANING

Some aspects of the reading act are less well understood than others. Reading comprehension certainly qualifies as one. This does not mean that nothing about it is clear and that teachers are therefore unable to help pupils improve their reading comprehension. What it does mean is that we must distinguish between what can be demonstrated and what appears to be less substantial, and that some judgments about reading comprehension are more tentative than others. Such conditions do not preclude a continuing search for teaching strategies even though theories supporting them have not been fully demonstrated.

One hypothesis on reading comprehension holds that interaction among hierarchical levels of subabilities reassembles and processes information stored in the brain. According to the theory, knowledge of words and the concepts they symbolize are the most important elements at the highest level in the hierarchy of abilities. At the second level is a set of factors—information, word sense, reasoning, knowledge of roots and affixes—on which word knowledge depends. Factors of the second level depend on others at the third. Comprehension occurs during reading when interaction among the elements at each level proceeds smoothly.

According to a communications model, sound patterns (words) are processed into language units whose meaning is tied to syntactic and semantic controls. Within the reader's memory are the rules that govern language, and sentence (surface) structures are processed according to these rules. These transformed structures are integrated with the semantic components in the reader's memory to convey meaning. This model includes the reader's cognitive abilities, attitudes, and feelings that influence the final outcomes of this integration.

Most other models seeking to explain reading comprehension imply if not state the importance of cognitive processes in the reading act. According to one model, the reader's own modes of thought, which operate consciously or unconsciously—inductive and deductive reasoning, convergent and divergent thinking, and judging—enable him to perceive relationships among the ideas the writer expresses and thereby to understand them. Another model refers to mental processes that the reader uses to establish rapport with the writer. These processes, which involve knowledge and reasoning, seem to occur in some sequence; the extent to which comprehension occurs depends in part on what phases of the reasoning processes occur. Other models describe comprehension as the product of a series of intellectual operations involving cognition, memory, divergent and convergent thinking, and evaluation.

It is entirely possible that no single model can explain the complexities of comprehension; in any case, it appears that for the present we can only infer what is occurring as a reader scans lines of print and demonstrates that he comprehends the messages they carry. There seems little doubt that we may view reading as a thinking and problem-solving process during which ideas are received and produced. Reading and thinking possess common roots, and to the extent that the reader processes information, reading and thinking seem indistinguishable. In essence, then, to teach children how to read is to teach them how to think.

In order to develop reading comprehension we must consider its many aspects and describe them in behavioral terms so that they can become goals to be sought. Therefore we refer to literal comprehension, which might be thought of as simple cognition, interpretive or inferential comprehension that involves convergent and divergent thinking and produces ideas, and evaluation, which is the assessment of ideas. Each of these comprehension strands has components, which when expressed behaviorally serve as focal points for instruction. Thus we speak of the ability to understand multiple meanings of words, figurative language, and ways in which ideas are expressed; the ability to see cause and effect relationships and make generalizations; the ability to discern author's intent and recognize opinions. These are only some of the areas on which teachers can concentrate their efforts to improve the reading comprehension of their pupils.

Marjorie S. Johnson deals with the related question of sequence in the development of reading comprehension. To identify a sequence is no easy task; she does postulate two sources on which sequence can rest: psychological and logical. She believes that "[sequence in the development of reading comprehension] must evolve from the accumulated knowledge of the perceptual-conceptual bases of thinking and comprehension, of language-experience relationships, of the sequence of language development, and of sound principles of learning." She believes, moreover, that it is possible to analyze the skills on which reading comprehension rests and to deduce from them the direction a sequence can take.

She shows that it is unrealistic to view sequence as a straight line, to assume that one can progress easily from a first level of difficulty to a second level, from a second to a third, and so on. Within any level of comprehension it is difficult to establish a sequence of development that progresses from the simple to the complex. However, it is not too difficult to agree on the progression when considering the basic levels of comprehension. Who would question the wisdom of making certain that literal meanings are understood before dealing with ideas that grow out of the meanings that have been established?

Another point Johnson makes is that the difficulty of the materials children read should not determine the sequence for developing comprehension skills. She appears to be questioning the desirability of assigning given comprehension skills to specified grade levels. Higher level thinking skills are not reserved for upper reading levels. Experience demonstrates the wisdom of confronting young children with thinking tasks that challenge them and lay the groundwork for more complex ones. Preschool children can and do make inferences; as they mature they continue to learn to make others.

Objective reality versus symbolic representation, oral language versus written language, rich experience versus inadequate background, simplicity versus complexity, independent versus interdependent abilities—all these considerations are involved in trying to fix some sequence for reading comprehension. Implied in these conditions is the recognition that children move through sequences at different rates, that some are ready for one set but not for another. What is not implied is the realization that progress toward maturity depends on the guidance teachers provide—guidance that leads to self-evaluation and independence in thinking.

Although Constance M. McCullough's treatment of reading for meaning is not a book of recipes, it does indicate the kinds of understandings a teacher who wishes to teach children to comprehend what they read, must possess about his own language and how these understandings can help him to facilitate the process. One of them is that words, phrases, sentences, or even paragraphs generally cannot be isolated if the meaning of what one is reading is to be understood fully. The reader must seek meaning not from bits of information but from the totality. And if he can perceive the style or mood of the writer, his ability to gain information will be enhanced.

Another clue to meaning is found in the way ideas are organized. This seems to make the difference between the ease or difficulty with which a reader comprehends. Just as the meaning of isolated words is not firm, so the meaning of single sentences is unsupported. Grouped they form a meaningful unit. McCullough would have teachers make a habit of recognizing units of thought patterns so that they could train children to do the same.

Language explains, clarifies, expands, highlights. In addition, it has an "echo" effect. Realization that language functions in these ways leads to the conclusion that the meaning of one sentence can be found in another. The implication for teaching seems evident.

Another observation about language is that at times it is unpredictable. It does present words that could signal an expected meaning—words such as since, both, however—but even these words could mislead the reader when used in special ways. In McCullough's opinion, "the language is full of untrustworthy characters" that suggest caution in interpreting them.

If reading is thinking—and most of us support this notion—then Hilda Taba's explanation of her efforts to help children master cognitive skills complements McCullough's treatment of language roles and their relation to comprehension. Taba set out to determine if training could have an effect on the time at which formal thought occurs. She identified three cognitive tasks for treatment: concept formation, development of generalizations and inferences, and explanation and prediction of new phenomena.

Operating on the assumption that thinking is an active process in which the learner must participate and that sequence is an important factor in learning to think, Taba developed a schema in which the teacher became a guide to discovery rather than a dispenser of information. By programing a series of questions about social studies content, she found that children with no special intellectual abilities could be taught to perform thinking tasks involving literal and inferential meaning. Her findings add weight to Johnson's views about the importance of sequence in the development of reading comprehension and the wisdom of including the wide range of comprehension skills at every stage of reading development.

As we have stated earlier, evaluative reading is a third strand of reading comprehension. It involves judgment of the truthfulness, accuracy, and worth of what is read and follows literal and/or inferential reading. Evaluation or critical reaction cannot occur unless the reader possesses some reasonable standards he can use as yardsticks to measure ideas gained through reading.

Helen M. Robinson defines critical reading in a similar fashion. She not only establishes the abilities children need in order to learn how to read critically but also the conditions in learning climates that make progress possible. She too makes the point that young children are quite capable of reacting to what they read and that "this ability may increase throughout life, as background and experience develop ever-higher standards against which to judge what is read."

Sequential Development
of Reading Comprehension

MARJORIE S. JOHNSON

The importance of strong programs for the development of comprehension has been recognized by virtually every individual concerned with reading. Many encouraging steps have been taken to clarify the whole field of thinking and comprehension and to provide materials which will lead toward greater emphasis on growth in this area. However, at least one major question appears to plague both the teacher and the diagnostician as they focus on reading comprehension—"What kind of sequence exists within the seeming morass of abilities involved?"

For the diagnostician, it would be most comforting to be able to find a pattern of development of comprehension abilities. This would allow him to structure his evaluation so that he could, with at least a fair degree of assurance, determine the point in this systematic development which a child has reached. Thus, by inference, he could determine those abilities the child has mastered and those with which he is now ready to proceed. If no such pattern exists, he can, at best, merely sample the child's performance in handling various kinds of demands on his comprehension. Finding that the child has mastered one specific ability may, however, give no information about his functioning with another.

For the teacher, too, there would be a large measure of security to be found in a structured sequence for the development of comprehension. Many authors have provided such a pattern for the teaching of word perception and recognition abilities. Availability of a similarly systematized plan for comprehension would allow teachers to follow this to "guarantee" that the child would get sequential help, missing no essential steps or abilities necessary for adequate performance.

Unfortunately, it appears that there is very good reason for the nonexistence of this kind of prescriptive pattern of comprehension abilities. Facets of the total comprehension complex other than the abilities per se are strong determiners of the sequence in which an individual deepens and expands his thinking in reading situations. It is the purpose of this paper to present some of the considerations basic to sequential development of comprehension and some of the major determinants involved.

SEQUENTIAL DEVELOPMENT OF READING COMPREHENSION by Marjorie S. Johnson. From *Reading and Thinking,* Proceedings of the 22nd Annual Reading Institute, Temple University, 1966, ed. Marjorie S. Johnson and Roy A. Kress, pp. 45–52. Reprinted by permission.

BASIC CONSIDERATIONS

Reading comprehension is the result of thinking which is triggered by visual language symbols. The fundamental concerns, then, must be with thinking processes and their application in reading situations. The processes themselves are the same whether their use is required in reading, in listening, or in appreciating objective reality. In fact, only a relatively small change is required for the adaptation of these processes to speaking, writing, and other actively expressive situations. Obviously, therefore, the basic considerations in a program for sequential development of reading comprehension are equally necessary ones in those designed for promoting growth in thinking in other situations.

Psychological Foundations

In the final analysis, a logical plan for the development of all the abilities required for good reading comprehension must rest on and take its structural, sequential pattern from what is known about language and mental development. Specifically, it must evolve from the accumulated knowledge of the perceptual-conceptual bases of thinking and comprehension, of language-experience relationships, of the sequence of language development, and of sound principles of learning.

Perceptual-Conceptual Bases.   All comprehension is dependent upon the individual's manipulation of relevant percepts and concepts, formed in the course of his previous experiences, in pursuit of the meaning of current stimuli. How he perceives the situation of the moment, what it comes to mean to him, and how he can fit it into a larger pattern are all determined by the combined effects of the stimulation of his receptive mechanisms and the higher mental processes set in motion by this stimulation. Variations in comprehension, both of degree and of kind, occur in accordance with the individual's perceptual-conceptual reservoir. In essence, then, his comprehension is limited by the sensory data he has acquired in his previous experiences, the nature and degree of processing of this data, and the stock of meanings that he has already built. To the extent that he has organized his previous experiences along flexible lines, he will be able to dip into his perceptual-conceptual reservoir for relevant material which will allow him to understand the present stimulus situation.

Language-Experience Relationships.   Understanding of and through language is possible only when the referential or symbolic nature of words is recognized. In the final analysis, one does not comprehend the language, but rather the realities of things or ideas which the words represent. Until one appreciates the function of words as mere symbols to make communication of meanings possible, he can develop no real comprehension of language. Acquisition of language proceeds as a process of learning to associate accepted symbols with meanings which have already been established. As more and more facility with handling language-experience relationships develops, words become tools of organization as well as symbols to represent particular perceptual experiences or concepts. This important function is lost, however, to the individual whose language is inadequately based in experience.

Sequence of Language Development. Normal human development takes place in an orderly fashion as part of the total maturation of the organism. In the area of language, there are four basic functions to be developed—listening, speaking, reading and writing. Two of these use oral language; two, visual symbols. The nature of the organism is such that ability to handle oral language develops long before the eyes are ready to deal with printed symbols or motor coordination has reached the point required for writing. Likewise, the mind becomes receptive to and able to interpret spoken words before the speech mechanism has matured to the point of organized vocalization. Although the child begins early to experiment with the production of speech sounds and, on a somewhat random basis, probably manages to form all of them, his learning to communicate through speech must wait on further maturation and the acquisition of wide experience with language. In the same fashion, his ability to read, to decode visual language symbols, forms the basis for his ability to write, or encode in visual language symbols. Development of comprehension in reading, then, is dependent not only on an adequate experience base for language but also on the understanding at the oral language level.

Sound Principles of Learning.   If adequate thinking abilities are to be developed for comprehension in reading, instructional activities must be planned in terms of what is known about learning. The tasks placed before the child must be suited to his maturity level. They must be ones he has a readiness, in terms of previous learnings, to master. The child must approach the task in a purposeful manner, with real recognition of what this mastery of it can mean to him. He must be sufficiently involved, on a personal basis, that he can muster the attention and concentration to participate actively. Without real reaction to the stimuli which are present in the situation, he cannot hope to learn. Only with active, purposeful involvement will he be able to recognize his accomplishments and gain satisfaction from the mastery of the task which faces him.

One further consideration of learning phenomena is essential in a good program for development of thinking abilities. A child learns what he does, what he practices. Learning errors in or superficiality of thinking must be avoided. As he approaches a learning task, he must be guided so that he will be able to complete it successfully. Leaving him to flounder through is apt to lead to the production of many errors to be learned. Likewise, attempts to teach by presenting errors to be corrected are to be avoided, lest the child learn these errors. Only when an individual has mastered a particular task or process can he be expected to perform independently. As he learns, he needs careful guidance so that he will take the right steps in the right way.

Logical Foundations

Within the framework of these psychological foundations, a logical analysis of the specific abilities required for good thinking and reading comprehension leads to certain conclusions about these abilities and their sequential development.

Impossibility of Exact Scaling.   The sequence of development of thinking abilities cannot be conceived as a straight line from one most basic and simple ability through many others in an ascending scale of difficulty, comprehensiveness, or complexity to a final one which represents the apex of functioning. The abilities simply are not of the type which allows this kind of scaling. Moving from one ability to another is, in most instances, not an additive process, for instance. Nor is it always the case that theoretically "more advanced" abilities necessarily represent refinements of "more basic" abilities.

Choosing a few reading comprehension abilities at random may serve to illustrate the barriers to exact scaling. Suppose one were to attempt to scale the following five: ability to use context to determine the meaning of a particular word or phrase; ability to use clues from typography and punctuation to get meaning; ability to follow a sequence which is determined by cause-effect relationships; ability to evaluate the relative importance of ideas; ability to interpret such devices of style as subtlety, allegory, sarcasm, satire, or irony. What criteria could be applied to determine which of these belonged first on the scale of difficulty? On the surface, perhaps the use of context to determine meaning seems easiest or most basic. At one level of thinking, this may well be true. None of the other abilities could be mastered without attaching to words meanings which were appropriate to the contextual setting. At another level, it must be recognized, however, that application of any of the other abilities chosen might, in a particular situation, be a necessary part of using the context to get meaning. One could not ascribe suitable meanings to the words of Pope's title, *The Rape of the Lock,* without appreciation of the significance of his mock heroic style. Nor can the full meaning of the definite article, and therefore, the real idea, be apprehended in the following sentence without understanding of the significance of the italics: He is *the* person I could recommend.

With almost any group of abilities selected as "test cases" similar findings would result. A scale of priority in learning cannot be established for reading comprehension abilities. Factors other than any inherent characteristics of the abilities themselves determine the learning sequence.

Relationships of Abilities and Materials.   The sequence of development in comprehension cannot be established through any direct link between a particular ability and a particular difficulty level of the material to be read. In the area of word analysis, certain abilities obviously are needed at specific reader levels because the nature of the words included demands this kind of analysis for successful work. Other abilities would be inappropriate for instruction at the same level because the materials contain no words which require the use of the analysis techniques they entail. In the area of comprehension, however, there is no ability which can be assigned to one level to the exclusion of others. Any one comprehension ability may well be needed for full appreciation of materials at any reader level.

No comprehension ability or thinking process can, in reality be mastered for all time so that it is then available for use in understanding all situations or all materials. One does not learn once to appreciate chronological sequence and then find no difficulty thereafter in following an organization pattern determined by chronology. One does not master inferential thinking, getting specific information, evaluating an author's competence to write on a topic, or interpreting figurative language and then function adequately in these areas every time they become focal needs for good comprehension. Rather, one finds oneself needing constant readjustment or modification in the manner of use of previously acquired abilities so that they can be applied to present situations.

Further, the nature of the situation or materials may be such that known techniques—abilities which have been "mastered"—cannot be used. Such things as lack of relevant experience or acquaintance with technical vocabulary as well as too great a burden of structural complexity in the material might interfere with application of certain abilities. The following paragraph from the introductory material of Taylor's *The Behavioral Basis of Perception* will probably illustrate the point for most readers:

> A *multistable* system is a large system containing many subsystems, each of which is ultrastable. A large multistable system cannot adapt in a reasonable period of time if all its step-functions have to arrive simultaneously at the appropriate values, but if one of the subsystems can be isolated from the rest for a time, it can adapt as if it were completely independent. Ashby envisages two types of relationships between the subsystems, which we may call the *parallel* and *serial* arrangements. In the first, the subsystems can adapt independently of one another and in any order, including simultaneity. In the second arrangement, adaptation of the first subsystem is a prerequisite for adaptation of the second one.[1]

The word forms of this paragraph are certainly not troublesome for adult readers. However, the technical setting in which familiar words or word

[1] Taylor, James C. *The Behavioral Bases of Perception*. New Haven, Conn.: Yale University Press, p. 5.

elements are used makes their meanings puzzling to the individual without adequate relevant experience and information. Well-known techniques for arriving at understanding fall far short of completely successful application. Consideration of the root word and prefix seems to lead to a fairly satisfactory "meaning" for *ultrastable*. One may, somewhat mistakenly, even feel that one really has some knowledge of the nature of a system if it is "exceedingly permanent." However, it is unlikely that the same kind of semantic analysis will bring equally satisfactory results when applied to *multistable*. Is this *multi* as in *multimillionaire, multilevel,* or *multidisciplinary*? What is a system when it is multistable? At this point, one may not even be sure what a system is at all. With all this difficulty, it is not likely that the "uninitiated" would be able even to retain specifically stated information from this paragraph, let alone use any of his comprehension abilities which involve true manipulation of ideas.

It must be recognized, then, that each thinking ability is, in reality, being learned and being used at every reader level if adequate reading comprehension is achieved. None can be learned once and considered to be mastered. None can be "put off to the higher levels." Instead, each has some factors and uses which are important from the very beginning reading experiences and, in fact, before reading ever begins. Each is also subject to everlasting extensions and adaptations. The infant learns early to infer (from sounds and facial expressions, for instance), yet the boy and man, too, constantly learn to infer. What the infant learned about inferential thinking forms the foundation for the man's learning, but in itself it is not enough. To function successfully, the man must continually *learn* to think inferentially.

DETERMINANTS OF MULTIPLICATE SEQUENCE

Progress toward truly effective instruction in the area of reading comprehension appears to be dependent not on finding a sequence of abilities, but rather on planning in terms of the psychological and logical factors which have been discussed. To deal with all of these requires not a single-track sequence, but one which deals simultaneously with many determinants.

Obective Reality VS. Symbolic Representation

When a new thinking ability is introduced, the starting point should be real things rather than the language which represents them. Suppose the particular ability is that of classifying according to essential similarities. The best learning situation for the child will be one in which he has a real need to classify in order to accomplish a recognized end. The purpose of his classification will determine which elements of the whole are the essential ones. He can then, if he is dealing with reality rather than symbols, make direct observations about particular characteristics or elements. Until he can be guided to classify in this kind of situation, efforts to teach him to classify verbal symbols will be pointless. If a child cannot look at or handle a group of actual objects and group them according to whether or not they will burn, he could hardly be expected to do a similar job with symbolic representations of these objects. The degree of objective reality in the situation involved must therefore be one of the factors taken into consideration in the instructional sequence.

Oral Language VS. Written Language Symbols

In accordance with the natural development of language, the child learns to deal with the oral symbols before he masters their visual representations. Written language symbolizes the oral symbol which represents the reality. The child should move gradually, progressing in the use of a particular thinking ability from its application to real objects through manipulation of oral symbols and finally to employing it in reading and writing. He cannot be expected to abstract essential characteristics on the stimulation of a printed symbol for an object unless he can do the same job when the stimulus comes from a spoken word or group of words. To function at the written language level, he must be able to bring to mind the oral symbols and the realities they represent, before he can find the pertinent similarities and classify on the basis of them.

Rich Experience VS. Inadequate Background

A third determinant of sequence in comprehension is the amount of relevant experience the reader has to bring to the situation. To learn a new thinking process demands that the child have sufficient background of information and experience to perform in the required way. Again, the task of classification offers suitable illustrations. A child may be able to deal adequately with printed statements about familiar things or events and arrive at a good set of classification labels for them. At the same time, he may be completely helpless to deal with the same kind of classification even at the level of objective realities when the things or events are utterly strange and meaningless to him. He must first discover what, in the broad sense, these things or events are before he can possibly move on to the stage of deciding what basic characteristics of them are similar and form a basis for grouping them.

Simplicity VS. Complexity of Raw Materials

Uncomplicated, discrete items are generally easier to handle than are more intricate items or involved ideas. As a new ability is learned, it should first be developed in relation to raw materials which, in themselves, present little or no potential for confusion and difficulty. To group boards of equal length is easier if the boards are separate than if their absolute lengths are camouflaged by the relationships with other boards put together into triangular forms. In the same fashion, the child may be able to deal with individual labels for physical entities more easily than he can handle verbal descriptions of complex ideas or events. Classification of names of generals, battles, etc., of the Civil War would appear to be an easier task than classification of causes or effects of that war in terms of their major area of impact as social, economic, etc. The job is still one of abstracting essential similarities, but the demands placed on the reader by the materials to be classified dictate the sequence in instruction.

Independent VS. Interdependent Abilities

Some few abilities may be virtually independent of others in the sense that the thinking processes involved do not overlap. In most cases, however, one finds that one thinking ability or process actually includes another. The process of classification has been used repeatedly as an example so that by now it should be amply clear that other abilities are subsumed in it—detecting similarities, detecting differences, using purpose to determine importance of particular characteristics, etc. The sequence of teaching, then, is obvious. Classification cannot be taught before the other abilities which are a part of it. In the same fashion, skimming to locate a particular name, date, title, etc., can be learned as soon as a child is capable of the visual matching task which is involved. However, skimming to find an idea cannot be taught until a child has acquired certain other abilities. He may need to suggest to himself possible key words which would signal the presence of material related to this idea. In that case, instruction on key words would have to precede specific instruction on skimming to locate an idea—a title which might indicate that the article was about birds, a sentence which tells about what birds eat, or a listing of birds native to Pennsylvania.

Sequence is, therefore, sometimes determined by the interlocking or interdependence of abilities. The more inclusive the ability, the more preceding steps there will have to be in the sequential development.

TEACHING-SUPPORT

One final caution must be added at this point. For adequate learning in the form of eventual mastery of all required thinking processes, there must be very direct instruction. *Teaching* is necessary. Teaching is too often confused with testing or with the assigning of work to be done independently. If the child is to move from no grasp of a particular ability to mastery of it, specific instructional techniques must be devised. These must be so structured that the child moves gradually toward independence in carrying out the processes involved. First, he will have to move through the process with a competent teacher who can take the responsibility. He must be involved if he is to learn, but he cannot be expected to direct the process. After he has been lead "by the hand" as often as is necessary, he must be expected and allowed to take over whatever steps he can. Support must be withdrawn when it is no longer necessary. Through gradual lessening of the amount of responsibility taken by the teacher and, therefore, gradual increase of the responsibility taken by the child, he moves toward independence. The child must not be deprived of the opportunity to do as much as he can. On the other hand, he cannot be expected to do things he has not as yet learned to do.

With true instruction, the child can move at his own maximum rate toward eventual independence. This independence will never be complete in terms of total mastery of all necessary thinking. However, it can reach the point of self-structuring of thinking processes and recognition of the degree of success achieved. Thus, the child will never be in the position of feeling he has done a good job when his thinking has not been adequate to achieve his purposes. He will have learned self-evaluation as part of good thinking.

CONCLUSION

A wide variety of factors must be considered in arriving at a suitable sequence of activities for the development of thinking and reading comprehension. Final decisions on the sequence must be based on the characteristics of the individual to be taught, the ability to be learned, and the nature of the situation in which the understanding must be achieved. To search continually for a series of steps which could be prescribed for all people on the path to good thinking and reading comprehension is futile. Real progress toward achievement of a logical, structured, sequential program in this area can come only out of the application of knowledge of people, language, thinking, materials, etc., to good diagnostic teaching.

Linguistics, Psychology,
and the Teaching of Reading

CONSTANCE M. McCULLOUGH

I.

With every contribution and every criticism from relevant disciplines, the teaching of reading has the opportunity to improve. All you have to do to realize this is to see what happens in classrooms in which there are poorly informed teachers as compared with classrooms in which well-informed teachers continuously reassess their practices in the light of new information. Historically and hysterically, as these contributions and criticisms have come, we have tended to go overboard, doing too much of the new thing or applying it in ways and at times that are not best or even desirable for reading growth. Materials have appeared which stress the new, and completely ignore some very worthwhile elements in the total reading program. They are welcomed like manna from heaven. Sometimes I wonder which is worse—to be poorly informed or to be caught in the hysteria of the new bit—though ordinarily I try not to say this aloud.

The thing we must learn as teachers is that there is no perfect contribution or perfect material; there is only a perfect teacher; and that perfect teacher is the one who evaluates each contribution to see what it can be and mean in an entire program which consists of much more than any one contribution.

As teachers we have been trained in the application of psychological principles to classroom procedures. We might be said to be amateur psychologists. Certainly we have had a great deal of help from psychologists in the teaching of reading. But most of us have had little training in the linguistic concepts which now clamor to be recognized. We have been flying on one wing. Somehow, now, in mid-air, we must assemble that other wing—of appropriate size and shape and timing to provide balance and efficient progress in flight.

It is interesting to note that when children have difficulty learning to read, we tend to blame material or method, and a critic comes along and says,

"Do *more* of *this*." More phonics, for example. Actually, instead of doing more of what we have been doing, we should be exploring for the missing parts that we haven't known and haven't used. This is what Marianne Frostig did in developing her tests and materials for the identification and improvement of subskills in visual perception, and what Samuel Kirk did in developing his tests of psycho-linguistic abilities in young children. There are plenty of parts still missing in our knowledge of language. There is much still to explore. And I believe it will be only when the teacher of reading informs herself of the new findings in linguistics and psychology, and studies the possibilities of their congenial application, that a program superior to the ones currently used will emerge. It is in that belief that I present this paper.

II.

At the recent Dallas meeting of the International Reading Association, I had the good fortune to hear a paper by Lee Deighton of Macmillan Company. Deighton is an editor and author who explores the problems of language and learning, and as you probably know has made some very helpful contributions to vocabulary development.

In his paper he reminded his audience that, while the reading eye progresses in a series of pauses and movements, from left to right, in the case of English, it cannot during any one pause take in more than about an inch of print. On many occasions it may not view a whole word in any one pause. It may even see the back end of one word and the front end of another. The speed at which the eye performs in this manner is relatively limited, especially in unfamiliar material in which guesswork about the words the eye has skipped can be fatal to meaning.

The brain, meanwhile, is champing at the bit. It must assemble all of this garbage into something meaningful. While the eye trots earnestly along, the nerve impulses which process its findings may be going at as great a rate as 200 miles an hour. Various estimates have been given by various sources. For the nerve impulses it must be worse than wiping dishes for a meticulous washer. But the point that Deighton made is that the brain has a chance to do a thorough job of mulling over meanings, a chance to be right and wrong several times about the author's meaning. He speaks of it as a circular movement, though I am not sure that "circular" exactly describes it and I suspect he is not either.

But with the example of an expression like "the little white house," he shows that the ideas of "little" and "white" are modified when the eye comes to "house," for a little house has not the littleness of a little dog, and the whiteness of white paint is not the same as the whiteness of feathers in a little white feather, or the whiteness of a stone in a little white stone. Therefore, Deighton believes that the mind holds in abeyance certain ideas as it explores the effect of other ideas upon them.

Let's see how Deighton's theory works on a sentence which I shall now read. My first word is *In*. I shall continue slowly to add words, and you as a listener try to determine what adjustments your thought has to make to grasp the meaning of this sentence: "In . . . its . . . hose-like . . . gray . . . trunk, . . . the . . . little . . . figure . . . on . . . the . . . matchbox . . . carried . . . a . . . Republican . . . banner."

The word *In* has several different meanings, such as that referring to time, place, manner, or state of being. *Its* suggests possession by an inanimate either in a previous sentence or in the current one. Linguists call *its* a noun determiner and expect a noun to follow it sooner or later. *Its* confirms the fact that *In* is being used as the beginning of a phrase. *Hose-like* has an attributive form implying that a noun is soon to come, but is puzzling in meaning because there are several kinds of hose. *Gray* is another attributive form which still does not identify the hose. *Trunk* is a surprise, for the usual trunk into which one puts things is not shaped like a hose of any kind and is not ordinarily owned by an *it*.

My pause, which is here signaled by a comma, marks the end of the phrase, and gives hope for the coming of a noun. *The,* indeed, signals that coming. *Little,* another attributive word, is again a puzzler, this time because littleness is relative. *Figure* qualifies as a noun and as an inanimate; *its* must refer to *figure*. But *figure* has several meanings, too. Does a figure eight have something in a hose-like gray trunk? Or is the word *figure* used as a general term for a shape of some kind? If *hose-like gray trunk* has suggested *elephant* to the listener, the reference to a little figure is indeed baffling. The listener feels still worse when he hears that the little figure is *on the matchbox,* for now the size is whittled down to nothing like an elephant.

Carried follows the noun phrase in the expected position for the verb in a Noun-Verb-Noun type of basic sentence (NVN), and confirms this hunch with its *d* ending. But there are different meanings for *carry* too. The listener must settle for the idea that this *carry* is used in the sense of "hold in a stationary position," for you can't go far on a matchbox. *A* denotes the coming of another noun. *Republican* is in either an adjective or noun position. The sentence could stop there. But *banner* proves that *Republican* is an adjective, and the listener does not have to imagine what kind of square a Republican would have to be to fit on a matchbox. *Republican* confirms the hunch that the figure is an elephant after all; the trunk belongs to the elephant. The *In* at the beginning of the sentence means the trunk was curled around. It is an embracing *In*. The listener must imagine what the banner may have on it, who might own such a thing, whether the little figure is a statue or a picture, upright or prostrate, attached or unattached, and so forth.

The listener who had had no experience with the Republican emblem would not get the meaning of this sentence at all. Or if, in listening, he did not catch the word *Republican*—if, in reading, he skipped over it—he would be mystified. The African listening to this and knowing the Republican emblem might still see in his mind an African elephant; an Indian, an Indian elephant.

Now, what did you smart people have to be able to do to get this message clearly? You had to listen carefully. It is said that we catch seventy-five percent of the sounds we could hear, and that we then add the missing links by context or situation, to realize the intended words.

You had to note the similarity of my Indiana English pronunciation to that to which you were born or are accustomed. You had to invest these spoken symbols with the meanings your experience has given them. You had to group into meaningful English units—that is, words, phrases—the stream of sounds you heard. Intonation and pauses peculiar to the English sentence helped you. In reading, of course, you would have had to reinvest the *symbols for sound* with intonation and pauses.

Familiarity with the structure of the English sentence helped you. The little words, like *in* and *on* and *the*, were important clues, also. You had to know what they signaled and what they might mean if they were words of multiple meaning. You had to catch the signal for the past tense of the verb *carry*, in order to know the time of this observation. You had to know the function of a pronoun and be able to reason that *its* referred to *figure* and not to *matchbox* or *banner*.

If this sentence had carried an emotional intent, you would have had to be sensitive to that, also. As it was, if you are a Democrat, you simply had to restrain yourself.

III.

The English language is literally laced with signals, or lacily littered with signals, however you like it. In a composition of ten sentences, it is quite possible that an *it* in the last sentence refers clear back to a noun in the first sentence. Phrases and synonyms echo one another from one sentence to another, the same meaning sometimes serving even different functions.

Our study of meaning, therefore, cannot be confined to one word or one phrase or one clause or one sentence or even one paragraph. The meaning and even the pronunciation of some words depend upon the purpose of the speaker or author. Some of the things which we have thought of as niceties—perhaps to be observed and taught, and perhaps not—such as the style or mood of the speaker or author—even deliberate ambiguities—cannot be optional if, as in many cases, clear reception of meaning cannot be gained without them.

What I have been saying is that all of these skills and knowledges, all of these dimensions of concepts, are the concern of teachers of reading. The readiness of the young child for reading, the readiness of the college student for a science text assignment, depend upon such preparation. And in passing I should like to observe that what Robert Lado has done for the understanding of the language needs of a Spanish-speaking child in learning English, what Claude Wise and others have done to compile the linguistic needs of children from still other backgrounds, must be put in a form readily useful to teachers. Houghton Mifflin's *Introducing English* for the reading readiness of Spanish-speaking children is a step in the right direction. But *is* it not possible to produce comparable material with suggestions and additions to accommodate the needs of children of other language groups as well?

IV.

Meanwhile, back at the ranch, psychologists and educators have tried to extend their understanding of the reading process. You probably know of the work of Irving Lorge at Columbia University, who investigated certain vocabulary problems with Thorndike, and on his own developed a formula by which the difficulty of reading material could be roughly determined. His formula was one of several, such as the Flesch, the Dale-Chall, and the Spache, by which school systems and teachers can estimate the difficulty of textbooks and tradebooks before perpetrating them on youngsters.

Lorge was aware that elements were missing from the formula. Obviously conceptual difficulty was one. But he believed that organization of material was also a potent factor. From John Carroll, the well-known linguist at Harvard, he obtained some paragraphs from essays written for College Board Examinations. He selected passages of equal length and difficulty according to this formula. The vocabularies, the sentence length and complexity, the topic treated, were the same. The only apparent difference, as far as Lorge could tell, lay in organization and in clues to organization. He tested students on the meaning of these passages and found that they were better able to answer questions on passages well-organized *and* bearing clues to organization.

I read his unpublished paper on this experiment in, I believe, the fall of 1960, and it so aroused my interest that I have really never recovered from the fascination of this problem.

It led me back to the work of James McCallister at Chicago Teachers College thirty-five years ago, in which he identified nine different kinds of paragraph organization which students should learn to recognize to facilitate their reading of textbooks. I studied a set of textbooks in science for the elementary school and found two kinds of patterns throughout the series—one in which an illustration is followed by a statement of principle, and one in which the steps in an experiment are enumerated. In a tenth-grade chemistry text I identified twelve different patterns of paragraph organization.

The problem, as I saw it, was to make teachers aware of these patterns and of ways to teach them so that students would not read everything the same way and come out with the main idea every time—sometimes useful and sometimes not so useful. You know, we have hypnotized our students and ourselves for years by stopping with "the main idea and a few significant details" instead of considering the author's trend of thought.

Of course, the flaw in my thinking at the time was that I hoped to find comparable patterns in every text, whereas the truth is that each author tends to have a habit pattern of his own. The teacher must be able to recognize the patterns the author habitually uses if she is to help students to recognize and use them. The problem is to find the units of thought, composing patterns.

Unaware of Bloom's now famous taxonomy or of Guilford's now famous cube of cognitive processes, I produced empirically from my observations of textbooks in science and social studies a schema of the cognitive ingredients which are expressed in such material. To distinguish it from the creations of other great geniuses throughout history, I entitled it "McCullough's Excelsior"—referring, of course, to the analogy someone once made, likening the action of ideas in the brain to the dumping of a raw egg into a box of excelsior. A linguist will tell you that this schema may be true of English speakers and not of speakers of some other languages, and so as I describe it you must realize that I am a prisoner of my own language.

Here it is: The brain of a human being receives sensory impressions of objects and living organisms in patterns of events and situations, modified by his own thought-and-feeling predispositions and reactions. He becomes conscious of various relationships: whole-part, cause-effect, sequential, comparison-contrast, and coordinate-subordinate. From these he can develop certain products of the mind: theories, laws and principles, generalizations, summarizations, definitions, classifications, and procedures. These, in turn, he can support with examples, elaboration, and application.

The order in which he does any of these things is individual.

This schema does not include processes, such as induction or deduction, because I was concerned about what was on a printed page, not about how it got there. Neither does it include such topics as evaluation or analogy, for they are special cases of existing categories.

When you think of *words,* in connection with this schema, you see many more possibilities for the development of concepts and vocabulary relationships than we have ever used before. Dictionary definitions begin to look extremely sick, by comparison—as indeed they must be if the book is not to weigh a ton.

You also begin to see that if reading is thinking, then we should be sure that a child cannot only *speak English* but think in the various ways in the English language before we expect him to *decipher the print* and think in it. And if the child is to keep fresh the various ways of thinking, then our daily activities should offer this variety over a period of time. For example, what happens to other thought patterns when some preschool and kindergarten programs emphasize the use of context clues? This is good, but what is being done about other elements?

And if, in word-analysis, we use a set of cards on which the child must analyze words and then put them under headings, such as "toys" and "food," what are we doing to balance this with experiences in which *he* must decide the heading under which certain words he selects might belong; and what are we doing to give him equal exercise that is not simply a classification experience? You begin to see that in giving the child fifteen minutes of this and ten minutes of that in the classroom all of these years, we have been making decisions without knowing it—decisions that distort his readiness to meet the thought challenges of the reading task.

As I tried to identify the types of thought in sentences within paragraphs, I discovered for myself some very important facts about language in habitat. Let me give you an example. Take the sentence, "He ran." This is a statement of fact. It does not reveal the situation in which "he" is. Now add, "As he looked back over his shoulder he could see that the bear was still after him." This second sentence does a lot. It suggests why he ran and tells what he did next:

> The bear came after him.
> He ran.
> He looked over his shoulder.
> The bear was still coming.

So "He ran" is not only a statement of an event but also a statement of the effect of a cause.

If, instead, the sentences read, "He ran. Each step was the biggest he could possibly take," the second sentence describes the way he ran, elaborating the first. The first sentence may be a summary or generalization of the series of descriptive sentences to follow.

If, instead, the sentences read, "He ran. She skipped after him," you have two statements of event, one event following another, and providing a contrast. You don't know the human motivation for this—whether they were both going toward the candy store, whether she just liked him, or whether he had learned early to stay away from women.

The upshot of this is that, just as the linguists have discovered that the sound of a letter depends upon the situation of the letter in the word—"back, bake, bark, balk"—and as Deighton found that the meaning of a word is altered by its relationships with other words—"The bare branch could bear the bear no longer"—so I found for myself that the meaning of a sentence, the contribution of a sentence, the classification of a sentence, depends upon its surroundings. The student who reads sentences like a string of beads, each at its isolated face-value, is headed for trouble. The teacher who confines her help to only what she considers the new, hard words, is missing many of the serious problems that confront the student. The elements of language are not islands. They create a fabric whose very open spaces are significant.

V.

Another fascinating observation you can make if you *study* language instead of just using it, is that a second sentence seems sometimes to put a spotlight on a word or phrase in the preceding sentence. In "He ran. She skipped," the contrast of *he* and *she, run* and *skipped,* stresses both of these elements. But in "He ran. Each step. . . ." "Each step. . . ." features the *ran.* In some paragraphs you can follow the author's progress in stressing first one dimension, then another, as though you were watching fireflies on a summer night. Language also contains an echo effect:

> August was a very *dry* month.
> The *thirsty* cattle stood by the *empty troughs.*
> Farmers looked for *clouds* in the *blazing* skies.
> But *no rains* came.

Listening activities can sharpen a student's sensitivity to types of ideas. I have enjoyed considerable enlightenment from listening activities myself. There is a person who has always reduced me to utter silence. I realize now that she has an intimidating habit of sounding like God but with less wisdom. Her emphatic judgmental statements about everything render further comment unnecessary if not unwelcome. I have also followed conversations in which the same person tells the same story to a succession of different people. With one partner who attempts to placate him, comment by comment, he becomes disgusted at what he interprets as lack of sympathy. With another partner who adds fuel to his fire—"How outrageous! . . . Well, I never! . . . *etc.*"—he is more angry at the end than he was at first. Students can learn a good deal about *sources of ambiguity* in language by recording conversations in which remarks have been misunderstood and misinterpreted. They don't have to leave home to get ample evidence for analysis in class.

Hilda Taba, as you know, in her effort to encourage the use of higher thought processes in class discussions, has charted the level of challenge of teacher questions and the quality of student comments, with some very insightful results. And Hayakawa has shown how the insertion of certain loaded words can trigger feelings and reactions.

VI.

Now, how can we help students gain some mastery over the linguistic problems in reading? If you wish to prove to your students that there is no telling where an author will go from one sentence to the next, give them a sentence and ask each student to say or write what might sensibly come next. In spite of the unpredictability of an author's next step, students must form hunches about what the author will do. You can give them a typical opening sentence for a paragraph of classification or comparison or cause and effect or illustration of a principle or definition or description or interpretation, and ask them to say what may happen next and why they think so.

Students of limited English background are not ready for the many ways in which English can express a single thought. They need experience in listening and reading to find duplication of thought in different wording.

If you wish to prove to your students how dependent they are on signal words, word order, and word endings in unfamiliar material, you may be inspired by Lewis Carroll or C. C. Fries to give them a sentence like this: "The lorks of the inksy anks glom sterb stonk by co-glickent gunding." They'll never guess that the atoms of the common gases form diatomic molecules by co-valent bonding, but they will know something about the relationships of the words and the nature of the statement.

Carl LeFevre in his helpful book, *Linguistics and the Teaching of Reading* (McGraw-Hill), gives lists of signal words. What he does not tell you is the frequency with which they don't signal what you expect. For example, "both . . . and" are coordinates in the sentence, "He was both clever and wise." But in the sentence, "They were both clever and wise," "both" may be referring to *they,* signaling backwards instead of forwards to "clever and wise." The language is full of untrustworthy characters. Take the word *since:* "Since you left the company, much has happened." Is the *since* causal, with the meaning that nothing could happen as long as a bottleneck like you was around, or is it temporal, indicating only the passage of time? And what about the word *by,* an innocent-looking word which we have often passed over as we dwelt upon the rare noun which followed? "Come by ten o'clock. Come by train. Come, by the way. Come by the house. Come by sometime." The dictionary lists ten uses of *by* as a preposition alone, and several more as an adverb. In unfamiliar material the student should be cautious—should hold in abeyance, as Deighton says, his decision about its meaning.

For years we have told students that the word *however* signals a change of direction, a reversal; but it doesn't always. In written material, the questions, "However did you do it?" and "However, did you do it?" show their different intent only by the presence of the comma. And in many sentences, *however* adds to or limits the preceding idea rather than controverting it. We have had students look up hard words in the dictionary. Sometimes we should have them look up the easy ones to see the many meanings that are well established, not to speak of those which may be gathered in time.

How can we tell when "you were" is singular and when it is plural and when it is condition contrary to fact? How can we tell that a question in a textbook is a question even before we come to the mark at the end? How can we tell the passive voice is being used and the subject is not the actor? What are the signals for the remote past that help us sense flashbacks and time change?

If the author uses signals such as *first, next, finally, on the other hand, besides, another point, in summary,* his organization is easy to follow. That is, it is easy if the student recognizes the signals. But if an author just as well-organized does not give these helpful signals, the reader has to sense them. How can the student sense that a new point is being made, not just an addition to the old? How can he tell that a subordinate point is being made? How can he tell that now the author is telling all the negative things about a topic, having just told all the positive things? How can he tell the flavor of a generalization from a specific fact, a definition from a statement of function, a principle from an illustration? By ear training and by visual analysis, students must learn how to detect such differences: but if we ourselves do not know the points to be observed, we cannot teach students to follow the ideas of the author.

A characteristic of English is the use of pronouns or alternate words instead of repetition of the same word. What proof is there that the pronoun refers to *this* word and not to *that*? What tells the reader that two words are being used synonymously?

Some nouns like *reindeer* and *fish* have the same form for singular and plural. In what situations do these dual purposes create reading difficulty and a dependence upon signals?

VII.

I do not have to tell you that this kind of learning can be done only by children who are well-acquainted with the English language. We should expand our idea of the disadvantaged to include all of us: children who do not speak English, children who do not recognize "book English," children unready for the concepts in assigned texts, and teachers unready to help them decode the meanings they encounter.

The reading act requires the decoding of written symbols into the sounds which those symbols rather inaccurately represent. The decoding of written symbols into sounds gives the reader the original speech-symbol for an idea. The interaction of these ideas, appraised by a knowledge of the order of English, the signals of relationship, and the possible meanings each word or phrase or clause may have in a variety of contexts, gives the reader what, from his experience, the author has meant to say. If the reader stops here, he will be fair game for any propagandist and will never produce ideas of his own. Now he must use his thought processes upon what he has observed and gathered, to develop products of his mind stimulated by this reading. The last step in the reading act is the use or expression of these ideas, these products, and the testing of them to see their validity.

In this paper I am concerned mainly with the second step, the decoding of meanings. But it is only one part of the total process. We should never magnify it to the exclusion of other important parts. Neither should we neglect it, either as teachers or as students of the language.

One wonderful contribution that this study of meaning can make is that it can vitalize some of the erstwhile deadly parts of the English program, those whitened bones set in orderly rows on the blackboard, defying utility and interest. Who hasn't hated the so-called irregular verbs: *drink, drank, drunk; see, saw, seen?* But Archibald Hill in his classification of verbs in his book, *Introduction to Linguistic Structures* (Harcourt Brace Jovanovich), shows fifteen or more patterns in which verbs are found. One realizes that the so-called irregular verbs are friends in disguise, with built-in signals to tense, whereas a verb like *cut,* which we have always appreciated for its dependability, gives no clue. We can realize the "signal" advantage to the child-who-*sounds* these endings or internal changes *correctly.*

The structural approach to English, used by many teachers with foreign students and the disadvantaged, is notoriously dull. Here is a who-dun-it I wrote in India, in structural English: "This is a man. This is a robber. This is a knife. This is a murder. This is a jail." I couldn't get a publisher. But if children can make discoveries about verbs, about structure, about the ways language works—in listening, speaking, reading, and writing activities—the language arts program will get a better Hooper rating. Curiosity will supplant lethargy, and discovery will replace boredom and inefficiency in learning. Practice will have more meaning.

I believe that we are on the verge of a great awakening in the language arts. (Perhaps it is niggardly of me not to say "RE-awakening.") There are more reasons for thinking this than I have time to convey. If we inform ourselves about the nature of our language, if we are curious and interested ourselves, neither we nor our children will need the artificial stimulus of color on letters, or the evasive crutches by which we first teach a symbol for the symbol of a symbol, and then the symbol of a symbol that the symbol for the symbol stands for. While some linguists would have us start with the alphabet, others with "Nan can fan Dan," and others with children's natural language, we should be good enough specialists in the teaching of reading to know that none of these alone is sufficient.

Let the linguist tell us about the language in his orderly way. Let the psychologist tell us how children learn. Let us then use this information to make a more suitable program for learning than either can conceive. Let us be curious about our own language so that the zeal created by our own efforts of discovery will electrify our classrooms. Let us have the restraint not to impose the fruits of our discoveries in dull little lists or artificial sentences upon children whose being cries to express itself. Rather, let us set the stage so that the discovery can be theirs and the learning confirmed by the intensity of their attention at the moment of insight.

Twenty-three years ago I reported the discoveries my college students had made about seven types of context clues to the meaning of unfamiliar words. *My* thinking stopped with theirs. I realize now that we were seeing only the top of the iceberg. Nine-tenths of the signals suggestive of meaning were hidden by our ignorance of other supportive linguistic clues. Those context clues are still valid. But think how much more you and I can do today to give our children power through insight.

References

1. Bloom, B. S., ed., *Taxonomy of Educational Objectives*. New York: McKay, 1956.
2. Booth, A. D., *et. al.*, "Aspects of Translation," *Studies in Communication 2*. London: Secker and Warburg, 1958.
3. Context Clues, entire issue, *The Reading Teacher*, volume 11, April 1958.
4. Enkvist, Nils E., *et. al.*, *Linguistics and Style*. London: Oxford University Press, 1964.
5. Firth, J. R., *Papers in Linguistics 1934–51*. London: Oxford University Press, 1957.
6. Fries, C. C., *Linguistics: The Study of Language*. New York: Holt, 1962.
7. ———, *The Structure of English*. New York: Harcourt, 1952.
8. Frostig, M., *Developmental Test of Visual Perception*. Los Angeles: the author, 1961.
9. Gleason, H. A., Jr., *Linguistics and English Grammar*. New York: Holt, 1965.
10. Halliday, M. A. K., *et. al.*, *The Linguistic Sciences and Language Teaching*. London: Longmans, 1964.
11. Harper, Robert J. C., *et. al.*, *The Cognitive Processes*. Englewood Cliffs, N. J.: Prentice-Hall, 1964.
12. Hayakawa, S. I., *Language in Action*. New York: Harcourt, 1941.
13. Hill, Archibald A., *Introduction to Linguistic Structures*. New York: Harcourt, 1958.
14. Hunt, Kellogg W., *Grammatical Structures Written at Three Grade Levels*. Champaign, Ill.: National Council of Teachers of English, 1965.
15. Kirk, Samuel A. and James McCarthy, "The Illinois Test of Psycholinguistic Abilities: An Approach to Differential Diagnosis," *American Journal of Mental Deficiency*, 56 (November 1961) 399–412.
16. Lado, Robert, *Linguistics Across Cultures*. Ann Arbor: University of Michigan Press, 1957.
17. ———, *Language Teaching: A Scientific Approach*. New York: McGraw-Hill, 1964.
18. LeFevre, Carl, *Linguistics and the Teaching of Reading*. New York: McGraw-Hill, 1964.
19. Loban, Walter, *The Language of Elementary School Children*. Champaign, Ill.: National Council of Teachers of English, 1963.
20. McCallister, James, "Reading Ability of Junior College Freshmen," *Chicago School Journal*, 18 (1936) 79–82.
21. National Council of Teachers of English, *English for Today*. New York: McGraw-Hill, 1962.
22. Newsome, Verna, *Structural Grammar in the Classroom*. Oshkosh, Wisc.: Wisconsin State College, 1962.
23. Roberts, Paul, *English Sentences*. New York: Harcourt, 1962.
24. Russell, David H., *The Dimensions of Children's Meaning Vocabularies in Grades Four Through Twelve*. Berkeley, Calif.: University of California Press, 1954.
25. Shuy, Roger, ed., *Social Dialects and Language Learning*. Champaign, Ill.: National Council of Teachers of English, 1964.
26. Strang, Ruth, "Secondary School Reading As Thinking," *The Reading Teacher*, 13 (February 1960) 194–200.
27. Whorf, Benjamin L., *Language, Thought, and Reality*. Cambridge, Mass.: M. I. T. Press, 1964.
28. Wise, Claude, *Applied Phonetics*. Englewood Cliffs, N. J.: Prentice-Hall, 1957.

The Teaching of Thinking

HILDA TABA

Educators have long said to themselves and to others that the proper business of school is to teach students to think. Yet this objective has remained a pious hope instead of becoming a tangible reality. A variety of factors have militated against developing a serious and well thought out strategy for helping students to become autonomous, creative, and productive thinkers.

Perhaps the most serious inhibiting factor has been the hazy conceptualization both of what is meant by teaching and what thinking consists of. Thinking has been treated as a global process which seemingly encompasses anything that goes on in the head, from daydreaming to constructing a concept of relativity. Consequently, the problem of defining thinking is still before us. The distinctions between the various types of thinking have been defective also. Even the more serious educational thinkers fail to distinguish the strategies of thinking, such as problem solving, from the basic cognitive process and skills, such as generalizing, differentiating, and forming concepts. These processes are the necessary ingredients of problem solving if this strategy is to amount to anything beyond sheer formality.

Implementation of thinking as an educational objective also has been handicapped by several questionable assumptions. One rather widely accepted assumption is that reflective thinking cannot take place until a sufficient body of factual information is accumulated. Teaching, which follows this assumption, stresses factual coverage and burdens the memory with unorganized and, therefore, rather perishable information.

An equally unproductive assumption is that thought is an automatic by-product of studying certain subjects and assimilating the end products of someone else's disciplined thought. Some subjects are assumed to have this power independently of how they learn or are taught. Inherently, memorizing mathematical formulae or the steps in mathematical processes is assumed to be better training than memorizing cake recipes, even though both may be learned in the same manner and call for the same mental process—rote memory (15).

The analysis of teaching suffers from similar difficulties. Teaching is still viewed largely as communication of knowledge, and often knowledge is

THE TEACHING OF THINKING by Hilda Taba. From *Elementary English,* 42 (May 1965), pp. 534–42. Copyright © 1965 by the National Council of Teachers of English. Reprinted by permission of the publisher and the estate of Hilda Taba.

equated with descriptive information—the "what," "who," and "when" questions are the main diet of classroom instruction. As a consequence the current methods of teaching tend to be shaped by this emphasis. Research on teaching has skirted the actual process of teaching and has concentrated instead on such matters as personal characteristics of good teachers and *a priori* criteria for rating effective teaching (6).

It is no wonder, then, that despite the widespread acceptance of thinking as an educational objective little consideration has been given to the ways in which learning to think differ from the ways in which students learn knowledge or content of various sorts.

Recent research is producing changes in both of these areas. Studies of cognition are under way, which promise a more precise analysis of the processes and of the psychological dynamics of the mental activity we call thinking. Some of these studies are concerned with styles of labeling (12), others with strategies of concept formation (2), and still others with what amounts to the styles in strategies of thinking (7, 10). Important as these studies are, as yet their results cannot be easily translated into the methods for modifying the ways of thinking. But at least they are opening up the possibility of a scientific approach to the analysis of thinking.

The development of thinking has received renewed attention also, as exemplified by the recent interest in the work of Piaget and his followers. Piaget's theories regarding the nature of thought and the sequences in the transformation of the patterns or modes of thinking have influenced such enterprises as Bruner's (3) analysis of the process of education and Suchman's (13) experiments with inquiry training.

Some progress is being made in the study of the teaching process also. Recent studies of teaching have focused on teaching as it occurs in the classroom instead of inferring its effectiveness either from *a priori* notions of good teaching or from the characteristics of good teachers. Studies by Hughes (8), Flanders (5), and Bellack (1) focus on describing and cataloguing the teaching acts and on inferring from these descriptions their impact on learning in general, on classroom climate, and on achievement.

This article is a description of a study of classroom interaction designed to examine the relationship between teaching strategies and the development of cognitive processes (16). The study, conducted under a grant from the Cooperative Research Branch of the U.S. Office of Education, focused on several hypotheses. The central hypothesis was that it is possible to train students in the processes of thinking, provided that the trainable cognitive skills could be identified.

The studies of thinking cited above seemed to have one difficulty in common as far as the application of their findings to instruction in the classroom is concerned. The findings regarding the styles of thought fail to shed light on the processes by which these styles are acquired or to describe the skills on which these styles are founded.

Another hypothesis was that under optimal conditions this training would result in an acceleration of the usual developmental sequence, such as the appearance of abstract or formal thought. The studies of the development of thought and intelligence by Piaget and the Geneva school (9^1, 11, 14^2) suggest that the evolution of thought takes place in three stages, essentially: (1) the sensory-motor stage or the preverbal intelligence; (2) the stage of concrete operations or thinking with objects and concrete events, which stage lasts from around two to eleven years of age; and (3) the stage of conceptual or formal thought which is established between eleven years of age and adolescence. There is a question, however, whether training would alter these age placements since the available data recorded the performance of untrained children, or those with only a minimum of training, such as in the study by Ervin (4). It seemed reasonable to assume that if both the curriculum and teaching strategies were addressed to the development of thought, formal thought could appear earlier.

The third hypothesis was that with adequate teaching strategies the possibility of abstract thought would be opened to students who are now considered to have too low an IQ to be capable of higher levels of mental activity.

The study was conducted in elementary classes which were using a curriculum in social studies that systematically stressed the development of an ability to generalize and to use generalizations productively. What remained to be done was to specify the necessary teaching strategies and to train the teachers in their use, in order to become adept at these processes themselves, and to learn how to induct children in the mastery of the required cognitive skills.

THE CONCEPT OF COGNITIVE TASKS

In an effort to arrive at teachable and learnable aspects of thought, three cognitive tasks were identified: (1) concept formation, (2) the development of generalizations and inferences through interpretation of raw data, and (3) the explanation and prediction of new phenomena by applying known principles and facts.

Concept Formation

In its simplest form, concept development may be described as consisting of three processes or operations. One is the differentiation of the properties or characteristics of objects and events, such as differentiating the materials of which houses are built from other characteristics of houses. This differentiat-

[1] Chapter 6.
[2] Pp. 107–112.

ing involves analysis in the sense of breaking down global wholes into specific properties and elements.

The second process is that of grouping. This process calls for abstracting certain common characteristics in an array of dissimilar objects or events and for grouping these on the basis of this similar property, such as grouping together hospitals, doctors, and medicine as something to do with health care or according to their availability as an index to the standard of living. Naturally, the same objects and events can be grouped in several different ways. For example, hospitals, X-rays, and surgical equipment can be grouped together as health facilities, as types of services, or as indices of standard of living, depending on the purpose of the grouping.

The third process is that of categorizing and labeling. This process calls for the discovery of categories or labels which encompass and organize diverse objects and events, such as evolving the concept of a unit measurement from measuring with a cup, a yardstick, a plain stick, and a rubber band. It also involves the process of super- and subordination; that is, deciding which items can be subsumed under which category.

In classrooms this cognitive task occurs in the form of enumerating or listing, such as identifying a series of specific items noted in a film or reported by a research committee, then grouping similar things, and, finally, labeling the groups.

Interpretation of Data and Inference

Essentially this cognitive task consists of evolving generalizations and principles from an analysis of concrete data. Several subprocesses are involved. The first and the simplest is that of identifying specific points in the data. This process is somewhat analogous to the listing or enumeration preceding grouping. The second process is that of explaining specific items or events, such as why ocean currents affect temperature, why Mexico employs the "each one teach one" system in eradicating illiteracy, or why the way of life in California changed when its harbors were opened for free trade. This process also involves relating the points of information to each other to enlarge their meaning and to establish relationships.

The third operation is that of forming inferences which go beyond that which is directly given, such as inferring, from the comparison of the data on population composition with data on standards of living in certain Latin American states, that countries with predominantly white populations tend to have a higher standard of living.

Interpretation of data and formulation of inferences take place in the classroom whenever the students must cope with raw data of one sort or another, such as comparing the imports and exports of several countries or analyzing and synthesizing the factors which determine the level of technological development in a given culture by examining the tools and techniques used in the production of goods.

Application of Principles

A third cognitive task is that of applying known principles and facts to explain new phenomena or to predict consequences from known conditions. For example, if one knows what a desert is like, what way of life it permits, and how water affects the productivity of the soil, one can predict what might happen to the desert way of life if water became available.

This cognitive task requires essentially two different operations. One is that of predicting and hypothesizing. This process requires an analysis of the problem and of the conditions in order to determine which facts and principles are relevant and which are not. Second is that of developing informational or logical parameters which constitute the causal links between the conditions and the prediction and, in fact, make a rational prediction or explanation possible. For example, if one predicts that the presence of water in the desert will cause cities to be built, one needs also to make explicit the chain of causal links that leads from the availability of water to the building of cities. These chains may consist of logical conditions, such as that the presence of water is the only condition to make the soil productive, or from factual conditions, such as whether the desert soil contains salt or not.

These predictions and explanations are of different orders of generality and complexity: for example, the prediction that cities will be built as a consequence of a water supply represents a greater leap than does the prediction that grass will grow.

In order to develop criteria for effective teaching strategies it was necessary to evolve a theoretical construct. In the light of this construct these processes and their development were viewed.

Space permits the description of only a few principles in this theoretical construct. First, the learning of thinking was viewed as essentially an active transaction between the individual and his environment. The nature of this transaction is only partly controlled by the nature of the immediate stimulus. Partly, it is controlled by whatever mediation is available either in the form of models offered or of guidance that is available. Chiefly, however, the individual must develop for himself both the conceptual schemes and the processes of using them. In other words, the environment and training become available to the individual only to the extent that he performs certain operations on what he receives. These operations cannot be "given" in the ordinary sense of the word. An individual may, for example, imitate a model of the "if-then" reasoning. But this model remains unproductive unless he internalizes and elaborates this process himself.

Second, the development of thought follows a sequence in which the simpler and the more concrete operations must precede and prepare for the more complex and the abstract. The elementary school child, for example, must work out the idea of cause and consequence on concrete material before he can evolve an abstract concept of causes and consequences. It appears also that the elementary school years are the period during which the concrete thinking, or thinking with concrete objects and events, is being transformed into formal thinking or thinking with symbols. For this reason an emphasis on the development of certain basic cognitive skills on this level is crucial.

The idea of a sequential order applies also to the mastery of the skills involved in the cognitive tasks described above. As a matter of fact, the skills as described above could be seen as a series of sequential steps in which each preceding one is a prerequisite for the success in mastering the next one. For example, in interpreting data the differentiation of specific points is a prerequisite to comparing and contrasting these points or to seeing relationships between them. The latter is, in turn, a prerequisite for making inferences, and so on.

Finally, the conceptual schema undergo a constant reorganization. The dynamics of this reorganization can be visualized as a rotation of intake of information into the existing conceptual scheme and the extension or reorganization of the scheme whenever the problem or the information received creates a dissonance because it does not fit the scheme. For example, a child whose concept of relationship of altitude and temperature is that the higher one goes the colder it gets is jarred into modifying this concept when faced with the fact of high altitude combined with high temperature. He now needs to extend this concept to include the concept of geographic zones.

Piaget (11) calls these two processes "assimilation" and "accommodation," and these terms will be used in the discussion that follows. This rotation of assimilation and accommodation seems to describe the psychological dynamics or mechanism for the gradual maturation of thought, and, as such, is extremely important in the strategy of training.

Hunt (9) points out, in addition, that this rotation requires a proper match between the existing conceptual scheme and that which is required by the new information or task. When the requirements of the accommodation are too far beyond the existing conceptual scheme it is impossible for the child to make a leap. When it is too close there is no challenge for reorganization.

TEACHING STRATEGIES
FOR COGNITIVE GROWTH

The concepts of the cognitive tasks together with the principles which govern the development of the cognitive skills have interesting implications for the formulation of teaching strategies.

First, the concept of thinking as essentially an active process, in the sense that it can be learned only by doing, sets the process of teaching into a new perspective. If students are to develop a cognitive structure by their own efforts, the usual role of teaching and of the teacher has to be reversed. Instead of teaching consisting primarily of communication of information, with the role of the teacher as a fount of that information, he needs to become an adroit guide of the heuristic process. In this kind of teaching strategy the art of asking questions assumes a crucial role. Questions, furthermore, need a double focus: on the substance of what is being discussed and on the cognitive operations. A question such as, "What materials do we use in building houses?" focuses on the materials and excludes other characteristics of building houses such as tools and labor. This question also asks for enumeration of these materials rather than explanations of why these materials are used. Other questions are addressed to explanation, such as why women in certain primitive tribes carry things on their heads or why some countries fail to use the natural resources they have.

The concept of sequence and of the rotation of assimilation and accommodation suggests, further, that teaching acts, such as the questions, need to be programmed to foster an appropriate sequence of learning. If the learning to apply knowledge to explaining new phenomena involves mastering certain modes of thinking in a certain order, then the questions the teacher asks and the remarks she makes need to follow that order. If there is to be rotation of intake of new information with tasks that require changing the conceptual structure, then the teaching acts need to be organized to stimulate such a rotation. If time and pacing of transitions from one mode or level of thinking into another is essential, then the teaching strategy must manage this pacing. In other words, teaching needs to be addressed first to the objective of thinking; second, seen as a series of acts, each of which has a specific pedagogical function; and, finally, viewed as a strategy or organization of these functions.

In the study described above, *Thinking in Elementary School Children* (16), two groups of teaching functions were identified which seemed to affect the development of cognitive skills, either positively or negatively. First are questions or statements made by the teacher or the students which are psychological or managerial in their function and unrelated to the logic of the content. Statements of this type included approval, disagreement, disapproval, management, and reiteration. Second are teacher questions or statements which give direction to discussions and are related to the logic of the content and of the cognitive operations sought. This group of functions included focusing, refocusing, change of focus, deviating from focus, extending thought on the same level, lifting thought to a higher level, and controlling thought (16[3]).

Focusing questions or remarks establish both the content topic under consideration and the cognitive operations to be performed. They set the cognitive task. For example, a question by the teacher such as, "If the desert had all the water it needed what would happen to the desert way of life?" establishes the central content topic for discussion and calls for prediction of consequences. However, to prevent students from indulging in associative thinking which follows a single line and opens up new dimensions, a change of focus may be needed. Refocusing may be necessary to bring the discussion back to the original topic.

Extending thought on the same level fulfills the requirement of allowing

[3] Chapter 7.

a sufficient amount of assimilation before thought is lifted to another level, such as making a transition from description of specific points noted in a film, to explaining why certain events took place in the film or from prediction to establishing its validity. This is essentially a strategy in which a number of students are induced to respond to the same question instead of proceeding from an answer by one student to a question to the same one, as is usual. Extension of thought on the same level also assures the participation of the slower students. This engages them in the initial step of the process and thus prepares them for participation in the next step.

Lifting of the level of thought occurs when the teacher or child either gives or seeks information that shifts the thought to a level higher than the previously established one. Thus, making a transition from enumeration to grouping and from grouping to labelling represents lifting of thought. However, pursuing each of these steps by engaging more students or by seeking clarification and elaboration would represent extension.

Controlling thought occurs when the teacher gives what the students should do for themselves, such as suggesting a category or classification or giving explanations of phenomena observed instead of seeking explanation from the children.

The examples below illustrate the function of focusing, extending, and lifting thought:

(1) C Malobi took the money home with her. (Child gives specific information.)
(2) T What did Malobi do with the money? (Teacher seeks specific information.)
(3) C She saved it. (Child extends thought on the level of specific information.)
(4) C She put it underground. (Child extends thought on the level of specific information.)
(5) C She put sticks and tin over it. (Child extends thought on the level of specific information.)
(6) C Before she did that she put it in a little pot. (Child extends thought on the level of specific information.)

In the following example the teacher attempts to lift the level of thought from the giving of information to explanation:

(1) C They carried things in baskets on their heads. (Child gives specific information.)
(2) T Explain why. (Teacher lifts thought to the level of explanation.)
(3) C I suppose they can carry more things that way. (Child gives an explanation.)

The combination of these functions together with the pacing of assimilation and the timing of lifting thought to a new level is what constitutes the teaching strategy. This strategy is determined by recognizing that it takes time to learn the skills involved in these cognitive tasks. They are not in the class of instantaneous learning. Furthermore, presumably there are individual differences in the speed with which these skills can be mastered. Some students may make a clear distinction after a few attempts at enumeration, while others need to "mess around" for a longer time to discover what is at stake and what the model of differentiation is. Teaching strategy, to be effective, must allow variation in pacing each step, determining how long to continue on the plateau of each step, and when to make a transition to the next one.

In order to assess the effectiveness of these pedagogical functions, the verbal remarks of students were rated as to level of thought in each of the three cognitive tasks. In effect, these ratings described the successive cognitive operations involved in each of the tasks described previously. Presumably the process of making inferences is a more complex one and of a higher order than is identification of the points in the information presented, the latter being a prerequisite to the former. In the task calling for inferring from data, a teacher may seek, first, specific information. She may then attempt to lift the level of thought to that of explanation, and follow with questions designed to elicit inference, *etc.* The success in eliciting appropriate responses constitutes the measure of the effectiveness of the teaching strategy.

The charting of this flow of teaching acts and of the level of students' responses describes visually the relationship of the two. For example, when the teacher attempts to raise the level of thought too early in the discussion, this typically results in the children's returning to a lower level and in their inability to sustain discussion at the higher levels of thought. On the other hand, an effective strategy of focusing, extending, and lifting thought, combined with appropriate pacing of extensions and properly matched lifts, will result in a gradual movement toward higher levels of mental operation by the majority of the students. A frequent change of focus produces an alternation between several levels, a lack of sustained thought at any level, and a gradual return to the most primitive one. The same result occurs when the teacher inserts controls of thought by giving students what they should be doing for themselves. The figure on the opposite page illustrates some of these strategies:

Pattern A represents a strategy in which the transitions are paced appropriately, with the result that the class follows the transitions from one level of thought to the next and sustains the thought on each. In Pattern B the lifting of thought occurs too early, with the result that when the few students who could follow it have exhausted their ideas the class settles down to the lowest level. Pattern C illustrates a discussion in which the focus is lost, and the teacher is forced to keep the discussion alive by constantly changing the topic, without being able to sustain thought on any.

What, then, can be said about the merits of this approach to teaching thinking? First, the specification of thinking as an object of educational effort permits a clearer analysis of the appropriate pedagogical functions necessary to make this objective both more realistic and attainable. A more clearly focused target together with more articulated pedagogical functions may also permit a more effective training of teachers than is possible when both the nature of cognitive processes and of the appropriate teaching strategies for them are vague and obscure.

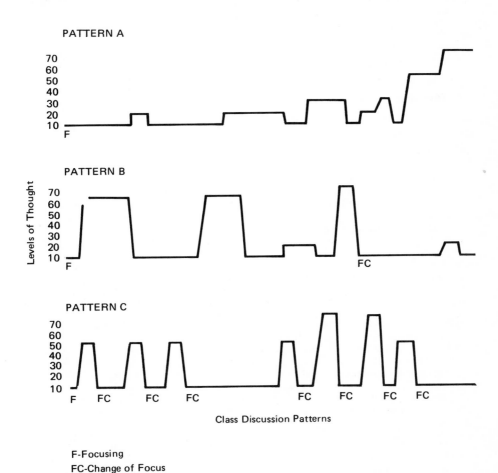

Class Discussion Patterns

F-Focusing
FC-Change of Focus

Second, it seems that a similar analysis of other educational objectives, such as the enhancement of the ego concept, the growth in affective domain, and the development of a creative approach to literature and art, might eventuate in the kinds of description of instructional processes which may provide the material for the development of a generic and a functional theory of learning and teaching.

Finally, such an approach to teaching thinking may reach students who are now relatively untouched by instruction. The results of the study described here indicated a lack of correlation between the performance on the test of Inference in Social Studies and the students' IQ. Analysis of tapescripts suggested that a careful structuring of the sequential steps in mastering the basic cognitive skills and an appropriate timing and pacing of the transitions from one level of thought to another are the chief ingredients to opening the possibility for a higher level of mental functioning to students of low ability (as measured by tests of intelligence). Analysis of a few individual cases indicated the possibility that among the so-called slow students are many who are only slow absorbers. Evidently, when the amount of information to be assimilated is reduced and opportunity is provided for systematic processing of that information, such students can function on abstract levels of thought.

Bibliography

1. Bellack, A., et al., *The Language of the Classroom*. New York: Institute of Psychological Research, Teachers College, Columbia University, 1963.
2. Bruner, J. S., Jacqueline J. Goodnow, and G. A. Austin, *A Study of Thinking*. New York: Wiley, 1956.
3. Bruner, J. S., *The Process of Education*. Cambridge: Harvard University Press, 1960.
4. Ervin, Susan M., "Training and Logical Operation of Children," *Child Development*, 31 (1960), 555–563.
5. Flanders, N. A., *Teacher Influence, Pupil Attitudes, and Achievement*. Prepublication manuscript of a proposed research monograph for the U.S. Office of Education, Cooperative Research Branch, Washington, D.C., 1960.
6. Gage, N. L. (Editor), *Handbook of Research on Teaching*. A Project of The American Educational Research Association. Chicago: Rand McNally, 1963, Chap. 11.
7. Guilford, J. P., "Basic Conceptual Problems in the Psychology of Thinking," *Annals New York Academy of Science*, 91 (1961), 9–19.
8. Hughes, Marie, et al., *Development of the Means for the Assessment of the Quality of Teaching in Elementary School*. (Mimeo.) Salt Lake City: University of Utah, 1959.
9. Hunt, J. McV., *Experience and Intelligence*. New York: Ronald Press, 1961, Chaps. 5–9.
10. Peel, E. A., *The Pupil's Thinking*. London: Oldbourne, 1960.
11. Piaget, J., *The Psychology of Intelligence*. New York: Harcourt Brace Jovanovich, 1950.
12. Sigel, I., *Cognitive Style and Personality Dynamics*. Interim report. Merrill-Palmer Institute, 1961.
13. Suchman, J. R., *The Elementary School Training Program in Scientific Inquiry*. U.S. Office of Education, Title VII, Project 216. Urbana: University of Illinois, 1964.
14. Taba, Hilda, *Curriculum Development. Theory and Practice*. New York: Harcourt Brace Jovanovich, 1962.
15. Taba, Hilda, and F. F. Elzey, "Teaching Strategies and Thought Processes," *Teachers College Record*, Vol. 65, No. 6, March, 1964.
16. Taba, Hilda, S. Levine, and F. F. Elzey, *Thinking in Elementary School Children*, U.S. Office of Education, Cooperative Research Branch Project No. 1574. San Francisco: San Francisco State College, 1964.

Developing Critical Readers

HELEN M. ROBINSON

Most teachers and reading experts agree that critical reading is one of the significant goals of reading instruction. Some educators use other terms and descriptions as did Chase[1] when he referred to "higher illiteracy" as the inability to relate the content of verbal communication to events which at each moment are shaping our future. He stated that "I hold that the values which thoughtful men cherish are more endangered by illiteracy than the atomic bomb and its offspring."

Among the characteristics Chase attributed to higher illiteracy are two which have pertinence for this paper: "the higher illiterate can absorb and repeat ideas found on the printed page, but he has not developed the ability to relate these ideas to the life around him. He does not engage in the kind of dialogue which will test the relevance of what he has read to his own personal experience, to the lives of those he meets, or to the behavior of individuals or social groups in general."[2]

While few others have related the significance of critical reading to the atomic bomb, many have rated this ability as essential for the survival of a free world.

WHAT IS CRITICAL READING?

A cursory examination of approximately a hundred references reveals that critical reading is usually mentioned, included in some sequence, or described; but it is seldom defined. At times it is lumped with the "higher level" reading skills or designated as critical thinking applied to what is read. One who plans to do research on critical reading or a teacher who wishes to teach this ability may be confused by reading many of these references because of the vague descriptions of the process and skills or because of sharp differences in opinions about the definition.

Some examples of definitions of critical reading which reveal the differences are offered in the following paragraphs.

Fay wrote that "the essential element in critical or evaluative reading that distinguishes it from literal comprehension is that the critical reader must react to what he reads. He must do something more than merely absorb

DEVELOPING CRITICAL READERS by Helen M. Robinson. From Dimensions of Critical Reading, Proceedings of the Annual Education and Reading Conference, University of Delaware, 1964, ed. Russell G. Stauffer, pp. 1–12. Reprinted by permission.

261

what the author is telling him."[3] After an extensive review of the literature on the nature of critical reading, Sochor[4] concluded that literal and critical reading could be differentiated only on the basis of the reader's purpose—to understand what is stated or to deal with the ideas in some way. Later she differentiated the two types of reading by defining literal reading as "the ability to obtain a low-level type of interpretation by using only the information explicitly stated" while critical reading was described as "the ability to obtain a level of interpretation higher than that needed for literal interpretation."[5] Both of these definitions or descriptions are vague and offer little direction in determining the unique characteristics of critical reading as opposed to inferring meanings, arriving at conclusions, and other similar abilities.

A more precise, but narrow, definition was given by Gans[6] who considered critical reading comprehension as the selection or rejection of reference material for use in solving a problem. Russell included critical reading, along with other skills, in creative reading, which he defines as "the process of integrating and organizing materials in order to come to some conclusion or synthesis or to solve some problem."[7]

The next two definitions come to terms with the more specific aspects of critical reading.

De Boer stated that "critical reading involves the search for relevant materials, the evaluation of the data, the identification and comparison of sources, and the synthesis of findings. It involves the capacity for suspended judgment and the interpretation of the writer's motives. But chiefly it involves a sufficient background of knowledge to provide a sound basis for judgment. Critical reading implies the existence of appropriate criteria in the mind of the reader."[8] In De Boer's description of what is involved in critical reading, there is a distinct implication that to read critically one must have experience sufficient to develop criteria for judging the validity or worth of the materials read.

Gray developed a conceptual framework for the total reading act which includes critical reading. He referred to the four major aspects as (1) perception of words, including both recognition and meaning; (2) grasp of meaning of continuous discourse, both stated and implied; (3) thoughtful reaction to ideas gleaned; and (4) assimilation, or fusion of the new ideas with those already acquired. In this framework, Gray included critical reading in the third aspect—thoughtful reaction. He described it as "the evaluation of what is read in the light of sound criteria or standards."[9] He added that critical reading involved the wise selection of facts or standards needed in making specific evaluations. Of primary importance are clear thinking, weighing of values, and rigorous checking on the validity of the conclusions reached. He added that the reader will accept or be guided by that which is sound and meritorious, and reject or disapprove that which is untrue or of questionable value.[10]

The dictionary definition of *critical* suggests harshness of judgment, but states that "in precise use, critical implies an effort to see a thing clearly and truly in order to judge it fairly."[11] Based on the precise use and the definitions and descriptions already given, a definition of critical reading has been adopted for this paper. It is judgment of the veracity, validity, or worth of what is read, based on sound criteria or standards developed through previous experiences.

SKILLS AND ABILITIES
BASIC TO CRITICAL READING

Most investigators and theorists agree that critical reading is based on, or is an instance of, critical thinking. In this respect, there is great similarity to critical listening. For this reason, there is some objection to including this ability as a part of reading. Nevertheless, reading offers tremendous opportunities for insuring the development of critical thinking. Although thinking has been defined many ways, the description used in this paper is "to exercise the powers of judgment, conception, or inference; to reflect for the purpose of reaching a conclusion."[12] Acceptance of such a choice is in contrast to imagining, planning, envisioning, and realizing. The assumption is frequently made that critical thinking and by implication, critical reading, is closely related to intelligence level as measured by tests. In Russell's[13] review of the research as well as in more recent investigations, the coefficients of correlation between intelligence test scores and critical thinking have not exceeded .50 and most have been considerably lower. The discrepancy may be based on the nature of the tests used, or may be due to lack of development of critical thinking abilities on the part of those who are capable of learning critical thinking. The consensus of writers is that critical thinking and critical reading are greatly facilitated by intellectual maturity but that even persons of below average intelligence may learn the simpler levels of critical reading.

Several types or levels of complexity of abilities basic to critical reading have already been given. Gray proposed three requisites. The first "is an attitude of inquiry concerned with such items as the soundness or worth of the ideas expressed, the actions of a character or the literary quality of the material read." The second "is an adequate background or basis for evaluation which includes information, specific facts and established principles. . . . "[14] A third requisite "is ability on the part of readers to make sound judgments, in evaluating what they read."[15]

De Boer recognized three general levels of critical reading, each successive one implying more complex abilities than the others. First is the relevancy of materials to a specific question or topic. At the second level is evaluation of the accuracy of an item of fact or the reliability of a source of information. Third is the ability to appraise the validity of a conclusion reached by an author. This level calls for not only the relevancy, accuracy, and validity of facts and arguments but also a decision as to whether pertinent information has been overlooked or suppressed.[16]

Russell suggests four conditions as essential to critical reading: (1) a knowledge of the field in which reading is being done; (2) an attitude of questioning and suspended judgment; (3) some application of the methods of logical analysis or scientific inquiry; and (4) taking action in light of the analyses or reasoning.[17]

Heilman proposed that "Almost all of the prerequisites for, and obstacles to, critical reading are related to the two skills of discerning a writer's purpose and drawing inferences. The presence or absence of bias, a lack of background, the habit of accepting that which is in print or that which is allegedly backed by authority, and the lack of experience in dealing with controversial topics, all help to determine whether critical reading can take place."[18]

An interesting description of many skills and abilities called into use comes from Strang. The following quotation is illustrative: "In reading to obtain proof on any point the student will first formulate the assumptions which are to be studied. Then he will select, as he reads, the ideas significantly related to the assumptions. He will search for evidence in support of or opposed to the assumptions and weigh each bit of evidence as he reads. If evidence accumulates against one of his original assumptions, he will change it."[19]

So far, in this paper, little attention has been given to the familiar reading skills requisite to critical reading. Many of the writers already mentioned have detailed the skills and abilities needed. Some writers separate the skills and list ten to twenty. Others group them into classes. For example, Heilman lists ten abilities, but in summary says that "the reader must know the meaning of the words used and the different shades of meaning words have in different contexts. He must separate main thoughts or ideas from qualifications; he must detect the author's purpose, bias, and intent."[20]

In one of his last publications, Gray[21] brought together, in diagrammatic form, the essential skills. To summarize his views, he said that it is necessary to perceive words accurately, knowing both the proper pronunciation and the appropriate meaning in a given context. Comprehension calls for fusing smaller meanings into larger ideas and noting the relationship and organization of the ideas. Both literal and implied meanings must be secured. The type of material must be recognized and inquiries appropriate to it should be made. The inquiries include identifying the author's purpose, mood, and attitude toward his topic. These abilities are often known as reading the lines, reading between the lines, and reading beyond the lines. Furthermore, these reading skills must be sufficiently developed so that they can be applied automatically with major attention given to the mental processes suggested earlier in this section.

The intellective and reading skills and abilities must be supplemented by a consideration of the attitudes of the reader. McKillopp[22] found that, among 11th-grade students, attitude had very little affect on literal meaning. However, when judgment, evaluation and prediction were required, attitude was a very significant factor.

In grades 7–10, McCaul found that the stronger the pupils' attitudes the greater was the effect on interpretation. He concluded that "he (man) is not purged of emotion, prejudice, and attitudes just because he has a book in his hands. When he reads he is as much a dupe of his attitudes as he is under any other circumstances."[23]

At the adult level, a plethora of studies have been made of the effects of strongly held beliefs (biases) on understanding an author's argument or reasoning.

Thus, attitudes combine with experience to contribute to individual differences in critical reading.

Therefore, to develop critical readers, it is essential that the skills and abilities in reading for complete understanding be combined with (1) an inquiring attitude; (2) a background to supply knowledge about the topic, field, or area to provide standards or criteria for evaluation; (3) the ability to suspend judgment until the writer's message is fully secured; (4) the ability to follow the organization or logic of the presentation, recognizing what is included and what is omitted; (5) awareness of the author's qualifications, and intent; and (6) recognition of the publisher's commitments. Inductive and deductive reasoning, analysis of language, and appreciation of quality of writing seem to be essential ingredients. All of these abilities will be influenced by the reader's attitudes.

CONDITIONS FOR CRITICAL READING

The first essential condition is a commitment on the part of the school or school system to develop critical readers. Such a commitment will be reflected in the aims and goals of reading instruction and in all content areas in which reading is used.

Second, the materials provided for reading must be appropriate for children and youth to use at various levels of maturity. For example, a single textbook, selected by the teacher as authentic, is not conducive to critical reading. Books, magazines, and newspapers presenting different points of view and kinds of writing are helpful in developing critical reading. For example, Engle[24] stated that "A curriculum for reflective thinking is one which selects and organizes instructional materials and experiences in such a way as to maximize the opportunities for students to make intelligent and thoughtful decisions with respect to what to hold valuable, what to believe, what guiding ideas or principles to accept as true and what courses of action to follow. . . . In contrast, a curriculum antithetical to reflective thinking selects and organizes materials on principles which emphasize the memorization of specific pieces of information in relative isolation from other similar data. . . ."

Third, the teachers must be able to read critically, value an inquiring attitude, and be ready to foster the kinds of discussions which reflect differing views. Austin et al[25] found that there was general agreement that critical reading should be one of the goals of instruction, but that few college teachers felt secure in guiding classroom teachers so as to reach the goal.

A fourth requisite is the ability on the part of teachers to ask the right kinds of questions. In this connection, there is general agreement that reproducing isolated facts deters critical reading. The questions must be appropriate to the selection, calling for critical evaluation of the materials. Teachers should be prepared to expect differences among responses, especially those based on value judgments. In each instance, teachers should consider both the response to the selection and the standard or criterion for making the judgment. When children and young people become adept at answering a wide range of questions requiring critical judgment, they should be led gradually to formulating their own questions before they read, while they are reading and after they have finished. This step is greatly facilitated when teachers foster an inquiring attitude throughout the school years.

A fifth requisite is willingness to take the time necessary to help pupils develop adequate criteria for critical reading, for reading slowly enough to weigh the evidence, for discussion which helps clarify similarities and differences in conclusions reached. In other words, it is essential to "uncover the ground rather than cover it" as others have said.

WHEN TO TEACH CRITICAL READING

The discussion so far has emphasized the need for a broad background of experiences and a fund of information. Obviously, background is built from infancy, in the home; and it is a continuous function of the school. In addition, background needs to be related to what is read at all developmental levels.

Preschool children are capable of critical thinking before they read, according to Smith.[26] To be sure, the critical level is simple and the topics are sufficiently familiar that children have information so as to judge validity or worth. It follows then, that beginners in school may be taught to read critically as soon as they have acquired sufficient competence in the undergirding skills. They may learn to compare and contrast ideas as soon as they are sufficiently mature to identify clearly, likenesses and differences. At the primary grade level, McCullough[27] compared pupils' abilities to answer questions of detail, main ideas, and sequence with those requiring creative reading. At this level she used questions requiring pupils to draw conclusions, pass judgments, and see relationships. She found significant relationship among the skills with no special difficulty in what she called creative reading.

As pupils progress in school and read many easy books, they can learn to be critical of the materials selected for their personal reading, going beyond the responses that they like or dislike the story or informative material.

Nearly a quarter of a century ago, Gans[28] demonstrated that middle-grade children could judge relevancy and authenticity of materials, especially when relationships were close or fairly obvious. They were less successful with remotely related materials. Other aspects of critical reading can be taught at this level, but we have just begun to explore the possibilities.

A great deal of attention has been given to propaganda analysis, sometimes in the middle grades, but more often in junior high school. Perhaps the reason is that more than 20 years ago, the Institute of Propaganda Analysis reported seven sly techniques used to influence readers: (1) bad names, (2) glad names, (3) transfer, (4) the testimonial, (5) plain folks, (6) stacking the cards, and (7) the band wagon.[29] The simplicity and structure of this list seems to help teachers "get hold of" this aspect of critical reading.

Even though sixth-grade children learn to identify propaganda devices, Nordelli[30] found that the pupils did not change in their abilities to resist the propaganda. Osborn[31] showed that knowledge of the methods of propaganda was not enough to provide resistance to them.

To some writers, teaching propaganda devices is the essence of critical reading. It would be exceedingly unfortunate if instruction stopped at this level, using only a small segment of the range of possibilities. But this example suggests the necessity for clearly identifying other areas of critical reading so that they, too, may be taught.

In the secondary school, all of the content of the curriculum offers tremendous opportunity for teaching critical reading. Literature is an example, because as Gainsburg[32] points out, critical reading is the foundation of appreciation. Social studies provides a rich source of materials for critical reading. In science and mathematics, critical reading becomes essential.

Colleges and graduate schools are likely to expect critical reading, often in areas where students lack the background to read critically. In fact, in my own doctoral courses to which only excellent students are admitted, critical reading of research must be developed. This is done by exposing graduate students to excellent and poor research, making comparisons and contrasts, evolving standards for judging research, redesigning published reports to improve them, and offering a great deal of practice in the application of all of these abilities.

It seems clear to me that if an attitude of inquiry is fostered and if the techniques of critical reading are taught, this ability may increase throughout life, as background and experience develop ever-higher standards against which to judge what is read.

TEACHING CRITICAL READING

Three general approaches to teaching critical reading were pointed out by Huelsman.[33] The direct approach is one in which teachers plan for and systematically develop the attitudes, skills and abilities of critical reading.

The second approach may be called incidental in that teachers are developing critical reading as a by-product of the inquiry into content. Using the unit or topic in which many references are read requires some aspects of critical reading.

The third is the functional approach which emphasizes the evaluation of primary source material rather than securing information from secondary works.

So far, no evaluation of the relative effectiveness of the three approaches has been made. In fact, few studies to determine how well the elementary and secondary schools combine efforts to develop critical reading can be found.

One study seems worth a brief reference at this time. Rogers used for her subjects 30 high school sophomores and 30 seniors. She compared their performances in an undirected reading situation, reading a magazine as one would in a dentist's office, with that of a school assignment where questions about the selection were anticipated. Articles were paired from three issues of the *USSR* magazine for reading level, human interest and content interest. A descriptive rating scale for level of competence permitted her to ascertain the level of the use of critical reading as revealed by the responses. She reached the following conclusions:

1. "There tended to be a focus on 'remembering facts' to the exclusion, in many instances, of evaluative thinking about what was read." For example, students were asked to tell what they thought about an article but responded with the content of the article.
2. "There was little awareness of the need for evaluative response." This behavior was exhibited especially when direct questions were not asked. The students showed no curiosity about the purpose of the magazine, or its publisher, but accepted its slanted content fully.
3. "The subjects demonstrated question-answering skills rather than reading skills." The subjects attempted evaluation of the selections, with varying degrees of skill, only when questions triggered this response. Without the teacher or a test, critical reading did not appear to function.[34]

From this study, it seems clear that the teachers' emphasis and the kinds of questions used will markedly influence the development of critical reading.

A second study by Smith[35] using high school seniors revealed that they set purposes for reading by their teachers' tests and the questions or the ones students anticipated.

The limited evidence available strongly suggests the necessity for direct instruction, for the frequent use of questions which promote critical reading, and for developing independence on the part of students in reading critically.

TESTING CRITICAL READING

Undoubtedly one of the greatest deterrents to critical reading has been the nature of standardized tests. Most of the elementary reading tests, as well as the bulk of high school reading tests require reproduction of material stated, with few of the evaluative or critical types of questions. Because students rank high on these tests, teachers are not moved to the difficult task of teaching critical reading.

Judging from the problems reported by those who have attempted to construct tests of critical thinking, it will not be easy to add tests of critical reading to our present survey tests. Yet without them, few teachers will do more than express their opinions that critical reading is important. Furthermore, experiments and practices in teaching reading will be difficult to appraise without tests.

CONCLUDING STATEMENT

Critical reading is one of the least understood and most elusive of the reading skills and abilities. At the same time critical reading is reported to be basic to appreciation of literature, to arriving at sound conclusions concerning personal and social problems, to scientific investigation—in short—to the educated man. Piecing together the scanty reports, there is evidence that critical readers can be developed but that time and effort must be directed toward instruction for this purpose throughout the school years. Self-understanding of biases and an independent inquiring attitude may contribute to continued development of critical reading throughout life.

References

1. Francis S. Chase, "Demands on the Reader in the Next Decade," in *Controversial Issues in Reading and Promising Solutions.* Supplementary Educational Monographs, No. 91. (Chicago: University of Chicago Press, 1961), p. 9.
2. *Ibid,* p. 11.
3. Leo Fay, *Developing the Ability To Read Critically.* Reading Promotion Bulletin, No. 28 (Chicago: Lyons and Carnahan), p. 1.
4. E. Elona Sochor, "The Nature of Critical Reading," *Elementary English,* XXXI (January, 1959), pp. 47–58.
5. E. Elona Sochor, "Literal and Critical Reading in Social Studies," *Journal of Experimental Education,* XXXVII (September, 1958), p. 50.
6. Roma Gans, *A Study of Critical Reading Comprehension in the Intermediate Grades.* Teachers College, Columbia University. Contributions to Education, No. 811. (New York: Bureau of Publications, Teachers College, Columbia University, 1940).
7. David H. Russell, *Children Learn To Read* (Boston: Ginn and Company, 1949), p. 305.
8. John De Boer, "Teaching Critical Reading," *Elementary English Review,* XXIII (October, 1946), p. 251.
9. William S. Gray, "Sequence of Reading Abilities," in *Sequential Development of Reading Abilities.* Supplementary Educational Monographs, No. 90. (Chicago: University of Chicago Press, 1960), p. 17.
10. *Ibid,* p. 19.
11. *Webster's New Collegiate Dictionary* (Springfield, Mass.: G. & C. Merriam, 1951), p. 197.
12. *Ibid,* p. 883.
13. David H. Russell, *Children's Thinking* (Boston: Ginn and Company, 1956), p. 292.
14. Gray, *op. cit.,* p. 17.

15. *Ibid*, p. 19.
16. De Boer, *op. cit.*, p. 252.
17. David H. Russell, *Children Learn To Read* (Boston: Ginn and Company, 1956), p. 308.
18. Arthur W. Heilman, *Principles and Practices of Teaching Reading* (Columbus, Ohio: Charles E. Merrill Books, 1961), p. 312.
19. Ruth M. Strang, *Problems in the Improvement of Reading in the High School and College* (Lancaster, Pa.: Science Press, 1938), p. 190.
20. Heilman, *op. cit.*, p. 313.
21. Gray, *loc. cit.*
22. Anne Selley McKillop, *The Relationship Between the Reader's Attitude and Certain Types of Reading Response* (New York: Teachers College, Columbia University, Bureau of Publications, 1952).
23. Robert L. McCaul, "The Effect of Attitudes Upon Reading Interpretation," *Journal of Educational Research*, XXXVII (February, 1944), p. 456.
24. Shirley H. Engle, "A Curriculum for Reflective Thinking," *The Indiana Social Studies Quarterly*, XIV (Autumn, 1961), p. 21.
25. Mary Austin *et al.*, *The Torch Lighters* (Cambridge, Mass.: Harvard University Press, 1961), pp. 48–50.
26. Madorah E. Smith, "The Preschool Child's Use of Criticism," *Child Development*, III (June, 1932), pp. 137–141.
27. Constance M. McCullough, "Responses of Elementary School Children to Common Types of Comprehension Questions," *Journal of Educational Research*, LI (September, 1957), pp. 65–70.
28. Gans, *loc. cit.*
29. "How To Detect Propaganda," Propaganda Analysis I. Publication of Institute of Propaganda Analysis (November, 1937), pp. 1–4.
30. Robert R. Nordelli, "Some Aspects of Creative Reading," *Journal of Educational Research*, L (March, 1957), pp. 495–508.
31. Wayland W. Osborn, "An Experiment in Teaching Resistance to Propaganda," *Journal of Experimental Education*, VIII (September, 1939), pp. 1–17.
32. Joseph Gainsburg, "Critical Reading Is Creative Reading and Needs Creative Teaching," *Reading Teacher*, XV (December, 1961), pp. 185–192.
33. Charles B. Huelsman, Jr., "Promoting Growth in Ability To Interpret When Reading Critically in Grades Seven to Ten," in *Promoting Growth Toward Maturity in Interpreting What Is Read*. Supplementary Educational Monographs, No. 74. (Chicago: University of Chicago Press, 1951), pp. 149–153.
34. Bernice Rogers, "Directed and Undirected Critical Reading Responses of High School Students," (Unpublished Doctoral Dissertation, Department of Education, University of Chicago, 1960), p. 209.
35. Helen K. Smith, "Research in Reading for Different Purposes," in *Changing Concepts of Reading Instruction*. International Reading Association Conference Proceedings, VI. (New York: Scholastic Magazines, 1961), pp. 119–122.

6   Suggestions for Further Reading

Few books are devoted wholly to the teaching of reading for meaning. For some understanding of the factors involved in bringing meaning to, and taking meaning from, the printed page, see Richard L. Henderson and Donald Ross Green, *Reading for Meaning in the Elementary School** (Prentice-Hall, 1969). Mildred A. Dawson (compiler), *Developing Comprehension including Critical Reading** (International Reading Association, 1968); and Martha L. King, Bernice D. Ellinger, and Willavene Wolf (eds.), *Critical Reading** (Lippincott, 1967), are collections of articles on the nature and teaching of comprehension. Other publications that consider selected aspects of comprehension include Russell G. Stauffer (ed.), *Reading and the Cognitive Processes* (International Reading Association, 1967); Russell G. Stauffer and Ronald Cramer, *Teaching Critical Reading at the Primary Level* (International Reading Association, 1968); Doris Lee and others, *Critical Reading Develops Early* (International Reading Association, 1968); and Marjorie S. Johnson and Roy Kress (eds.), *Reading and Thinking* (Temple University, 1966).

Meaning and its relation to the reading of literature are the subjects of David Russell, "Comprehension: Literal and Interpretive," in Robert B. Ruddell (ed.), *The Dynamics of Reading* (Ginn, 1970), 151–77. The content and methods and materials for developing comprehension are the subjects of Helen M. Robinson (ed.), *Sequential Development of Reading Abilities** (University of Chicago Press, 1960), 51–99; Russell G. Stauffer, *Directing Reading Maturity as a Cognitive Process* (Harper and Row, 1969), 59–84, 474–82; Albert J. Harris and Edward R. Sipay, *Effective Teaching of Reading*, 2nd edition (David McKay, 1971), 333–64; and Clifford L. Bush and Mildred H. Huebner, *Strategies for Reading in the Elementary School* (Macmillan, 1970), 95–158.

* Available in paperback

7

READING IN THE
CONTENT FIELDS

When teachers are urged to regard the teaching of reading in conjunction with study in subject areas as an integral part of the reading curriculum, three basic principles are assumed. The first is that general reading ability is a necessary foundation for reading all kinds of materials. The second is that the possession of general reading ability does not assure ability to read all kinds of materials. And the third is that some special reading abilities are associated with materials in subject areas. These assumptions are outgrowths of data obtained from investigations, demonstrations, and actual classroom experiences. To deny that the skills of reading are related cannot be supported by present knowledge; to deny that some skills possess sufficient individuality to warrant special treatment is equally tenuous.

Why are we so concerned with providing reading instruction in the content fields? Possibly the most direct answer to this question lies in our pupils' inability to meet the subject-matter demands we place upon them: to master and remember difficult concepts and their related information and to become independent learners. This weakness is associated with a number of problems. Many pupils find that subject-matter materials are more difficult to read than those which tell a story because they are passive readers; they are unfamiliar with the language; and their facility in reading is complicated by the author's style. Put another way, pupils often lack purpose in reading content, and their reading of science, social studies, mathematics, and other subjects is hindered by their inability to deal with technical vocabulary and concept load. In addition, readers often find the idea density much greater in these materials. Often these ideas are only partially explained and understood. Furthermore, they come so rapidly that many pupils feel overwhelmed.

Pupils have to be able to apply their basic reading skills with greater precision to content materials than to story-type materials. This means that they must have a good command of the higher-level word identification skills —structural analysis and use of the dictionary—as well as those skills related to phonics, context, and sight vocabulary. Moreover, to grasp the meaning intended by the authors and evaluate information and ideas, they must be able to use context clues efficiently, to recognize and infer relationships among ideas, and to apply standards to measure them.

In addition to these skills that are needed to read all kinds of materials are those having particular relevance for reading content and for engaging in independent learning activities—the study skills. Stated in behavioral terms they include the following abilities: to establish purposes for reading by making surveys; to locate information from several sources; to select information by recognizing its significance; to organize and remember information through outlining, summarizing, and notetaking; to understand the significance of graphic materials by comprehending their literal and implied meanings and by seeing relationships between the text and the graphic materials; to follow directions by understanding the relationships between the directions and the readers' purposes; to vary reading rates and styles in accordance with the readers' purposes and the nature of the materials. Pupils who learn these skills and apply them will be better able to cope with the requirements for reading in the content areas. It seems only natural for teachers to help pupils develop these and any other reading skills they need as they read in the content fields.

As Helen Huus points out, reading has no content of its own. Reading is a vehicle by which information and ideas from various fields are acquired. Reading enables pupils to build a background of experiences needed to make judgments and generalizations and to expand their knowledge. Success in any subject area depends in great measure on reading ability.

Most textbooks in social studies have internal problems such as the number and compactness of concepts introduced, the presentation of ideas without clues to their relative importance, vocabulary used in technical ways, and content that lacks appeal for some pupils. Problems exist in the pupils too: limitations in intelligence, background of information, vocabulary, command of language patterns, proper attitudes. All these have an effect on how successful pupils will be in mastering social studies content. Teachers can help pupils overcome some of the limitations by guiding them to develop vocabulary, reading flexibility, and higher comprehension. To these Huus would add another ingredient—the expansion of concepts through wide reading. While she limits her examination of reading requirements to social studies, her comments and suggestions are equally important for reading in other subject areas. Nearly all reading skills have some applicability to all content fields. Pupils merely must use some skills more often than others when reading specialized materials.

Mathematics is one subject area in which reading seems to receive hardly any recognition. This may be due in part to the fact that suggestions for reading mathematics have been limited mainly to the treatment of technical vocabulary and concepts. While there is no question that the vocabulary of mathematics involves complex relationships and symbols denoting abstract ideas, other problems in reading it are present. N. Wesley Earp notes the parallel structure of the text and worked-out examples so common in mathematics textbooks and urges that teachers "develop in children a real attitude of aggressiveness and thoroughness in discerning and following the relationships of verbal and mathematical symbols." In a sense this is similar to reading in science where diagrams parallel the text and pupils must move from text to diagram and back in order to follow complicated explanations.

Purpose in reading mathematics is important too. Children need to read for single purposes and successive purposes; they might read a problem without regard for numerals in order to determine its basic nature and then reread it to see if the problem contains all the information needed to solve it.

Teachers can train children to read mathematics problems so as to reduce the possibility of failure to solve them because of reading weaknesses. Earp suggests five steps involving several readings of the problems that pupils should follow. In addition, teachers can help children become familiar with the text's organizational structure and its typographical features. Both of these elements are there to make the textbook more useful and understandable, and pupils should learn to use them properly.

The development of work-study habits and skills is the subject of the excerpt from the article by George D. Spache. He, like others, believes that training in these habits and skills "is an absolute essential in the elementary . . . reading program." Many basal reading programs do not prepare children for the kinds of reading they must do in the content fields, and therefore teachers must add such work to the reading curriculum.

In order to make the training interesting and relevant, study skills instruction should be based on the study materials pupils are reading at that time—their own textbooks, reference materials, magazines, newspapers, and so on. Pupil requirements should determine the nature of this instruction. Teachers should observe pupils to determine how they function in study situations; pupils may be able to verbalize some of their problems.

Spache refers to study skills that are used to identify, collect, and reconstruct information. These classifications involve library and dictionary skills, using book parts, outlining, summarizing, notetaking, and retaining information. Each major skill has its own complement of subordinate skills that some pupils lack and that teachers must help pupils obtain. Included in this article are a number of suggestions for teaching the study skills.

Reading speed and comprehension (reading flexibility is a much better way to think about reading rate) are dependent on the reader's background of experience vis à vis the material, his purposes for and interest in reading, his familiarity with the writer's style, plus such factors as the physical characteristics of the material, the clarity of writing, the complexity of ideas, the reader's abilities, his personality, and his physical state. Each of these factors can play a significant role in the way a person reads.

Because reading flexibility has not been given the attention it deserves, many children cannot adjust their reading to their purposes, nor do many of them know how to read materials in order to better achieve their purposes.

They tend to read all materials at the same rate even though the levels of difficulty may vary. Many do not realize the importance of stopping or re-reading when they fail to grasp the meaning of a passage.

In order to attack the problem, J. Harlan Shores suggests that we teach middle-grade children more about the reading act so that they will know when they are reading efficiently for a given purpose. There are various reading rates, none of which is clearly defined; instead, each one varies with the reader's purpose and the nature of the material. Fast readers are not necessarily the best readers; the ability to change reading styles to fit reading needs is the mark of a superior reader.

Reading

HELEN HUUS

The ability to read is a complex process that is basic not only to education in school, but also to the acquisition of many out-of-school learnings. Although the Western World has attained a fairly high standard of literacy, there are still misconceptions regarding the nature of reading.

Reading is not merely recognizing the printed symbols and pronouncing the words correctly; it is not merely being able to reproduce verbatim or in digested or summarized form what the author has stated; it is, as Strang, McCullough, and Traxler state, "more than seeing words clearly, more than pronouncing printed words correctly, more than recognizing the meaning of individual words. Reading requires us to think, feel, and use our imagination. Effective reading is purposeful. The use one makes of his reading largely determines what he reads, why he reads, and how he reads."[1]

If a broad concept of reading is accepted, the line between reading and thinking becomes only faintly drawn. While all thinking is not reading, all reading will require thinking. Where the dividing line occurs is not within the province of this chapter; nor are all aspects of reading discussed here, for some are found elsewhere in this book. Here emphasis is placed upon vocabulary development, rate of reading, formation of relationships, and wide reading.

Reading itself has no content of its own. It is principally a skill or process by which ideas on the printed page become the reader's own. The ideas may be drawn from a variety of fields, as science, history, geography, sociology, anthropology, mathematics, and art. What makes reading important is its function as the vehicle by which the authors of any age communicate their ideas to contemporary and succeeding generations.

Since the social studies courses in schools today draw from many different disciplines and sources, the need for students to be competent readers assumes added significance. So much of the information in social studies comes from books, magazines, newspapers, pamphlets, government reports, and other

[1] Strang, Ruth; McCullough, Constance M.; and Traxler, Arthur E. *The Improvement of Reading*. New York: McGraw-Hill Book Co., 1961. p. 1.

READING by Helen Huus. From *Skill Development in Social Studies*, 33rd Yearbook of the National Council for the Social Studies, 1963, ed. Helen M. Carpenter, pp. 99–114. Reprinted with permission of the National Council for the Social Studies and Helen Huus.

printed sources dealing with a wide range of subjects that the student must put his reading skills to use if he is to acquire the background he needs to make judgments and generalizations.

Reading not only contributes to the background of information of the student and gives him practice in using the skills he has, but this background becomes, in turn, the springboard for expanding his knowledge and further enriching him. Thus the dual purpose of information and motivation is served. In addition, attitudes may be developed, reinforced, or changed through reading; and students can become acquainted with the literary heritage and cultivate a lasting interest in personal reading.

The ability to read is important for the student's success in social studies work. According to Fay, at least fourth grade reading ability is needed for social studies reading in the middle grades (four to six).[2] Rudolf found that eighth grade students who had been given specially prepared materials on certain reading skills showed greater gains in social studies knowledge, study skills, and reading comprehension than a comparable group that had no such help.[3] In a study of eleventh grade students of American history, Aukerman found that good history students were better in general reading ability than poor history students, and that social studies achievement and the ability to find the main idea of a paragraph were related to general reading ability.[4] These are but a few of the studies that show the relation between social studies and reading and emphasize the necessity for good reading habits on the part of students.

PROBLEMS OF READING IN THE SOCIAL STUDIES

While there are certain skills and abilities necessary for good general reading—such as word-analysis techniques, vocabulary and paragraph comprehension, and library skills—some of the reading skills and abilities are especially pertinent to the social studies, though many are also important in reading any specialized subject matter. The special applications lie in two directions—in the material to be read and in the reader himself.

The Reading Material

Most textbooks in social studies make heavy demands on the reader because of the number of concepts introduced in a relatively small space. The

[2] Fay, Leo C. "What Research Has to Say About Reading in the Content Areas." *The Reading Teacher* 8:68–72, 112; December 1954.

[3] Rudolf, Kathleen Brady. *The Effect of Reading Instruction on Achievement in Eighth Grade Social Studies.* Contributions to Education, No. 945. New York: Bureau of Publications, Teachers College, Columbia University, 1949. 72 pp. plus 12 unnumbered pp.

[4] Aukerman, Robert C. "The Reading Status of Good and Poor Eleventh Grade American History Students." *Social Education* 11:351–53; December 1947.

background needed by the reader to interpret briefly noted events, places, and ideas is greater than most students possess, and as a result, difficulties occur. Because the information is not explained or expanded, much of it becomes mere verbalism without images or meaning.

Another reason for difficulty in reading in social studies stems from the rapidly changing nature of the material. What becomes printed today will in a short time be past history. Two difficulties result: the lack of perspective in viewing material that was prepared in the heat of the moment before the long view could be seen, and the fact that the content will soon be superseded by a current commentary. Information regarding prehistoric life is a good example, for as methods of scientifically measuring the age of fossils are advanced and as new discoveries are made (such as the exposure of the Piltdown man hoax), the previously known facts must be reviewed and reorganized. Yet rarely are clues to the relative importance of ideas given except in the gradation of type faces used in the headings in most textbooks. Students who have access only to limited and out-of-date sources will suffer as a result.

Still a third difficulty with social studies material is its complicated style of presentation. Sentences are not only packed with information, but may be long and involved; they may use inverted order; or they may include allusions and figures of speech that need interpretation. In addition, the vocabulary load is very high, for many words are used only once or twice and thus do not give enough repetition to become fixed in the student's mind. Furthermore, technical words are often defined in such a complex manner (either in the text itself, in the glossary, or in the dictionary) that it is difficult for students to ferret out the meaning. Shortened forms, such as abbreviations, letters like NDEA or OEEC, or the symbols used in tables, and the new forms accompanying documentation, such as italics, footnotes, and bibliographical citations, need special attention even for good readers. While these problems are not unique to social studies materials, they do pose difficulties for students.

Since social studies material is usually written by experts who are committed to their field of interest, what they put in textbooks is of interest to them but may not be of much interest to sudents who read it. In the middle grades, the objective approach in the writing is also a departure from the kind of material which most of the pupils have used in learning to read, and consequently adjusting from fiction with characters and story content to factual material becomes another hurdle. The problem is further complicated in that the factual material usually deals with events which are removed from the pupil either in space or time.

Instead of dealing with the here and now or the immediate community, pupils read about explorations of the 16th century, or of colonial America, or of Latin America today. In higher grades, the curriculum includes other areas of the world—the Far East, Australia, Africa—that are remote from firsthand experiences of the majority, and other times—prehistoric man or the age of the vikings—that are difficult for students to conceptualize. Although textbook publishers have made notable efforts to provide interesting, well-illustrated books for social studies, often space limitations restrict the amount of detail and explanation that can be included, and the treatment of the topic is all too brief.

While the inclusion of much graphic material adds to the meaning, it may also pose problems in reading. The legends under the photographs may require deciphering, for often these have been streamlined to conserve space. The references to other pages in the textbook, or to "Fig. 1" (which sometimes is never explained but eventually comes to be interpreted as "Figure 1"), or to maps and charts found on other pages, or to statistics and tabular data need explanation and practice in interpretation if they are to serve their best use.[5]

Thus it appears that many of the difficulties found in social studies reading lie in the nature of the materials themselves. Hence, it behooves teachers carefully to select material which will provide for the best understanding by the pupils.

The Reader Himself

Other limitations in reading are inherent in the reader himself—his intelligence, his background of information, his vocabulary and command of sophisticated language patterns, his attitudes and value pattern. The nature of the material to be read demands of the reader sufficient intelligence and background not only to derive literal meanings but also to infer hidden meanings and to make applications from what is read.

Intellectual ability is required for a reader to sift facts from opinion, to analyze the point of view from which the author is writing, to be aware of biases (both his own and the author's), and to recognize when enough facts have been presented that a valid conclusion can be drawn. His background of information serves as a reservoir from which concepts are recognized, recalled, and compared with the content being read in order to make the meaning clear. Practice is necessary to obtain competence in these skills of inference and application, and even students with a high level of intellectual capacity need instruction in order to acquire such competence.

Studies show that readers tend to remember best those facts and ideas that reinforce their own views and to reject or ignore material on other sides of an issue, whether it be political, religious, racial, or ethical.[6] The development of attitudes and the acquisition of information are, to a great extent, dependent upon firsthand experiences. As attitudes are gradually acquired and as value patterns unconsciously begin to take shape with increasing age, young people bring to their reading the products of their heredity and

---

[5] Other problems involved in learning to read graphic material are discussed in Chapter XI.

[6] Crossen, Helen Jameson. *Effect of Attitudes of the Reader upon Critical Reading Ability.* Chicago: Departmen of Education, University of Chicago, 1946. 133 pp.; Eller, William, and Dykstra, Robert. "Persuasion and Personality: Readers' Predispositions as a Factor in Critical Reading." *Elementary English* 36:191–97, 202; March 1959.

environment—their family and friends, their neighborhood and community, their state and nation. The approach they take, the interpretations they can make, and the ideas they accept or reject are permeated by their feelings and beliefs.

What the reader obtains from his reading and thinking about what is read is difficult to assess completely. Tangible evidence of the effect of reading, however, can be seen in behavior such as willingness to share, improvement in social courtesies, interest in civic improvements, and concern with national and international issues.

If reading is an important means of social studies learning, if the materials for social studies present unique problems in reading, and if the reader is the product of his heredity and past experiences, what can a teacher do to help? The school offers many opportunities for teachers to guide students in developing reading skills as achievement in social studies progresses; especially important are the skills of vocabulary development, rate of reading, formation of relationships, and extension of reading. These skills are discussed in the sections that follow.

DEVELOPING VOCABULARY

Types of Difficulty

Problems in the social studies vocabulary are principally those of pronunciation and meaning. In the first category are the many proper names met for the first time: in primary grades, names like Pilgrim, Puritan, Samoset, Massasoit, Plymouth Colony, Massachusetts Bay, and Elder Brewster; in the middle grades, words like Antarctic, Amazon, Switzerland, Colorado, Illinois, and Arkansas; in junior high, such words as Indonesia, Saudi Arabia, Angola, Committee of Correspondence, and Reconstruction; and in senior high or college, words like Aristotle, Attila, Renaissance, and Byzantine. It matters not at what level the word is first met; correct pronunciation and definite meaning are still required.

In addition to proper names, terms like *shelter, community, patriotic, interdependence, transportation, industrial, guild, conservation, colonization, imperialism,* and many others need to be interpreted. Students need to learn to use word-recognition techniques—context clues, analysis of structure, and phonetic elements—and to check their best estimates against the authority of a glossary or the dictionary. In many schools today, students are given adequate help in learning to unlock words of one syllable, but so many of the words in social studies have more than one. All too many children have no systematic method by which they can analyze multisyllabic words and arrive at a reasonable pronunciation. Giving help on recognition skills is the responsibility of teachers, even of those above the beginning levels; secondary teachers, too, need to check the recognition skills to detect areas of need. This is true even when helps for pronunciation are included in the material.

Students should be helped to recognize known word elements like pre-fixes, roots, and suffixes; once the word is thus stripped down to the chassis and the framework located, the synthesis can proceed systematically. Take the word "Alhambra," for example: Students can subdivide it into syllables, and those who know that divisions are usually made between double consonants will have no hesitancy. They figure out "Al-ham-bra" and proceed from there. Or take the word "Indonesia": Using the same generalization, the first syllable becomes "In," and the pupils who knows the generalization that a syllable usually ends *before* a single consonant will be able to separate the word into "In-do-ne-sia." If he knows that a syllable ending with a vowel is usually long, he should be able to arrive at a fair pronunciation, which he can check against his own experience or against a glossary or the dictionary.

Teachers who work with grades above the third would be wise to include in their word study the variations in pronunciation due to derivations from Greek, Latin, French, Spanish, or German. Just a few generalizations will aid the student, and the teaching can be done when the various countries are studied for the first time.

For many words in social studies the pupil already has at least one meaning, but not the meaning that fits the situation—words like *branch, cape, mouth, source, range, plain, belt, cancer, gap, pan,* and *quarter.* To extend the pupil's vocabulary so that he acquires additional meanings is both important and necessary. Too often, however, both teachers and pupils skip over known words, assuming the meaning to be clear, but pupils who are taught to demand meaning from the very start will check words that appear not to make sense when met in a new context.

To complicate matters still further, some words shift their meanings in the same selection, and the reader must keep abreast of the changes. Most usual of these shifts are the pronouns *it* and *that,* which shift their referents, or words like *regular* when applied to winds, mountain ranges, trade routes, or the army.

But the most complicated of the vocabulary problems stems from the myriads of new words—words unknown both in pronunciation and in meaning. Here the reader must apply his word-recognition techniques to acquire pronunciation, then use context to try to define meaning. Later he can check against the glossary or dictionary, or he can use what association he has and continue reading to see if the concept will clarify itself. If he uses the dictionary, he may need to try several of the meanings for "fit" before he finds the one that suits. When the vocabulary load becomes burdensome because of the large number of new words, it is easier for students to skip along, hoping that the meaning will be clarified in later discussions with little effort on their part. This becomes the plight of the slow learner and the poor reader, and eventually, when the vocabulary load has become too large, they simply quit trying to read.

A recent issue of *National Geographic,* a magazine often used in the secondary school as well as in upper elementary grades, contains the following unusual words or phrases in the space of a few pages in an article on New Zealand:[7] "Rotorua," "thermal district," "Polynesia," "cold tussock deserts," "Thames," "Chelsea," "nomad," "after a spell in Spain," "bush," "kauri gum," "kiwi," "Maori," "Cape Maria van Dieman," *"Heemskerck,"* and "Governor General." Some of these terms ("bush," "thermal," and "spell") are known words whose meanings can be inferred from context. Others, however, such as "tussock," meaning a "tuft of growing grass," are likely to become intelligible only through use of the dictionary. Words like "Cape Maria van Dieman" and *"Heemskerck"* require some knowledge of foreign pronunciation. The necessarily heavy vocabulary load of materials that deal with foreign cultures or times past complicates the process of reading and learning.

To add to the difficulty, there are phrases and abstract terms that require interpretation, such as "the Crown's representative," "flung lonely, as by some giant hand," "a treasure locked in vast ocean," "gift of the sea," "dominion," "sovereignty," and "eating up 2000 acres of good farmland." To make sense from these in context demands attention and concentration, plus bringing to bear the pertinent past experiences.

Practical Aids for Vocabulary Development

Many opportunities for providing direct experience as an aid in understanding the meanings of words and phrases are at hand for the teacher who can recognize them. In the primary grades, classes can take excursions into the community to such places as the bus station, the grocery store, and the airport to see at first hand some of the service units and agencies. On their return to school, the pupils can make charts containing a list of the new words learned, and the charts can be continued as they learn additional words that fit into the same context. Firsthand experiences of this kind also clarify children's concepts of abstract terms and relationships, such as the processes employed in distributing mail or in putting out a newspaper, the work done by various employees, the physical environment in which work is done, and the specialized equipment that is necessary.

While the purpose of the educational excursion may be the same for the various grade levels, the length and complexity of a tour will increase with the age of the students. Even though pupils at all levels may visit the airport, for example, those in the higher grades acquire information in more areas and in greater detail and abstraction, learn more technical terms, and understand more complex relationships, such as the financial aspects or the airport's contribution to community economics, than do children in the primary grades.

The middle grades also profit from somewhat more complex excursions

[7] Shadbolt, Maurice. "New Zealand: Gift of the Sea." *National Geographic* 121:465–511; April 1962.

to the dairy, factory, newspaper offices, and docks, while secondary school students may take a day's trip to a nearby historical site, a museum, a governmental agency, or a city. Some schools have provided student exchanges for several days at a time with another school in another city.

Other types of firsthand experiences that increase meaning vocabulary can be acquired by students at all levels without leaving the classroom. Inviting visitors to come to the class, or having an exhibit relating to units being studied, gives students a chance to hear explanations or see products and specimens that clarify meanings. When they were studying Mexico, one sixth grade class collected a serape, a sombrero, horses made of straw, silver jewelry, glassware, pottery, hand-embroidered blouses, and other objects made by Mexicans. These same objects could have been used by a third grade or a tenth grade for an exhibit of *their* study of Mexico, but the arrangement, the relationships, and the labels and legends for the various items would vary with the purpose and the maturity of the learners.

When firsthand experience is impractical or impossible, simulated experiences that come as close as possible to reality will serve the purpose. The many filmstrips, films, recordings, models, pictures, pictorial maps, graphs, and charts are in this category. Let the teacher add these to put meaning into the printed symbols and to give the student a feeling of actually living in another place or during another era.

Helpful also, and it requires no additional materials, is the use of discussion, explanation, or exposition to clarify and extend vocabulary and meaning. Helping children make associations between what they already know and what is new can aid not only in understanding, but also in remembering, if the presentation has been vivid enough. Teachers should create or locate colorful, clear explanations, examples, and analogies that help the pupil understand new terms, new information, and new ideas, so that these become real enough for him to identify himself with the situations. The teacher will need to decide how many of the terms and ideas in one lesson he should explain and which are the ones most needed by the pupils. The number will depend upon the complexity of the ideas and the rate at which they are introduced, but there is danger of misunderstanding or confusion when too many terms are introduced too fast.

Some teachers get good results in vocabulary development by encouraging pupils to keep individual lists of interesting or difficult words. In the primary grades this might take the form of a picture dictionary, while in later grades it could become part of a larger word-study project where derivations are discussed and related words coming from the same root (*script, describe, conscription, inscription, subscription,* and *scribe,* for example), are listed. Pupils extend their vocabularies by repeated use of new words, and opportunities to utilize them in exercises or in compositions should be provided. Regular use of the glossary and dictionary and special exercises employing these aids are other ways to improve vocabulary, and teachers can sometimes use a series of words from social studies as a springboard. For example, *government, parliament, capital, kingdom, empire, republic, nation,* and *country* are terms that need to be distinguished, and a glossary or the dictionary can be used to advantage to compare the specific meanings and to help children develop accurate concepts.

Junior and senior high school students might construct other lists containing certain types of words, such as "fighting words"; or words connoting speed, prestige, depression, or other emotional reactions. Study of words of this type is basic to detecting how authors create mood or tone in such materials as editorials, advertising, or reports of political activities. Helping students recognize and interpret these is a teacher responsibility that continues through graduate courses.

If students can get meaning from words in context, they have the basic element for interpreting what they read. Without the basic building blocks, however, this skill cannot be developed.

ADJUSTING OR ADAPTING RATE OF READING

A reader's rate of reading is affected by his mental capacity and basic reading skills, his familiarity with the field of study, and the level of difficulty of the material, as well as by his purpose for reading. Versatile, mature readers will vary the speed according to their purposes. A slight story in a popular magazine will not be read at the same rate as study material in a social studies textbook. Neither will all parts of the newspaper, such as the editorials, the advertisements, or other features that are of interest to the reader at the moment, be read with the same intensity.

Different rates from the fastest to the slowest have been variously labeled, but there appears to be general agreement that there are at least four levels in rate of reading: (1) skimming, (2) cursory reading, (3) study reading, and (4) critical reading.

Skimming

The most rapid kind of reading consists of merely looking for key words in order to locate the exact place where information may be found, to obtain a general survey, or bird's-eye view, of a longer selection before settling down to read it carefully, or to determine whether the selection is relevant to the problem under consideration. Location skimming is used primarily in reference work with dictionaries, atlases, encyclopedias, almanacs, or directories, while survey skimming is used to decide what the framework of the article is and what parts are pertinent to the problem at hand.

For example, teachers can ask students to make a list of topics covered in the sections about Central and Southern Africa found in their textbooks or in an encyclopedia article on Africa, and then to indicate which part of the lesson or article deals with certain aspects of the topic, such as coffee production in Ethiopia, the industries of South Africa, or the importance of Johannesburg or Cape Town.

Even first-graders can skim to find answers to questions on material they have read, to locate specific words on a page, to "find the part that tells . . ." or to review word-recognition skills. Later, elementary school pupils use skimming to locate words in the dictionary, places on maps, articles or sections of articles in the encyclopedia, or to hunt for such elusive data as dates, amounts of money, exact quotations, and the like. They use survey skimming to learn the length of an assignment, to see the general headings of the main parts of the lesson, or to find the part they want to read. In junior and senior high school the same skills are used, only the contents become more varied and increase in difficulty. This is true of nearly every skill in reading that can be mentioned: The beginnings lie in the primary grades, and problems of learning are different in degree, not in kind, from the primary grades through secondary school and college. This is contrary to a widely held but incorrect idea that the process of teaching reading skills moves in a sequence which introduces problems requiring higher levels of thinking at later grades, rather than one which permits the five- and six-year-olds to grapple with these problems at their level of development.‾

Asking pupils to "look" for the "part that tells . . ." rather than to "read" until they find the "part that tells . . ." is often helpful in getting them to skip around the print. Suggestions that they use such clues as a specific word (like "lumbering"), capital letters, dates, italicized words, words in quotations or in boldface type, guide words, or headings are also hints that may prove useful to them. In the long run, skimming contributes to good study habits, for it saves wasting time and energy on irrelevant material and facilitates the location of pertinent information.

Cursory Reading

Cursory reading, also, is used at all grade levels. In this type of reading, pupils read a selection through once as rapidly as they can, skipping over unknown words and pressing on to obtain a general overview or the main idea. This is akin to skimming but requires the reading of main units in more detail than skimming does. Cursory reading is also useful as a review of previously read material in order to make a summary, to generalize, to validate impressions, to check on the main idea, to formulate questions on the material, or to determine the relevance of the whole to the problem at hand. When pupils have trouble in acquiring the necessary rhythm to "scoot along" in cursory reading, it may be helpful to give them much easy material spaced in thought units or to have them pick out the thought units or groups of words in a selection that may be seen at one look.

Primary grade children use this type of reading when they prepare to dramatize a story, when they reread to choose their favorite story, or when they read to formulate questions of their own. Middle-graders often utilize cursory reading as the first step in their study, as recommended by the "Survey, Question, Read, Recite, Review" (SQ3R) technique. In secondary school, and to a greater degree in college, the rate of reading becomes increasingly important as the assignments increase in length. Students with poor word-recognition techniques, who are word-by-word readers, and who lack a background of experience necessary for easy comprehension will find their rates of reading much too low for academic success or efficient study habits. Practical exercises in word attack, phrase reading, and firsthand experiences or browsing in well-illustrated books, looking at informational films, and using other visual aids are ways to improve reading rate indirectly. Once basic skills are attained, timed reading aids in increasing speed, but unless basic skills are established first, reading under the pressure of time will not bring the desired result in speed without loss of comprehension.

Study Reading

Study reading is a third type of reading to which rate must be adjusted at any grade level. This type of reading is done to obtain the greatest possible understanding, such as reading to visualize a scene, to comprehend directions, to follow an argument, to make an outline, to prepare a play, to get information for making a mural, to write entries for a fictitious diary, to take an open-book examination, or just to remember and organize what has been read. Teachers can have young children draw a scene that is described in the story; older pupils can construct dioramas, from miniature size in a shoe box to the almost life size demanded for stage scenery.

Most of all, however, students need to be able to read with optimum speed and concentration as they prepare their daily class assignments. In the middle grades, pupils can be helped to note how the structure they found as they were skimming the selection is completed with explanation, elaboration, and example, and how the parts fit together to make the whole. They can perceive how events build up to a climax—whether it be a revolution, a new discovery, or the fall of an empire—then list the significant events in order to see the gradual, logical progression. With such understanding, making an outline is merely putting these ideas down in written form according to a prescribed pattern. Without this understanding, outlining becomes merely a confused listing of topics identified by numbers and letters.

Many activities that follow from reading can be accomplished only when pupils have paid attention to the details in the lesson and have remembered them. This type of reading is an essential tool for effective study, and unless it can be done with enough ease and speed to keep abreast of assignments, achievement will suffer.

Critical Reading

Critical, or reflective, reading proceeds at the slowest rate of all, for here the reader pauses to recall and associate, to reflect and compare, to ponder over an apt saying and appreciate the author's skill, to note and evaluate the style of writing, the mood created, or the author's purpose. This kind of reading is typical of readers who savor what they read and hesitate to quit, for they are truly making what they read their own.

Critical reading begins in the primary grades when children are given a chance to relate what they read to their own experiences. They can compare the farms in the stories with those they have seen, or the contributions of community helpers with their own policemen, firemen, and postmen. Even at this level they can use several sources for their information, note similarities and differences, and decide which book gives them the clearest and most complete and interesting information.

In the later elementary grades, pupils can note relationships, images, or feelings identified by allusions and references like *Spice Islands, kaiser, Caesar, czar,* and *the bread basket of America.* In secondary schools, as students delve into the whole realm of adult writings, they are faced with even more complex patterns of style. Secondary school students, too, need to track down allusions, to note the emotional appeal of words like *colossal, incredible, elegant, infallible, extravagant, restless, oppressed, poverty-stricken,* and *harsh,* and to recognize the author's point of view and purpose. Is he trying to convert or debunk? Is he presenting factual information or only his opinion? Is his style direct and straightforward, or is he writing "tongue in cheek?" These are only a few of the kinds of analyses that critical reading requires. Others are discussed in the following section.[8]

In each of the four types of reading discussed above, teachers should encourage students to read at their optimum rate without comprehension loss. While improvement of rate of reading is not the crucial skill in the elementary school that it becomes in secondary school and college, nevertheless attention to the four types of reading and the purpose of each should aid a student in adjusting his rate for each purpose which, in turn, should improve his study habits.

FORMING RELATIONSHIPS

Basic to the acquisition of concepts through reading in social studies or in any field of study is the ability to recognize the way in which the material is organized, whether in sequence or logically, and to see the relationships that are stated directly or implied; to analyze connections between events so that inferences can be made as to cause and effect; to form mental

---

[8] See also Chapters III and V.

images of space and distance; to recall and make judgments from the perspective gained by combining past experiences with present knowledge; and to see similarities between what is read with what has been previously experienced or [to] determine what can be applied to present-day life. The remainder of this section describes a few ways by which such relationships can be developed.

Relationships Inherent in Organization

Unlike stories typically found in many basic readers, social studies content may be written in an objective, reportorial fashion, which presents an account of events as they occurred. In the lower grades, pupils can obtain practice in understanding the idea of sequence by retelling stories or events in order, by giving directions, and by making picture charts, flow charts showing events in a series, or time lines with appropriate notations in the right segments. Children's understanding of chronology is thought to develop relatively slowly, and it is not until the child is 11 or 12 that he begins to have a clear notion of chronology, and then only for a limited span. Time lines in the fourth grade do show pupils' relative position, but the relation between the early explorations and the late 19th century is still quite vague to most of them.

In lower grades, studying a specific period, such as "Pioneer Days in the Middle West" or "Children of Colonial Days," helps pupils obtain a feeling of what it might have been like to have lived then, and to realize that the people who did live then are not necessarily to be pitied or envied, but rather to be understood. When the period being studied can be related to the child personally, perhaps to his own family or to the local area, a firsthand connection of this kind can be most useful in concept development. By secondary school age, some students may be sufficiently interested in family genealogy to trace their own heritage and relate it to historical development.

As the pupil gradually fits together the pieces of history he has been studying, he assembles in the mosaic of his memory a picture of the development of civilization. By the time he reaches high school and college, not only should he understand the chronological development of various segments of the world, but he should be able to see the cross-sectional view as well.

The logical development of an idea by the building-up of a reasonable line of argument can be begun with materials for the primary grades and continued on to adult books. Students can tell whether main ideas succeed each other in proper order, whether one idea evolves from the preceding idea, whether all ideas are substantiated, explained, or expanded with appropriate detail.[9] It should be emphasized, however, that the beginnings of

---

[9] See Chapter V, which treats this topic more fully.

the concept underlying logical organization can be started even before children learn to read—as they classify objects and ideas at home or in kindergarten. In the first grade, children can make simple outlines of main ideas and their related details by drawing lines between the main idea in one column and the appropriate details in another column, by helping make a group outline, or by making a mental outline of the three (or more) things to say when given a chance in "Show and Tell."

Primary grade children, like older ones, can also write sentence or short paragraph summaries, and can note signals like *first, second,* and *third* that give warning when the author is about to make a shift. Later on, such signals include words like *next, then, another, finally, moreover, yet, still, at last, meanwhile, furthermore,* and *later.*[10]

In secondary school, even more subtle hints of shift in topic can be pointed out, such as the phrases *on the other hand, in addition to, opposing this,* and *in contrast to.* Individual students could be encouraged to keep a list of such phrases, or the class might compile a master list from their collective efforts.

Cause-Effect Relationships

Seeing the connection between events and results is basic to the interpretation of facts in the social studies. Such relationships may be chronological, and students at any age can make double-column charts lining up events on one side and results on the other, or make a list of events as they build toward a climax.

Beginning in the middle grades, an understanding of cause and effect in geography can result from studying a physical map and noting how features such as terrain, coast line, drainage basins, and relative location may be helpful in predicting population centers, occupations the land can support, and what products will probably be available for trade. With the addition of temperature, rainfall, and prevailing wind data, students should be able to make even more accurate predictions, which can then be checked against political maps and industrial and commercial statistics. Making such an analysis of a map not only gives students practice in seeing relationships, but also shows them a method for making logical deductions from data and for interrelating several items of data in order to arrive at a conclusion.

Space-and-Distance Relationships

The relationships of space and distance, both on the surface of the earth and in the atmosphere, also come within the scope of social studies

[10] Cansler, Gleamon. "Readiness for Reading in Content Fields." *The Reading Teacher* 8:73–77; December 1954.

content. The beginnings of these concepts can be found in the lower grades as pupils compare the distances they travel to school, to the shopping center, to church, or to the city. They make maps of local neighborhoods, put these on the floor and suddenly see their community as a whole. Later, they study road maps, physical and political maps, product and rainfall maps, and maybe even hydrographic and astronomical charts, and compare distances on these with what they already know. They build mental images of space, but not always too clearly: even adults have difficulty in grasping how far away the sun, moon, and planets really are, or the relative distance between San Diego and Seattle as compared with that between New York and Minneapolis. Such a simple technique as using a piece of string and a globe can show the reason why a great circle route appears curved on a flat map. Using maps with various projections and comparing distances with those on the globe helps students understand the distortion inherent in most flat projections. All of these activities aid students in their acquisition of ideas about space and distance.[11]

Relative Importance of Ideas

Determining the relative importance of several main ideas found in a selection or judging which of several causes are the crucial ones requires not only an effective reading approach but intelligence as well. Primary grade children have practice in this when they first choose main ideas in stories heard or read, then line up the ideas in sequence and decide what the story is about. They also have experience in placing concepts in more general categories: so "community" may be a larger grouping than "town" or "farm," and "city" is a larger grouping than "neighborhood" or "shopping center."

At higher grade levels, importance may be determined by having students analyze events and decide the "point of no return" in the procession toward a goal or action. In retrospect, students can interpret and speculate on what might have happened. For example, suppose Marco Polo had not gone to China: How long might it have taken to create widespread interest among Europeans in products from the Orient?

Relative importance may be judged in another manner by reading accounts from more than one source and noting which events are always mentioned and which are sometimes omitted. Frequency of mention does not necessarily indicate importance, yet the very fact that several writers deem an event of sufficient consequence to be elaborated does aid students in judging importance. Such comparisons can be started in primary grades as pupils pursue a unit using several sources, including both trade books and textbooks. The learning can be carried forward through elementary

[11] These and other aspects of developing skill in understanding concepts of place and space are discussed in Chapter IX.

school, secondary school, and into college as students read widely and compare. It is only from such a background that valid techniques for judging importance can be fostered, and teachers should aid students in developing a perspective from the limited view they possess.

Application to Personal Experience

Still another way of seeing relationships is to apply what has been read to personal experiences—for validation, assimilation, enjoyment, or utilization. Young children read stories of airplane trips, relate these to their own experience with airplanes and airports, then build the images into a mental framework in which each individual may visualize sequence along a kind of horizontal time line, with specific reference points of significance to him, or on a vertical pattern with steps or stages progressing upward according to defined levels—perhaps by centuries or decades, or according to significant events like grandmother's golden wedding anniversary, the first voyage of Columbus to the New World, or the fall of Rome. As new information is acquired, it, in turn, is stored away in its proper place for future reference.

Young children and immature learners need more concrete experiences and utilize inductive reasoning more than do older children and mature learners, who can shift to the abstract and to deductive approaches.[12] As the child progresses through school, he becomes increasingly independent of firsthand experience as the basis for building concepts and begins to deal with symbols and abstractions. With increasing age and conscious application the ability to relate expands, so that by adolescence he can relate not only to himself, but also to the larger group and to society.

Learning to make sequential, logical, cause-effect, and space relations and to determine their significance and application are important tasks of reading in the social studies, for otherwise many facts would remain unordered and the impact of their interactions would be lost or misinterpreted by students.

EXPANDING CONCEPTS

One of the best ways to expand the concepts of students and to enlarge their store of information is to promote wide reading from various sources. The unit method provides this and encourages pupils at the start to read in order to learn enough to raise pertinent questions for study. Thus in introducing a unit at any level, it is good procedure to provide for browsing materials that will aid students in formulating their questions. Answering these questions becomes, in turn, the purpose for further reading. This

[12] Vinacke, W. Edgar. "Concept Formation in Children of School Ages." *Education* 74:527–34; May 1954.

arouses interest which sparks additional reading, raises other questions, and the circle continues until the unit is culminated.

Students read many types of material—biography, fiction, almanacs, journals, newspapers, textbooks, reports, government documents, for example. They compare and relate, they judge quality and style, they analyze and organize. Then they synthesize their findings and share what they have found through oral reports, written compositions, booklets, articles, murals, charts, graphs, slides, or other pictorial means, and in turn receive the benefit from the work produced by their fellow students.

Many beautiful library books contain the human elements, the story detail so often lacking in a paragraph of text that dismisses a decade in one sentence.[13] Students at all levels, of all abilities, need books that give them a chance to identify themselves with ancient Rome or Norman England, or with the inhabitants of present-day Lebanon or India. It is books such as these that form the woof of the tapestry woven into the warp of the text. And beautiful illustrations not only give aesthetic satisfaction, but often clarify meanings as the student reads.

Perhaps the most lasting value, however, is the development of a liking for books and of the habit of reading that persist long after students leave school. Such permanent use of reading, wisely done, is one of the major reasons for teaching reading, and the interest engendered through wide reading in social studies offers one spur to continual use of books.

SUMMARY

Reading *is* important to the social studies. The broad concept of reading requires not only that the reader obtain the literal meanings, but also that he interpret and apply what he reads. The developmental reading program is concerned with the basic skills of word recognition and full comprehension; but there are special applications that must be made to reading in the social studies because of the number and compactness of concepts introduced, the relative importance of the ideas presented (often with no clue), the objective and symbolic style of the language used, and the lack of appeal of the content to some students. The main avenues to improvement in reading discussed in this chapter are the development of

[13] Carpenter, Helen McCracken, and Gaver, Mary Virginia. "Making History Live Through Reading." *Interpreting and Teaching American History.* (Edited by William H. Cartwright and Richard L. Watson.) Thirty-First Yearbook. Washington, D.C.: National Council for the Social Studies, a department of the National Education Association, 1961. pp. 398–414; the World History Bibliography Committee of NCSS, Alice W. Spieseke, chairman. *World History Book List for High Schools: A Selection for Supplementary Reading.* Bulletin No. 31. Washington, D.C.: National Council for the Social Studies, a department of the National Education Association, 1959. 119 pp.; and Huus, Helen. *Children's Books To Enrich the Social Studies: For the Elementary Grades.* Bulletin No. 32. Washington, D.C.: National Council for the Social Studies, a department of the National Education Association, 1961. 196 pp.

vocabulary, the improvement of rate in relation to purpose, the formation of various types of relationships, and the expansion of concepts through extended reading.

If teachers help students catch the spirit of people down through the ages and in the world today, if history and geography are changed from cold facts to human beings continually striving toward progress, and if through reading, each student begins to realize his own place in this continuum of civilization, then truly reading has made its contribution.

Suggestions for Further Reading

COVELL, HAROLD M. "Reading and the Social Studies." *Social Education* 21:14–16; January 1957.

> This report of a study of the characteristics of good and poor readers of social studies material at the eleventh grade level lists nine points of difference between them. Several ways by which teachers can work to improve the reading ability of students, as implied by this study, are also included.

DALLOLIO, HELEN CAREY. "Trends in Geographic Content Re-Emphasizes Difficulties in Reading." *Journal of Geography* 58:144–49; March 1959.

> Difficulties of vocabulary, concept formation, and problems of location and distance and of organization are discussed. Some suggestions for helping pupils overcome these difficulties are given, especially in the section on organization.

FAY, LEO; HORN, THOMAS; and MCCULLOUGH, CONSTANCE. *Improving Reading in the Elementary Social Studies.* Bulletin No. 33. Washington, D.C.: National Council for the Social Studies, a department of the National Education Association, 1961. 72 pp.

> Nine questions often asked by teachers form the chapter titles of this pamphlet. The answers give suggestions for coping with individual differences, utilizing the textbook effectively, teaching the use of charts, graphs, maps, pictures, reference books, and library resources, and helping pupils develop good reading and work-study skills so that they become thoughtful, critical readers.

GROSS, RICHARD E., and BADGER, WILLIAM V. "Social Studies: Reading in Relation to the Social Studies." *Encyclopedia of Educational Research.* Third Edition. (Edited by Chester W. Harris.) New York: The Macmillan Co., 1960. p. 1310.

> This section presents a summary of research studies relating to the reading of material in social studies. It is most useful as an overview and for locating specific studies pertinent to a problem.

HARRIS, ALBERT J. *Effective Teaching of Reading.* New York: David McKay Co., 1962. Chapter 12.

> Chapter 12, which is devoted to the development of efficiency in functional reading, deals with skills in locating information, reading specific subject matter, and organizing and summarizing and with the effective use of these skills.

HEILMAN, ARTHUR W. *Principles and Practices of Teaching Reading.* Columbus, Ohio: Charles E. Merrill Books, Inc., 1961. Chapter 8 (pp. 268–98) and Chapter 9.

> The last part of Chapter 8 includes many ideas for teaching reading in the intermediate grades that can also be adapted for use in the secondary school, such as the development of concepts and pronunciation, improvement of the rate of reading, and development of study skills. Chapter 9 defines the prerequisites for critical reading and includes a section on "What the School Can Do."

PRESTON, RALPH C.; SCHNEYER, J. WESLEY; and THYNG, FRANC J. *Guiding the Social Studies Reading of High School Students.* Bulletin No. 34. Washington, D.C.: National Council for the Social Studies, a department of the National Education Association, 1963. 79 pp.

Discusses importance and need for guidance of reading, together with techniques for meeting individual differences for improving comprehension of social studies textbooks and for stimulating wide reading of nontext materials.

STRANG, RUTH, and BRACKEN, DOROTHY KENDALL. *Making Better Readers.* Boston: D. C. Heath and Co., 1957. Chapters 3 and 5.

Chapter 3 includes suggestions for teaching paragraph comprehension, outlining, word meanings, and critical reading at the high school level. Chapter 5 applies reading techniques to various subjects in the high school curriculum. While only one section (pp. 220–42) relates specifically to social studies, other suggestions in the chapter may also be adapted and applied to this field of study.

Procedures for Teaching Reading in Mathematics

N. WESLEY EARP

All teachers, Yoakam has said, should be reading teachers regardless of their content specialization [12]. The reading teacher specialist can effectively work on some content skills, but the only place to teach some of the reading pertinent to a content area is in the class dealing with that material. Teachers of self-contained classes, moreover, must be committed to the fact that reading instruction must go on all day—out of the social studies text and the arithmetic book, from reference materials, from all the symbolic sources the child encounters.

Suggestions dealing with reading in arithmetic follow. There is significant agreement among researchers and authorities on the importance of these ideas [3, 4, 5, 9, 10, 11]. Teachers will be able to discern from some of them the actual procedures that might be used in classrooms to furnish instruction. With respect to others, teaching activities need to be devised and tested.

Research has demonstrated that concerned researchers and teachers can bring about improvement in reading in mathematics even using empirically devised procedures. Perhaps the next thrust of research then, should be to seek out and prove teaching procedures in a carefully controlled way. Even

PROCEDURES FOR TEACHING READING IN MATHEMATICS by N. Wesley Earp. Reprinted from the *Arithmetic Teacher*, November 1970 (vol. 17, p. 575–79), © 1970 by the National Council of Teachers of Mathematics. Used by permission.

from the general treatment possible at this time, however, the thoughtful teacher engaged in classroom practice should be able to create effective learning experiences.

Children must be brought to understand the nature of verbal arithmetical material. They must recognize that it is conceptually packed material with a high density factor which requires at least three kinds of adjustment: adjustment of rate (this material must be read much slower than narrative materials), varied eye movement (much more in the way of right-to-left and other types of regressive eye movement will be used), rereading (even the most advanced reader may need to read a problem or explanation several times).

The nature of arithmetic material is also such that the child is likely to be dealing with two or three sets of symbolic meaning within one context. The child who synthesizes conceptual meaning for regular verbal symbols, numerical symbols, and literal symbols in one passage is dealing with a complex task. One of the lesser obstacles with which he must deal is that of applying word-attack skills. He must have the proper conceptual background for understanding the verbalism and the arithmetical symbolism before he can read effectively. His need of background for the latter must be met by the arithmetic teacher. The child who has a weak conceptual background in the vocabulary, signs, and symbols of arithmetic will read poorly no matter how much reading instruction he has had.

One additional point on the nature of printed arithmetical material: Often there is a parallel structure where the reader must follow both verbal context and a worked-out example or where he must relate context to tabular material. For instance, in the most recent edition of a popular arithmetic series a page on the multiplication algorithm has two worked-out computations. In a related paragraph of verbal and numerical symbols twelve questions are raised concerning the two samples [8, p. 37]. In the same text children are asked to work on one page in terms of data shown by both table and graph on two different pages [8, pp. 255–56]. Children often have difficulty with such an arrangement. Phillips has suggested that using hands as well as eyes might be helpful to children who are in the learning stage of relating the two kinds of language [9]. However we do it, we must develop in children a real attitude of aggressiveness and thoroughness in discerning and following the relationships of verbal and mathematical symbols.

In regular reading instruction the child is asked to read for some particular purpose. He can concentrate on one thing at a time. Spencer and Russell suggest that the child seldom reads in arithmetic for just one purpose [10]. Here his purposes are frequently many: to grasp the total idea, to note sequence, to relate two significant ideas, and to find the key question—to name a few. For this reason, in the subsequent section on problem solving, several readings are recommended.

Authorities do suggest, however, that children should at times be given a single purpose or successive purposes for reading in the arithmetic text-book. This may be done by asking a question or giving a particular direction. As an example, consider this problem: "A family left home at 8 A.M. They reached their destination, 335 miles away, at 4 P.M. What was their average speed in miles per hour?" [8, p. 140]. The child may be asked to read with-out concern for the numerals involved to determine the basic nature of the problem (averaging). Or the child may be asked if the essential information for averaging is present. A different purpose for each of two or three readings of the passage could be stated.

Symbolic devices such as graphs, charts, and diagrams are related to all areas of the curriculum but are more pertinent to mathematics than to any other content field. Noting and using the relationship that is usually being portrayed in these devices is invaluable training for reading in arithmetic. The child should be taught to read all titles and labels and to note the means used by the writer to show various relationships. Using these aids as a corol-lary to verbal context to furnish needed data in problem solving is a worth-while procedure. In the typical classroom youngsters could doubtless learn much more about charts and graphs by making them. At any time that data are available in the routine work of the class, the information should be organized in some such form. The author recently observed first grade groups successfully making and reading graphs. Second graders can readily chart such factors as weather information.

Every content area has its own technical language. Arithmetic has more distinctly technical language at the elementary level than any other school subject, with the possible exception of science. Thus there is no alternative to the consistent, planned, and thorough teaching of vocabulary. The hear-say-see-write approach can be effective in teaching the actual terms, but in-ductive work where possible is additionally recommended in order that children develop the concept underlying the terminology. Even the child who can give a textbook definition of a vocabulary item may have little grasp of the concept involved. The teacher must seek to learn whether, in terms of performance, the children in the class understand both vocabulary and the underlying conceptual structure.

In teaching vocabulary and conceptual development special attention is due specific uses of common words. Langer has pointed up the problem in this way: "Many of the most common words are also the most difficult. These abstract, multiple-meaning words indicate relationships . . . among words and their accompanying concepts" [7, p. 452]. Children, in reading, must be pressed to explain meaning. "What does this word mean as used here? . . . Does this familiar word make sense as it is used in this problem?" Imagine, for example, the confusion of the child who applies common meanings to the words "greatest possible error" in attempting to interpret this statement: "The *greatest possible error* in a measurement is one-half of the smallest unit used in making the measurement" [8, p. 157]. Conceptually he must also deal with ". . . one-half of the smallest unit. . . ."

The numerals, signs of operation, signs denoting relationships, literal numbers, abbreviations, and special symbols such as π are all parts of the vocabulary of mathematics. One would conclude, of course, that these represent major mathematical teaching tasks. But there are reading problems involved. The child must have experiences in which these symbols are viewed as a part of reading. Again the conceptual interrelationships must be stressed. In work with these the teacher teaches *both* mathematics and reading.

One form of mathematical expression—the verbal problem, word problem, story problem, or whatever one might choose to call the problem in a short paragraph setting—has particular difficulty for children. Reading has consistently been shown by research to be a factor in poor performance in this area. From the initial work with verbally stated problems children should never be given the idea that a single reading will be adequate to discern the total situation. Frequently children left to their own procedures read only until they encounter a number; then they work with that number and any other they see (usually using the computational process then being studied) without actually reading the entire problem.

Insofar as reading procedure is concerned the following steps are widely prescribed in the literature on problem solving:

1. *Use a first reading to visualize the situation,* to get a general grasp of it. The child need not pay much attention to the actual numerals during this reading. He may, in fact, be asked to read orally and leave the numerals out of this reading. For example, he can say, "Tom has *some* stamps . . ." rather than "Tom has 123 stamps. . . ."
2. *Reread to get the facts,* paying particular attention to the information given and the *key* question which is the basis for programming the problem.
3. *Note problem vocabulary or concepts* and explore these with the help of the teacher.
4. *Reread as a help in planning the steps for solution.* On this reading some arithmetic authorities have the child state the situation in a mathematical sentence. A sensible estimate of the answer may be made also prior to actual processing of the problem. Screening out irrelevant data or noting the need to seek out additional data may be involved in this very careful reading. (Problems containing irrelevant data and also those in which the child must seek elsewhere for relevant data should be included in the arithmetic program.) Teachers should be able to see many key questions and statements they can use to set specific purposes for children in the various readings. Often the problem should be read orally and developed through extensive class dialogue as a means of teaching effective reading, with the teacher actually guiding the discussion.
5. *Read the problem again to check your procedure and solution,* to

note if all work has been done. The child must be taught to do this even after the processing is complete.

Thus several readings are entailed in properly approaching problem solving in arithmetic. Various other helpful techniques may be used, such as having the child state a problem in his own words, after two or three readings, to check his understanding of concepts and vocabulary. The alert teacher will actively work on this process by having specific lessons using the text and related materials.

For many children the arithmetic text is merely an exercise book. Few really know the organizational structure of the text. Too often the child must be directed specifically to use such an aid as the glossary. The child who needs review to recall an idea or process may have no idea how to seek this out in the text. Thus occasional work designed to help the child learn to use parts of the text should be planned by the teacher. Finally, the special typographical aids such as italics, indentations, bold type, or underlining should be studied by the class and used by both teacher and children.

The preceding paragraphs set forth some procedural suggestions for teaching reading in mathematics. That teaching in this area can be effective is borne out by research. Ideas for teaching are being increasingly publicized. Substantial action in classroom implementation is distressingly belated. Seven years ago, in *The First R,* Austin and Morrison entitled the final chapter "Will Tomorrow Be Another Day?" [2]. With reference to this, Kress and Johnson recently editorialized that the authors knew

> that repeated advice along these lines had not been heeded. Has tomorrow now come? If it has, did tomorrow turn out to be another day? If it did, another day of what? Are we, like King Hassam, still sleeping in the faith that tomorrow *will* be another day? Sleeping in that faith hardly seems the way to prevail" [6, p. 264].

Action on reading in content fields must find its way into elementary and secondary classrooms.

At least two forms of action could become effective and, let us hope, make tomorrow another day:

Teacher training must be "beefed up" in the total area of reading in the content subjects. Course time and practice in reading in mathematics must be given to undergraduate teacher-trainees. One general course in reading or the language arts does not allow time for teaching the specialized skills. Recommendations 5 and 6 of *The Torch Lighters* [1] point up the direction but fall short of the need.

In-service programs for practicing teachers must be used to help broaden classroom reading programs. Reading specialists, supervisors, and curriculum experts should be brought into play to work with teachers in devising programs for teaching content-area reading skills which the teachers can use in the classroom. In-service programs in reading, like training courses in reading, tend to emphasize fundamental reading skills. The proposed program would be an intensive one dealing with reading specifically related to each content area. In-service teachers and teachers-in-training must be informed of the reading skills needed for understanding the content subjects and impressed with the importance of teaching these skills.

Ultimately, any effective action in making children better readers of mathematical content must be taken by classroom teachers. Thus the theme of these paragraphs suggesting what might be done for and by teachers is fitting. Perhaps effective teaching procedures will not prove to be obscure. The demand is probably great for an awareness of the critical need for good content-area reading and the consistent search for those procedures that work and their persistent application.

References

1. Austin, Mary C., et al. *The Torch Lighters*. Cambridge: Harvard University Press, 1961.
2. ———. *The First R*. New York: Macmillan Co., 1963.
3. Call, N. J., and M. A., Wiggin. "Reading and Mathematics." *The Mathematics Teacher* 59 (February 1966), 149–57.
4. Harlan, Charles L. "Years in School and Achievements in Reading and Arithmetic." *Journal of Educational Research* 8 (June–December 1923), 145–49.
5. Johnson, Harry C. "The Effect of Instruction in Mathematical Vocabulary upon Problem Solving in Arithmetic." *Journal of Educational Research* 38 (October 1944), 97–110.
6. Kress, Roy A., and Marjorie Seddon Johnson. "Another Day of What." *Reading Teacher* 22 (December 1968), 210, 264.
7. Langer, John H. "Vocabulary and Concept Development." *Journal of Reading* 10 (April 1967), 448–56.
8. Morton, Robert L., et al. *Modern Mathematics Through Discovery*. Morristown, N.J.: Silver Burdett Co., 1970.
9. Phillips, Jo McKeeby. "Reading Mathematical Content." *Instructor* 77 (March 1968), 120, 136, 138.
10. Spencer, Peter L. and David H. Russell. "Reading in Arithmetic." In *Instruction in Arithmetic*. Twenty-fifth Yearbook of the National Council of Teachers of Mathematics. Washington, D.C.: The Council, 1960.
11. Wilson, Estaline. "Improving the Ability to Read Arithmetic." *Elementary School Journal* 22 (January 1922), 380–86.
12. Yoakam, Gerald. "The Reading-Study Approach to Printed Materials." *Reading Teacher* 11 (February 1958), 146–51.

The Development of Work-Study Habits and Skills

GEORGE D. SPACHE

I think you will all agree that training in study skills is an absolute essential in the elementary and the secondary reading program. In my opinion, this training can begin in the very first grade and be gradually broadened and continued throughout the first twelve grades. As you know, the reading tasks we ask of our children proliferate rapidly and assume a great variety and complexity as they move over into reading in the content fields, particularly about the fourth grade. Most of the previous training in the basal reading program does not prepare the child for the types of reading tasks that he has to do in the content areas. Thus, the immediate goal of training in the study skills is really to prepare the child to do the types of reading other than those that are commonly encountered in the basal or primary reading program. If we look at the performances of upper elementary or junior high school students, we find that there are obviously a great many difficulties in applied reading or in the application of reading skills. You remember the studies of James McAllister who attempted to identify, by interviewing the students, the particular problems that they were experiencing.[1] Over half of the fifty different kinds of reading difficulties in the content fields that he identified were due to inappropriate methods and inappropriate teachniques in the use of reading as applied by the pupils. A great many other studies show that growth in effective study skills does not continue during the secondary school, largely, perhaps, because of lack of training. Our students do not become more efficient and more effective in the application of reading merely because they acquire a few more years of schooling. There are, moreover, marked differences in the study practices of the academically successful and the academically unsuccessful students, especially in the extent of the sound learning procedures that they use. Yet, even very successful students are not completely efficient or free from ineffectual practices for which they compensate by burning the midnight oil.

[1] James M. McCallister, *Remedial and Corrective Instruction in Reading* (New York: Appleton-Century-Crofts, 1936).

THE DEVELOPMENT OF WORK-STUDY HABITS AND SKILLS by George D. Spache. From *Reading Attitudes and Skills Needed for Our Times*, 1st Annual Reading Conference, University of South Carolina, 1960, ed. Paul C. Berg, pp. 37–55. Reprinted by permission.

For example, Cuff[2] found that high scholarship students do not take notes while reading, while Brink,[3] in another study, observed that high scholarship students usually read the entire assignment before outlining. Now in difficult material, these particular practices would probably not yield a high degree of comprehension. And yet, although relatively ineffectual, these practices appear to be possible for the students of superior mental ability. Unsuccessful students, academically speaking, on the other hand not only use ineffectual and disorganized study practices, but also lack the compensatory native ability which might enable them to counterbalance this. My point is that directive training in the study skills is desirable not only for weak students, but also for the competent, the academically successful student as well. In schools where this type of training is attempted, the indications are that improved grades and better personal adjustment to school are the results of training for both poor and weak students. In my opinion, this training program should begin, as I have already suggested, as early as the first grade and should continue on through the secondary level. In fact, it may well be extended through the early college years as many collegiate institutions do.

If a program is going to be of such duration and involve, as we will see, a wide variety of tasks, skills and materials, then, obviously, integrated planning is absolutely essential. The objectives and teaching procedures must be coordinated over the entire elementary and secondary level at least. (Of course, nobody can cooperate with college teachers, so we don't expect to be able to plan with them, but they are a breed to themselves!) But, certainly, in the elementary and secondary level, we can expect that planning can be coordinated. In planning the study skills program, we must, I think, be cognizant of the significance of pupil personality and attitudes toward study practices. Study skills are not simply a body of facts or information that the student absorbs. For example, several studies which have analyzed achievement tests, including study skills tests, do not identify a factor for study skills. In other words, study skills do not constitute a body of knowledge such as arithmetic does or language skills do. Rather, they reflect some hidden element. Study skills that the child or the high school student uses are not only due to his knowledge of what is good practice or his verbalization of what is good practice, but are a reflection of his academic motivation and how much he identifies with the goals of the school. They are a reflection of his habits of work, and they are probably a reflection of such personality traits as anxiety, compulsiveness, stability and self-confidence. In the study I mentioned a moment ago, Cuff notes such compulsive traits among high scholarship students as the use of complete sentences while writing. In other words, there is a general tendency for compulsiveness on the part of high scholarship students not to write in simple phrases or

---

[2] Noel B. Cuff, "Study Habits in Grades Four to Twelve," *Journal of Educational Psychology*, XXVIII (April 1937), 295–301.

[3] William G. Brink, "Study Techniques of the Best Students," *Nation's Schools*, XLV (May 1950), 40.

in abbreviations, but to write complete sentences when notetaking; or, another practice, the student reads each topic until it is clearly understood. Now these practices may be desirable, but they probably reflect a certain amount of internal pressure about academic achievement as much as anything else. Evidence, for example, also indicates that re-reading is not highly profitable; yet we see students of high academic standing being compulsive about it. They must read until they thoroughly understand, even if they re-read three and four times, as they also must write in complete sentences while taking notes. Academically successful students are noticeably more cautious, more persistent and meticulous in their study practices. Because they differ in their habits and their motivation, rather than in the knowledge of what constitutes good study practice, poor students can mouth the principle and the rules of good study and tell you what they should be doing or what the books on how to study say they should be doing. They are as aware of these facts, this informational aspect of it, as good students, but they do not have the habit, the attitudes and the feelings which enable them to put these practices into effect consistently.

PRINCIPLES OF TEACHING STUDY SKILLS

If I justify the practices of study skills, let's talk a little about how to teach them. In general, there are several principles which might be kept in mind. First of all, the training must be interesting and realistic to the student as contrasted with extended practice or drill in artificial tasks. The student must constantly see the relationship between this desirable habit or this desirable skill and his daily work, or it becomes again a pure verbalization rather than a practice which he can see reasons for. Thus, wherever possible, practice materials in study skills should be drawn from the student's own study material—his current assignments, for example, or, perhaps, from a file of exercises, such as Helen Scott of Rhode Island has suggested, drawn actually from current types of assignments that students would normally practice with.

Other methods for enlisting the thinking of the student are pupil autobiography from high schools, and particularly from colleges. Ask the student, guided by a list of pertinent questions, to write the story of his study habits or his reading problems. Coupled with interviews with the student and observation of him at work, this will help the teacher to increase the relationship between training in study skills and the actual needs of the student. One study has shown that when training in study skills is individualized, the results are superior to when it is done in a formal, group fashion with all children receiving the same instruction.[4] This again em-

---

[4] Daisy Marvel Jones, "An Experiment in Adaptation to Individual Differences," *Journc'* *of Educational Psychology*, XXXIX (1948), 257–72.

phasizes the importance of individual differences in this particular kind of training.

SKILLS TO BE TAUGHT

Now what type of skills shall we teach? What kind of general classification might we give students? Stone has an interesting way of labeling or classifying study skills.[5] He calls them identifying, collecting and active reconstruction. I think these are very apt terms, although they are not in general use. Identifying involves, for example, skimming, recognizing main ideas, formulating idea families and comprehending the author's organizational scheme. Collecting includes, of course, notetaking, collating and organizing materials, while active reconstruction, as the term implies, suggests implementing the purpose for study by review, self-recitation, and re-reading. Other classifications which are more common in the literature include locating, organizing, and retaining, and these will be used in this discussion.

Locating Information

Library.   Obviously, under locating information the first major group is that of library skills, including a whole host of subordinate and major skills which we attempt to teach the students. Among the more significant ones, of course, are general understanding of the library—its arrangement, its major facilities, the Dewey decimal system, and the card catalog. Cleary makes the point, although it may seem perfectly obvious, that certainly children need to be aware that fiction materials are commonly arranged by the author, and non-fiction by subject, yet this comes as a dramatic unfolding to some individuals.[6] Students certainly should understand the significance of the shelf heading and the call number, the subject title and the author card. These are almost absolute essentials.

How do we usually approach this kind of instruction? Some of us will purchase a workbook on how to use the library; others of us will take our children to the library, as we do at our University, give them a Cook's tour and hope that this introduces them to its facilities. Others of us will constantly try to employ assignments which require the library and, then, in terms of how adequately the student does the assignment, try to judge his library practices. In other words, we try to observe actually what he can do with a piece of material which requires use of the library and then help him to repair the knowledge or information that he doesn't have. The

[5] David R. Stone, "Teaching Three Functions of Study-Reading," *Journal of Developmental Reading*, III (Winter 1960), 137–41.

[6] Florence Damon Cleary, *Blueprints for Better Reading* (New York: H. W. Wilson, 1957).

University of Michigan recently had a symposium on the subject of reading interests under the title, "Reading for Life," and there were three or four papers on the role of the library in reading interests of the future.[7] Comments indicated that our librarians are thinking about even the physical arrangement of the library, and it was interesting to note that many thought that our current libraries are not arranged for the best possible uses. It was suggested that the large room in which a number of students sit is not conducive to study, but rather to distraction, and that we need many, many, small rooms. We need refreshments; we need places to smoke; we need different hours in the library. These are not my opinions; these are quotations from those who should know how libraries should be. In one institution the library remains open until two o'clock each morning except Saturdays because of the tendency among young college students to study early into the morning. Thus the library can play a most significant part. To sum up the symposium's findings, most of the writers were discouraged about the amount of reading that an average college or high school student does.

Dictionary.   Let's go on to another kind of locating skill—the use of the dictionary. Here, again, we often assume that after the third or fourth grade, the child is perfectly competent in the use of the dictionary, and that he can use it for meanings, for spelling, for pronunciation, for derivation, and to distinguish usage. Actually, this is not true. In a college level textbook which Dr. Berg and I made out of our experiences with college students, we have included the kind of exercises on use of the dictionary which most people think a fourth grader can do.[8] Actually, most college students do not get anything like their money's worth out of the dictionary that they use. The average student, when asked if he can find the spelling of a word in a dictionary will look at you as though you were just a little silly. Of course, he says, you can't find a word you do not know how to spell. This is one of the good, legitimate uses of the dictionary for which many poor spellers are entirely incompetent. You talk to him about meaning —he feels that there is one meaning, and that's it. The fact that almost all our words have multiple meanings which are related to the particular context has not occurred to him. You talk to him about derivation and it is all Greek as far as he is concerned, and so on. Actually, the dictionary should be a most significant locating tool, particularly for vocabulary development right on through the high school and college. I am suggesting that we must continue to direct instruction in its use as long as our students are available to us. We have built a dictionary test in the book just mentioned which attempts to sample the student's ability to use a real dictionary

[7] J. M. Price, editor, *Reading for Life* (Ann Arbor: University of Michigan Press, 1959).
[8] George D. Spache and Paul C. Berg, *The Art of Efficient Reading* (New York: Macmillan, 1955).

page—one which he is not likely to be familiar with. We have now stand-ardized this for the high school as well as college students, and there is very little growth, very little difference in the ability of the average twelfth grader and the ability of the average eighth grader in his use of the dic-tionary. Perhaps our attitude toward the dictionary has not made it an interesting book—was it Mark Twain who made that comment about it? It is dry reading; yet, as you know, it has a wealth of information. We have come to feel about the dictionary as though it were an arbitrary prescriptive instrument. We feel it has the final word on things and, therefore, we go to it only in dire extremity, rather than recognizing that dictionaries them-selves are in a state of flux and are constantly being rewritten, that terms are constantly being redefined, and that the dictionary is not a prescriptive tool but a descriptive one.

Books and Periodicals.   A third group of skills in locating informa-tion is the care and use of books. I won't bother you with the details of how to open a new book or to take care of it, to cover it, etc. You are more familiar with this than I am. Understanding the content and the charac-teristics of a book, the ability to use the glossary, the index, the table of contents, and all of its constituent parts can be extended not only to a book, which is our most basic tool, but probably should be extended to include the average newspaper. In other words, our children not only should be taught the care and use and understanding of books, but also the same probably is true for the newspaper. If we think of the future reading of the average adult, it will be most probably in the newspaper and the picture magazines rather than in books. Less than ten per cent of Americans buy books in one year anyway. So, I would suggest that while we train children to care for, to use books, and to understand their parts, that we extend our training to the newspaper and whatever magazines we feel are appropriate.

Maps.   A fourth kind of locational skill is that of map reading. Here the research has very little to say. We know maps are hard to read; we know there are a number of specific skills in the use of maps—the symbols, the colors, the grid, the understanding of directions, longitudes, latitudes, and so on. Yet if we look for suggestions as to when or how to teach these skills, we find very few definitive answers. About the only thing we can say is that since maps are difficult, since there are a great variety of them, and since their reading is an essential part of life for anyone who even drives a car, we should start early and we should continue to attempt to help our children to read maps more intelligently, rather than assuming that by the time they are of junior and senior high school age they can read any and all kinds of maps. This is a group of skills which needs a great deal more attention, a great deal more planning. Most of us take for granted that it is accomplished in our social studies textbooks, for example. Actually, this is not true. When you give formal tests of map reading at the junior or senior high school level, you find that the average individual cannot read them well.

Tables, Charts and Diagrams.   Another major area of study is in the reading of tables, charts and diagrams. Again, here the research indicates that most children find graphs, tables, diagrams and charts very difficult to read. Most pupils never seem to develop any real facility in dealing with these materials. And, even when they are combined, as a diagram which is supposed to clarify a table, or vice-versa, few students seem to know how to read them. It doesn't seem to make the situation more simple, but rather more difficult, for the average individual. For example, you have the kind of graph or chart which indicates change, such as a bar. You have graphs and charts of relative proportions or time; you have those that employ picture symbols; you have those depicting time or flow, or comparison or relationship, or those which are completely composed of pictures. This is a very simple listing, and actually the variety that is met by our students is much greater. About all that we can say is that it seems to be helpful to give children practice in constructing their own kind of charts and diagrams and to help them to clarify them. This kind of training should begin by the fourth grade at the latest and continue successively through the rest of the school years.

Organizing Information

Outlining.   A first skill in organizing information is outlining, and here we again get into an area where we haven't very definitive facts. Most classroom and remedial teachers have witnessed improvement in childen's retention and comprehension when they have been trained to incorporate outlining into their study techniques, and this to a degree is supported by the research on the values of outlining in many of the content fields. Yet, we know very little about the effects of kinds of outlining or when to do it. For example, if you would retain more of what I have said today, would it be better to make your outline while I am talking or after I have finished? Actually, we don't know. For some people, one method seems to be more effective; for some, another method. Or, strange as it may seem, would it be better to take no notes, no outline at all? The controlled research which has been done has been unable to tell us whether listening to a lecture and taking notes during the lecture, after the lecture, or no notes at all is better, or whether these notes should be firmly organized in an outline fashion. We don't seem to be able to prove very clearly what kind of or-ganization is best. We do know that when we teach students, particularly those of lesser ability, to utilize outlines, that they seem to improve in their study habits or their study results. For example, with college students, I make it a practice to teach them to use the outline while they are reading—

not wait until the end of the chapter. While they are going through read-ing the headings, and the subheads and the opening of each paragraph, they should begin the outline. In other words, translate the headings and subheads into the headings of the outline, leaving space to fill in the details during the reading of the entire chapter. Now, sometimes, of course, one whole chapter is too much; it should be half of a chapter, or it should be a section of a chapter. This is something that you have to find out by experimentation with the individual student. Sometimes one just can't outline a whole chapter at a sitting even though he is of college age or presumably of college ability. We have evolved our teaching procedures of outlining more or less by trial and error. We start with such things as "what's a good title for this paragraph" or "what's another way of saying what these few sentences say," or "what would be a phrase that would tell us what this paragraph or this group of sentences says." And, then later, we teach the student not only to fill in the main idea, but major details also in a two-step outline. It is customary, beginning about the fourth grade, to in-troduce this type of instruction. The amount of material is gradually in-creased during the fifth grade, while in the sixth grade normally we expand the outline to three steps—a title, a major head, a sub-head and a sub-ordinate head, and we also begin to introduce the idea of a summary para-graph of the material. This is all very logical and seems to be fairly effective, but, as I have said, we do not know whether perhaps this might be done more efficiently some other way. We don't know which is a better method—underlining or just summarizing, although we think either is better than disorganized notes. It is not surprising that when we start to examine students as to how they use outlines and how well and in what fashion, they turn out to be just about as confused regarding this as we are. What we do is logical, but not psychological, not necessarily positively desirable.

Summarizing.   Let's take another kind of organizing—summarizing. Again, we don't know whether writing a summary in order to organize material is really a highly effective procedure. Sister Mary Richard, for example, takes a story and reads it to her children at the first grade level and has them write four sentences with a mental picture in mind of each major portion of the story.[9] In other words, she has the students write what amounts to a four-sentence summary and then they compose a sentence and polish it while she does a picture to illustrate each of the four sections of the story. It sounds very interesting; what it does, I don't know. It does, of course, tend to pull the story together and to provide some degree of organization, but how valid it is for long range training, we have no way of knowing. But, we see that training and summarizing begins quite early in the primary grades, even with written summaries, and gradually increases

[9] Sister Mary Richard, "Summarizing Stories," *Elementary English,* XXXVII (January 1960), 43–44.

from the simple sentence or two to a more complete treatment and to a larger body of material to be summarized. About all that we can say about it is that it probably is more profitable for the student to write the summary in his own words, rather than just naively copying what the book or the lecturer has said. This does seem to make a difference. Presumably, in order to write it in his own words, he has done some thinking, so we have made him think a little about it and reorganize it in his mind.

Notetaking. Notetaking is another kind of organizing problem and, as I said, if we look at what people call their notes, they are as decorative sometimes as they are an exhibition of what they have learned from a particular body of material. We don't know whether it is more profitable to take notes during a lecture, after, or no notes at all. Experiments show no real difference in the amount of retention for the average student relative to the kind of notes he takes. Some of us will train our students to take down only the main idea of the speaker or only the main ideas of the chapter. Some of you are frustrated because you cannot take many details, and some teachers attempt to have their students copy as many details as well as the main ideas. Again, we see no difference in the retention or comprehension of the student, whether he sticks only to main ideas or tries to add some details or only the speaker's jokes. Preston, in a study on the teaching of study practices, suggests that notes be on main topics while reading and then filled in later with details.[10] He suggests that notes should be brief and they should certainly be expressed in the student's own words, rather than a copy of the text, and that they should be revised and reorganized shortly after they are finished while they are still fresh in the student's mind. All of this we would probably agree with on a logical basis. It sounds sensible to do it this way. Stone has an interesting approach and suggests that each notetaking task demands certain decisions of the students.[11] He must decide, for example, how full his notes should be. He must decide how closely he will follow the source, text, or speaker. And, therefore, he has to give some thought to the amount of detail he needs to get what he wants from the material. And, he must decide whether he will follow the author's organization or use a different one, whether he will write his own headings or merely paraphrase what the speaker or writer had said. In this kind of originality, many of you will evolve a time-saving device of abbreviation, dropping the second and third syllables from words or abbreviating terms that constantly recur by a single letter or two or symbol. I once tried to learn to do this by using the system by which one drops all the vowels. It just didn't seem to make any sense not to have any vowels. I would rather abbreviate in my own fashion by dropping perhaps the last syllable

[10] Ralph C. Preston, *Teaching Study Habits and Skills* (New York: Holt, Rinehart and Winston, 1959).
[11] Stone, *op. cit.*

or two. There is a system which you can learn that, as I say, consists largely of deleting the vowels and writing only the consonants. It's a kind of short-hand-longhand writing, but, again, this is something that has to feel natural to you, and so most students evolve a fairly satisfactory system of abbreviations or shorthand which makes sense to them; if this is readable later, it's good. If it is not, and it often is not, even to the person who wrote it, then, obviously, the student needs to be trained out of the practice or taught how to abbreviate so that he himself can read it.

Retaining Information

Memorizing. In the third major skill, that of retaining and using information, we get into the question of how to memorize. There are here a great many principles that can be supported and can be affirmed quite dramatically. Memory is much better if the person becomes interested or tries to cultivate an interest in material, and this is a primary requisite for study. This means that no matter how he does it, the student has to try to find a reason to like, or enjoy, or become in some degree interested in his particular assignment, if he wishes to retain it with any degree of confidence. Next he must understand the total picture before he begins with the details, again reaffirming our idea of surveying material before actually trying to read it for detail.

Spaced Study. Spaced study is better than single sessions. Despite the frequency of their practice, all night study sessions are not particularly profitable; study spaced over a period of time is preferable. Overlearning aids retention. Forgetting also is retarded to some degree by repetition, by talking it out with oneself, a friend, classmate, or other person. If you wish to retain anything for any length of time, you have got to go back to it again within a reasonable period. This stops the curve of forgetting. You remember perhaps some of the experiments of the Russian whose work in forgetting shows us that unless our ideas are closely tied to experiences or other learning, we lose about fifty per cent of what we have just learned in twenty-four hours. Unless the material is vitally interesting and meaningful and closely tied in with other facts so that it becomes part of our general body of knowledge, we will not remember it. In other words, if I were to teach you ten French words this moment and then ask you to repeat them within twenty-four hours without any review or self-recitation, most of you would have forgotten at least five of them. You would probably have no recall of them at all unless you were a French student, unless you could tie them to their English cognates, or in some other fashion get a clue that would enable you to retain them. Our curve of forgetting is much faster than our curve of learning.

Self-Recitation. When we get into this retaining of material or information, the problem of re-reading often comes up. Most students attempt to improve their retention, particularly when they find something difficult, by re-reading it several times, in fact, re-reading successively one time right after another. Unfortunately, for all their good intentions, the second or the third or the fourth or the fifth reading is of little or no value. The indications are that what one learns in the first reading may be added to by about five per cent by successive re-reading. Unfortunately, this most common practice of re-reading is not a very efficient procedure. It would be much more profitable to read something only once and use questions to guide the reading. These questions may be set up by the teacher, they may be contained in the textbook, or they may be constructed by the student while studying, but indications are that one reading is just as profitable as a number of readings if one reads to answer specific questions.

Reports. Another problem that we face is that of preparing reports, or, as we dignify it in the elementary school, we have our children do "research." We start telling them that they are doing research and committee work. Formal training in the preparation of reports probably cannot occur much before the fifth grade, because we have some real problems in terms of maturity and organization involved—such things as recognizing the problem itself and then formulating and stating it, and then knowing and finding appropriate resource material. Actually to prepare some kind of a report the individual must be able to define what he is trying to solve; he must be able to know where the sources are, to go to these sources, to collate them, and then to bring all this material together and organize it. I am not talking simply about two children who go off to exchange ideas about a book, but rather the actual preparation of a report to be presented. An article in the *English Journal* of May, 1960, gives an interesting device for helping students in this kind of work. The writer of the article suggests a series of letters to aid in an intelligent preparation of a report. The symbols are S, A, O, W, R, RW. Unfortunately, these letters do not resemble any common word, which doesn't make them easier to remember, but they do outline the actual steps the student should follow in preparing a report. "S" means, of course, to select materials; "A" means to assemble them and sort them; "O" means to organize them in an outline; "W" means to write the first rough draft; "R" means to revise this first rought draft; and "RW" means to re-write in final form.[12]

[12] Father William F. Wiebler, "Gimme a Gimmick," *English Journal*, XLIX (May 1960), 343–44.

Dimensions of Reading Speed
and Comprehension

J. HARLAN SHORES

I

It may be that our conceptualization of the reading process is at once too simple and too complex. It is too simple when we think of it as word recognition or even as understanding what the author wrote. It is too simple when it neglects critical evaluation and interpretation of what is read or when it neglects the fact that reading and thinking are inseparable processes when the printed word provides the stimulus for the thought. The reading process is also conceptualized too simply when it is regarded as a mechanical process apart from the purposeful motivation of the reader, when reading rate and reading comprehension are separated in measurement or when the definition does not include basic study skills with printed materials.

On the other hand, our conception of reading is too complex when it goes beyond printed materials, and it is much too complex when the reading process itself is defined to include all the factors related to reading success.

Shortly before his death, W. S. Gray wrote that "Basic research in reading seeks to secure a clearer understanding . . . of the nature of the reading act." I am sure that this was not a new idea with Dr. Gray. He emphasized it many times in his writings. He was simply pointing once again to the fact that theory and research directed toward a more adequate understanding of the reading act will pay larger dividends in the long run than will experiments with methods and materials.

One small but positive step in the direction of a better understanding of the reading task may come from making a clear distinction between those factors that are *related* to the ability to read, and those factors that are actually reading itself.

The point was just made that as complicated as the reading process is, it is sometimes made too complex by including in it all the factors related to it—by including in it all the skills and abilities involved in thinking as

DIMENSIONS OF READING SPEED AND COMPREHENSION by J. Harlan Shores. From *Elementary English*, 45 (January 1968), pp. 23–28, 43. Copyright © 1968 by the National Council of Teachers of English. Reprinted by permission of the publisher and J. Harlan Shores.

well as those related to the learning and use of printed symbols. Consider for a moment just a few of the factors that may help to determine how rapidly you read and how well you comprehend. Some of these are directly related to the physical characteristics of the material—size of type, type style, blackness and sharpness of print, quality and tone of paper, size of page, organization on the page, amount of white space, kind of illustrations, placement of illustrations on the page, relations of illustrations to text, heading and subheadings, and overall organization and design.

Other factors that may affect speed and comprehension are related to less tangible aspects of the material—the clarity of the writing, the field of knowledge from which the writing is drawn, the complexity of the ideas being developed, the author's style and choice of words, the kind of writing (poetry, narrative, descriptive, *etc.*), the rapidity with which ideas follow one another, and the extent to which ideas are fully developed.

Still other factors that determine reading speed and comprehension are directly related to the reader, his personality, and his environment while reading—how he feels (whether he is sleepy, alert, healthy, ill, calm, nervous, relaxed, tense), and what he has on his mind, his emotional stability, his vision, whether he likes to read, his mental abilities, his reading skills, his ideals, his biases, his prejudices, his freedom from distractions. All these and many more he brings to his reading job and each may help to determine how he reads.

But most important of all to both reading comprehension and speed are those factors that relate the reader to the material he is reading—the background of experience he has for this material, his purpose for reading it, his interest in this field and especially in the part of it about which he is reading, his mental set with respect to this job and to this material, his familiarity with the peculiarities of style and phraseology of this author and this field, whether these new concepts are compatible with or contrary to those he already holds.

II

It is impossible to say which one of these or the many other factors that may affect a person's reading is most crucial in reading. For any one person, nearly any one of them could play a major role. A child who can't see well enough to distinguish word forms can't read. The emotionally upset child may not be able to read or think until his emotionality is more stable. The person with strong prejudices may not even be able to understand an opposing argument. A person with no background for his reading is imagining meanings. The reader with no purpose in mind collects trash and jewels alike and often doesn't know one from the other.

It seems to me that there is a difference in kind between these factors that are in one way or another related to the reading task. When one considers what a person has to know or what he has to be like to be successful with the reading task, one comes up with the fact that he must know the meanings of words. He must be able to recognize words in various type faces and in both capitalized and lower case forms. He must be able to associate words with objects. He must be proficient with various phonic, structural, context, and other clues to word recognition. He must have some interest in the material—some motivation for reading it. He must have adequate experience background for understanding it. And this list could go on and on. Each of these skills, knowledges, abilities, is a part of the reading process in much the same way that each aspect of one's personality structure is a part of one's behavior. However, it is probably important to note that none of these parts of reading is reading itself. They are instead the *relational elements* of the reading process.

The point here is not that relational factors are unimportant to reading. They are extremely important, but they are not reading itself, and we too often delude ourselves by thinking that we have understood the reading process when we have accumulated much data about factors related to reading. He has a good vocabulary. His experience background is adequate. He is emotionally stable. His vision and hearing are normal. He recognizes words well by several techniques. His interests are broad. But can he read? What can he do with the reading skills? Can he understand what he reads? Can he distinguish main ideas from subordinate ones? Can he evaluate, criticize, use a dictionary, find his way with a map? These are the behavioral definitions of reading, and it might be observed that much less attention has been devoted up to this time to these behavioral elements than to the relational ones. Each is a productive area for theorizing and experimenting.

III

Just for a few moments let us turn our attention specifically to one relational factor, the reader's experience background, and to one *functional* factor, the reader's purpose for reading, as two of the most vital factors affecting reading comprehension.

What one gets from reading depends heavily upon what he brings to it. Without adequate experience background for a passage, adequate comprehension is impossible. Perhaps this is easiest seen in its extreme. If the reader has no meanings in his experience for the words he sees, there can be no understanding, no interpretation, no evaluation. In fact, there can be no thinking about these words, except perhaps a vague wondering of what it is all about.

A rich program of learnings at home and at school and a good reading program are not different things. They are two sides of the same coin. When there are the beginnings of a chemistry lab in the basement, or a few seeds in a flat box, or an active science program at school, the rich backgrounds of meanings are being developed that must be there if the reading of science is to provide the understandings, interpretations, and evaluations that make comprehension a thinking process.

While the reader's experience background provides a basis for comprehension and thought, the reader's purpose sets the conditions for doing the job efficiently. A good reader may cover material at two thousand words a minute and do an excellent job if all he wants is a general idea of what the passage is about. He may cover the same material at fewer than a hundred words a minute and also do an excellent job if he now wants to recall all the ideas of the passage in sequence and relate them to another sequence that he has in mind from another book. He is using different reading skills during these two readings, and he is using them efficiently in both instances. The difference, of course, is in the job he set for himself. It is a difference in his purpose for reading.

IV

There is some evidence to indicate that children in the upper grades of the elementary school are not only unable to adjust adequately their reading skills to the purpose for which they are reading, but they also don't know how they should have read the materials to achieve better their purpose. In connection with a study of purposeful reading that I want to report later, I thought it might be interesting to find out how two groups of sixth-grade students reading the same material for different purposes thought that they read the material. Were they reading more or less rapidly than usual? Did they read at the same speed throughout or did they read parts more rapidly or more slowly than other parts? Did they pause one or more times while reading? Did they look the material over before reading it? Did they begin with the first word? Did they reread all or parts of it? Did they use a hand or finger to mark the place while reading? Was the purpose performed while reading or after reading? Did they read the material out loud to themselves—that is, did they vocalize or sub-vocalize? Was it interesting? Was it difficult?

We talked over what these questions meant before they responded to them on a multiple-choice questionnaire. When the two groups were tested again on similar material the following day, they were asked to respond to a little different type of questionnaire. This time each question asked how an ideal reader—"the best reader in the world," "the best reader you could imagine" would have read this material for this purpose. Each group had read the same passage but one had read it for the main idea and the other had read to keep in mind a series of ideas in sequence. Later I had fifty able adult readers read the same materials and respond to the same questionnaires.

This, of course, is not very secure data. The first part is introspective and the second is a very rough indication of goal orientation. But it is interesting, and if we don't take the results too seriously, they may provide straws in the wind. I'll spare you the specific percentages of those who responded in one way or another to these questions, but you might be interested in two general conclusions:[1]

First, children have not achieved the flexibility of rate and comprehension adjustments that characterizes the able adult reader when he reads for rather different purposes. Examples of this are the numerous instances where the sixth graders reported using the same techniques when reading for each of the two purposes in this study whereas adult patterns varied with the purpose. The able adult reader has learned when to reread, when to pause, when to slow down, and even when to finger point and vocalize. Most children are not so sophisticated in their reading habits.

Second, children's goal orientation with respect to purposeful reading is unclear and confused. Sixth-grade children have very fuzzy and erroneous ideas of how the very best reader would read for main ideas or to keep in mind a series of ideas in sequence. When one considers the lack of empirical evidence concerning these matters, it isn't strange that this confusion exists, but it is disturbing. Evidence of confused goal orientation is apparent in the divergence of opinion concerning what an ideal reader would do in a reading situation. It is also apparent in the often wide discrepancy between what the children thought the ideal reader would do and what the able adult reader actually reported that he did.

Even regarding this kind of data as tentative, it surely would suggest that we would do well to teach intermediate-grade children much more than we do about the nature of the reading process so that they would know when they are reading well for a given purpose. Arthur Gates makes this same point in the December, 1958 issue of *The Reading Teacher* when he writes:

> The emphasis should be shifted from teaching the child how to learn by being taught—that is, waiting to be told what exercises to do, what books to read, what details to study—to learning how to learn by himself. This is what a youngster strives to do when he learns to play baseball or tennis or to swim. He tries to figure out how to go about it himself. He strives to understand how the good pitcher or swimmer performs and what he as a learner is doing wrong. There is a strong suggestion in the results of research and in observations of expert teaching in dancing, music, and athletics, and in the theatre and elsewhere, that we have greatly underestimated the school child's capacity for achieving insight into the nature of good and poor techniques. He can learn under his own steam in reading—provided he has a teacher shrewd enough to help him.[2]

When Gates says that children can help to teach themselves to read, he implies, of course, that children know what they are doing—that they

---

[1] Shores, J. Harlan, "Reading of Science for Two Separate Purposes as Perceived by Sixth Grade Students and Able Adult Readers," *Elementary English*, (November, 1960), pp. 461–468.

[2] Gates, A. I., "Improvement in Reading Possible in the Near Future," *The Reading Teacher* (December, 1958), p. 86.

have purposes in mind while reading and are judging their performance on the basis of how well the purposes were fulfilled. To do this requires a clarification of purposes as well as instruction in how to read efficiently for various purposes.

V

How fast should a person read? He should read as rapidly as possible and still meet the comprehension specifications that he sets for himself or that the task sets for him. How fast is this? For most tasks, no one knows what the upper limits are. In fact, for most tasks we don't even know what rate to expect as an average. There probably are some reading tasks where 200 words per minute is very rapid reading, and there may be others, if we include skimming, where 1,000 words per minute is too slow. There are norms of reading rate for relatively simple material with comprehension at 70 to 80 percent accuracy in getting main ideas and simple facts during a single original reading that indicate an average reading rate of about 200 to 250 words per minute for the upper intermediate grades and about 300 to 350 words per minute for adults. If a person reads any other kind of material for any other purpose, we don't know how rapidly he reads in comparison to other people.

Realizing that some readers go through the materials once rapidly and then reread all or part of the material for the specific purposes set by the comprehension questions, an adequate measure of reading rate must provide three scores—an original reading rate, a time for reading the questions, rereading the materials, and answering the questions, and a total time which is the sum of the previous two.

The question then, "Are fast readers the good readers?" needs to be broken down into several questions. Defining a "good reader" as one who comprehends well, we need to ask, "Are good readers those who read rapidly during an initial reading?" Do the good readers read rapidly when dealing with the study-type comprehension questions and when rereading to answer the questions? Are the good readers those who take less time in total to read, reread, and answer questions? A single answer is not adequate for these three questions and they in turn give rise to others. Are the fast readers the good readers on each of these measures regardless of the difficulty of the material and the purpose for reading? It is to these questions that I wish to speak briefly.

In the January, 1950, issue of *Elementary English,* Dr. Kenneth Husbands and I reported an investigation concerned with the relationship between reading speed and comprehension. The general conclusion of this study was that there is no relationship between reading speed and comprehension when the task is difficult. The fast reader was not the best reader when he was reading biological science material in order to solve a problem. In fact, under these conditions the efficient and able reader slowed his rate to that of the inefficient reader.

Since these findings are quite a bit at variance to the often stated generality that the fast reader is the good reader, the speaker did a much more intensive study ten years later also at the sixth-grade level with better instrumentation and with a comparison group of able adult readers to see whether it was possible for both of these generalizations to be true. Actually, they *are* both true. When speed and comprehension are measured as they are in tests of general reading ability, there are good, strong positive correlations between reading speed and comprehension. However, when the task becomes difficult either because of more difficult materials or a more demanding purpose, or both of these, the relationship between speed and comprehension drops to one that could easily be explained by chance factors.

VI

Let me report this study to you. It involved a rather intensive testing program for two matched groups of sixth-grade students and a less intensive testing of one group of able adult readers.

All forty-six sixth graders of a K–12 consolidated school on the southeastern coast of the United States comprised the student population. Even though the "tourist trade" was the largest industry, each of the children included was a permanent resident of the county. The children were of average age in grade and were somewhat above average in intelligence and reading achievement. In terms of their mental ability the group may have been slightly underachieving. The two sixth-grade groups reading the same material for different purposes were closely equivalent in chronological age, mental age, measures of general reading abilities, and science achievement.

With the sixth grades, four reading rate measures provided ten rate scores, and five comprehension measures provided 11 comprehension scores. Two of the rate and comprehension measures were taken in 20 separate testings, so the rate measures on these two represent 20 separate rate measures of 200 to 400 words each or a total rate measure of 8,000 to 16,000 words on these two tests.

The adult group was taken from several advanced undergraduate and graduate university-level courses dealing with the teaching of reading. A few of these 51 students were juniors and seniors in the program preparatory to teaching in the elementary grades. The majority were experienced teachers and administrators working toward graduate degrees.

The adult comparison groups read the same science materials for the same purposes as did the sixth-grade groups. The only difference in the treatment was that the adults responded to only five of the twenty reading selections and did this at a single sitting whereas the children responded to only one passage at a sitting for twenty sittings.

Let me report only five general conclusions from this study.

1. Fast readers are the good readers when reading some kinds of materials for some purposes. When reading other kinds of materials for other purposes, there is no relationship between speed of reading and ability to comprehend. In general the fast readers are the good readers on the reading tasks presented in the standardized tests of general reading ability. There is no relationship between speed of reading and comprehension for either sixth-grade children or well-educated adults when reading scientific materials for the purpose of solving a problem, getting the main ideas, or for keeping a series of ideas in mind in sequence.

2. When either adults or sixth-grade children read the same materials for two different purposes and when the purpose for reading is set for the reader in advance of the reading, the purpose for reading influences the speed with which the reading is done. This finding is supported in Roossinck's study of the reading of scientists and sixth-grade children, and in Troxel's study of reading eighth-grade mathematical materials for different purposes.

3. There is no relationship for either adults or sixth-grade students between comprehension and rate of the work-study reading involved in responding to the comprehension questions. In other words, those who work rapidly on the rereading and question answering are not necessarily the best readers.

4. Efficient adult readers are much more flexible in adjusting reading rate to the demands of the task than are sixth-grade students. In comparison to the adults, the children read relatively more rapidly as the task becomes more demanding with a consequent loss in relative comprehension. The efficient adult slows his rate and rereads as necessary in keeping with the demands of the task. Sixth-grade students need to develop this type of flexibility.

5. Inasmuch as there are different relationships between rate and comprehension when rate is measured as an original reading time and when rate is measured to include rereading and question-answering time, it is important to define what is meant by reading rate. This finding also suggests that authorities in the field of reading would do well to attempt to standardize a practice for measuring reading rate. Since rereading and reorganizing what is read is both necessary and time consuming when reading for some purposes, the most meaningful measure of rate would be one which offered both an original reading time and a time for rereading and answering questions. The total time, which is a sum of these two, destroys some of the specificity of the composite parts and is useful only as an indication of the total amount of time taken to complete a work-study reading task.

7 Suggestions for Further Reading

There are some useful publications whose content is devoted exclusively to reading in the subject areas. Although intended mainly for the secondary school teacher, the guides and aids they contain may be applied to the elementary school curriculum: Ralph C. Preston (ed.), *A New Look at Reading in the Social Studies* (International Reading Association, 1969); Harold L. Herber (ed.), *Developing Study Skills in Secondary Schools* (International Reading Association, 1965); H. Alan Robinson and Ellen Lamar Thomas (eds.), *Fusing Reading Skills and Content* (International Reading Association, 1969); and David L. Shepherd, *Effective Reading in Social Studies* and *Effective Reading in Science* (Row, Peterson, 1960).

Among textbooks that contain suggestions for teaching reading in the content fields are John J. DeBoer and Martha Dallmann, *The Teaching of Reading*, 3rd edition, (Holt, Rinehart and Winston, 1970), 228–98; 393–425; Robert Karlin, *Teaching Reading in High School*, 2nd edition (Bobbs-Merrill, 1972); Paul McKee, *Reading: A Program of Instruction for the Elementary School* (Houghton Mifflin, 1966), 316–76; 405–35; George D. Spache and Evelyn B. Spache, *Reading in the Elementary School*, 2nd edition (Allyn and Bacon, 1969), 274–320; and Miles A. Tinker and Constance M. McCullough, *Teaching Elementary Reading*, 3rd edition (Appleton-Century-Crofts, 1968), 204–23, 237–84.

8

READING FOR APPRECIATION
AND ENJOYMENT

Many years ago, the content of reading textbooks consisted mainly of selections that were regarded by their compilers as literature. Children read these selections which were used as vehicles to teach them the basic reading skills. Thus children were exposed to folk tales, fables, fairy tales, Bible stories, poetry (which they often were required to memorize), and so on, with the view to developing their reading ability and to teaching them the moral values conveyed by many of the selections.

More recently we have seen a complete change in the nature of our reading textbooks. While some still contain narrative selections, few of these selections would be regarded as literature. More and more space in these books is devoted to factual and informative selections, with the result that many pupils have little exposure to literature in the normal course of their reading programs. Undoubtedly, the recognition that literature ought not to be used to develop basic reading skills has a real influence on the contents of basal readers. But at the same time pupils are being denied the satisfactions of reading and listening to literature unless the appreciation of literature is an integral part of their reading curriculums and planned experiences in reading and listening to literature are offered throughout the elementary grades.

One of the main goals of any reading program should be the development of an appreciation of quality writing and the promotion of permanent interest in reading. Appreciation can lead to greater interest and greater interest to appreciation since each supports the other, but they are not one and the same. Environments that offer opportunities for extensive exposure to books and reading can promote interest in reading, while experiences that enhance one's knowledge of quality writing and sensitivity to it help to develop appreciation. Some of us assume that wide reading leads to appreciation. For some pupils this may be so, but for the majority, opportunities to acquire a knowledge of literary forms and uses of language and to learn how to assess their worth are the means by which they will reach this objective.

Charlotte S. Huck makes a case for reading interest and appreciation of literature. She firmly believes, as do others, that if children learn to read but do not do so, we will have wasted our time and theirs and developed a nation of "illiterate literates." She would make books and reading a natural part of the school environment, expect teachers to serve as models who read and know books, to demonstrate their enthusiasm for them, and to read to children of all ages. She would also allow time in each school day for independent reading, reading just for pleasure, and time for children to talk about books.

Reading in depth builds appreciation for literature. A beginning in this direction could be made by exploring how children respond to a story, how they feel about the story, what it means to them. Once they begin to deal with the "whys" of their feelings, they will touch on the ways in which the author builds plot and develops characters and the way he uses language to create meaning and feeling. The children will develop new insights into meaning and literary style by comparing and contrasting the stories and poems they read.

Bernice D. Ellinger and Sister Mary Julia MacDougall believe that the primary grades are the right place to begin to teach children how to select good reading materials, and that the way to do this is to teach them to read them critically. As was pointed out in section 6, there is no justification for delaying instruction in critical reading. We know that young children can and do think critically, and that there are ample opportunities even in the first grade for promoting the development of critical reading. Certainly the evaluation of materials ought to be one element of critical reading.

Ellinger and MacDougall suggest a number of critical reading activities that will lead children to distinguish forms of literature, to recognize the devices of literary forms, and to develop criteria for evaluating them. What they really advocate is the application of critical reading skills to the reading of literature. This, they believe, will help children to develop a love for good literature and the ability to identify quality in literature.

Poetry is one form of literature that we often neglect. Perhaps this is due to the negative attitudes teachers have toward poetry, attitudes that were fostered by unpleasant experiences with it. How one teacher overcame her children's dislike for this literary form is told by Margaret Koch in "Poetry in the Fourth Grade." Here are some of the children's reasons for liking poetry now:

"This year we could choose the poems we wanted to read. We didn't *have* to memorize poems. But then we did anyway and liked it."

"You read us the poems we liked, not just what you read when you were a little girl."

"We had lots of poetry books in our room so we could read poems by many different poets."

"Yes, and each of us had a paperback poetry book of our own. . . ."

The identification of children's books that have literary merit is a formidable task in view of the fact that more than a thousand are published each year. How to identify potentially favorite books (favorite books are considered good books) of children was the subject of an investigation by Vera Ohanian. She analyzed three known favorite children's books for their apparent and hidden stories and concluded that these books seem to reflect the problems that are common to childhood, and they show that these problems can be dealt with. These problems are revealed through the hidden story and have an impact on children's attitudes toward life. One possible way, then, to judge the quality of this literature is to determine if it contains characteristics that appeal to children. If Ohanian's analysis is accurate, then teachers have a basis for selecting books that children will want to read and that can be used to develop an appreciation of literature.

One major justification for following an individualized reading program is the apparent stimulus it gives to the development of interest in books. This goal will not be realized fully unless the books that appeal to children are made available to them. To know the reading preferences of children, L. F. Ashley claims, is to know also their reading dislikes and the times at which preferences and dislikes peak. He offers data showing what boys and girls in grades four through seven say they prefer to read and what they seem to avoid. Of course, there may be better ways of determining what children *really* will read than by asking them what they prefer and dislike, but Ashley's data do show that a reading program, whatever its nature, must not delay in nurturing good attitudes toward books. To wait is to lose the opportunity to encourage suitable reading habits and tastes.

Strategies for Improving Interest and Appreciation in Literature

CHARLOTTE S. HUCK

If we teach a child to read, yet develop not the taste for reading, all our teaching is for naught. We shall have produced a nation of "illiterate literates"—those who know how to read, but do not read. The major purpose for teaching children to read is to help them become readers who readily turn to books for information and enjoyment. Nearly one hundred and fifty years ago, Sir John Herschel in an address at the opening of a library at Eton said

> Give a man a taste for reading and the means of gratifying it, and you cannot fail to make him a happy, as well as a better man. You place him in contact with the best minds in every period of history, with the wisest and the wittiest, the tenderest and the bravest, those who really adorned humanity. You make him a citizen of all nations and a contemporary of all ages.

Developing interest and appreciation in literature are not the same things, although they are mutually supportive. Interest in reading is developed through the opportunity for *wide reading,* for listening to many stories, through exposure to many books. Appreciation for literature requires knowledge and understanding of fine writing and grows out of the opportunity for reading *in depth.* A child may develop an interest in books independently, whereas the appreciative reader is the informed reader. Discrimination is developed gradually over a period of time; it requires sensitivity to the idea of the book, and sensitivity to the means of expressing that idea. While enthusiasm and interest in good books may be caught, appreciation and discrimination are almost always taught. At the same time we cannot develop appreciative readers until we have captured their interest in reading; and hopefully, appreciation for literature should increase interest. Someone has said you do not enjoy a poem until you understand it—you cannot understand it if you do not enjoy it. Obviously, while interest and appreciation are different in kind and degree, they are closely interrelated and interdependent.

STRATEGIES FOR IMPROVING INTEREST AND APPRECIATION IN LITERATURE by Charlotte S. Huck. From *Reaching Children and Young People Through Literature,* ed. Helen W. Painter (1971), pp. 37–45. Reprinted with permission of the International Reading Association and Charlotte S. Huck.

324

THE READING ENVIRONMENT

How then do we develop this taste for reading; how do we create an interest in books? First we begin very early to make books a natural part of the child's surroundings. Before a child can talk, he should be read to and exposed to good books. While I do not agree with the undue emphasis that is placed upon teaching children the alphabet and how to count on the TV program "Sesame Street," I do commend them for the selection of books that they read to children. For many boys and girls who come from bookless homes, this will be their first exposure to stories and nursery rhymes.

When the child is old enough to come to school, he should enter an environment that invites reading. While central libraries in every elementary school are an absolute necessity, every classroom should have a changing library of two hundred or more books. Many of these could and should be paperback, for paperbacks have a very special appeal for some children. Hopefully, the day will come when each classroom is equipped with a listening center where children may listen to a recording of a book at the same time they read it. Older boys and girls should have an opportunity to listen to various readings of poems or interviews with authors. Films and filmstrips should also be a part of this reading environment since children may come to an appreciation of literature through a variety of media. The private ownership of books can be encouraged through book clubs and school bookstores of paperbacks. Research studies consistently point up the importance of the accessibility of books. If good reading material is constantly available, children will read.

SIGNIFICANT ADULT MODELS

A few children discover books by themselves; in most instances a parent, teacher, or librarian has served as the catalyst for bringing books and children together. As children grow up seeing significant adults as readers, they become readers. Show me a teacher who is enthusiastic about children's books, and I will show you a class of children who enjoy reading. Invariably, the teacher who reads, who knows books, and who shares her enthusiasm with her students will inspire a love of reading.

Teacher education must assume the responsibility for producing informed, enthusiastic teachers. Much needs to be done to improve the teaching of children's literature at both the preservice, inservice, and graduate levels of education. There is much to be learned in the field of children's literature. Students develop real respect for the quality of writing and illustrating in children's books. Since nearly 3,000 children's books are published each year, inservice and graduate courses in children's literature are greatly needed. If a teacher hasn't taken a refresher course in this field in the past ten years, she may have missed 30,000 books!

READING TO CHILDREN

The enthusiastic teacher knows that one of the best ways to create interest in books is to read to children every day. Children should hear many stories before they are expected to read. As they discover that books can produce enjoyment, they gradually develop a purpose for learning to read. Even boys and girls in the middle grades should have a regular story hour. For this is the time their teacher reads the books "too good to miss," or introduces them to several books by just reading enough to capture their interest, or provides depth and balance in their literature program by reading a satire such as Jean Merrill's *The Pushcart War* when many of the students are engrossed in reading sports stories.

Recently, I taught an inservice course in an inner-city school. After I had suggested that each teacher read aloud to her children regardless of grade level, a sixth grade teacher told me that he couldn't read aloud to his children, that they wouldn't listen. I challenged this statement and the next thing I knew, I had agreed to go in and read to them myself. After worrying all the next week about what I would read to them, I selected *Stevie* by John Steptoe. It was short, written and illustrated by a young talented black, and contained the universal theme that we seldom discover how much we like or enjoy a person or object until we have lost it. Before I read the book, I told the class about the author and asked them to decide if he was a good writer and illustrator. I have never read to a more attentive class! Afterwards I asked them if Robert had liked Stevie and one girl replied, "I think he thought he was a nice nuisance." In two words she had summarized the major theme of that story. Of course you could read to that class, but you had to select a story that spoke to the hearts and minds of those children.

SELECTING BOOKS FOR CHILDREN

Books that we read aloud to children should be carefully selected in terms of creating interest in reading and developing appreciation for fine writing. Too frequently the teacher pulls anything off the library shelf to keep the children quiet on Friday afternoons. Other teachers select books to read aloud that will enrich the social studies program. In fact, a recent dissertation completed at Ohio State University by Chow Loy Tom found that nearly 80 percent of the middle grade teachers who do read aloud to their students select books that correlate with social studies. This suggests that little attention is given to the literary experience of hearing *The Courage of Sarah Noble,* or *Carolina's Courage,* but that the emphasis is placed upon the facts of pioneer life and the westward expansion. Children may not be asked to *feel* as Sarah did when she was left alone with the Indians. They may never understand the symbolic meaning of Sarah's cloak, or appreciate the fine use of words by Elizabeth Yates in *Carolina's Courage.* This is using literature for wrong purposes and will never result in an increased understanding and appreciation for it.

Another method by which teachers select books to read aloud is to choose their favorite stories and poems. This approach at least allows the teacher to share her enthusiasm for that particular book or poem. The disadvantage of such an approach is that it provides for no particular balance in what is presented to children either at that level, or at various grade levels. In one survey of a school, we found *Charlotte's Web* was read aloud to the children in second, fourth, fifth, and sixth grades! *Charlotte's Web* is one of the finest children's books of our times, but even so, I question the time spent in reading it aloud that often! Primary teachers will be reading many stories to their children; I hope a minimum of one a day. Hopefully, middle grade teachers will present parts of many books as book teasers to interest children in reading the books. But how many books will teachers read in their entirety? An educated guess might be that starting in the third grade when teachers begin to read longer continuous stories to boys and girls, an average of some four to five books are read aloud during the year. This means that from third grade through sixth grade, children may hear only some twenty books presented by their teacher. Surely, those twenty books should be selected carefully in terms of their relevance for the particular group of boys and girls and for the quality of their writing.

PROVIDING TIME FOR BOOKS

If we are serious about creating an interest in books and a love of reading, we must provide the time for children to read books of their own choosing every day. Plato once said that what is honored in a country will be cultivated there. Go into the typical middle grade classroom and you will find students reading texts for information and instruction, but seldom will they be reading books for pleasure. Interest in reading is created by opportunity for wide reading. If we are as interested in making readers of our children, as in teaching them *to read*, we shall provide as much time for recreational reading as we do for instructional reading.

Interest in books is contagious, so we shall want to provide time for children to share their favorite books. This does not mean requiring a child to write a deadly dull book report or give an oral report every time he has finished a book. We should not penalize children for reading. It does mean providing time for children to get together and share their genuine enthusiasm for a book. I recall one nine-year-old boy who could hardly wait to talk about *The Island of the Blue Dolphins* with his friends. He started his discussion by taking a poll to see how many of five boys in the group had read this book. When he found that some of them had, he said, "Well, you may wonder why I'd like a book with a picture of a girl on the cover, but this isn't like any other story I've ever read, and it is *so* good I've read it four times!" He then went on to discuss what Karana had done for the eighteen years that she had lived on the island alone. His enthusiasm for the book was genuine, his interest was obvious, and needless to say, the other boys in his group could hardly wait to read his book.

READING BOOKS IN DEPTH

Wide reading is necessary for creating interest in books, but reading a book in depth is required for building appreciation for literature. Appreciation for literature is based upon more than enjoyment of books, it is founded upon knowledge and understanding of the idea of the book and the art of writing. Growth in appreciation is gradual and cumulative. The development of taste for literature results from long experience with good books.

Teachers need to know how to teach for literary appreciation. Always, I would begin with the child's response to the story, the way the story made him feel, its meaning for him. Only when I thought children were ready for it, would I ask "How did the author or poet create meaning?" Too frequently teachers do not know how to explore either the feeling or thinking levels of a book, but move children away from the book with extraneous concerns instead of back into the book for enrichment.

This fall I observed a teacher aide who asked all the wrong questions about Yashima's well-known story *Crow Boy*. Her first question to a group of inner-city fourth grade children was, "Where did the story take place?" There was a mad dash to the globe as everyone wanted to point out Japan. She then asked what Japan was, finally eliciting the word she wanted, namely "an island." Her next question concerned Crow Boy's lunch—"Why did he eat rice balls instead of a hamburger?" Eventually they got from an island to growing rice, but Crow Boy was lost along the way. At this point, I could no longer refrain from entering the discussion. I asked the children to recall how Chibi felt at the very beginning of the story. We looked again at the first picture of Chibi hiding under the schoolhouse, and the next one that showed him cowering from the schoolmaster. Then I read them the last two pages that told of a grown-up but still shy Crow Boy who went back to his mountain home giving the cry of the happy crow. We talked about the way Chibi had changed and what had made him change. Looking at the end-papers of that book, I asked the children why Mr. Yashima might have painted a butterfly and blooming branch to represent the story. There was no response, so I asked one final question which was: "What was a butterfly before it was a butterfly?" One boy brandished his hand wildly and said in an excited voice. "It was a caterpillar and it *changed* into a butterfly, just like Chibi changed!"

The questions I asked redirected the children's thinking to the story and helped them see the interrelationship between Chibi's character change and the events that happened to him. Children discovered for themselves the symbolic meaning of Yashima's endpapers. They had read a story in depth, and rather than have a geography lesson, they had *experienced* literature.

COMPARING AND CONTRASTING

Children may develop new insights and discover new meanings in books and poems when they compare and contrast them. Sixth graders could explore the various dimensions of survival by comparing such books as *Island of the Blue Dolphins, The Cay,* and *My Side of the Mountain.* In which of these stories was survival the most difficult? How did enduring the hardships change the characters? Which story was the most believable?

Even young children can compare the theme of sibling rivalry as presented in the realistic story of *Peter's Chair* and the delightful fantasy of a family of badgers in *A Baby Sister for Frances.* In these books, primary children learn that not all baby brothers and sisters are immediately loved and accepted by their older siblings. They can also see how the same theme of the importance and individuality of every member of a family can be the basis for different plots.

Boys and girls may discover that excitement depends upon one's point of view in *Nothing Ever Happens on My Block.* The text of the farcical little book reflects Chester Filbert's dull point of view that nothing exciting ever happens on his street, while the detailed pictures by Ellen Raskin portray amazing happenings at 5264 West One Hundred and Seventy-Seventh Street. Older children can identify the change in point of view in the Benéts' poem of "Abraham Lincoln," in which Lincoln's contemporaries complain that they need a man for troubled times but they have no idea where to find one. In the last verse of that poem, the point of view shifts to that of the modern poet who comments, "That is how they met and talked/Knowing and unknowing,/Lincoln was the green pine,/Lincoln kept on growing."

PLANNING A LITERATURE PROGRAM

Appreciative response to literature does not develop from an in-depth study of one book. It results from the cumulative effect of hearing good books read aloud, discussing and comparing books, and reading and reacting to them from kindergarten through college. Such a program should not be haphazard and incidental. It should be planned and sequential in terms of the background and experience of the children and teachers. If teachers can agree on what literary skills should be taught, such as identification of types or genres of literature, knowledge of such literary constants as theme, characterization, plot, style, and setting, they can use a variety of meaningful books to teach these concepts. Flexibility and choice of books must be kept open, however, for nothing would kill interest in literature faster than to require all children in the elementary school to read certain books. (Look what happened to *Silas Marner!*) The literature program should be planned for each school, for each grade, and consequentially throughout the grades. Growth in appreciation is gradual and cumulative. The development of interest in and taste for literature results from a lifetime love affair with good books.

Bibliography

Benét, Rosemary and Stephen Vincent. *A Book of Americans*. Holt, Rinehart and Winston, 1933.
Dalgliesh, Alice. *The Courage of Sarah Noble*. Scribner's, 1954.
George, Jean. *My Side of the Mountain*. Dutton, 1959.
Hoban, Russell. *A Baby Sister for Frances*. Ill. by Lillian Hoban. Harper, 1964.
Keats, Ezra Jack. *Peter's Chair*. Harper, 1967.
Merrill, Jean. *The Pushcart War*. W. R. Scott, 1964.
O'Dell, Scott. *Island of the Blue Dolphins*. Houghton Mifflin, 1960.
Raskin, Ellen. *Nothing Ever Happens on My Block*. Atheneum, 1966.
Steptoe, John. *Stevie*. Harper, 1969.
Taylor, Theodore. *The Cay*. Doubleday, 1969.
White, E. B. *Charlotte's Web*. Harper, 1952.
Yashima, Taro. *Crow Boy*. Viking, 1955.
Yates, Elizabeth. *Carolina's Courage*. Dutton, 1964.

Reading Literature Critically

BERNICE D. ELLINGER
SISTER MARY JULIA MacDOUGALL

INTRODUCTION

A child who reads one book a week during his entire elementary school career would even then only become familiar with 300 books. With the few outstanding books amid the 3,000 published for children each year, he could easily miss ever reading a really good book. Who could say that the primary grades are too soon to help children improve their ability to select good reading material? The child who recognizes the hallmarks of good writing will be much more likely to read some of the best books that have been writ-

READING LITERATURE CRITICALLY by Bernice D. Ellinger and Sister Mary Julia MacDougall. From *Critical Reading*, ed. Martha L. King et al. (1967), pp. 301–12. Published by J. B. Lippincott Company. Reprinted by permission.

ten for him. Those who help a child to read literature critically are therefore guiding him to the selection of high quality books.

Rationale for Teaching Critical Reading

Doubt has been expressed that direct instruction in critical reading skills is appropriate at the elementary school level. Some people fear that such instruction will contribute to the increasing number of youthful cynics and objectors. Critical reading as it is defined by today's educators implies a positive approach to the printed page, one in which the reader is open to a number of possible alternatives. It is only after careful examination of all the available options that a trustworthy decision can be made. The purpose of reading critically in literature is not to destroy or dissect the work, but to enhance one's appreciation of it. An understanding of the components of fine literature should contribute to a deeper appreciation of the totality of the work.

In this sense, critical reading involves an evaluation of the quality and significance of literature. For such thoughtful reading, certain skills are needed, skills that are different from those used in reading informational material. Because critical reading is comprehensive in nature, effective utilization of it necessitates the ability to determine which skills are appropriate for use. For example, the reader would look for factual accuracy in a history book but not in a book of children's fantasy. Such ability to discriminate is constantly necessary. From the long list of critical reading skills which could be enumerated, only those related to the reading of literature will be discussed here. Even within this limitation, only a cursory explanation of the selected skills can be presented in this article. Illustrative situations are provided which were taken from actual incidents which occurred during the experimental phase of the Critical Reading Project entitled "The Critical Reading Ability of Elementary School Children."[1] Although the experimental treatment included analysis and evaluation of informational materials and literature, the discussion here is restricted to Literary Form, Components of Literature, and Literary Devices, the three major phases of the work with children's literature.

LITERARY FORM

Skills taught in the area of literary form are those which students use (1) to distinguish between types or forms of literature, (2) to recognize the characteristics of specific literary forms, and (3) to develop criteria for evaluating these forms. Ways of teaching some of these skills are illustrated here.

[1] "The Critical Reading Ability of Elementary School Children," supported by the U.S. Office of Education. The principal investigators are Willavene Wolf, Charlotte Huck, and Martha King.

Comparing Fact and Fiction

A teacher who concentrated early efforts in critical reading on helping pupils to assess accuracy and authenticity in informational material made the transition to literature study by helping the second grade group to distinguish between informational books and books of fiction. The focus was thus placed on the form of the work. After *Ducks Don't Get Wet* by Goldin had been read in class during a science study, and McCloskey's *Make Way for Ducklings* had been read aloud for enjoyment, the children compared the two books. They noted that both books contained facts, but that the two authors used the facts in different ways. In comparing the reasons for the illustrations, the children decided that McCloskey used his portrayal of the authentic Boston scenes and of the duck family to help him tell an amusing story, while Goldin used drawings to show the reader what she was explaining in the text. The children further discovered that, although McCloskey's ducks think, talk, and generally act like people, there are no imaginary elements in Goldin's informational book.

The following questions helped to clarify the differences between the two literary forms for these second graders:

How are the two books different?
What did the author intend to do in each book?
How can you tell that a book is fiction?

Developing Criteria for Fiction

Certainly, knowing that a book is fiction is only the first step in learning to read literature critically. A much more important phase of the process is discerning whether the book is *good* fiction. This involves the complex skill of developing criteria. One fourth grade class, when faced with the problem of deciding what makes a book worthwhile, thought they needed a set of standards to use as a measuring stick. The set they developed served as a guide for some of their earliest literary judgments. They considered a book worthy of their time if:

It tells a good story.
The characters seem real.
There is meaning behind the story.
The story is told in an interesting way.

Categorizing Fiction

Within the realm of fiction, children can be helped to see that there are two basic categories: fantasy and realistic fiction. Realistic fiction remains true to the nature of the characters involved; fantasy allows behavior which is not true or even possible in real life.

Children need the fanciful, but taste for it frequently has to be cultivated; likes and dislikes are strongly expressed in this area. The modern child may early come to believe that "the facts" are all important, that books of fantasy are a waste of time when there is so much to learn about the real world. Elementary school children may need help in wondering, questioning, venturing into unknown times and places. The wise teacher guides them to fill this need with imaginary literature.

It is easy for children in the primary grades to identify with Francisco and his desire for a pet dog in *Amigo*. Rather stark reality is displayed in the early text and pictures as the young boy learns some of the deprivations of poverty. About midway through the book, however, there is a subtle change to fantasy. By this time the young realist is so intent upon the budding friendship between Francisco and a prairie dog that he would not exchange this fantasy for all the informational books available.

According to the maturity and experiences of the class groups involved, children can be led to see further subdivisions in fantasy and realistic fiction. Within the first category are the folk tale, fairy tale, fable, myth, and modern fantasy; the second includes historical, biographical, and modern fiction.

Fifth and sixth graders feel quite competent in the process of identifying forms of literature when they can separate historical fiction from biography by knowing, for example, how to correctly classify *Johnny Tremain* and *America's Paul Revere*, two of Esther Forbes' books for young people. Then there is autobiography that they can learn to keep separate from fiction written in the first person. A sixth grade boy was asked about the literary form of *Trace Through the Forest* after the class had enjoyed that book.

> Well, Lafe is telling the story, but since the author is Barbara Robinson, I know it's not an autobiography. It must be fiction then, but it's based on fact. Colonel Zane did cut a road through the wilderness. Since it took place in 1796, it must be historical fiction.

Such reasoning is indeed complicated, but children can work their way through such a process as they clarify ideas about books and stories. They learn to look for different qualities in the various types of literature. They learn to demand accuracy in historical background if the book rests in fact, but they will accept a character from the author's imagination if the hero is believable and true to the life of his times.

As children learn about literary form, poetry need not be slighted. Boys and girls in the primary grades can enjoy more than just the story line of *Amigo*. Since the book is written in verse, the children can have the added joy of listening for the sounds of the ending rhymes. They discover not only that poetry can be enjoyable, but that it can heighten the delight of an already enticing tale. After a happy experience with narrative poetry, lyrical forms may have more appeal. When the children know what to look for, they may find that poetry can be fun.

COMPONENTS OF LITERATURE

The major components of literature identified in the Critical Reading Study were (1) characterization, (2) plot structure, (3) theme and setting with careful analysis of these as an over-arching purpose. Materials were selected from children's literature to illustrate the use of each component.

Appraising Characterization

Since believable characters are a vital part of good literature, attention to characterization is necessary. The carefully delineated character in Stolz's *Dog on Barkham Street* and *Bully on Barkham Street* change during the story, but they meet the criteria of being both possible and believable changes. Fourth grade students found that they could understand why Martin Hastings acted as he did, once they had read the story told from his point of view. Characters who behaved the same at the end of the story as they did at the beginning were contrasted with ones who changed or developed during the story. First graders recognized that Madeline acted the same way at the end of the book *Madeline* as she did at the beginning, whereas Chibi had changed his behavior by the end of *Crow Boy*. The changes were made gradually and believably. Flat, stereotyped characters were compared in several books with well developed, believable ones in order to show the contribution the latter make to the quality of literature.

Sperry uses nine ways to reveal the character of Mafatu in the first chapter of *Call It Courage*. Fifth graders easily recognized the selections in which the author revealed Mafatu's thoughts, described him, his surroundings, and his actions, showed what others said to Mafatu and how they reacted to him. They used these ways of revealing character in their own writing as a way of becoming familiar with the techniques of characterization. The original stories were read aloud and the class members identified the approach used by each pupil. Books which had been read by the group were evaluated to determine how well the author had done in producing a believable character. Examining methods of developing characterization proved to be a useful approach to the study of this important component of literature.

Identifying Plot Structure

Lessons on plot structure were developed to help students see why an author puts a story together as he does. Elements such as the introduction, build-up, climax, and ending of a story were identified by the children and viewed as a basic framework for a story. Children can see how each part of the story gets bigger and more fantastic as it progresses through the snowballing "tall tale" approach used by Dr. Seuss. In the Seuss selections of "Marco Come Late" and *To Think That I Saw It on Mulberry Street* there is a sudden drop in suspense at the end of the story when the main character comes back to reality with his tale.

Accumulative plot structures were found in Nic Leodhas's *All in the Morning Early,* and *Always Room for One More,* and Galdone's *House that Jack Built.* In these books, each event builds upon the preceding one until a peak is reached; then the action backtracks or ends with a dramatic climax. Books such as *Homer Price* and *Little House in the Big Woods* where the action begins and ends in each chapter were viewed as episodic. Some such books have a continuity in which one episode necessarily follows another, but each story stands independently in the chapters of *Homer Price.*

Parallel plot structure was illustrated in McCloskey's *Blueberries for Sal.* In this story, the author switches back and forth from Sal and her mother to Little Bear and his mother as both pairs go blueberry picking. The climaxes in the two plots appear one after the other and the stories end separately. The story of either Sal and her mother or of Little Bear and his mother going blueberry picking would not have been particularly interesting, but the crossing of the parallel plots made the tale an exciting one.

Becoming Acquainted with Story Theme

Teachers who had allowed children to read at a literal level were not able to get them to identify the theme of a book easily. When a question such as "What is the main idea of this story?" was asked, these children would begin telling what happened in the plot. Only after illustrating with obvious themes in simple picture books could the teacher get the children to discover a message which goes beyond the plot of the story. The idea that we really ought to be ourselves is portrayed in *Dandelion, Little Rabbit Who Wanted Red Wings, Harry, the Dirty Dog,* and *The Unhappy Hippopotamus.* When first graders realized that the same basic idea came through in a number of different stories, they could make the distinction between theme and plot.

Comparing fairy tales proved to be a useful way to illustrate story themes. *The Emperor's New Clothes* and "Master Till Paints a Picture" both show that most people do not want to admit that they have anything but the highest virtues and qualities. In each story, a cruel hoax is exposed by one person's truthfulness.

Recognizing Story Setting

A component of literature which is fairly easy for children to identify is story setting. The relevance of the setting to the plot can be illustrated by discussing the kinds of things that can happen in the story. If the time and place concern pioneer days in the west, one could not suddenly arrange an airplane flight. When the reader knows the time and place of a story he may to some extent predict what events will take place. He may even predict what a person will do, for he realizes that people are influenced by the circumstances in which they find themselves. The critical reader asks, "Why does the character think, act, and talk the way he does in the story?" and "Would the character have acted differently under different circumstances?" The fine work that is produced in some historical fiction is the result of meticulous planning of details. Jean Lee Latham studies reports of the period about which she writes. Treating the facts as a framework, she skillfully weaves her story among them. Many of the details do not appear overtly in the story, but they provide the backdrop of information as she writes. The critical reader evaluates how well the author stayed within the stricture of the time and place he has chosen and also determines how the setting affects the action and character development of the particular story.

LITERARY DEVICES

In the third section of the literary study an attempt was made to put the child in the place of the author and to help him think as an author thinks about writing. Some topics of study were: (1) devices for story development, (2) ways of achieving mood, and (3) characteristics of writing style. Children examined the techniques an author uses in the production of literature and began to evaluate his effectiveness. Examples of beginning classroom efforts at such evaluation follow.

Learning About Story Devices

Some first graders learned about an author's use of foreshadowing in story development with Keats' *The Snowy Day*. After reading the page which tells that Peter put the snowball in his pocket, the teacher asked:

What will happen to Peter's snowball?
Will Peter be disappointed?

After the children's prediction had come true, the teacher questioned further:

Why was Peter sad?
Did he understand what happened to his snowball?
How did *you* know what was going to happen?

These children gained only the beginnings of an understanding of the foreshadowing technique from this story, but they showed that they understood a character's feelings better because they had gained some hint of them ahead of time.

Boys and girls who read widely discover that authors choose to present their stories from various points of view. Presenting the action from a definite perspective is a necessary element in story development and children can learn to grasp its importance. Some excellent books for fifth and sixth graders have been written in the first person; *Island of the Blue Dolphins* is but one example. Everything comes to the reader in this book through the words and thoughts of Karana. The reader gains an understanding of the character from this technique which could hardly be achieved in any other way. With guidance, children can critically consider the effectiveness of an author's choice of point of view.

A third grade teacher used *Where the Wild Things Are* to help a group learn about an author's use of symbolism. The pupils learned that ordinary things—such as the food that was still hot in the story discussed—can stand for complicated ideas. Here a mother's love and forgiveness were symbolized effectively by a warm supper for her son. This experience with symbolism in a picture book may open the door to richer experiences with literature. It is difficult for children to get the idea that one thing "represents" another, but numerous illustrations with stories in which this is done help.

Only three of the many devices an author may use in developing his story have thus far been mentioned. A fourth is essential in a discussion of children's literature: an author's treatment of fantasy. This actually involves a number of techniques; one of the most intriguing is how the author makes fantasy believable. Of what good is a story which does not hold a reader's interest and, at least to some extent, his credibility?

Charlotte's Web was studied by a fifth grade at this level of analysis. Some of the key questions of the discussion were:

1. What type of literature does the book start out to be?
2. When and how does the fantasy begin?
3. How is Fern's appearance in the story treated after the fantasy is introduced?
4. Does Fern understand the talk of the animals?
5. Does Fern ever talk to the animals?

As children watch a story which begins in a realistic setting subtly turn into fantasy, they become aware of the skill of a master at work. Animals talk to each other and the story becomes quite involved, but people never talk to the animals, and for those who have not lost the wonder of childhood, the story remains believable to the end.

Detecting Mood

The mood of a book is a very subtle "feeling" that the reader gets as he reads or it may be considered the spell that is cast by a book. The pictures and the language in *The Moon Jumpers* combine to cast a spell of a warm summer moonlit night. Words such as "drowsy," "tired," "fall asleep," and "dream" contribute to the feeling of a late evening in the yard while the misty, dusk-like illustrations extend the eerie feeling of being outside late at night after others have gone to bed. The book has the effect of poetry; it creates a mood in a very few lines.

The language of a story generally carries the mood to the reader. From the first page of *Rabbit Hill* there is a feeling of excitement and suspense. Phrases such as "the hill was boiling with excitement," "new folks a' coming, new folks a' coming" quickly ensnare the reader in the mood of the story. Wojciehowska uses short snatches of conversation by unidentified townspeople to build up the feeling of expectation for Manola in *Shadow of a Bull*. "It's the eyes. He has exactly the same look in his eyes. The same sad eyes."

Books which describe a unique ethnic group or a particular period of history use authentic speech to help create a mood. The Amish in *Wonderful, Nice* use words such as "rootch over, Katy," and "Lost you are, maybe?" to create the mood in the story. *The Blind Colt* depicts life on the western plains and includes the words "critter," "yo'all," "little feller," and "young'un" to help the reader feel that he is really in the setting of the story.

Appreciating the Author's Style

Children can evaluate dialogue and authentic speech to see if they contribute to or detract from the story. Some of the spelling necessary to depict authentic speech makes reading difficult, but it is acceptable if it contributes to vivid characterization. Regional stories would not be authentic if their characters spoke standard English.

Metaphorical language contributes to writing style and can bring numerous mental pictures to the reader. The poet who wrote "The Moon's the North Wind's Cooky; He bites it day by day" certainly did not intend to be taken literally. Children are generally literal readers and act much like Amelia (in *Amelia Bedelia* by Peggy Parrish) as she follows her employer's list of housecleaning chores. To her, "Dusting the furniture" meant sprinkling dusting powder on the pieces.

Writing style is related to the point of view from which a story is told, the mood that it creates, and the content of the book. Children learn that an informational book should not try to couch facts in poetic, metaphorical terms, nor should a book of fantasy be written in terse declarative sentences. Books such as *May I Bring a Friend* and *Madeline,* which are written in rhyme, appeal to young children. Children frequently can supply the rhyming word or can join in a repetitive phrase such as "Hundreds of cats, Thousands of cats, Millions and billions and trillions of cats" from Gag's *Millions of Cats*. Children can also evaluate the writing style in relation to the type of book, the mood that it attempts to create, and the purpose for which it was written.

CONCLUSION

After a series of experiences in evaluation of literature, children were given reviews of children's books written by adults. The children read the book themselves, wrote their own reviews and then compared their reviews with those of adults. This technique of criticizing the critics provided an opportunity for the application of a number of the skills of literary analysis. Children were motivated to take a stand on a book and either recommend it or not recommend it and tell why they chose as they did. Critical reading involves taking a stand, making a judgment, and giving criteria for the stand taken. This kind of exercise was helpful in encouraging children to do these things.

Critical reading, then, involves skills which contribute to the development of criteria for evaluating literature. It requires that the reader go beyond the literal level of getting meaning from a printed page. It involves recognizing the hallmarks of good writing and gaining some understanding of the components of good literature. Primarily, the purpose of reading critically is to enhance or deepen the reader's appreciation of literature, and all activities that are directed toward critical reading must contribute to this over-arching purpose. Shallow teaching could distort these worthwhile goals and result in children's superficial ability to "label" components, devices, and forms of literature. At the elementary school level, the labels are not as important as the full enjoyment of literature. Inspired teaching can help children develop a love for good literature and can help them to recognize it in the morass of annual publications.

Bibliography of Children's Books

Hans Christian Andersen, *The Emperor's New Clothes*. Illustrated and translated by Erik Blegvad. New York: Harcourt Brace Jovanovich, 1959.
C. S. Bailey, *Little Rabbit Who Wanted Red Wings*. New York: Platt and Munk, 1931.
Ludwig Bemelmans, *Madeline*. Illustrated by author. New York: Viking, 1939.
Beatrice Schenk de Regniers, *May I Bring A Friend?* Illustrated by Beni Montresor. New York: Atheneum, 1964.
Esther Forbes, *Johnny Tremain*. Illustrated by Lynd Ward. Boston: Houghton Mifflin, 1943.
———, *America's Paul Revere*. Illustrated by Lynd Ward. Boston: Houghton Mifflin, 1946.
Don Freeman, *Dandelion*. New York: Macmillan, 1964.
Godfrey Freeman, "Master Till Paints a Picture," in *The Owl and the Mirror*. New York: Duell, Sloan and Pearce, 1960.
Wanda Gag, *Millions of Cats*. Illustrated by author. New York: Coward-McCann, 1928.
Paul Galdone, *House That Jack Built*. Whittlesey, 1961.
Dr. Theodore Seuss Geisel, "Marco Comes Late," in *Treat Shop*. Edited by Eleanor Johnson and Leland Jacobs. Columbus, Ohio: Charles E. Merrill, 1954.
———, *To Think That I Saw It on Mulberry Street*. New York: Vanguard Press, 1937.
Augusta Goldin, *Ducks Don't Get Wet*. New York: Thomas Y. Crowell, 1965.
Ezra Jack Keats, *The Snowy Day*. Illustrated by author. New York: Viking, 1962.
Robert Lawson, *Rabbit Hill*. Illustrated by author. New York: Viking, 1944.
Sorche Nic Leodhas, *All in the Morning Early*. Illustrated by Evaline Ness. New York: Holt, Rinehart and Winston, 1963.

————, *Always Room For One More*. New York: Holt, Rinehart and Winston, 1965.

Robert McCloskey, *Make Way For Ducklings*. Illustrated by author. New York: Viking, 1941.

————, *Homer Price*. Illustrated by author. New York: Viking, 1943.

————, *Blueberries For Sal*. New York: Viking, 1948.

Nancy Moore, *The Unhappy Hippopotamus*. Illustrated by Edward Leight. New York: Vanguard Press, 1957.

Scott O'Dell, *Island of the Blue Dolphins*. New York: Houghton Mifflin, 1960.

Peggy Parrish, *Amelia Bedelia*. New York: Harper, 1963.

Barbara Robinson, *Trace Through the Forest*. New York: Lothrop, Lee and Shepard, 1965.

Glen Rounds, *The Blind Colt*. Illustrated by author. New York: Holiday House, 1941.

Byrd Baylor Schweitzer, *Amigo*. Illustrated by Garth Williams. New York: Macmillan, 1963.

Irma Selz, *Wonderful, Nice*. New York: Lothrop, Lee and Shepard, 1960.

Maurice Sendak, *Where The Wild Things Are*. Illustrated by author. New York: Harper, 1963.

Armstrong Sperry, *Call It Courage*. Illustrated by author. New York: Macmillan, 1940.

Mary Stolz, *A Dog on Barkham Street*. New York: Harper, 1960.

————, *The Bully on Barkham Street*. Illustrated by Leonard Shortall. New York: Harper, 1963.

Janice Udry, *The Moon Jumpers*. Illustrated by Maurice Sendak. New York: Harper, 1959.

E. B. White, *Charlotte's Web*. *Illustrated* by Garth Williams. New York: Harper, 1952.

Laura Ingalls Wilder, *Little House In The Big Woods*. Illustrated by Garth Williams. New York: Harper, 1932; 1953.

Maia Wojciechowska, *Shadow of a Bull*. Illustrated by Alvin Smith. New York: Atheneum, 1964.

Taro Yashima, *Crow Boy*. Illustrated by author. New York: Viking, 1955.

Gene Zion, *Harry, The Dirty Dog*. New York: Harper, 1956.

Poetry in the Fourth Grade

MARGARET KOCH
and Her Fourth Grade Class

MRS. KOCH: We have been invited to tell you about poetry and the way we have approached poetry in our fourth grade. We have been reading a lot of poetry this year, and we have learned to know a great many poets.

If you could visit our class, you would see many paintings which have grown out of our reading of poetry. The mural back of us was created in our class by boys and girls who enjoyed "The Jumblies" by Edward Lear. On a table near the window, we have our collection of poetry books which children may borrow whenever they care to. Often that table is bare—which

POETRY IN THE FOURTH GRADE by Margaret Koch. From *Teaching Reading—Not by Decoding Alone*, Highlight of the 18th and 19th Annual Reading Conferences, Lehigh University, 1971, ed. Joseph P. Kender, pp. 107–14. Published by The Interstate Printers and Publishers, Inc. Reprinted by permission.

simply means the books are tucked in the children's desks or are in use in some poetry project.

We find that we enjoy poetry more when we have our desks in a circle. (*to the children*) Can you explain how we came to use the circle plan?

CHILDREN: It's more interesting when you can see the faces of the people who read. . . . You can hear better too. . . . Yes, and you can act out poems in the middle of the circle. I like that.

MRS. KOCH: What kinds of poems do you like best?

CHILDREN: Funny poems. . . . Like "You Know Who" by John Ciardi. . . . And "Hey Bug" by Lilian Moore. . . . Well, I like "Ants Were Here" even better.[1]

MRS. KOCH: Are there other kinds of poems you enjoy too?

CHILDREN: Animal poems. . . . My favorite is "Missing" by A. A. Milne. It's about a mouse. . . . I like "Kittens" by Eve Merriam. . . . And don't forget "Little Turtle" by Vachel Lindsay. . . . The one I like best is "Lone Dog" by Irene Rutherford McLeod.

MRS. KOCH: Can you think of any poet who writes chiefly about nature— animals, insects, plants, and all the rest?

CHILDREN: Aileen Fischer. . . . She wrote a book I like called *Listen, Rabbit!* . . . *Cricket in a Thicket* is good too because it has lots of little poems.

EUGENE: We read sad poems too.

CHILDREN: Some are not really sad, just serious, like "This Is My Rock" by David McCord. . . . And "The Snare" about a rabbit that is caught in a trap. That one made me want to cry.

MRS. KOCH: It's strange, but sometimes we like a poem that almost makes us cry. I wonder why.

CHILDREN: Well, you like to feel the way the poet feels. I mean poets seem to be just like us. They feel. . . .

MRS. KOCH: Can you think of a poet—or a poem—that shows the poet feels the way you do?

SHARON: Karla Kuskin wrote a poem about waking up in the morning. That's just the way I feel.

JEFF: Lilian Moore called her book of poems, *I Feel the Same Way*.

MRS. KOCH: Jeff, I think you have become a real Lilian Moore fan. It's good to have one poet you know all about, isn't it?

[1] Throughout the discussion, the children read and recited many poems not quoted here.

CHILDREN: My favorite is John Ciardi. . . . Mine is Harry Behn. . . . Don't forget A. A. Milne, he's for me.

MRS. KOCH: People always ask about memorizing poetry. This year no one has been required to memorize a poem. Yet I think many of you could stand up here and recite an entire poem, maybe half a dozen. How many of you really find it is fun to memorize a poem? (About two-thirds raise their hands.) I never liked to memorize a poem when I was in school so I always wonder why you boys and girls respond in a different way. Can you explain this?

CHILDREN: For one thing you let us choose the poems we memorize so each of us can pick a favorite. . . . Then we all have different poems, and you don't have to listen to the same poem over and over again, maybe 30 times. . . . I like to hear people recite their poems when they get lots of expression in the lines. That's fun.

MRS. KOCH: What are some of the other ways to have fun with poetry?

CHILDREN: Sometimes we read poems in parts. I mean maybe the boys read the first two lines, and the girls read the next two. Like that. . . . Acting out a poem is the best.

MRS. KOCH: What poems have you found to be good for acting out?

CHILDREN: "Buckingham Palace" by A. A. Milne. . . . "Puppy and I" by Milne, too. . . . "The Owl and the Pussy Cat" . . . "The Jumblies" . . .

MRS. KOCH: Would you like to act out one of these poems for our friends here today? Yes? Which one?

CHILDREN: "The Jumblies" (children act this poem out).

MRS. KOCH: Every now and then I find a surprise on my desk in the form of a poem one of you has written. One of the first people to try his hand as a poet was Rod Sassaman, who is a racer. He has won several county championships in three-quarter midget racing. Rod . . .

ROD: Well, my first poem is called "My Racer."

> *Does my racer ever*
> *get tired of turning*
> *its wheels round and round?*
>
> *Does it ever feel like quitting*
> *in front of the finish line*
> *and let me feel*
> *like a sitting duck?*

MRS. KOCH: One day I received a poem from David McKalip. Will you tell us about how you wrote this poem, David?

DAVID: I wrote it in two parts. When I finished the first half, it seemed like it ought to have music with it. Our music teacher helped me fit it to the autoharp so now it really has music. Then I kept thinking about it, and I wrote the rest of it and made up the chords to that too. It doesn't have a title so I'll just read it.

> *The stars*
> *are like the pearls*
> *in a deep, dark sea*
>
> *But the moon*
> *is a glowing shell*
> *that shines on me.*
>
> *There are many mysteries*
> *in the sounds of the night—*
> *that I shall never hear*
> *with the morning light.*

MRS. KOCH: Some of us get inspiration for poems from the poetry books we have read. One of those books is *See What I Found* by Myra Cohn Livingston, who tells of finding a piece of string, a paper clip, and many other things that we might call junk. After we read that book, we decided to bring in our own basket of junk and write about the things we found. Will you read some of those poems?

LEE ANN:

> *See what I found! An egg box.*
> *A magical land with mountains to climb.*
> *A box to keep my secrets in.*
> *A place for my dolls to have fun.*
> *A little tent to hide inside.*
> *A giant inside swimming pool*
> *   for me to swim in.*
> *A forest of tree stumps*
> *   for me to sit on.*
> *See what I've done,*
> *   you try it too.*

EUGENE:

> *See what I found! A trivet.*
> *an arrow that belonged*
> *   to an Indian—*
> *a rocket going to the moon*
> *or a knife to kill an animal.*

ROD:

> *See what I found! A tulip bulb*
> *it could be a snake—*
> *a cobra—*
> *a piper is piping*

> *the snake is climbing*
> *out of its basket.*
> *Now it's sticking out its stinger*
> *It's climbing around*
> *and then back into his basket*
> *Ready for the next show.*
>
> *Good-night.*

DANNY: Another book that gave us ideas for poems is *Prayers from the Ark.* . . .

MRS. KOCH: Yes, after we read that book, we made a list of animals not included in the book. Then we tried to think what each animal might pray for, and many people in this class wrote prayers in the style of the poet, Carmen Bernos de Gasztold. Danny, we all remember yours.

DANNY: Mine is the prayer of the racoon.

> *O Lord,*
> *Why did you put this mask*
> *on my face?*
> *Hunters like to shoot me.*
> *Animals like to eat me.*
> *And all I do is*
> *roam the woods*
> *and mind my own business.*
>
> *Amen.*

MRS. KOCH: One day Rod came in to class, and said, "I love poetry." I'll never forget that day because so many of you said you felt the same way. Some of you even said you used to hate poetry, but now you like to read poetry. I wonder why.

CHILDREN: This year we could choose the poems we wanted to read.

We didn't *have* to memorize poems. But then we did anyway and liked it.

You read us the poems we liked, not just what you read when you were a little girl.

We had lots of poetry books in our room so we could read poems by many different poets.

Yes, and each of us had a paperback poetry book of our own—*The Arrow Book of Poetry.* . . .

I liked hearing the recordings of poets reading their own poetry—like David McCord and Aileen Fischer.

We could act out poems, too, or do whatever we wanted, like painting a mural or having a poetry pantomime.

When somebody got us started on a poem, we all wanted to read more. It was neat.

(After 50 minutes of discussion and reading of poetry the fourth graders withdrew, and a panel of three teachers commented on their use of poetry in the elementary grades and answered a number of queries from the audience.)

MRS. GORDON: After hearing these fourth graders read poetry, no one should think he needs special training in speech to do a convincing job. Enjoyment and appreciation are the only factors needed to read aloud for the enjoyment of others. Each of the children who read today sparked the reading of the other children.

MRS. RAFAELLI: One of the poetry books that has helped my second graders write their own poems is *Hailstone and Halibut Bones* by Mary O'Neill. Each poem is unrhymed and about a different color. Let me read a color poem written by a seven-year-old, Chris Pivnichny:

> *Brown*
>
> *I like brown*
> *because paper bags*
> *are brown*
> *And Negroes*
> *are brown*
> *sitting in the sun.*
> *I like brown*
> *because roots are brown.*

When children learn that a poem doesn't have to rhyme, they feel free to say just what they mean in their own poems. They are no longer tied down with trying to find words that will rhyme.

MRS. HORVATH: My sixth graders wrote a number of color poems, too. For example, let me read one by Charles Rugh:

> *Red is a house on fire*
> *And the flames shooting*
> *Left and right.*
> *Red is the sun—*
> *Burning with fear.*

Boys seem to enjoy poetry just as much as the girls—sometimes even more. Also, some of my really slow readers responded to poetry as enthusiastically as the very best readers. Sixth graders who read on a third-grade level, according to the tests, write some of the most interesting and imaginative poetry.

MRS. KOCH: Sometimes they read poetry aloud better than children in the top group who go so fast you can't understand half [of what] they say.

MRS. RAFAELLI: One way to help those youngsters who are slow readers—and even slower writers—is to let children work in groups when they write poetry. Sometimes the whole class will work on a poem. One or two children start off and that seems to spark the others. Even the slowest learners come in with their ideas. They see their lines added to the poem I am putting up on the board. Here is a class poem my second graders wrote.

The Color of Spring

Spring is the color of buds laughing in the trees
The animals waking from their deep sleep
A fluffy cloud in the sky of blue
Of grass getting green
Of flowers blooming
Of geese honking north again
Of raindrops splattering in puddles
Of butterflies fluttering in the sunshine
Of Easter eggs in a basket
Of snow melting
Of days growing warmer and longer
Of buttercups and pussywillows
And the ladybugs crawling on a twig.

AUDIENCE: When do you find time for all of this poetry? Do you have a regularly scheduled poetry period on a certain day of the week, for example?

MRS. HORVATH: I find that poetry just comes up without scheduling. It becomes part of the language arts program—whenever we read or write or listen, we seem to include poetry.

MRS. GORDON: It has to come naturally. Sometimes the class will be gung-ho on poetry for a week or two—have it every day—and then not include poetry for a couple of weeks.

MRS. HORVATH: One of the nice things is that poetry can be correlated with everything else—art, music, social studies, and even physical education.

MRS. GORDON: There are poetic implications in almost every discipline—even math.

MRS. KOCH: The secret of this is for the teacher to be so well aware of the poems children like that when a subject comes up—or an incident occurs in the class—you think to yourself, "There's a poem about that," and so you bring it out whether you are teaching social studies or science or just talking about the rainstorm last night. You don't say you're going to teach poetry every day for 40 minutes. Just a few minutes with a poem you enjoy and that fits into the theme of the moment is better than 40 minutes creating a hatred for poems by dissecting them.

Cherished Books of Children:

What Makes Them So?

VERA OHANIAN

Close to 1410 books were published for children in 1969. The exploding book population complicates the problem of separating the literary gem from the chaff. The geegaws must be found for the pile clearly labeled Not-For-The-Taking and the literature of worth For-Children's-Savoring.

THE PROBLEM: IDENTIFYING POTENTIALLY FAVORITE BOOKS FOR CHILDREN

Identifying the contemporary literature of worth is a task important to parents and teachers. How can such books be known? Books beloved by children appear to be a logical source. The established literary heritage, the books which have passed the test of time and children's reading, yields models useful to understanding the nature of potentially favorite books.

It is pertinent to review *what* literature affords children in the judgment of a professor of children's literature and a psychoanalyst. Leland B. Jacobs states:

> Literature has great possibilities for helping the young reader in his search for self. As one identifies his character he begins for the moment to walk in the shoes and live in the skin of another person and in so doing he begins to forge ideas about himself. (3:1)

Lili Peller, in a penetrating revelation, asserts:

> At the core of every successful story there is a universal day-dream. The tale begins, the curtain rises, the reader identifies with the hero, and enjoys experiences inaccessible to him in reality (5:430)
> Before he encountered the story, his own daydream may have been unconscious or conscious or have lost access to consciousness (becoming repressed), and now regains it or comes close to consciousness. (5:415)

CHERISHED BOOKS OF CHILDREN: WHAT MAKES THEM SO? by Vera Ohanian. From *Elementary English,* 47 (November 1970), pp. 946–52. Copyright © 1970 by the National Council of Teachers of English. Reprinted by permission of the publisher and Vera Ohanian.

It appears that literature offers unique possibilities for discovering and better understanding the self. That is to say, literature permits children to investigate and know deep-most thoughts, beliefs, feelings, fears, and wishes that exist about the self. It helps children to explore and comprehend inner space as opposed to *outer* space, i.e., to know the self in distinction to knowing of Sputniks, rockets, turtles, and the moon.

EXPLORATION OF THE PROBLEM

To understand the nature of favorite books, three known choices of children, Armstrong Sperry's *Call It Courage,* Rumer Godden's *Impunity Jane,* and A. A. Milne's *Winnie-The-Pooh* are explored. A brief resume of the apparent story, an analysis of the significance of story events, and a summary are presented.

Call It Courage: The Apparent Story

Call It Courage is a story about a fifteen-year-old Polynesian, Mafatu, the son of Tavana Nui, Great Chief of Hikueru. It takes place before the dawn of recorded history in the Pacific South Seas. Mafatu is unable to master the male activities of his tribe because of a fear of the sea acquired at the age of three in a near-fatal drowning during a hurricane which took the life of his mother. Taunted by his peers for his inability and saddened by his father's silence, Mafatu steals away from the island in an outrigger canoe with his only friend, his dog Uri, resolved to conquer his fear of the sea. Mafatu survives a hurricane, eluding Moana, the sea god. He is washed ashore unclothed and unarmed on a desolate island where he fends superbly for himself. He escapes from the eaters-of-men to return to his father and his island-home very obviously a man.

The Hidden Story

The less apparent story is woven along with the more obvious. The covert story deals with the problems of feeling or being found inadequate and unacceptable and its resolution. Feelings of inadequacy and incompetency stem from a condition basic to childhood, the hurdles and continually increasing tasks faced in growing up. Explored in *Call It Courage* are the persistent questions facing the child, "Am I up to it? Can I make it?" An examination of story events which support the interpretation are listed below:

1. The sharp contrast between the status of the father and of the son suggests the enormity of the demands perceived by Mafatu in the task of growing up. The father is the Great Chief of Hikueru, and the son, Mafatu, meaning Stout Heart (which again underlines the demands felt in the direction of

growing up), is in reality a weak heart. For fifteen years following his birth, Mafatu has failed to fulfill the expectations suggested in his name and befitting the first-born son of the Great Chief. The discrepancy between expectation and achievement identifies the problem.

2. Mafatu's failure to achieve, clearly and logically accounted for, lends reality to his child-like and helpless status. A trauma of near-drowning at age three during a hurricane which took the life of his mother and left Mafatu with a haunting fear of the sea explains his inability to achieve and win acceptance. His fear of the sea is reiterated in persistent fantasies and strong accompanying physical reactions. While the surf pounds at night, Mafatu hears the threat made by Moana, the sea god, "You cheated me once, Mafatu. Someday, someday I will claim you." And Mafatu's hands become damp and cold; his knuckles whiten, as his nails dig into his palms.

3. His relationships are indicative of his unacceptable status. His step-mother knows "little sympathy" for Mafatu; his father is silent, grim, and ashamed of him while other elders of the community whisper about his inability. His step-brothers openly scorn Mafatu, and his peers laugh at him, making his heart feel "like a stone." Indeed, it is as if people are dead to him and he to them. Mafatu is portrayed as a youth isolated from human contact.

4. His associations with two animal friends are further revealing. Both animals are defective. Mafatu's dog, Uri, is "non-descript," and Kivi, the albatross with one foot smaller than the other, is heckled and pestered by other birds but befriended by Mafatu. Why is Mafatu's dog unclassifiable? Is not Uri's non-descriptiveness a reflection of Mafatu's plight? Mafatu, like Uri, does not belong. And, is there not strong similarity between the heckled and pestered Kivi and the scorned and laughed at Mafatu?

5. Mafatu's fantasies reflect his intense need to build status to win his father's approval and to feel comfortable with himself. Mafatu fantasies his father saying, "Here is my son, Stout Heart. A brave name for a brave boy." And so that his father may be proud of him, he imagines others saying, "There goes Mafatu. He killed the wild boar single-handed."

6. Mafatu's desperate need to flee Hikueru, to ride out a fierce hurricane in an outrigger canoe and to land on a strange island, alone, stark naked, equipmentless, and weaponless testify to the intense feelings of inadequacy evoked by the insurmountable difficulties perceived in the task of growing up, of mastering. His condition upon arrival at the island poignantly communicates profound feelings of being unequal to the challenge.

7. His near unbelievable and too numerous achievements once on Forbidden Island suggest the urgency to accomplish, to grow, and thus to earn acceptance. Why must he make a fire, a shelter, a dugout canoe from a tree felled by his own hands, and all array of tools, and a raft necessary for survival? Why must he also kill a boar, hammer-head shark, and an octopus? And why must he further top his achievements by invading the Sacred Place of the Eaters-of-Men to steal a spear? And why must he be pursued by black figures in war canoes only to elude them, to return home the proven son of a Polynesian chief?

Call It Courage has been designated an "exciting action tale" and Mafatu, "the son of a Polynesian Chief, rejected by his people for his cowardice." Mafatu is regarded as "a hero for city-raised children to encounter." (5:418) Indeed, Mafatu is an ageless hero for children in any corner of the earth. *Call It Courage* states a problem common to childhood, the finding of acceptance and belongingness, through the successful resolution of the tasks continually faced in growing up. It enables the ten- and eleven-year-old, with whom the book is popular, to identify with Mafatu, even to take on the powers of a fifteen-year-old in solving one of the most basic of problems. The child reader accompanies Mafatu who actively goes out and proves himself. Feelings of powerlessness aroused by failure are counteracted through Mafatu's fantastic achievements. Essentially, *Call It Courage* expresses the continual challenge children perceive in growing up and the apprehensions they experience regarding their adequacy to deal with the next task.

Impunity Jane: The Apparent Story

Impunity Jane, a delightful volume by Rumer Godden, is about Impunity Jane, a four-inch pocket doll of thick china with movable legs and arms and a wig of yellow hair. Her life begins in London, England, in the late nineteenth century when gas lights are in mode and lasts half a century to the time of T.V. Impunity Jane is purchased by a grandmother for her granddaughter, Effie, to play with in her doll house, but Jane is unhappy not only with Effie but all her other female players, Elizabeth, Ethel, and Ellen. It is not until she is stolen by Ellen's boy cousin, Gideon, that life, after fifty years of boredom, becomes exciting and joyous.

The Hidden Story

Ostensibly, *Impunity Jane* is a story of a pocket doll who finally finds a pocket in which she is happy. But what is the less apparent story, which is not as easily told but more readily felt? The hidden story of *Impunity Jane* reveals a universal phenomena, the curiosity which boys and girls experience regarding each other's sex world. The girls' interest in and envy of the life of boys is more dominantly expressed. Gideon is curious also, but his curiosity is not mingled with feelings that a girl's world is more desirable. His interest runs to the degree of finding out about a girl's world. Story situations which spell out this interpretation are listed:

1. Impunity Jane's curiosity in and desire for the life of a boy is suggested in the first passage when she asserts that she belongs in a pocket and not in a doll house as everyone else thought. The desired pocket is not Grandma's (for she needs to peek out and look beyond it), but Gideon's. The male pocket serves as a vehicle for exploring a boy's life.

2. Her desire for exploring a boy's life is further revealed in her affinity for such adventurous toys as a skipping rope, a telescope, and a sailing ship and more strongly in her desire to be these male toys. Indeed, it is almost as if Impunity Jane desires to be a boy, "to go," "to see," and "to enjoy" the vigorous life of a boy. And as Jane recites "I'm, imp-imp—Impunity Jane," her desire to be a tomboy is more subtly suggested. Is not Jane's wish to become a boy naughty and unrealistic, the work of magic? Is not her fear in having her wish fulfilled assuaged by asserting that she can escape without harm forever?

3. Dissatisfaction with the world of girls is none-too subtly expressed in the fifty years spent in a doll house, the symbol of imprisoned feelings and confinement. Effie's beaded cushion feels like pebbles to Jane and Elizabeth's stitches more like carving knives. Ethel's efforts to educate Jane secure half-hearted attention. And life with Ellen reaches its lowest ebb as Jane sits in the doll house collecting dust. Such hardships underscore Jane's distaste for a girl's world. Her envy for a boy's life is further indicated when Jane attends to Ethel's brother with hoop in hand and when she wishes to be the train with which Elizabeth's brother is playing.

4. Jane's wish to be rescued from the doll house by Gideon, a seven-year-old boy, clearly bespeaks her desire to venture with boys and to know of their world. Life both inside and outside Gideon's pocket is exhilarating. Inside his pocket she jostles very much at home with string and corks, sweets and sweet-papers, an important message, and for a long time, a snail. Outside his pocket she runs, spins, sails a yacht, rides an airplane, and is carried aloft attached to a balloon.

5. Gideon's interest in exploring the world of a girl is clearly evidenced from the moment of entry into the nursery where he is drawn to the doll house to steal Jane so that he, too, may know of a girl. However, Gideon is uncomfortable in expressing such curiosity, hence his fear that he will be called a sissy if discovered with Jane in his pocket.

Impunity Jane has been described as a sensitive story. To what? To the curiosity which a doll and a young guy have about each other's world and the consequent fantasies manufactured to define what it is like to be a boy or to be a girl. Perhaps such curiosity and fantasies are most intense during latency, roughly ages eight through eleven, when boys associate almost exclusively with boys, and girls with girls. Thus through *Impunity Jane*, little girls can know of the more adventurous world of boys, and little boys can learn through Gideon what it is like to play with a doll. Hence, *Impunity Jane* offers children the opportunity to deal constructively with their curiosity regarding the life of the opposite sex.

Winnie-The-Pooh: The Apparent Story

Now, let us consider the perennial favorite, *Winnie-The-Pooh*. The characters, stuffed animals belonging to Christopher Robin, a five-year-old, are Pooh or Edward Bear, Piglet, Eeyore, the donkey, Owl, Kanga, Baby Roo, and

Rabbit. They live in a forest in the present or at any time the book is read. Though stuffed toys, the animals act very much alive. They share in the problems of living, make visits, have exciting adventures, and even go on expeditions. Do you recall the time Pooh Bear visits Rabbit, successfully hints to be served honey, of which he licks too much, and gets stuck in Rabbit's door hole as he attempts to exit? Rushed to the rescue, Christopher Robin reads to Pooh, who waits for the passage of time and reduction to respectable proportions. Who can forget the famous expedition to the North Pole proposed under the strangest circumstances? No member of the expeditionary force has the faintest idea of where the Pole is located or what it looks like! They march along and when Pooh Bear grabs the first long pole to catch Baby Roo who is being carried downstream by a strong current, Christopher conveniently decides upon the identity of the pole. The North Pole of course!

The Hidden Story[5]

And so *Winnie-The-Pooh* continues, but what is the true message conveyed to children? The real meaning is a denial of several great problems and pressures experienced in a parent-child relationship, in sibling and peer rivalry, and in accepting maleness and femaleness. The story events supporting this interpretation are explored below:

1. A denial of human problems is suggested through the major role played by animal characters. Nine of the ten characters, including the Heffalump and the Woozle, are animals. And it is they who carry out the plot. The one human character, Christopher Robin, is incidental to the story. He remains on the fringe, his feelings undepicted. He is important only to help the animals carry out the plot. Why, then, do the animals play the major role in *Winnie-The-Pooh*? Is it not to frustrate the possible occurrence of human problems? Certainly animals do not have social-emotional problems on the scale that humans do.

2. A further denial of human problems is achieved by employing one animal of a kind, with the exception of Kanga and Baby Roo. Each animal character lives alone in his own house and is independent and autonomous. Each animal character possesses unique abilities, strengths, and weaknesses. Kanga is big and powerful; no other animal competes in size. Piglet, fearful and small, manages feats impossible to Kanga. In such an arrangement the possibilities for conflict are mostly eliminated. There are also no parents to give orders to be obeyed, no siblings and peers to fight or compete with.

Further security is achieved through the inclusion of positive aspects of family life—togetherness, loyalty, and support. Though the animals live apart, they are readily available to help each other. The *one* human in the story, though a child, serves the role of a parent. Even in fantasy, it is too frightening to children to remove completely adult succor. Thus, Milne includes Christopher Robin, a giant among animals, used by them when needed.

3. Human problems are denied also through the simple and carefree life portrayed. Difficulties are readily solved. Recall how easily Eeyore's birthday gift is procured by Pooh-Bear—an empty, discarded, still sticky, honey jar belatedly offered. And that's all it takes to make Eeyore happy. Remember, too, how conveniently Owl's bell pull just turns out to be Eeyore's dropped tale! Even their expeditions are effortless and nothing more calamitous occurs than Baby Roo slipping into a stream. Their enemies, the Heffalump and the Woozle, turn out to be imaginary and non-existent.

4. Problems of sex are ignored. Early in the story Milne reveals his deliberate intent to conceal the sexes of the animals:

> When I first heard his name, I said, just as you are going to say, "But I thought he was a boy?" "So did I," said Christopher Robin.
> "Then you can't call him Winnie?"
> "I don't."
> "But you said—"
> "He's Winnie-Ther-Pooh. Don't you know what 'ther' means?"
> "Ah, yes, now I do," I said quickly; "and I hope you do too, because it is all the explanation you are going to get." (4:7–8)

And so Milne closes this subject.

5. Problems associated with aging or with growing up are denied, too. Story characters remain undeveloped. They neither grow old nor die.

Winnie-The-Pooh has been described as "a clever fantasy for the youngest" and "a game of let's pretend put into story form." (1:306) But *what* is to be pretended? The foregoing analysis provides the answer. The characters and story events deny the existence of the critical problems experienced by the young child in parent, sibling, and peer relationships, in accepting one's sex, and in growing up and old. The stories are built around fantasies which seem to say, "Let's pretend these problems do not exist. Don't let them bother you." Fundamentally, then, *Winnie-The-Pooh* deals with problems burdensome to the child between the ages of three to seven and offers a way of coping with them, through escape, and thus demonstrates mastery through denial.

SUMMARY

Based on the foregoing interpretation, favorite books seemingly mirror the sensitive, feeling problems common to childhood and, more importantly, demonstrate a way of mastery. For example, in *Call It Courage* children can identify with Mafatu and his most crucial of problems, feeling or being found unacceptable. They can learn from Mafatu that failures in achievement can be overcome by direct solution and acceptance can be earned. *Impunity Jane* affords children the opportunity to explore their curiosities about each other's sex world. When Gideon steals Impunity Jane from the doll house, he affords boys an experience in knowing about girls and vice versa. Subtly, the book sanctions the expression and exploration of a universal curiosity. *Winnie-The-Pooh,* on the other hand, demonstrates to children how to deal with some of the most troublesome and persistent problems involved in parent-child and sibling relationships and those created by sex differences. These stories illustrate mastery through denial. That is, they seem to say, "Just pretend these problems don't exist, and they won't bother you."

It would seem then, that favorite books explore problems common to childhood and permit their solution. The presentation of such universal problems is veiled. It is implicit and hidden in the apparent story. Nevertheless, the covert story constitutes the fundamental core and vitality of the book and impinges on the child's feeling and fantasy life. Clues to the impact of the emotional significance of the story on children are clearly visible. The cheeks become heightened in red, the eyes glazed, the skin transparent, and the breath suspended. The "secret" story communicates in the realm of the lesser known realities, putting the child more closely in touch with the inner self. Thus, the reaction of children to literature of worth is intuitively perceivable by teachers and parents. The foregoing discussion of *Call It Courage, Impunity Jane,* and *Winnie-The-Pooh* reveals the qualities critical to books of worth and provides guides useful in selecting them from the emerging literature.

References

1. Arbuthnot, May Hill. *Children and Books.* New York: Scott Foresman, 1947, 626 pp.
2. Godden, Rumer. *Impunity Jane.* New York: The Viking Press, 1954, 48 pp.
3. Jacobs, Leland B. "Literature Stages A Comeback" *Curriculum Letter No. 25.* Middletown, Conn., Wesleyan University, May 1956.
4. Milne, A. A. The World of Pooh. New York: E. P. Dutton & Co., Inc., 1957, 314 pp.
5. Peller, Lili. "Daydreams and Children's Favorite Books" *The Psychoanalytic Child Study of the Child,* Vol. xiv. New York: International Universities Press, Inc. 1959, pp. 414–433.
6. Sperry, Armstrong. *Call It Courage.* New York: The Macmillan Company, 1962, 95 pp.

Children's Reading Interests
and Individualized Reading

L. F. ASHLEY

Like stockmarket speculators, we in education often plunge enthusiastically into 'new' ventures without quite understanding what we are letting ourselves in for. I am thinking particularly of this matter of individualized reading and the optimism it has already engendered. Many teachers—and many
faithful P.T.A. members—will undoubtedly be in high hopes that 'I.R.' will
solve most, if not all, our problems in reading—much as the inception of the
U.N. was automatically thought to ensure the successful resolution of vexatious
international issues. I am thinking, too, of the fact that only five per cent of
North Americans can be thought of as habitual readers (1) or, to put it rather
more urgently, ninety-five per cent of all those who attend school will probably
never take to reading as a matter of habit. How, then, will individualized reading affect this melancholy fact of life? If we assumed, fairly, that we could hope
to raise the five per cent to ten (and lower the ninety-five to ninety) we would
double the proportion of habitual readers-to-be but we would certainly not
halve the problem. We would still face a massive task of converting a host of
unwilling literates, a task, moreover, that needs to be seen in relation to existing and future population figures. With rising numbers of young people we
might, hopefully, turn our five per cent into ten—yet still have more in actual
numbers to cope with than before. With these thoughts in mind it will pay us
to look realistically at individualized reading—and especially at two considerations which it seems to me are fundamental to any worthwhile program: familiarity with children's reading interests and patterns; and a reasonably active
involvement with their literature. I want to discuss reading interests in the
light of a continuing personal study; some of the inter-relationships of reading
and literature will be touched upon later.

First, let it be said that reading interests cannot effectively be studied
without reference to reading *dislikes*: merely to investigate the one is to know
only half of the reader. For this reason, a representative sample of 900 elementary children in grades 4 through 7 were asked to indicate likes and dislikes of
forty reading topics (or kinds of reading—see Table 1). The children gave their
preferences—first choice, second choice and third—without guidance from

CHILDREN'S READING INTERESTS AND INDIVIDUALIZED READING by L. F. Ashley. From *Elementary
English,* 47 (December 1970), pp. 1088–96. Copyright © 1970 by the National Council of
Teachers of English. Reprinted by permission of the publisher and L. F. Ashley.

adults, and every effort was made to preclude the need for explanation. Hence, 'famous people' was substituted for 'biography', and 'life in the past' for history or historical fiction. Of the 900 children responding the breakdown by grade and sex was

Grade		Boys	Girls	Total
4		112	97	209
5		130	135	265
6		104	119	223
7		94	109	203
	Totals	440	460	900

Table 1 shows the popularity of the forty topics in ranking order. Clearly, mysteries are first in popularity, with a raw score of 266 from both sexes (29.55% of the total of 900 respondents). 'Peak of interest' refers to the grade and sex showing the most preference for any given topic. Hence, for mysteries, girls in grade 5 showed the highest response with 72 out of a total of 135 giving first preference (53.33% of the girls in that grade). Again, a total of 56 boys and girls gave talking animals as a first choice (6.22% of the 900) with the peak of interest in grade 4 girls (19 out of 97 girls in that grade—19.58%). Studying these peaks of interest by grade and sex shows the following:

Grade	Sex	Peaks of Interest
4	boys	nil
	girls	4 . . . . total 4
5	boys	18
	girls	17 . . . . total 35
6	boys	2
	girls	nil . . . . total 2
7	boys	nil
	girls	1 . . . . total 1

(The total comes to more than the forty topics because of an occasional identity of response. For instance, boys and girls in grade 5 and boys in grade 6 gave the same response for encyclopedias.)

While tables like this are obviously susceptible of many interpretations and to many variables, two aspects of Table 1 are worth noting: the preponderance of reading interest peaks at the grade 5 level, for both boys and girls; and the fact that series books such as "Nancy Drew" and the "Hardy Boys" are not given top place—which fact seems to indicate honesty of response by the children. In view of the many opinions that girls read more than boys it ought to be noted that, in this study, boys show somewhat more interest than girls. Of the many questions to be asked of Table 1 there is room here for two: Why are stories about real animals almost three times as popular as those concerning animals that 'talk'? Why is science fiction half as popular again as science?

Table 1
Relative Popularity of Areas of Reading Interest

		Boys' and Girls First Choice Total response out of 900	Grade	Base: 900 children Grades 4–7 Peak of Interest Sex	Response
1	mysteries	266	5	G	72
2	adventure	232	5	G	62
3	ghost stories	197	5	G	52
4	comics	186	5	B	45
5	science fiction	155	5	B	43
6	horse stories	150	5	G	45
7	animals—real	147	5	G	37
8	jokes	145	5	G	41
9	humor	144	5	G	41
10	Nancy Drew (series)	137	5	G	58
11	fiction	131	5	G	33
12	sports	128	5	B	49
13	Hardy Boys (series)	126	5	B	41
14	war	123	5	B	48
15	riddles/puzzles	113	5	B	30
16	life in the past	111	5	G	32
17	science	105	5	B	26
18	hobbies	104	5	B	30
19	love stories	93	7	G	32
20	famous people	83	5	B	20
21	non-fiction	79	5	B	24
22	encyclopedias	76	5/6	BGB	15
23	myth and legend	75	5	B	18
24	stories of Canada	71	5	B	17
25	stories of families	70	5	G	31
26	jobs	69	5	G	21
	westerns	69	5	B	20
27	exploration	67	5	B	18
28	pirates	60	5	B	21
	short stories	60	5	B	15
29	Bobbsey Twins (series)	58	5	G	22
30	travel	57	5	G	15
31	animals—talking	56	4	G	19
32	poetry	55	4	G	16
33	fairy tales	52	4	G	24
34	magazines	50	6	B	11
35	newspapers	48	5	B	12
36	people of other lands	46	5	G	11
37	fables	33	4	G	13
38	grade readers	24	5	G	7

Table 2 shows the extent of the children's specific dislikes, in order of unpopularity. So far as I am aware, this is the only table of its kind offered as evidence of *children's* opinions. It will be seen that a total of 469 stated that they did not like stories involving love (52.1% of the 900) and the greatest dislike

Table 2

Relative Dislike of Areas of Reading Interest

					Base: 900 children Grades 4–7
	Boys' and Girls' Last Choice Total response out of 900			Peak of Dislike	
			Grade	Sex	Response
1	love stories	469	5	B	101
2	Bobbsey Twins (series)	446	5	B	101
3	grade readers	411	5	B	81
4	war	403	6	G	99
5	Nancy Drew (series)	395	5	B	112
6	pirates	394	6	G	92
7	animals—talking	382	5	B	85
8	poetry	380	5	B	89
9	fairy tales	367	5	B	88
10	westerns	360	6	G	59
11	jobs	346	5	B	74
12	fables	339	5	B	79
13	sports	306	5/6	G	59
14	Hardy Boys (series)	282	5	G	55
15	exploration	277	5	G	54
16	family stories	272	5	B	74
17	encyclopedias	268	5	G	52
18	newspapers	261	6	G	56
19	travel	258	5	B	49
20	magazines	255	5	B	55
21	science	253	6	G	59
22	people of other lands	250	5	B	61
23	hobbies	246	5	G	58
24	myth and legend	236	6	G	49
25	horse stories	225	5	B	66
26	famous people	224	5	B	46
27	animals—real	218	5	B	50
28	stories of Canada	213	5	B	37
29	short stories	209	5	B	43
30	non-fiction	195	6	G	42
31	science fiction	193	6	G	42
32	life in the past	184	6	G	33
33	riddles/puzzles	173	6	G	33
34	humor	164	6	B	32
35	fiction	147	5	B	25
36	ghost stories	146	6	B	37
37	jokes	123	6	G	25
38	adventure	97	6	B	20
39	mysteries	85	6	B	15
40	comics	84	6	B	18

came with grade 5 boys (112 out of a grade total of 130=82.9%). Again, sports were disliked by 306 boys and girls (34.0% of the 900) with the greatest dislike shown by girls in both grade 5 and 6 (43.7%-grade 5 girls; 49.5%-grade 6 girls and incidentally, a greater dislike still with grade 7 girls-51.4%). The tabulation of peak of dislike shows

Grade	Sex	Peak of Dislike
4	boys	nil
	girls	nil . . . . total nil
5	boys	19
	girls	5 . . . . total 24
6	boys	5
	girls	12 . . . . total 17
7	boys	nil
	girls	nil . . . . total nil

Putting the peaks of both first choice and dislike together we get

Grade	Sex	First Choice	Dislike	Totals
4	boys	nil	nil	nil
	girls	4	nil	4 . . 4
5	boys	18	19	37
	girls	18	5	23 . . 60
6	boys	2	5	7
	girls	nil	12	12 . . 19
7	boys	nil	nil	nil
	girls	1	nil	1 . . 1

Though Tables 1 and 2 confirm each other to a degree—for instance, mysteries are at the top of the first choices and almost at the bottom of the dislikes; ghost stories and comics are near the top of the first and the bottom of the other —they do not correspond exactly because of the allowance to be made for second and third choices. Both tables should, of course, be compared with findings in other studies of reading interests (2). However, it should be noted that too much reliance is placed on 'classic' studies of the 1930's and 1940's (3). In the tables here presented there are really no surprises. Surely, poetry *is* disliked by about 42% of all children in grades 4 to 7. With the war in Vietnam occupying so much space on the mass media it would be natural to see such emphasis reflected in girls' opinions—as indeed it is: an average of 71% of girls in grades 4 through 7 state an active dislike of books about war. (The comparable figure for all the boys is, oddly, exactly in reverse—17%.)

To refer back to the composite table of first choice and dislike peaks—it seems very striking that an overwhelming preponderance of both like and dislike comes in grade 5 and that boys should record very nearly double the number of peaks as the girls (37 as against 22). So contrary is this to some of the (older) studies of interests that I took another approach. Using responses from all four choices—first, second, third and dislike—I took six topics at random and tabulated the peaks of interest (Table 3). On the basis of decided opinion, one way or the other—like and dislike—I am tempted to wonder whether it is possible to derive what might be called a 'Reading Involvement Index'. This paper, of course, does not provide sufficient data for such an Index—which would, however, need to recognise the fact of *negative* involvement as an indication towards remediation.

Table 3
Sample Patterns through the Grades (figures are percentages)

Area of Interest	Grade 4		Grade 5		Grade 6		Grade 7	
	boys	girls	boys	girls	boys	girls	boys	girls
Poetry								
first choice	5	16	3	15	1	3	0	3
second	4	13	6	24	0	7	1	2
third	5	14	12	25	12	12	5	10
Disliked	33	16	68	24	49	60	50	35
Total	47	59	89	88	62	82	56	50
Animals—Real								
first choice	16	17	13	28	16	21	9	7
second	6	16	21	22	10	11	3	8
third	10	14	17	22	9	14	3	11
Disliked	21	16	38	18	39	19	26	15
Total	53	63	89	90	74	65	41	47
Hobbies								
first choice	13	8	23	9	22	3	10	3
second	11	6	15	8	11	8	6	4
third	5	17	19	22	9	11	9	6
Disliked	12	29	31	43	26	36	15	20
Total	41	60	88	82	68	58	40	33
People of Other Lands								
first choice	8	8	6	8	6	3	0	1
second	5	16	15	20	8	5	5	1
third	7	14	19	39	10	12	5	6
Disliked	15	18	47	19	27	38	26	27
Total	35	56	87	86	51	58	36	35
Science Fiction								
first choice	22	11	33	13	26	8	14	7
second	8	6	16	24	11	10	9	9
third	2	14	22	17	12	8	5	8
Disliked	12	36	13	30	15	35	9	17
Total	44	67	84	84	64	61	37	41
Myth and Legend								
first choice	11	6	14	11	6	5	6	6
second	7	10	20	24	9	17	5	1
third	9	16	21	22	18	7	5	7
Disliked	15	27	35	27	22	41	20	18
Total	42	59	90	84	55	70	36	32

Table 4
Sample Patterns through the Grades (figures are percentages)

Area of Interest	Grade 4 boys	Grade 4 girls	Grade 5 boys	Grade 5 girls	Grade 6 boys	Grade 6 girls	Grade 7 boys	Grade 7 girls
Fiction								
first choice	12	11	23	24	19	7	5	9
second	8	11	24	31	12	14	7	11
third	4	9	16	14	8	13	2	5
Disliked	16	25	19	16	22	16	9	7
Total	40	56	82	85	61	50	25	32
Non-Fiction								
first choice	13	9	18	14	4	3	2	3
second	6	12	27	27	14	13	5	4
third	5	11	18	19	12	8	5	5
Disliked	12	28	20	22	16	35	14	24
Total	36	60	83	82	46	59	26	36
Animal—Talking								
first choice	4	19	5	9	4	5	0	2
second	6	13	7	21	4	9	0	3
third	5	11	15	22	4	7	3	5
Disliked	31	25	65	28	61	39	52	39
Total	46	68	92	80	73	60	55	49
Short Stories								
first choice	7	11	12	10	4	3	2	4
second	6	13	19	26	9	12	4	5
third	7	8	21	27	14	16	5	7
Disliked	17	22	33	26	19	30	18	16
Total	37	54	85	89	46	61	29	32
Stories of Canada								
first choice	11	10	13	12	9	4	1	0
second	8	21	16	18	8	7	2	2
third	6	13	25	35	12	12	6	3
Disliked	16	9	28	22	31	27	22	30
Total	41	53	82	87	60	50	31	35
War								
first choice	22	6	37	5	24	2	11	0
second	9	3	18	9	13	4	9	0
third	7	4	16	7	13	5	9	3
Disliked	12	73	19	60	22	83	15	68
Total	50	86	90	81	72	94	44	71

Just in case my sample was too 'random' I took another six topics and tabulated them as before. Table 4 shows such a close correspondence with Table 3 that both are here summarised together:

	Grade 4	Grade 5	Grade 6	Grade 7
Boys and girls	52(52)	85(87)	61(64)	38(40)
boys only	42(44)	86(88)	60(62)	35(41)
girls only	63(61)	84(86)	62(66)	42(39)

(Percentages. First numbers are from Table 4; others in brackets Table 3).

Table 5

Percentage of Involvement — Likes and Dislikes
Boys and Girls — Grades 4 through 7 (Base: 900)

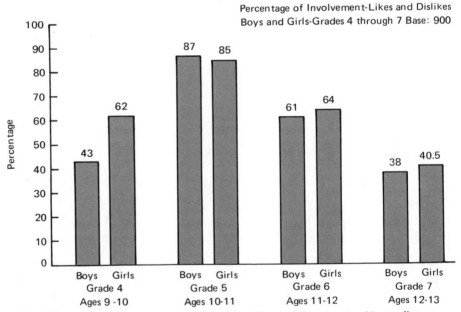

Note: Statistically, *children in grade 5 are more than twice as involved in reading as grade 7.*

Table 5 should be viewed in relation to a statement by Witty and Kopel (4), with which most teachers, today, would probably agree, that

> at twelve or thirteen years the amount and variety of reading activity of typical boys and girls approaches its peak. Children now show some interest in almost every field of literature. . . .

But—this was said in *1939,* thirty years ago but many teachers *today* will *still* assume it to be true. As was said, we place too much reliance on past studies of interests, despite taking for granted statements to the effect that 'children mature earlier than formerly'. Indeed, they do: about two years earlier if the tables in this paper are adequate evidence. Today, the 'peak and the amount' of reading comes in the 10 to 11 years range. Moreover, 'interest in almost every field of literature' pretty well falls away quite sharply in the latter half of grade 6.

For the teacher of individualized reading, then, there are several guidelines for consideration:

1. The best chance of encouraging good reading habits lies in—and before—grade 4.
2. There is still some hope in grade 5.
3. *There is very little chance at all after grade 5,* since by this stage reading tastes have become well-nigh crystallized.
4. After grade 5 the probable major task is one of *salvage.* I certainly question very much the worthwhileness, at this stage, of any attempt to 'push' the classics—at least, in their original versions.
5. If not 'recommended', series books ("Nancy Drew" and the like) ought to be recognised as a perfectly natural stage in most children's reading development. If we want children to acquire reading *habits* there is no doubt that the series books are pursued as a matter of habit.
6. The need for teachers to conduct their own studies in their own classes seems too obvious to discuss further. If one vital part of individualized reading programs is 'fitting the book to the child' how can it be done *at all* unless the interests *and dislikes* of the child are known?

One final comment: while an individualized reading teacher may do a very good job without taking a course in children's literature, the *children's* needs would likely be better understood for the investment.

References

1. Gore, Vidal, "French Letters: The Theory of the New Novel," *Encounter,* XXIX, December, 1967. p. 13.
2. For example: George Norvell, *What Boys and Girls Like to Read. Morristown, N.J.,* Silver Burdett, 1958; Jo M. Stanchfield, "Boys' Reading Interests as Revealed through Personal Conferences," *Reading Teacher* 16: 41–44, September, 1962. Boys—grades 4, 6 and 8.
3. *Readings on Reading Instruction.* Edited by Albert J. Harris. New York, McKay, 1966. Contains an excerpt from Thorndike's *Children's Reading Interests,* published in 1941 . . . long before television began its domination.
4. Paul Witty and David Kopel, *Reading and Its Educative Process.* Boston, Ginn, 1939.

8   Suggestions for Further Reading

Two comprehensive sourcebooks on children's literature and its teaching are May Hill Arbuthnot, *Children and Books*, 3rd edition, (Scott, Foresman, 1964); and Charlotte S. Huck and Doris Young Kuhn, *Children's Literature in the Elementary School*, 2nd edition, (Holt, Rinehart and Winston, 1968).

Several good monographs on the goals of teaching literature in the elementary school, the literature program, and the development of permanent reading interests have been published by the International Reading Association: Ruth Kearney Carlson, *Folklore and Folktales Around the World* (1972); Mildred Dawson (ed.), *Children, Books, and Reading* (1964); Dorothy Dietrich and Virginia H. Mathews (eds.), *Development of Lifetime Reading Habits* (1968); Helen Huus (ed.), *Evaluating Books for Children and Young People* (1968); Helen W. Painter, *Poetry and Children* (1970); and Harold Tanyzer and Jean Karl (eds.), *Reading, Children's Books and Our Pluralistic Society* (1972).

Collections of useful articles about children's literature and its values and teaching strategies will be found in these sources published by the International Reading Association: Jane H. Catterson (ed.), *Children and Literature* (1970); Helen W. Painter (ed.), *Reaching Children and Young People Through Literature* (1971); and Sam Leaton Sebesta (ed.), *Ivory, Apes, and Peacocks* (1968).

9

MEETING INDIVIDUAL
DIFFERENCES

According to the Harvard-Carnegie study on the preparation of teachers of reading, the majority of professors who teach methods courses in reading indicated that the topic "Adjusting Instruction to Individual Needs" should and is receiving the greatest treatment of all topics covered in such courses. One might assume from these data that teachers have learned their lessons well and truly are adjusting instruction in reading to the individual requirements of their pupils. But such is not the case. Too many children are locked into the same compartments and receive identical treatments.

How may we account for this state of affairs? Have teacher trainers been less than effective in preparing reading teachers? Do teachers have some reservations about the importance of addressing themselves to the question of individual differences? Do they fail to understand the implications of individual differences? Perhaps a little of all three. It is becoming increasingly obvious to many observers that providing for differences among children is in fact the classroom teacher's most difficult task. Moreover, demands on his efforts to help children progress at rates and in amounts appropriate to each child are as great in the primary grades as they are at higher levels.

It has been assumed for too long that teachers are cut from the same pattern and are replicas of one another. In reality, they are as different from each other in attitudes and abilities as the pupils they teach. Nevertheless, while we may not expect equal levels of performance in the classroom, it seems reasonable to aim for some minimal competencies in *all* teachers. The attainment of this goal rests with those who prepare teachers, those who have the responsibility of monitoring and upgrading instruction, and the teachers themselves.

There is no doubt that as far as reading is concerned, the individual needs of some children are being met to a greater degree than in the past. The merits of individual and group instruction have been debated, and many teachers rely on both. It is the problems associated with these plans that have not received the attention they deserve. The planning of multiple reading lessons, the gathering of appropriate materials, and the guiding of learning challenge the best efforts of any teacher. We must not lose sight of the fact that the dedicated elementary school teacher is making similar efforts in other curriculum areas too. What more teachers could use that some few enjoy are teacher aids who can gather and prepare instructional materials and work with the children both individually and in small groups under the teacher's supervision. Team teaching may also be a partial solution to the problem. And more effective use of the resources that are presently available to teachers may be another. Or perhaps as some have suggested, the adoption of the "open" classroom, which dispenses with rigid curriculums. Whatever the organizational and instructional adjustments, we must not lose sight of the fact that methods and materials are far more crucial than the patterns and plans we embrace.

Ruth Strang, in her review of ways of meeting individual differences in reading, suggests seven possibilities. Some are organizational adjustments, others are instructional. She explains how teachers can individualize in large groups and subgroups, in team teaching and team learning, and in learning laboratories. She makes a case for a composite program—one that includes whole-class instruction, flexible grouping, and individualization.

How can we help children to learn more effectively in groups? How can we guide children to self-direction in reading? There are no simple pre-scriptions for these questions, but there are some guidelines to follow that may facilitate the teacher's efforts and lead to greater learning. They involve knowing pupils, providing generous time allotments, moving slowly into new approaches, accepting more noise, recognizing failure and a need to start over, and accepting less than 100 percent adjustment. These are matters to which Theodore Clymer addresses himself. He believes that more learning in group settings will occur if children understand clearly the assignments and what their roles are in fulfilling them. In order for the children to assume and fulfill their responsibilities, these responsibilities must first be clearly defined by the teacher.

In the final article in this section, Elaine Vilscek addresses herself to philosophical questions, practical problems, and practical solutions concerning individualized reading instruction. No one form of organization nor instructional plan is advocated over another. Instead, teacher-prescribed, teacher-initiated, and teacher-paced instruction, together with pupil-initiated, self-paced instruction, are all treated as viable approaches to individualized instruction. No one reading philosophy or design has a monopoly on individualization. Programs and plans notwithstanding, "the teacher who sparks the interest of each child in learning and meets his needs . . . can truly be called 'master of his trade.' " This cannot be said often enough.

Effective Use of Classroom Organization in Meeting Individual Differences

RUTH STRANG

Students individualize their own instruction to some extent no matter what form of classroom organization the teacher uses. Some are clever in attending to the things the teacher wants to emphasize; others give overpotency to those parts of the period that interest them; still others "leave the field." This student-initiated individualization of instruction takes place even in a lecture. Suzie takes notes on everything the teacher says. Bill concentrates on ideas of special interest to him. Tony thinks about the escapades that his gang has planned for that evening. In a class, as in reading a book, the individual tends to pay attention to what is important to him at the particular time. The teacher presents the stimulus-situation, but the students make individualized responses to it. The role of the teacher is to accept and provide for these differences in students' responses.

PATTERNS OF ORGANIZATION

Both teacher-directed and student-initiated individualization can take place at any point in any type of classroom organization. The following patterns of classroom organization may be regarded as forming a continuum between the class as a whole and the individual member reading by himself:

1. A heterogeneous group, in which the teacher gives instruction to the class as a whole.
2. A horizontal grouping on a given grade level, now usually based on reading ability, or a vertical grouping that cuts across several age levels, as in the Joplin Plan, which reduces the range of individual differences in reading.
3. Team teaching, in which two or more teachers share responsibility for the instruction of two classes combined.

EFFECTIVE USE OF CLASSROOM ORGANIZATION IN MEETING INDIVIDUAL DIFFERENCES by Ruth Strang. From *Meeting Individual Differences in Reading*, ed. H. Alan Robinson, Supplementary Educational Monograph No. 94 (1964), pp. 164–70. Published by The University of Chicago Press. © 1964 by The University of Chicago. Reprinted by permission.

4. Groupings within a class—now known as "multiple-unit classroom design"—which may be formed on the basis of reading ability, reading difficulties or needs, interests, projects, or friendships.
5. Team learning, in which two or more students read and discuss a selection together or give each other practice in overcoming a difficulty.
6. Learning laboratories, in which the student learns by himself with the aid of workbooks, multilevel material, contracts (as in the Dalton Plan), programed material, or other kinds of guided independent study.
7. Individualized reading, in which each student chooses a book and reads it independently while the teacher holds conferences with individuals or works with small groups that have special problems.[1]

All these forms of classroom organization have potentialities for meeting individual differences. In addition we should not neglect the dynamic interaction that grows spontaneously out of the interpersonal relationships in the classroom; the learning that takes place in this informal way has barely been explored. Realization of the potential value of any of these forms of organization depends mainly upon three conditions: diagnostic teaching of reading, suitable materials for instruction, and competent, creative teachers who communicate genuine concern for the individual student.

LARGE-GROUP INSTRUCTION

It is no wonder that attempts to determine the most advantageous class size have been inconclusive. One teacher may treat a small class as an indivisible unit, whereas another teacher will find opportunities to individualize instruction even in a large class. If a teacher knows the abilities and backgrounds of his students and is sensitive to their motivations and ways of learning, he will meet individual needs in various ways, including the following as he teaches.

1. After choosing a selection that all the students can read with some satisfaction, the teacher will adapt his questions to individual students. He will encourage slow-learning Tom to ask and answer simple factual questions. He will stimulate Bill to delve more deeply into topics that are of special interest to him. He will try to relate the class discussion and the assigned reading to Tony's life out of school.
2. The teacher may provide for individual differences by encouraging the students to interpret the selection on different levels. For example, while he may be content to have Helen enjoy a given story

[1] These and other forms of classroom instruction are described in *Reading Instruction in Various Patterns of Grouping*, compiled and edited by Helen M. Robinson ("Supplementary Educational Monographs," No. 89; Chicago: University of Chicago Press, 1959).

as a simple boy-meets-girl romance, he will expect Betty to discover its deeper social significance, perhaps in relation to an understanding of some adolescent problem. The teacher may induce Tony, who rejects the story as a whole, to improve his oral reading by taking part in a dramatization of a single scene that appeals to him.

3. In a heterogeneous class the teacher will use the unique background of each student to enrich the discussion of a selection. For example, a boy who has been in a reform school may become the expert in a discussion of juvenile delinquency. The timid daughter of a migrant worker who has never lived in a real home may gain self-esteem by sharing with the class her experiences with camp fires. Disadvantaged students may learn to speak more acceptably as they extend their cultural horizons. Students from privileged homes may come to understand that people who appear very unlike them may have many unsuspected points of similarity.

4. From class discussions by teacher and students of problems of home relations, as these occur in their reading selections, individual students may develop the habit of looking below the surface of people's behavior. As a result of skilful class instruction, they may also learn to identify the author's style, intent, and purpose. By listening while the more able youngsters analyze the content of a story, the less perceptive may be introduced to a wider range of interpretation than they would have found by themselves; they will learn what to look for. They may also gain insight into the characters' motivations, the development of personality, and the symbolic meanings of certain words.

5. If he plans to teach the class as one unit, the teacher has one preparation to make instead of the three or four that are necessary when he divides the class into subgroups. Consequently he can spend more time selecting the assignment, planning the orientation, and formulating or, better still, stimulating the students to formulate a variety of thought-provoking questions.

6. In an undivided class the teacher can give a greater amount of instruction than in an individualized classroom pattern. He will do more teaching, less testing. He will have time to show the students how to read different kinds of materials for different purposes. He can explain the reading process, demonstrate it, illustrate it, and go through it with the whole class until all members have become proficient. It is better to teach an undivided class well than to teach three subgroups poorly. If the teacher expects all the students to learn, they will often respond by justifying his faith in them.

7. Some teachers guide as they teach. Recognizing that overage Ted needs to build up his self-esteem, the teacher will make casual, encouraging comments about his work. In unobtrusive ways the teacher can meet the emotional needs of some of his students.

We should not overlook the possible uses of large group instruction in meeting individual differences. The skilful teacher who knows his students can adapt the work to individuals by means of differentiated questions and assignments. He can also capitalize on the differences in ability and experience that are found in a heterogeneous group; he can use them to enrich the understanding of all and to challenge the reluctant learner to higher achievement.

This, obviously, is an ideal picture. There are, of course, many classes in which a vast amount of student time is wasted. Able readers tend to take over while the others "just look off into space." For some students the work will be too hard; for others, too easy. The main deterrents to successful learning in the ordinary heterogeneous class group are the wide disparities in reading ability, the lack of appropriate instructional materials, and deficiencies in the teacher's concept of teaching as well as in his preparation for the teaching of reading. (The latter deficiency is especially applicable at the high-school level.) Although we may reduce the range of individual differences in reading ability by using horizontal or vertical sectioning, many other types of individual differences will still prevail in any class.

TEAM TEACHING

There are a number of advantages in combining two or more classes into one group to be taught by more than one teacher. One teacher is free to observe individual students and to confer with them while the other teacher is giving instruction to the rest of the group. The two teachers can confer about the progress and problems of each member of the class. One teacher may be able to meet the needs and establish productive relationships with some individuals whom the other teacher may have found hard to reach.

SUBGROUPS WITHIN A CLASS

While giving instruction to the class as a whole, the teacher may note that certain students are finding the reading material too easy or too difficult. Observation of this kind, together with test results, is the basis for subgrouping according to reading ability. The superior readers are capable of reading books above their grade placement; and thus in their group they should raise preliminary questions about a given selection, read it silently, and discuss the answers they have found. Their written or oral reports will give the teacher evidence of their achievement. The other groups should follow similar patterns on levels of reading and thinking that are easy enough to prevent frustration but difficult enough to be challenging.

In class discussions the teacher should also note individuals who are encountering difficulties. He should then form subgroups for each kind of difficulty to provide the students with the additional instruction and practice they need. These groups will help each student to attain his reading goals.

As interests are revealed during class discussions, the teacher may form subgroups that will enable students of different abilities to work together on topics of common interest. These small groups encourage social attitudes; the students not only share their findings with one another but also may give other groups pertinent information they have found.

These varied, flexible groups have the following special values.

1. They multiply by three or more the individual student's opportunities for oral expression, depending upon the number of subgroups in which he participates. This is especially important for children from non-English-speaking homes, who must learn correct pronunciation and acquire familiarity with English sentence patterns. They will acquire oral English skills most naturally in the stress of living together.

2. The intimate, face-to-face relationships in the small groups encourage initiative as well as communication. The perceptive student will feel free to respond with genuine feeling to the author's message. Less sensitive members of the group will gain insight by hearing him tell how he felt and what he thought while reading the selection.

3. Participation in a small, friendly group also gives the individual more intimate opportunities to learn from others. When someone reads with expression, he will be stimulated to do likewise. When someone gives a better summary than he had in mind, he will see room for improvement. He will learn from the insights and mistakes of others. The small group stimulates active participation. The individual will be learning all the time, not just waiting for his turn to recite. However, these group skills must be taught. As one youngster said, "You have to learn how to learn this way."

The effectiveness of subgroups in meeting individual needs depends upon friendly, congenial relationships, adequate reading proficiency, careful planning by the teacher, and the availability of suitable reading material. Very useful are vertical files on many topics in the social studies, science, and health; the range of readability of the materials should be as wide as that represented in the group.

TEAM LEARNING

Two's a group. Buddies may learn together. One asks the questions; the other answers them. Then they reverse the process. For little children, team learning is like playing school. For two friends in the intermediate grades, it is an opportunity to help each other succeed. For adolescents it is a valuable social experience, especially for the young person who feels isolated or inhibited in larger groups. The teacher should usually prepare the learning task and a scoring key. The team then selects the kind of exercises on which it needs practice. As many as three or four may work together on material prepared for them. They will teach one another, and may sometimes do a better job than the teacher. Team learning also has other values similar to those already ascribed to other kinds of groups.

LEARNING LABORATORIES

In a sense every class is a learning laboratory. However, the particular form of organization referred to here is one in which the students work independently on workbooks, multilevel material, programed exercises, individual contracts prepared by the teacher, or projects and goals they have set for themselves. When students have been taught to read directions and have acquired whatever other reading skills they may need, they can go ahead with the assignment on their own. This form of classroom organization can contribute to the development of an individual's initiative and independence. If students are given freedom to choose their practice exercises or projects, and to progress at their own rate, they will begin to take more responsibility for their own learning.

One limitation of these independent study programs is that they consist chiefly of practice and testing. Instruction is likely to be neglected unless the teacher, in his role as guide, gives each student the instruction that he needs or unless the practice books combine instruction and practice. Another disadvantage of these forms of independent study, especially the workbook and programed types, is that they usually do not teach higher-level skills such as semantic interpretation and reflective thinking.

INDIVIDUALIZED READING

Individualized reading, which is now too familiar to need a detailed description here, is based on several assumptions: that the teacher makes a continuous study of each student and plans a course of study specifically for him; that suitable books are available; that the teacher can become familiar with all these books; and that the student has sufficient skills to read these books or that he can be taught the necessary skills in individual conferences. If the teacher is not at hand when he meets an unfamiliar key word, he must either unlock it himself with the word-recognition skills he has at his command or miss the meaning of the selection. He must have skill in sentence and paragraph reading, or he will fail to get the author's pattern of thought. He must know how to locate and interpret clues about character development, motive, and plot, or he will miss the deeper meanings of literature.

Individualized reading has many values. Like the independent study programs already described, it may stimulate the reader's initiative and interests. If his school experience accustoms him to choosing and reading a wide variety of books and magazines, he is likely to establish a lifetime friendship with books.

ADMINISTRATIVE FORMS OF ORGANIZATION

Only brief mention can be made of two administrative measures that affect classroom organization.

The non-graded primary unit, in which the grade barriers are removed between two or more grades, enables each pupil to progress at his own rate toward an appropriate individual goal. Some educators would like to see the ungraded system extended through the entire elementary school and even through high school. This form of organization focuses instruction and evaluation on the sequential reading development of each individual.

Special groups for retarded readers who have potential ability are still a common means of providing for individual differences. These groups are usually small; the atmosphere is friendly and optimistic; and the students receive personal attention and experience success in appropriate reading tasks. Under these conditions the retarded reader is free to learn.

Although these small reading groups are valuable as demonstration centers or laboratories in which new methods and materials can be developed, they can serve only a small proportion of the retarded readers who need help. Since all students need more effective reading instruction, there is a need for reading consultants who will spend the major part of their time working with and through teachers.

A COMPOSITE PLAN

A fluid method of grouping seems to be the best way to meet individual differences on any grade level. In any class, as an intrinsic part of the teaching process, the teacher gives the instruction and the practice the whole group needs.

Those who learn quickly can break away from the group, find books they can read, or become absorbed in some common interest—a dramatization, a report, an unanswered question from a science or social studies class. Those who need more instruction and practice may remain with the teacher for a little longer. Those who still have not caught on may form a little group with a "Future Teacher of America," who, having recently seen the light, may pass on the torch to one or more of his classmates.

At another time the class as a whole may meet to explore their interests. The teacher opens up the field. Suggestions for special reading projects pop up all over the room. Knowing the background of the students, the teacher may suggest additional topics and discuss ways of getting started on them. After the students get down to work, the teacher is free to go from group to group, giving all the help they need to complete their projects successfully.

To meet individual differences still more completely, the teacher may schedule periods of independent study and individualized reading. His conferences with each student, though limited in time, provide the most personalized kind of instruction.

A composite program of this kind includes some instruction of the class as a whole; varied, flexible grouping within the class; and independent study and individualized reading.

The composite method may be illustrated by an individual case. Maria, a sixth-grade student, was one of eight children in a Spanish-speaking home. Her father was periodically unemployed and often came home drunk. Although they were exceedingly poor, both parents were interested in their children's education. Maria cried often and seldom spoke to the other children. Since she sat quietly, apparently working on the exercise book the other members of the class were using, the teacher did not discover for a few days that the book was much too difficult for her. She then gave her a book on her present level of reading ability. In addition to listening to instruction given to the class as a whole, Maria had special instruction in a group working on comprehension, which was her main difficulty. She also teamed up with another friendly student who was having difficulty in spelling; they studied their spelling words together, each helping the other. In a class play, Maria was given a part that she learned to read well. She enjoyed the recognition and the feeling of belonging that participation in the play gave her.

The ideal program offers freedom for the individual to pursue his own special reading interests. It also includes much profitable informal interaction among the students in a close-knit unit in which each feels that he can and should make a contribution for the group. With such a program in action, the teacher is no longer haunted by the feeling that he is not doing his best to meet the needs of individuals.

Direction Toward Self-Direction

THEODORE CLYMER

It is the classroom teacher who, in the final analysis, makes the difference between good instruction and average instruction. The teacher holds the key to effective reading.

What procedures and techniques must be used in the classroom to enable the child to become an independent and effective reader, for surely the goal of self-direction must be the overriding one of all reading instruction? Eventually the value of an instructional program will be measured by the degree to which the child can operate independently or the degree to which he moves toward self-direction. The problem becomes one of deciding how classroom programs can enable children to become independent and able to direct themselves in the many reading activities, both within and beyond the classroom.

What about self-direction in the child who is in difficulty in reading? In the summer clinic program at the University of Minnesota there will be fifty to sixty elementary-aged youngsters with reading difficulties. If past years serve as a criterion, fifty to sixty of these youngsters will have difficulty in following directions and in working independently. Sometimes it seems as if remedial techniques foster this dependence on the teacher rather than helping students to become self-directing or independent. Could these children develop poor habits of following directions because in some classrooms directions are given which they cannot follow because of poor reading skills?

What needs must be taken into account by the classroom teacher in planning group instruction? What common classroom problems must be met if instructional groups are to be carried out effectively?

In terms of skills, in terms of interests, and in terms of general reading level, it seems clear that the typical elementary teacher must have different groups of students working on different assignments and in different materials. Thus, one of the major problems of adjusting to individual differences in the classroom is the complexity of classroom management.

Unfortunately, no definite prescription can be given for working with instructional groups. The authorities in the field have been extremely cautious in the directions and admonitions which they have given to classroom

DIRECTION TOWARD SELF-DIRECTION by Theodore Clymer. From *Developmental Reading: Diagnostic Teaching*, Proceedings of the 1967 Annual Reading Institute, Temple University, 1968, ed. Marjorie S. Johnson and Roy A. Kress, pp. 31–38. Reprinted by permission.

teachers. The reasons for this are clear. The variables are just too complex to be reduced to a set of principles which will be applicable to all learning situations which would be useful for all teachers and which would fit all pupils. Nevertheless, there are certain needs which must be taken into account in planning group instruction in the classroom. Some of these needs are discussed below.

THE NEED TO KNOW STUDENTS

A program of adjusting to differences with successful grouping in the classroom requires that the teacher have an intimate knowledge of his pupils. This information will include personal and social data as well as information on achievement in the various skills being developed under the teacher's direction. Certainly the procedures of the informal reading inventory are extremely appropriate here.

In addition to such procedures as the informal reading inventory, other avenues are available to the alert classroom teacher. Cumulative records, when they are well prepared, are often a valuable source of information about a pupil's strengths and weaknesses. Unfortunately, the typical cumulative record serves as a good source for the objective data which are recorded for all students—such things as grades, test scores, attendance, and health records. If anecdotal records form a part of the cumulative record folder, there is a tendency for negative aspects of behavior to be recorded more often than positive traits. The records may, therefore, reveal a somewhat biased picture of the student. In many elementary schools today the cumulative record will include notations about units carried out in the previous grade as well as grouping assignments in reading the textbooks and library material covered.

Teacher observation is, perhaps, the most useful source of information about the student. In many cases teacher observation is the only tool available. This observation can be systematized by means of a checklist or a rating scale, but most often informal observation procedures can be used to good advantage. Indeed, the real artistry of teaching is demonstrated by the teacher's ability to learn a great deal about a student from observing him for a very brief period of time.

If teachers are to carry out their assignments as instructional leaders, it is imperative that they know their students and that this information be utilized in organizing and directing the program of instruction. When such a philosophy is accepted, it is apparent that the number of students a teacher can work with successfully during the school day or the school year must be limited. The need to know students, to effectively plan an instructional program, and some of the new trends in curriculum organization in the elementary school are clearly in conflict.

THE NEED TO RECOGNIZE THAT NOT
ALL TEACHERS WILL ADJUST TO INDIVIDUAL
DIFFERENCES IN THE SAME WAY

Recognition and acceptance of individual differences among teachers is essential. Some techniques of grouping may be very effective when used by certain teachers while other teachers may find the same procedures difficult or even impossible to use. Occasionally, a teacher will develop a plan or a technique which is highly successful in his classroom. On the basis of the success of this approach for this one teacher, administrators may encourage, or even require, other teachers in the system to adopt the same approach. (There is always, however, a "pilot study" in the interim.) The overlooked aspect of such procedures is individual differences among teachers. One of the findings from the Cooperative First Grade Study is certainly the renewed attention to the importance of the classroom teacher as a variable in instruction. Principles of learning do not vary from classroom to classroom, but the manner or technique in which the teacher may most successfully apply such principles may differ from one classroom to another or from one instructional group to another.

THE NEED TO PROVIDE GENEROUS
TIME ALLOTMENTS

Time allotments of at least two types must be considered here. First, there must be a generous time in preparation for teaching. The need to collect materials appropriate to the interests of a group, the need to prepare a diagnostic exercise which might evaluate the group's success in a new word recognition technique, and the need to prepare corrective material will all require generous blocks of time on the part of the teacher.

In addition to the time required for preparation, the teaching day must allow generous time for carrying out these teaching plans. There is simply no alternative for sizable blocks of time for instruction. How this time can be found within the obese elementary curriculum is a special problem. The one essential ingredient to all successful plans of adjusting to differences in the classroom is the careful work which is done and the anticipation of any problems that are likely to develop. This approach does not indicate a lack of teacher-pupil planning or a classroom in which events unfold with deadly regularity; nevertheless, careful planning in anticipation of difficulties will prevent minor problems from becoming major ones. Probably one of the reasons beginning teachers fail in their attempts at adjusting to individual differences is that not enough planning and not enough anticipation of possible problems have taken place.

A careful planning program will involve more than classroom routine.

Planning necessitates an evaluation and an anticipation of instruction which must be given before beginning an activity project, or a lesson. In the elementary grades at least two questions must be asked: first, does the group have the necessary skills to carry out the assignment, and, two, is the group sufficiently mature so that they can work independently and in the ways in which the assignment requires? The ability to judge the difficulty of assignments and prerequisite skills will not come easily. Experience is, perhaps, the best teacher, but only through careful planning and anticipation can these problems be met.

Who does not recall amazing events which took place in his elementary classroom because he failed to anticipate what a set of directions might achieve? "Let's see how rapidly we can all put on our coats before we go out to recess." "Would the person who would like to pass the reading books please go to the cupboard and get them?"

THE NEED TO WORK EFFECTIVELY
WITH A GROUP AS A WHOLE

Our first responsibility as teachers is to work effectively with the entire class. Divide and conquer may be a suitable administrative technique, but it does not operate within the confines of the elementary classroom. No group work should be undertaken until the class is able to work effectively and for sustained periods as an entire group. This means that at the beginning of the school year, the very beginning, students will be engaged primarily in activities which involve the entire class. During this initial period their activities should provide the teacher with insight into specific needs and ideas as to how future instruction may be planned.

THE NEED TO MOVE SLOWLY INTO
ANY NEW PLAN OF ADJUSTMENT

Many teachers fail in their attempts to organize their classrooms because they move too quickly from old patterns and rush to new approaches, perhaps because of the stimulation of conferences such as this. "Make haste slowly" should be a cardinal principle in reorganizing approaches to instruction at the elementary grades. Two sets of problems make it imperative that changes in classroom procedures and routines be made slowly rather than rapidly. The first set of problems relates to the students. If the students have not been under a program like the one you are planning, they must learn to accept this program and, in addition, they must learn how to conduct themselves under these new routines. The problems are met easily and naturally in most classrooms, but in some situations students will need special help.

The second set of problems is obviously related to the demands made upon the teacher by the new instructional procedures. Perhaps the greatest problem here is the one of planning appropriate independent activities for students not under the teacher's direct supervision. The nature of these independent work periods will vary, of course, with the maturity of the student and the instructional resources available. Two criteria should be applied to any independent activities: they must be more than "busy work" and they should center on language related activities.

When the complexities of grouping are considered, a slow introduction of change in the routine with a testing of each approach as the class and the teacher find their way is a necessary and logical procedure. Some teachers become discouraged because they try to go too far and too fast in their beginning attempts at such instruction.

THE NEED TO ACCEPT NOISE, MORE CONFUSION

It seems that there are orderly classrooms and there are classrooms in which children are learning. While this is said somewhat facetiously, it does seem that a classroom which is perpetually neat is a classroom in which very little must be going on and very little learning must be taking place. Perhaps these statements are a defense for experiences when supervisors kept saying, "Mr. Clymer, you must pick up your room" or "Mr. Clymer, you must straighten up the work area of this classroom." Neat classrooms, attractive as they appear at first glance, are not classrooms which promote the maximum learning for students. Classrooms in which students gather to discuss ways to present their research findings are not as quiet or as orderly as classrooms where all students search a common textbook for answers to questions posed by the teacher. A number of groups working independently of the teacher creates more confusion and somewhat more noise than does the class-wide uniform assignment. However, at the sacrifice of a little orderliness, a great deal more can be accomplished in achieving the objectives of the curriculum.

Teachers are often embarrassed when visitors find the classroom in less than perfect order. Yet a few scraps of material inevitably fall to the floor during a construction period. Learning about the care of hamsters by having a family of them in the classroom is an effective learning experience but undoubtedly creates some housekeeping problems. The salt maps must dry somewhere and inevitably a little will adhere to the desks. When faced with a decision on perfect housekeeping versus effective learning, there is only one choice.

While it is inevitable that there be more noise, more confusion, and more clutter in classrooms where good instruction is going on, this does not suggest that there is any case for undisciplined confusion. A careful setting of standards by means of teacher-pupil planning and evaluation will go a long way in promoting proper conduct. Indeed, proper conduct and careful setting of standards is more important in situations where there is adjustment to differences than in classrooms where uniform assignments are the rule.

THE NEED TO RECOGNIZE
FAILURE AND TO START OVER

Not every attempt to adjust to individual differences will be successful. Indeed, perhaps most will not be successful. Not every attempt to work with groups with a variety of assignments will be crowned with success, in spite of what the textbooks say or the Professors of Education maintain. When failure occurs, the teacher should (a) attempt to learn the reasons why plans did not work as hoped, (b) adjust plans and procedures in terms of the reasons for failure, and (c) begin again. A single failure should not cause one to say, "It can't be done; it's impractical." A failure indicates only the need for a fresh start. The acknowledgment of a failure is not the mark of professional incompetence; it is the measure of a secure teacher who is willing to evaluate past mistakes and to move on to improve his instruction.

THE NEED TO ACCEPT LESS THAN
100 PER CENT ADJUSTMENT
TO INDIVIDUAL DIFFERENCES

It must be recognized at the outset that the goal of adjusting to individual differences is an ideal and that it will not be perfectly accomplished. It is not possible, and, perhaps in some ways, not desirable to adjust completely to individual differences. Nevertheless, in the classroom one can strive to do a nearly perfect job. However, it is simply not reasonable to expect that in every classroom for every period of the day each child will be challenged equally and that each child will be equally interested in everything undertaken. The reasons for this lack of perfect adjustment are apparent when the classroom situation is considered. The problem was well expressed by a beginning student teacher who, in speaking of his problems in working with his groups, said, "I think the problem is, Mr. Clymer, that there are more of them than of us."

THE NEED TO RECOGNIZE THAT
ADJUSTING TO INDIVIDUAL DIFFERENCES
CALLS FOR PLAIN HARD WORK

Adjusting to differences in abilities, needs and interests is a difficult task which calls for enormous resources of energy, talent, materials, ability and skill on the part of the classroom teacher. But most of all, adjusting to individual differences calls for hard work and lots of it. No teacher who has been successful in adjusting to individual differences has found an easy, slick, or sure way of doing it. Any successful program has as its foundation the attention and efforts of devoted teachers.

THE NEED TO WORK WITH CHILDREN IN A WARM AND COMPASSIONATE MANNER

While this need may sound maudlin, it is not intended to be so, and need not be so. It is amazing the way youngsters respond to some individuals who somehow, in ways yet unknown, are able to inspire children to do an effective job and to keep trying when their efforts are unsuccessful. Part of this need is met through knowing children, but probably a greater part of it is met through caring about children and accepting them for what they are and by being pleased with the performance even though it may fail to reach standards of perfection. How this need can be incorporated into programs of teacher education is not clear, but it is an important objective.

CONSIDERATION OF SOME COMMON CLASSROOM PROBLEMS

There appear to be two classroom problems which are perhaps the greatest impediments to successful individualization of instruction in the elementary classroom. The first of these problems is the children's knowing their responsibilities. The second of these problems is the children's remembering their responsibilities.

Children need help in knowing two kinds of responsibilities in the elementary classroom. First, they need to know the specific objectives which are to be accomplished in their lessons. These specific objectives may mean something as convergent as the pages of the workbook which are to be completed and corrected according to certain procedures or be as divergent as being prepared to discuss the points of view of two authors and how the child would represent the information in still another way. Whatever the objective, whatever the specific assignment, it is necessary that the child have a clear understanding of what his responsibilities are. One of the reasons for confusion, for wasted time, and for restlessness in classrooms is that children are not aware of their specific assignments which they are to complete. Second, children need to know their responsibilities related to behavior standards which are expected in the classroom. Children are anxious and unsure when they are unaware of the limits of their behavior. "What will happen if I get up and sharpen my pencil during the time the teacher is giving directions on how to complete the exercise which has been duplicated and distributed?" "What will happen if three of us go to the library at one time while the teacher suggested that only two should go?" Children seek limits for their behavior in the classroom and they should be given some help in knowing what these limits are. In addition, children are unaware of what their responsibilities are to other members of the group in terms of conduct. Teachers who discuss with their pupils the question of "Who is a good reading neighbor?" are teachers who assist youngsters in developing appropriate behavioral standards for the classroom. Without such help children are unable to develop these automatically. The failure of the youngster to perform adequately is sometimes a failure on the part of the teacher to inform him correctly.

A second major classroom problem is the child's remembering his responsibilities. Once the responsibilities have been assigned, once he has been informed, there is still the problem of remembering what it is he was to do. For every assignment the child should have some sort of independent reference source which will enable him to check back against that assignment. There may be times, of course, when part of the child's responsibility will be to keep the assignment in mind, but oftentimes teachers expect too much, particularly in terms of primary youngsters' remembering what their responsibilities are. At the beginning of the reading period it may help [to] review with each group the responsibilities which are to be carried out during the time they will work independently of the teacher. This may require a recitation of the questions to be answered in the basic book, the workbook pages which are to be completed, the reference books which are to be read, or the materials which are to be prepared for oral presentation. In all of these cases the child can be helped immeasurably if some source of bulletin board, chalk board, or oak tag reference is available for his use.

One additional point must be made which is related to the child's knowing and remembering his responsibilities. The point is this: never do anything for the child which he can do for himself. If the true goal is direction toward self-direction, the child must utilize his growing skills, his experience, and his increased maturity in solving problems on his own. Surely he will not be privileged to have a teacher with him always. The sooner he is prepared to work independently, to do things for himself, the sooner he is prepared for the real world and for his success in reading as well.

Individual Instruction

ELAINE VILSCEK

The demand for instructional diversity is more prominent today than ever before in the history of American reading instruction. Merely counting the number of times the term "individualized instruction" appears in the literature would be overwhelming. Is it probable that educators have deluded themselves into believing that the concept of "individualized instruction in reading" is desirable, is understood, and could be operational within the realm of public education? Is individualized instruction a myth, a misconception, a mirage, or an inevitable educational innovation?

Procedures related to individualized instruction are creative innovations that are less easily institutionalized than lockstep routine or systematized disorganization. Jules Henry (*23*), one of the contemporary educational critics, states,

> Schools cannot handle variety, for as an institution dealing with masses of children it can manage only on the assumption of a homogeneous mass. Homogeneity is therefore accomplished by defining the children in a certain way and by handling all situations uniformly.

Few educators today would accept Henry's dim perspective. The endorsement of a need for individualized instruction in reading would be nearly unanimous. Yet, as one observes behaviors of teachers and pupils, it is evident that "individualized instruction" is a concept more often verbalized than understood or applied. At one extreme are classrooms in which unique pupil responses, within some type of systematized uniformity, are the only evidence of instructional differentiation. While at the opposite end of the continuum one may observe pupils working solely within a segmented computerized environment. Consequently, longitudinal studies and surveys yield evidence that pupils who achieve are the "surviving fittest" (*17, 33*).

The impact of technology, the findings in educational behavioral research, the integrity of educators, the present magnitude of federal educational appropriations, and other factors will inevitably affect instructional diversification. In further exploring the topic "individualized instruction," the following will be considered:

INDIVIDUAL INSTRUCTION by Elaine Vilscek. From *Organizing for Individual Differences*, ed. Wallace Z. Ramsey, Perspectives in Reading No. 9 (1967), pp. 47–68. Reprinted with permission of the International Reading Association and Elaine Vilscek.

1. The evolving concept of individualized instruction
2. Individualized reading goals
3. Evaluation for individualized instruction and learning
4. Individually prescribed instruction
5. Related factors affecting instructional diversification
6. Individualizing instruction and learning within various approaches to reading and within various administrative provisions.

THE EVOLVING CONCEPT
OF INDIVIDUALIZED INSTRUCTION

If there is an instructional characteristic common to the Dame Schools of the 17th century and to the Responsive Environment Schools of the 20th century, it is that children learn in an individualized setting. Nila Banton Smith (25) describes practices of the Dame School:

> There was no particular philosophy or psychology which guided Dame School practice. The pupils who came to the Dame were at different stages of development and small in number, and there was no particular need for attempting to mold them into one achievement level for "mass production" purposes.

Differences do exist, similarly, among children of the 20th century whether they are within nongraded or graded instructional units. Appropriate pacing per pupil in learning to read is a major concern in accommodating masses of children. These concerns about meeting pupils' needs evolved over the years and contributed to changing concepts of "individualized instruction."

Between 1910 and 1950, individualized learning and instruction were expected as adjustments were made in curricular or classroom organization. The Winnetka and Dalton Plans are examples of curricular adjustments through which a child might progress at his own rate toward goals common to all pupils. Instructional practices reflected the philosophy that expectations and goals for pupils were common but could be individually reached in different lengths of time (25). Even in the "sixties" the residue of this theory is voiced in a demand for "equal educational experiences for all," when, in fact, the word *equal* cannot be rationally substituted for the word *appropriate*.

Educators of the "fifties and sixties" have extended concepts of accommodating learning in reading. The term *reading instruction* now comprehensively refers to teaching pupils to read as well as to directing or simulating an environment in which pupils learn to read through independent insights. As a result, the terms that represent an approach to and accommodations for pupils' needs and potentials in reading have been used synonymously to reflect totally different considerations. Included are labels such as individualized instruction in reading, individualized reading, individualized reading instruction, the individualized approach, individualizing reading instruction, personalized reading, individually prescribed instruction, and instructional diversification.

The chaotic effect of language semantics are evident as the term *individualized reading* is defined by Strang and subsequently by Lazar. Strang (27) concludes that "individualized reading" is a specific method of teaching reading. Lazar (19) states:

> Individualized reading is a way of thinking about reading—an attitude toward the place of reading in the total curriculum, toward the materials and methods used, and toward the child's developmental needs. It is not a single method or technique but a broader way of thinking about reading which involves newer concepts with class organization, materials, and the approach to the individual child.

These and other synonymous labels are confusing when one attempts to summarize and evaluate the related conflicting research findings.

For purposes of clarification in this paper, two distinctions between terminology are presented to the reader:

1. A descriptive label for a *learning approach in reading*
2. Descriptive labels of *accommodations for pupil differences within various learning approaches and within various administrative provisions.*

The term *individualized approach* will be used, exclusively, in referring to the first distinction. The terms *individualized instruction and learning, individually prescribed instruction*, and *diversifying instruction* will be employed as indicated in the second point of clarification.

INDIVIDUALIZED READING GOALS

Educators are becoming increasingly aware of the utility of well-designed blueprints of desirable instructional outcomes in the language arts. Foremost among published materials that represent a design for classifying learning goals are the *Taxonomy of Educational Objectives: Handbook I: Cognitive Domain* (5) and the *Taxonomy of Educational Objectives: Handbook II: Affective Domain* (18). Two major classifications of educational objectives are designated in the taxonomies, those encompassing the products and processes of knowing (cognitive domain) and those encompassing some personalized emotional response (affective domain). More specifically, objectives that reflect the acquisition of knowledge, understandings, habits, skills, and abilities are within the scope of the cognitive domain. Cultural-literary-aesthetic appreciations, values, and attitudes are classified within the affective domain. Such classifications of goals are of significance when attempting to formulate complete inventories of learning outcomes in reading.

Supported by school funds, funds from the U.S. Office of Education, or funds from the national foundations, educators have undertaken the task of compiling reasonably complete listings of desirable outcomes for pupils in the communicative arts. Such a project, sponsored by the Ford Foundation and directed by J. Steele Gow, was initiated in Pittsburgh in 1960. One facet of this Curriculum Continuity Demonstration Project in Pittsburgh involved the compiling of progressions of outcomes for potentially college-bound students, K–12, in reading and other language arts areas. The total language curriculum committee included teachers and supervisory personnel from the Pittsburgh Public Schools as well as University of Pittsburgh faculty from the departments of education, English, speech, and linguistics. Learning goals for pupils were listed under three major headings: understandings and knowledges, habits and skills, and attitudes and appreciations. The committee proposed and isolated five subcategories of knowledges and behaviors in reading. The subcategories were referred to as learning streams and were labeled *Thought Processes, Literary Appreciations, Study Skills, Mechanics,* and *History and Function of Language.* Specifics were included under each learning stream and some attempts were made to sequence them *(30).*

The listings of pupil-learning outcomes, prepared by the Curriculum Continuity Demonstration Project committee, were reevaluated and refined to serve as pupil goal guidelines in the U.S.O.E. Project, A Comparison of Basal and Coordinated Language Experience Approaches in Beginning Reading *(31).* Interrelationships between language outcomes were designated. The five learning streams, originally suggested, were redefined as seven channels of language transfer and were labeled as *Perceptual-Conceptual Development, Physiological Aspects, Mechanics, Functional Linguistics, Comprehension, Study Techniques,* and *Aesthetic Appreciations.* Definitions for the seven channels of language transfer, as quoted in the U.S.O.E. Cooperative Research Project No. 2729 Report, follow:

1. *Perceptual-Conceptual Development*—processes through which children learn to interpret and express everything sensed. Growth in this area is cloaked by past and present experiences and values; reflects cultural psychological, and biological influences; and is principally characterized by kind and degree of arousal of meaning.
2. *Physiological Aspects*—processes generally labeled as or associated with visual acuity, auditory acuity, kinesthetic acuity, posture, and visual manifestations of nonvocal dramatization.
3. *Mechanics*—processes that require use of one or more of the senses. Motor coordination, production of speech sounds, and other physiological aspects dictate the degree to which any child may or should be expected to master mechanics.
4. *Functional Linguistics*—those processes, overt and conceivably abstract, that necessitate understanding and application of linguistic

symbolism and structure. Abstractly labeling or generalizing perceptions would serve as an example. Other factors of functional linguistics might include recognition and generation of sentence patterning; awareness of pitch, pause, juncture; or attention to dialectic
or colloquial profiles.

5. *Comprehension*—growth in specific types of abilities including unit
and global considerations. Specific areas to be considered include
vocabulary, main ideas, following directions, creative interpretation,
critical evaluation, etc.

6. *Study Techniques*—processes established so that learning through all
six acts of language can be most effective. Study techniques may include ordering steps in perceiving, knowing how to utilize the differential between a speaker's rate and the author's rate, reference
methods, ways to convey information to others, etc.

7. *Aesthetic and Cultural Appreciations*—processes that directly reflect
growth in a pupil's sensitivity to beauty and to his literary heritage.
Learning in this channel will be overtly manifested through pupil
personality development, stimulation and breadth of interests, and
discriminative tastes.

A design, such as one of those described for classifying complete sets of
goals for pupils in reading, might serve as a grid within which a pupil's individual profile of variability could be observed and charted. But, considerations of an individualized profile of a pupil's goals in reading will be controlled by answers to three basic questions related to educational philosophy
and child psychology:

1. Do pupils possess an innate goal-patterning potential activated by
need and gauged by maturation when learning to read?

2. Should children be exposed to some hierarchy of instructional sequencing while learning to read through directed or discovery techniques?

3. Can a pupil's patterning potential be predicted or consistently observed, and what effects would this possibility have on instructional
sequencing in reading?

Conflicting answers to these questions are voiced in the literature. Some
are based on research studies while others are the product of speculation. Indirectly, too, these views are reflected in the instructional provisions set for
individualizing reading instruction. For example, use of self-directive, corrective kits such as the SRA Reading Laboratories would imply an affirmative
response to the second question of sequencing in learning to read.

A positive endorsement of a child's innate goal-patterning potential is
reflected in studies by Willard Olson (*21*). The terms "self-seeking," "self-
selection," and "pacing" were an outgrowth of his studies of child behavior.
These terms imply that each pupil, propelled by motivating forces, will seek

reading experiences congruent with his levels of maturation and interest. Characteristically, through such innate behavioral responses, the child is in fact patterning his own sequential progress and reaching individualized learning goals. According to Olson, the answer to question one would be "yes."

John Carroll (9) makes a dual recommendation about a child's patterning or his teacher's setting of learning sequences in reading. In part, Carroll supports Olson's conclusions as he compares relationships in reading and oral language, thusly:

> One major mystery is the fact that through an experience in which the child is presented with a tremendous variety of language utterances, not sequenced, ordered, or programed in any particular way, not even "taught" in the usual sense, the child is nevertheless able somehow to acquire the complex patterns of his language that linguists attempt to describe in terms of the phonology, the syntax, and the semantics of that language.

Accordingly, Carroll recommends the process of native language learning as "ideal" and questions:

> Could reading perhaps be acquired through conditions and experiences analogous to those by which the child acquires his native language, rather than by the slow, careful teaching processes which we have thought necessary?

He further states:

> When presented with a rather diverse set of stimuli, it is natural for the learner to pick out those which are easiest for him to learn and perhaps it is beyond the capability of any programer to predict exactly what these will be.

Yet, for years children have learned to read when sequences were presented or controlled. Levels of readiness and interest tempered the child's successes in learning to read. In defense of these facts, Carroll's final recommendation remains:

> The proper strategy, from this analysis, is to present a rich diet of reading materials at every stage, but as a parallel tactic also to call the child's attention to particular items or patterns, in a systematic way, so as to facilitate his own developmental progress through spiraling levels of complexity.

Thus, through contrasting the kinds of learning periods, controlled sequencing versus natural patterning, John Carroll contends that pupil progress in reading will be more adequately facilitated.

Of current significance in answering the question of how children acquire linguistic skills are studies by behaviorists such as Omar K. Moore (12).

One aspect of Moore's work involves the creation of new educational devices that permit the learner to explore freely, to be paced at a self-determined rate, and to discover independently various relationships within a structure. The child is allowed to set his own pace, explore, and respond within a prepared environment programed into the device. Moore's work also extends to an examination of the effects of prepared school and class curricular environments on a pupil's learning at the laboratory school in Hamden, Connecticut.

The question of scientifically reliable procedures for predicting a child's innate learning patterning in reading remains, hopefully, to be answered in the future. A step toward answering this question was proposed by Holmes and Singer in their study of the substrata factor theory of reading. Singer (24) states:

> The major developmental hypothesis of the substrata factor theory of reading states that as an individual learns to read, he sequentially develops a hierarchically organized mental structure of interrelated neuropsychological subsystems. . . .

Singer further indicates that subskills spiral toward a major skill and that these subsystems can be organized, reorganized, or mobilized. The fact that some readers achieve at higher levels may in part be attributed to a better integration or organization of subsystems. In a critical evaluation of the Substrata Factor Theory, Plessas (22) raised a number of questions that deserve attention. Among them are questions about the validity of test measures of pupil performance and questions about the rationale for considering reading products rather than the processes themselves. Plessas states:

> At this time there is no evidence to indicate that scores on a reading test reflect a high order of reasoning or intellectual skills in reading. Perhaps correct responses are actually a product of incomplete knowledge or partial guessing.

Quite obviously, individualized learning goals for pupils represent an educational ideal even though the procedures for goal anticipation, setting, and accomplishment remain questionable. Regardless of theoretical views related to this problem, teachers should become acquainted with the total goal perspectus in reading. A teacher cannot begin to encourage or accommodate for pupil differences and variability in reading unless she recognizes the total possible scope of maturity in reading.

EVALUATION FOR INDIVIDUALIZED INSTRUCTION AND LEARNING

Learning in reading can only be individualized if teachers employ instruments and procedure for determining a child's possible and current performance levels. Appraising a pupil's attitudes toward reading is as important as appraising his reading habits and skills. Yet, determining such a profile is useless unless teachers examine results, evaluate them, and subsequently make judgments related to individualized learning. Evaluations are important before the child is exposed to individualized instruction but are just as crucial as instruction and learning continue.

A teacher's judgments about a pupil's needs and accomplishments in reading should be based on an examination of standardized test results as well as results obtained through informal appraisal procedures. Both allow a means of measuring and evaluating how a pupil is progressing toward designated learning goals. This information should guide the teacher in initially structuring a learning environment and subsequently restucturing that environment in accord with findings from continuous evaluations.

If the information gathered about pupils is to be of value in individualizing instruction or learning, the measurement must be appropriate per pupil. Standardized and informal appraisal should be challenging to a student but not overwhelming. The degree to which present measurement instruments are appropriate for assessing reading potentials and achievements of pupils who have had diverse cultural, social, and educational experiences is often questioned. One of the many related questions is whether we are validly measuring uniqueness and breadth of pupils' reading vocabularies in standardized testing.

The instruments and techniques for appraisal in reading are being revised and improved. Numerous standardized and informal measures, currently available, deserve consideration by teachers. Leo Fay (*11*) classified the types of standardized reading tests according to their function in yielding information about what the pupil can read, how he reads, and how well he may learn to read. Respectively, the three categories of types of standardized reading tests included survey tests, diagnostic tests, and tests of reading potential. Fay describes survey tests as power tests for measuring general levels of comprehension and vocabulary, diagnostic tests as measures of strengths and weaknesses in specific reading skills, and tests of reading potential as measures of a pupil's expected level or readiness for learning. Comprehensive annotated lists of these tests appear in books and periodicals related to reading instruction.

Additional information about standardized reading tests at primary grade levels has been and is currently being evaluated in the cooperative research projects on beginning reading instruction. One experimental provision required of each cooperating project center was that selected group reading readiness tests, group reading achievement tests, and various individual tests be administered to participating pupils (*7*). In some instances longitudinal test data were gathered as pupils progressed for three years under varying experimental instructional conditions. Item analyses of responses to these tests by pupils who represented diverse social, intellectual, cultural, racial, and educational experiences could yield scientific implications for future test revision and construction.

To gain individual insights into pupils' reading behaviors, resourceful teachers maintain a balance between standardized and informal appraisal procedures. Informal appraisal procedures may include recording observations of pupil performance, using group or individual informing reading inventories, assigning individualized learning demonstration tasks to students, and eliciting pupils' indications of reading interests. Informal techniques, too, are important prior to and during reading instruction.

Charts, checklists, and anecdotal summaries serve as formats for recording observed behavior in reading. Individual pupil performance or attitudes in applying word recognition techniques, in employing study skills, in linguistic applications, in comprehending, and in demonstrating literary tastes can be noted and evaluated. As such subjective judgments are made, the evaluator should be guided by the criteria representing desirable progressive performance levels. Two of the problems in this type of informal evaluation are determining the consistency of a behavioral pattern and finding the time to record and analyze numerous observations per pupil.

Group and individual reading inventories such as those recommended by Betts (4), Strang (27), and Botel (8), are clues to grade level of pupil's reading performance. Betts and Strang suggest percentages of proficiency as criteria for assuming the level at which a student is instructed and the level at which he is able to read independently. A pupil's specific interest or lack of interest in selections that comprise the inventory will affect his level of performance on such inventories. Tests of phonics mastery, word mastery, and word recognition are separate features of the Botel Reading Inventory.

A third procedure for supplementing information about pupils is assigning individualized learning demonstration tasks to them. For example, an individualized demonstration of a pupil's skills in comprehending might be warranted. Such an assessment can be made with reading paragraphs graduated in difficulty levels. Each paragraph should be folowed by a task related to a specific comprehension skill. A pupil could be asked to demonstrate skill in stating a comparison, finding a nonsense detail, or evaluating plausibility in the selection. Any number of comprehension specifics could be assessed separately. Specific demonstration tasks should be assigned at a pupil's general instructional level as indicated by the Betts, Strang, or other inventories.

There are many ways teachers can find out what a student's interests are in reading. Kinds of materials pupils self-select are often testimonies of reading preferences. Using a technique that will result in a ranked order of pupil preferences is often advisable. Such a procedure could involve asking each pupil to create a modernistic collage of interests. To represent interests, pupils are asked to cut assorted forms and shapes from construction paper. The construction paper form or shape representing the subsequent degrees of interests should be scaled down in size. Each interest area may be labeled as forms and shapes are arranged on the collage. This activity also serves as a demonstration of a pupil's originality and associations.

A different kind of measurement can occur in computer-assisted instruction. The criterion test, as it is often called, is a go/no-go test that indicates whether a student is ready to progress to the subsequent study unit. As described by Coulson and Cogswell (10), these diagnostic items yield information about the mastery of subskills the program is designed to teach. If the program contains branching elements, test diagnostic items may also reflect which remedial branch the student requires. Idealistically, the investigators predict that computerized pupil diagnosis and data processing will be possible and economically practical in schools of the next decade. Much research on the role of computer-assisted diagnosis and data processing in reading remains to be initiated.

INDIVIDUALLY PRESCRIBED INSTRUCTION

The term "individually prescribed instruction" implies that each child's learning environment will be set, maintained, or modified in accord with his assessed progress toward individualized reading goals. To think of individually prescribed instruction as only tutorial in type would be completely unrealistic and impractical for the pupil education of large numbers of children. The gap between population growth and teacher supply is presently apparent when elementary class sizes number in the forties.

As a function of similarities in pupils' interests, goals, and needs at a common period of time, instruction can be prescribed and individualized justifiably for groups or pairs of pupils. There are occasions, though, when a teacher must work with a pupil entirely on an individual basis. But, sharing literature, feelings, and ideas with peers is essential in the process of learning to read. Discovering knowledge or acquiring a desirable common reading habit, skill, or attitude can be operational within group instruction for pupils at varying—age, ability, interest, and reading levels. Examples of contrasts in a group approach to individually prescribed instruction for acquiring a reading understanding, commonly needed by pupils, are charted below.

PUPIL UNDERSTANDING

Exaggeration is sometimes a device for creating humor in a story.

MATERIALS

Humorous caricatures
Tradebooks that are varied in interest level and grade level

CONTRASTING APPROACHES

1. Teacher Prescribed, Initiated, and Directed

Show the children a set of caricatures. Encourage the pupils to generalize that some figures are funny because they depict an element of exaggeration. Then, give each child a preselected tradebook in accord with his reading interests and independent reading levels. Ask each to read a designated page in his book (predetermined by the teacher) that is humorous. Suggest that each pupil note whether the humor is apparent or is created with exaggerations or some other device. Give the pupils an opportunity to share their findings.

2.   Teacher Prescribed, Pupil Initiated and Self-paced

Set the learning environment by making numerous caricatures and varied trade books available to the children. Permit pupils to self-select and pace themselves in these materials when they demonstrate an interest in humorous selections. After observing pupils using these materials, encourage each child to individually share his findings. Ask types of questions that elicit insights about the effect of exaggeration in producing humor.

In both of these approaches, learning was a function of prescriptive instruction, but the teacher's techniques of controlling and directing the learning environment differed. The time at which the prescription is fulfilled in the first approach is set by the teacher in accord with her evaluations of the pupil's need for the specific understanding. The timeliness of prescriptive instruction in the subsequent contrasting approach is determined by the child through his own goal-patterning potential.

Decisions made by the teacher related to her role in management of a learning environment are a critical part of individually prescribed instruction. The kinds of materials a teacher has in her classroom as well as her instructional philosophies will affect her decision making, and subsequently, the prescription. When programed materials, for example, are used by pupils, the teacher has made an initial prescription. This prescription is extended, hopefully, as a child works through programed materials in reading. The program author's proficiency in anticipating the pupil's subsequent learning sequence and his probable changing needs will affect the adequacy of the programed prescription.

An extensive study entitled "The Individually Prescribed Instruction Project" is now underway at one of the public school laboratories of the Learning Research and Development Center, University of Pittsburgh (13). The research study, under the direction of John Bolvin, involves individually prescribed instruction in reading, math, and science. Participating teachers and the research center personnel have cooperatively stated instructional objectives in behavioral terms. These objectives have been sequenced in view of student performance criteria. Instructional materials for reading, as well as math and science, that support the accomplishment of an objective were selected from those available commercially or were prepared by teachers and the research center personnel.

Pupil evaluations in this project are continuous and include general placement tests, periodic pretesting of specifics, and periodic post-testing of specifics. Teachers are taught how to examine pupil data, make evaluations, and subsequently write instructional prescriptions for groups and individual pupils. An evaluation staff, under the direction of Richard Cox and Mauritz Lindvall, supervises the collection of pupil data, the processing of pupil data, and the evaluation of curriculum materials and tests.

Since the initiation of the Individually Prescribed Instruction Project in 1964, many interesting observations have been made. The school plant itself is an architectural ideal. Collapsible paneled walls permit for large group, team type, teaching-learning experiences. Each classroom also contains a glass anteroom for small group or individual pupil study. The anteroom allows teachers to observe while managing instruction in the main classroom or vice versa.

Major instructional emphasis in reading is placed on knowledge, habits, skills, and abilities that can be behaviorally defined and measured. A portion of the prescriptive instruction seems related to use of work-type pages of material extracted from commercial sources or prepared by teaching and research personnel. Findings related to an analysis of prescriptions written by teachers are currently reported by Bolvin (6). Bolvin states that for writing prescriptions the following data are provided to teachers about children: (a) background information such as age, family, and past achievement; (b) placement profiles; and (c) pretest profiles. From an analysis of teachers' prescriptions the investigator concluded the following:

1. Pretest information was the most useful single type of data.
2. The prescriptions reflect teacher estimates and evaluations based on data available.
3. Prescriptions, typically, include the teacher's speculation about necessary degrees of practice and review for concept mastery.

A scientific evaluation of the feasibility and management of individually prescribed instruction within various learning approaches—such as, the basal approach, individualized approach, linguistic approach, language experience approach, and others—is, without doubt, a massive proposal. Concurrently, too, individually prescribed instruction within any one of the learning approaches must be tested within various public school administrative provisions, such as the Joplin Plan, Cross Grade Grouping, Team Teaching, the Nongraded School, Departmentalized Classes, and others. Reasonably controlled guidelines toward such a dual endeavor remain yet to be completely theoretically conceived and absolutely empirically sound.

Related Factors
Affecting Instructional Diversification

Issues and factors that affect instructional diversification remain, are changed, or are generated in a continuous but compounding fashion. Four of the many factors affecting the degree of probable individualized instruction are suggested through these questions:

1. What probable effects will technological developments have on reading instruction?
2. How will class size and school plant have to be modified to affect instructional diversification?
3. Do teachers possess competencies essential for accurate and discerning individualization of instruction? Can teacher limitations be resolved through in-service education?
4. What kinds of instructional materials are available to support extended concepts of individualized instruction?

An emerging educational phenomenon now unleashed by technological developments in our nation is commonly called the "computer." The far-reaching potential of this instrument could be an important factor affecting individualized instruction. As described by Patrick Suppes (28), computer-based teaching systems will be available in a variety of student-operated instructional devices at a reasonable cost in public education. The fact that presently thirty to forty students or classrooms can each work at a different task simultaneously, makes computerized instruction economically feasible.

These flexible instruments have the capacity to store, analyze, and organize masses of data that will enable the researcher to learn about individual students as they are in the process of learning. Current computers described by Suppes reflect three types of learning systems. The first is a Drill-and-Practice Systems that may supplement the teacher's role. Exercises at various levels of difficulty can be selected for a pupil by the instrument in accord with stored information about his past performance. A second type of learning systems, the Tutorial Systems, replaces the teacher in the main task of aiding a pupil to develop skill in the application of a concept. Computers now have the potential for assessing the validity of a pupil's stated inferences about material presented through the machine. The third learning systems, the Dialogue Systems, might even be able to accommodate the natural language of the student respondent and allow him to conduct a dialog. Research in this area is now directed toward the problems of speech recognition by the machine (28).

Atkinson and Hansen (2) describe proposed research on computer-assisted instruction in initial reading. The Stanford project involved 100 first graders for the 1966–1967 school year. The investigators proposed that 100 first graders would receive the major portion of their reading instruction under computer control. The Stanford Computer-Assisted Instructional System has the potential for presenting completely different sets of materials and instructional prescriptions for 16 students simultaneously. Thus, branching and self-pacing are featured within a predetermined, minute instructional sequence. The computer evaluates each pupil's responses and makes a decision about what to present next. All computer options must be preanticipated and written by the curricular programer as detailed lists of commands for the computer. In the Stanford Project, two hundred lessons were designed and read into the machine for the first year by a curriculum writing team. Consequently, pupil results at the close of one year will be affected by the adequacy of the prepared curriculum. Whether the program can appropriately anticipate and provide pupil diversity will attest to its adequacy.

Any comment except one of hope for improving procedures in individualizing instruction, with computers as one of the tools, would be premature at present. Computers can offer vicarious experiences but should never be a complete substitute for direct experiences. The sensations a pupil has in sharing ideas with a computer are not the sensations he has in sharing ideas with his teacher and his peers.

If our speculations about computer-assisted instruction become a reality, class size and school plant will come under completely reversed situations. Reducing class size will not be as critical, and the school plant may appear more like a manufacturing plant for educational production. Reasonably, it will be some time before the problems and mechanics of computer assistance are resolved. In the meantime, teachers are confronted with the tasks of individual assessment and prescriptive instructions.

It is a safe asumption at present that a reduction in class size could facilitate more accurate pupil goal setting, more frequent pupil evaluation, and better-designed instructional prescriptions. Charts of births, birth rates, and the total U.S. population between 1910 and 1970, prepared in the U.S. Department of Health, Education, and Welfare, are evidence that in 1972 there will be 15 percent fewer children in first grade than there are today (*32*). Teachers could reasonably expect class size reduced on an average of about five pupils per class unit. If the rate of teacher preparation continues to rise and the school economy permits, teacher-pupil ratios may even be smaller as first graders of 1972 move up through the grades. Whether this population decline will continue for first grades in subsequent years remains to be seen. Problems of school plant and space will concurrently be resolved in relationship to class size. Pupils function much more adequately in individualized instructional settings when there are fewer in the class and the school plant is reasonably modified to accommodate large group, small group, paired-pupil, and individual instruction.

Fewer pupils by 1972, more adequately prepared preservice teachers, and continued in-service for teachers would lend a fantastic boost to instructional diversification for pupils. The March issue of *The Reading Teacher*, 1966, is related to the need for continued in-service education. Austin (*3*), Aaron (*1*), Kasdon (*16*), Jan-Tausch (*15*), and Niles (*20*) either substantiate the present inadequacies of reading teachers, suggest areas of needs, and/or present suggested solutions. During the past two years, the current magnitude of federal appropriations for higher education, including teacher education, has amounted in excess of $640,000,000. This figure does not include programs such as Upward Bound and Head Start (*14*). With a continuation of funds and through sincere in-service teacher interest, progress toward teaching teachers about individualizing instruction can occur.

However, merely preparing teachers to better understand instructional diversification without improved instructional materials would produce a compounding educational effect. Various types of audiovisual-kinesthetic materials are available or are being prepared. Some of these can be called auto-instructional materials since they include means for pupil-response, registering, and checking at multi-achievement levels. Self-pacing is also permitted as pupils pursue prescribed instructional goals. Available materials that contain auto-instructional features include reading laboratory kits, representing high interest selections of varying difficulty; workbook materials with self-directive, self-corrective features; and audiovisual machines for controlled practice on rate of comprehension. Programed materials, tradebooks of high interest and varying levels of difficulty, records, films, filmstrips, and many other kinds of materials should be used to support the concept of individualized instruction. Care is recommended in the selection of such materials on the basis of quality. At present the purchase of materials that lend to instructional diversification has been possible, as never before, through federal educational funds (29).

INDIVIDUALIZING INSTRUCTION AND LEARNING WITHIN VARIOUS APPROACHES TO READING AND WITHIN VARIOUS ADMINISTRATIVE PROVISIONS

Perhaps a distinction can be made about the philosophies and learning psychology operant within various approaches to reading and within various administrative provisions. Individualized learning appears to be facilitated at or along a continuum. At one end of the continuum the teacher prescribes, initiates, and paces learning, while at the other extreme the teacher supervises or prescribes the environment in which the child self-seeks, selects, and self-paces his learning. The following chart of some learning approaches to reading and some materials illustrates the principal of an individualized instructional continuum.

In examining the chart, one should remember that the extent to which a pupil gains insight while learning may vary within teacher prescribed, teacher initiated, and teacher-paced instruction; and within teacher prescribed, pupil initiated, [and] self-paced instruction. Determining the degree to which a teacher should initiate and pace a pupil in learning, as contrasted with the degree to which he is self-motivated and can self-pace learning, is perhaps one key to individualizing instruction. The teacher's role and the child's role in instruction might also change in accord with the kind of understanding, habit, skill, attitude, or appreciation the child is acquiring. Similarities and differences in learning tasks that lend to a natural transfer or reinforcement of learning are also important considerations.

The arrows on the chart are presented to illustrate variations in interpreting and setting the conceptual framework of an approach or material. In classifying the approaches and materials, attention is directed to basic underlying philosophies and designs. When unsupplemented or employed in a singular fashion, the basal, phonetic, and linguistic approaches are largely implemented by the teacher. She initiates and paces instruction in accord with a set of directions that accompany the specific basal, phonetic, or linguistic materials.

INDIVIDUALIZED INSTRUCTION

TEACHER PRESCRIBED   TEACHER PRESCRIBED
TEACHER INITIATED, AND   PUPIL INITIATED, SELF-
TEACHER-PACED INSTRUCTION   PACED INSTRUCTION

APPROACHES

Basal Approach
Phonetic Approaches
Linguistic Approaches

←————————————— Individualized Approach

←————————————— Language Experience Approach

MATERIALS

Self-Directive, Corrective

Programed ————————————→

The individualized approach and language experience approach are placed at the far right of the continuum to illustrate that some advocates of these approaches perceive learning as primarily pupil initiated and self-paced. Arrows deflecting toward the left of the continuum indicate that other investigators have conceived variations of language experience and individualized approaches as tempered by a watchful teacher who takes a more active role when deemed necessary or appropriate.

When the approaches on the chart or others are employed in combinations, they can be placed all along the instructional continuum. For example, teachers using combination basal and language experience approaches to facilitate a pupil's learning may be simultaneously managing instruction at both ends of the continuum. If we could isolate the approach, the combination of approaches, or spaced rotation of approaches per child, learning might be more easily facilitated and instruction more appropriately individualized. We would, then, necessarily assume that a teacher would know how to consistently employ an approach or would know when and how to shift from one approach or combination of approaches to another according to pupil needs. Is this, in fact, a reasonable assumption in view of varied teachers' potential versatilities and competencies? Certainly a more scientific exploration of how pupils learn best and how individual teachers can facilitate learning best is warranted.

The task of classifying instructional materials is less complicated. The present complexion of the instructional materials on the chart determines their position. This placement changes as the materials themselves are modified. For example, self-directive-corrective materials, such as the SRA Reading Laboratories, hold a midposition since to a degree they can be pupil initiated and some self-pacing is recommended. Programed materials by their very nature set the learning sequence even though the child may pace himself within this lockstep pattern.

In this paper, individualized instruction has been treated as an instructional provision within various approaches rather than as an administrative provision separately. Approaches and combinations, such as, the basal approach, language experience approach, individualized approach, and phonetic approach, are employed within nongraded, team teaching, cross-graded, and other administrative organizations.

Administrative attention to approaches, to procedures, and to materials is nevertheless crucial in curricular planning. Basic philosophies and policies should be stated before planning ways to individualize instruction. But, regardless of approach, material, or administrative provisions, the teacher who sparks the interest of each child in learning and meets his needs through individualizing instruction can truly be called "master of his trade."

References

1. Aaron, Ira. "In-Service Help On Word Analysis Techniques," *The Reading Teacher,* XIX (1966), 410–414.
2. Atkinson, Richard, and Duncan Hansen. "Computer-Assisted Instruction in Initial Reading: The Stanford Project," *Reading Research Quarterly* (1966), 5–26.
3. Austin, Mary. "In-Service Reading Programs," *The Reading Teacher,* XIX (1966), 406–409.
4. Betts, Emmett. "Informal Inventories," *Handbook on Corrective Reading for the American Adventure Series.* New York: Harper and Row, 1952.
5. Bloom, Benjamin, (Ed.). *Taxonomy of Educational Objectives: Handbook I: Cognitive Domain.* New York: David McKay Co., 1956.
6. Bolvin, John. "An Analysis of Teacher Performance as a Step in Curriculum Evaluation," *Paper Abstracts* (1967 Annual Meeting of the American Educational Research Association), 104.

7. Bond, Guy, and Robert Dykstra. *Coordinating Center for First Grade Reading Instruction Programs,* (Final Report of Project Instruction Programs, Final Report of Project No. X-001), Office of Education, U.S. Department of Health, Education, and Welfare, 1967.
8. Botel, Morton. *Guide to the Botel Reading Inventory.* Chicago: Follett Publishing Co., 1961.
9. Carroll, John. "Some Neglected Relationships in Reading and Language Learning," *Elementary English,* XLIII (1966), 577.
10. Coulson, John, and John Cogswell. "Effects of Individualized Instruction on Testing," *Journal of Educational Measurement,* II (1965), 59–64.
11. Fay, Leo. "Formal Materials for Evaluating Growth in Reading Skills," *Individualizing Instruction in Reading* (A Report of the Twentieth Annual Conference and Course on Reading), University of Pittsburgh, 1964, 43–48.
12. Glaser, Robert. "The Responsive Environments Project," *Learning R & D Center Publication,* University of Pittsburgh, 1966, 12–13.
13. Glaser, Robert. "The Individually Prescribed Instruction Project," *Learning R & D Center Publication,* University of Pittsburgh, 1966, 4.
14. Howe, Harold. "Growth and Growing Pains," *Saturday Review,* (December 1966), 68–70.
15. Jan-Tausch, James. "The Team Approach to In-Service Education," *The Reading Teacher,* XIX (1966), 418–423.
16. Kasdon, Lawrence. "In-Service Education in a New Key," *The Reading Teacher,* XIX (1966), 415–417.
17. Kowitz, Gerald, and Charles Armstrong. "Patterns of Academic Development," *Journal of Educational Measurement,* II (1965), 207–212.
18. Krathwohl, David, Benjamin Bloom, and Bertram Masia. *Taxonomy of Educational Objectives: Handbook II: Affective Domain.* New York: David McKay Co., 1964.
19. Lazer, May. "Individualized Reading: A Dynamic Approach," *The Reading Teacher,* XI (1957), 75–83.
20. Niles, Olive. "Systemwide In-Service Programs in Reading," *The Reading Teacher,* XIX (1966), 426–428.
21. Olson, Willard. "Seeking, Self-Selection, and Pacing in the Use of Books by Children," *The Packet.* Boston: D. C. Heath Co. (Spring 1952), 3–10.
22. Plessas, Guy. "Substrata Factor Theory of Reading: Some Questions," *Reading and Inquiry,* (Proceedings of the Annual Convention of the International Reading Association), Vol. 10, 1965, 322–324.
23. Schrag, Peter. "Education's Romantic Critics," *Saturday Review,* (February 1967), 81.
24. Singer, Harry. "A Developmental Model for Speed of Reading in Grades Three Through Six," *Reading Research Quarterly,* I (1965), 29–49.
25. Smith, Nila Banton. *Reading Instruction for Today's Children.* Englewood Cliffs, New Jersey: Prentice Hall, Inc. 1963, 130–133.
26. Strang, Ruth. "Controversial Programs and Procedures in Reading," *School Review,* XLIX (1961), 413–428.
27. Strang, Ruth. *Diagnostic Teaching of Reading,* New York: McGraw-Hill Co., 1964.
28. Suppes, Patrick. "Plug-In Instruction," *Saturday Review* (July 1966), 25–30.
29. Vilscek, Elaine. "Self-Directive, Corrective Materials," *Individualizing Instruction in Reading* (A Report of the Twentieth Annual Conference and Course on Reading), 1964, 77–84.
30. Vilscek, Elaine. "Coordinating the Language Arts in the Primary Grades," *Reading and the Related Arts* (A Report of the Twenty-First Annual Conference and Course on Reading), 1965, 129.
31. Vilscek, Elaine, and Donald Cleland. *A Comparison of the Basal and the Coordinated Language Experience Approaches in the First Grade Reading Instruction* (Cooperative Research Project Report No. 2729), Office of Education, U.S. Department of Health, Education, and Welfare, 1964, 16–18.
32. Woodring, Paul. "There'll Be Fewer Little Noises," *Saturday Review* (March 1967), 54–55.
33. Wright, Betty. *Educating for Diversity.* New York: John Day Co., 1965, 29.

9   Suggestions for Further Reading

A thorough treatment of issues, problems, school practices, and implications in meeting individual differences among learners will be found in Nelson B. Henry (ed.), *Individualizing Instruction* (National Society for the Study of Education, 1962).

Most statements on methods of individualizing reading instruction are quite general in nature and fail to offer sufficient details to readers who might wish to adopt some of them. More clarification of various organizational plans designed to facilitate individualization of reading instruction appears in Wallace Z. Ramsey (ed.), *Organizing for Individual Differences* (International Reading Association, 1967). Group instruction in reading is covered in Albert Harris, *How to Increase Reading Ability* (David McKay, 1970), Chapter No. 6; and individualized reading is treated in Jeanette Veatch, *Reading in the Elementary School* (Ronald Press, 1966). For instructional adjustments in individualizing the teaching of reading, see C. M. Lindvall and John O. Bolvin "Programed Instruction in the Schools: An Application of Programing Principles in Individually Prescribed Instruction," in Phil C. Lange (ed.), *Programed Instruction* (National Society for the Study of Education, 1967), 217–54. Some applications from programing techniques to classroom teaching practices may be found in Richard C. Atkinson and Duncan N. Hansen, "Computer-Assisted Instruction in Initial Reading: The Stanford Project," *Reading Research Quarterly*, 2 (Fall 1966), 5–25.

10

OVERCOMING READING
DIFFICULTIES

Why do so many children experience difficulties in learning to read? How can we prevent reading difficulties? What methods can we use to overcome reading difficulties? These are questions whose answers are not as clear as we would like them to be. The fact that we are dealing with the complex human mechanism may explain why simple solutions only confuse and real ones elude us. There has been progress in preventing and overcoming reading difficulties, but there are still too many children for whom learning to read is a struggle, who never achieve enough to enjoy the benefits of a sound education, and who as a result are unable to assume suitable roles in society.

Surveys of research on the causes of reading retardation reveal conditions that *might* be related to reading failures. Clinical psychologists have established relationships between emotional development and reading success. Physicians have reported that physical and biological conditions account for reading problems. Sociologists explain reading progress on the basis of socioeconomic and cultural status. Linguists have been convinced that there is a strong tie between language factors and reading. And some educators have produced evidence that educational influences account for many reading difficulties.

Leon Eisenberg, a physician, classifies sources of reading retardation as sociopsychological and psychophysiological. Among the former he includes defects in teaching and deficiencies in cognitive stimulation and motivation. Among the latter are general debility, sensory and intellectual defects, brain injury, and "dyslexia," or specific reading disability. He believes that programs of intervention—maternal and child care, preschool health care and education, and revised curricula and classroom conditions—are needed to prevent and combat reading retardation.

It appears that evidence to support each explanation of the causes of reading difficulties can be found for isolated populations. But what cannot be supported with firm evidence are *causal* ties between one or more of these conditions and difficulties in learning to read. It is quite clear that what will adversely affect one learner will have no effect, good or bad, on another. It is also clear that many factors, singly and in combination, interfere directly with or produce obstacles to learning. This confused state of affairs has led some to the conclusion that to probe deeply for the causes of reading problems is an academic exercise that rarely leads to firm conclusions. Instead, they would concentrate their efforts on demonstrated conditions, that is, the reading difficulties themselves, and seek ways to treat them. Perhaps some middle course should be followed.

Recommendations for preventing or treating reading difficulties range from teaching children to creep and crawl, to providing perceptual training of one sort or another, to concentrating on phonics, to improving learning climates generally, to trying anything that seems to work. Prescriptions (drugs have been prescribed), recipes (exact procedures has been specified), guidelines, and practices vary widely since they originate in the bias of those who recommend them. Evidence to support each recommendation is easy to find; it is, however, equally easy to raise some doubts about each one.

Helen K. Smith offers several guidelines for remedial reading instruction: individualize instruction, begin at a level where the learner is, provide a climate in which progress can occur, concentrate on skills that are essential to immediate success and that provide balance in reading development, and offer meaningful practice in applying reading skills. She outlines measures for overcoming weaknesses in word recognition, vocabulary, comprehension, rate of reading, and interest in reading.

There is a body of research whose results do not produce dogmas but do suggest trends. The experiences of clinical workers and classroom teachers seem to confirm these results and give some support to the belief that many reading problems can be avoided by upgrading the quality of reading instruction generally. This means that more attention will be paid to the requirements of the learner, that no single "method" of teaching reading will prevail, and that a variety of materials will be used to develop skills and attitudes in reading.

There is also evidence that leads one to question some of the proposals for overcoming weaknesses in reading. There is a growing feeling that the real difference between "remedial" and developmental reading is more a matter of degree than of kind. Those who hold this view believe that children with learning problems require more precise evaluations of reading needs than are ordinarily made, and that teaching strategies require greater refinement than is typically offered. Inherent in these positions is the belief that there must be firm rationales for practices and that many common-sense judgments must give way to demonstrated realities.

These are some of the conclusions reached by Robert Karlin after surveying the research on remediation in reading and drawing implications for classroom practice from the results. He stresses the value of using informal reading tests to diagnose reading weaknesses, shows that group instruction has advantages that individual instruction lacks, and concludes that no one method of teaching word recognition skills works with all seriously disabled readers.

Survey of Reading Retardation

LEON EISENBERG

Today fully half the world's adults are wholly illiterate and not one third are "functionally" literate by the criterion of a fourth grade reading level (1). In 1956, by that standard, 11 percent of U.S. citizens could not read, the proportions varying by states from 3.9 to 28.7 percent (2). This is a measure of our failure and their failure, for to them are denied the riches of literature *and* the necessities of life. Employability is increasingly contingent upon literacy; those who fail to learn to read today will be the disadvantaged of tomorrow, impoverished in body and in soul.

METHODS

How many children are defective readers, and where are they to be found? What personal and familial characteristics are associated with reading difficulty? If the answers to these questions are to be interpretable, we must first consider methods of measurement of reading competence.

Surveys of reading performance are based upon group tests of reading such as the Iowa, Stanford, California, Gates, and others. Typically, the test is standardized by scoring the results of its administration to a sample of children drawn from selected and presumably representative communities throughout the United States. Practical considerations determine that the test must be given to groups of children rather than individually administered. The test must be relatively brief in order to avoid fatiguing the child and in order to commend itself to school administrators for periodic systemwide surveys. Scoring must be simple; hence stems the reliance on multiple choice answers which permit machine scoring. In general, the tests that are given to upper classmen assume reading competence at the elementary level, again in keeping with the necessity for brevity; consequently, a child may receive a minimum nonzero score simply by appearing for the test and signing his name to it. To this basement grade score may then be added additional credit for successful guessing at answers; most standard tests do not penalize for errors (the Gates is an exception). As a result, clinical reading specialists usually report functional reading levels based upon individual examination that are one or more grades lower than those derived from the group tests.

SURVEY OF READING RETARDATION by Leon Eisenberg. From *State Supervision of English and Reading Instruction,* Proceedings of the College Park Conference of State Supervisors of English and Reading, 1967, ed. Mary C. Rogers, pp. 43–57. Reprinted with the permission of the National Council of Teachers of English.

405

The skills measured by the elementary reading tests are different from those demanded for successful completion of the intermediate and advanced batteries. At the lower levels, little more is required from the child than the ability to decode the visual symbols into recognizable words. At intermediate and advanced levels, comprehension is called much more directly into play; in consequence, performance will vary with vocabulary, level of reasoning, and general intellectual facility. One would expect, therefore, that the child with limited exposure to intellectual stimulation would be progressively more penalized at ascending grade levels.

EPIDEMIOLOGY

With these general considerations in mind and the further restriction that comparisons between systems employing different tests must be made with caution (3), let us look at the facts and figures that we can summon. In Figure 1,[1] I have plotted the reading performance on the Stanford Test of the entire sixth grade population of a large urban center here named "Metropolis" (4). (It should be noted that children in special classes for mental retardation are *not* included.) Though the figures in this graph are precise and based upon actual figures from a single city, I shall not name the city, as naming would invite invidious comparisons. The findings serve to condemn not it but urban America. Twenty-eight percent of the sixth grade children are reading two or more grades below expected grade level, the conventional definition of severe reading retardation! With a median reading level of 5.2, the distribution is shifted significantly to the left; by definition of test construction, the median should lie at 6.5, the grade and month at which the test was administered.

Group intelligence tests administered to these children at the same time revealed a median I.Q. between 94 and 95. This may appeal to school personnel as a rationalization for the reading scores on the grounds that, had the children had the expected I.Q. median of 100, the theoretically constructed reading curve would be shifted well toward a more normal distribution. Before we buy this reassurance that all is well with the educational establishment, let us remember that the group I.Q. test requires reading for its comprehension; and success with it, no less than with the reading test, is a function of the educational experience of the child. It would be more accurate to state that *both* group I.Q. and reading levels are depressed in contemporary American urban school populations, given the circumstances of education and of life for the children who reside in the gray areas of our cities.

The epidemiologic significance of these data can be heightened by comparing them with those from other population groups. Figure 2[1] plots the reading scores for "Metropolis," for "Suburbia" (a county immediately out-

[1] The figures were not included with the printed text of the original article.—EDITOR'S NOTE.

side Metropolis), and for children attending independent (that is, private) schools in Metropolis. So enormous are the differences that one could almost believe three different biological populations are represented here; yet everything we know would indicate that the children of Metropolis have the potential to do at least as well as those of Suburbia and, I would add, almost as well as those of the independent schools. If this be so, or even approximately so, then we have here, in the difference between what the children of Metropolis do do and what they could do, a scathing indictment of the indifference of our cities to the education of their children.

Table 1
Sixth Grade Reading Levels by School System

| System | Test | % Retarded | | % Advanced |
		> 2 yrs.	> 1 yr.	2 yrs.
Metropolis	Stan.	28	57	9
Clinicounty	Cali.	15	35	8
Suburbia	Iowa	3	19	34
Independent	Stan.	0	1	82

Table 1 sets forth key reading parameters for the school populations of "Metropolis," "Suburbia," the independent schools, and "Clinicounty," a bedroom county (for exurbanite white collar workers) that includes pockets of rural, largely Negro, poverty. If we focus our attention on the percentage of children more than one year retarded in reading, Metropolis has failure rates ⅔ higher than Clinicounty, 3 times higher than Suburbia, and more than 50 times higher than the independent schools. Similar discrepancies obtain at the other end of the reading spectrum. Success rates, as measured by the percentages of children more than two years advanced in reading, are 9 times higher in the independent schools than in Metropolis or Clinicounty and 2.4 times higher than in Suburbia.

Let us now turn to other demographic characteristics as a basis for comparative analysis of population groups. Rates by sex (for Clinicounty) reveal that the number of retarded readers among boys (19.5%) is more than twice as high as that for girls (9.0%), a finding consistent with other surveys of reading performance (5, 6) and a point to which we shall return.

We have thus far examined rates by area of residence and by sex. What of rates by race? This question is not readily answerable for many urban school systems; for, although the schools may not be fully integrated, the records are, much, one suspects, to the relief of administrators when irate citizen groups raise questions about the adequacy of education for Negro children. The data from Clinicounty, however, did permit computation of rates by race. Whereas 12 percent of the white children were two or more years retarded in reading, a failure rate alarming enough in itself, the corresponding figure for Negro children was 36 percent, 3 times as great! (Within each ethnic group, the male rate remains significantly higher than the female rate, 16.8% to 7.1% for whites and 42% to 26% for Negroes.) These figures become somewhat more explicable when we add the information that only 7 percent of the white families in Clinicounty as against 62 percent of the Negro families fall into social class V, the very bottom of the economic heap.

SOURCES OF RETARDATION IN READING

Epidemiologic surveys employing a crude measure like group reading levels suffer from the inherent limitation that they treat by a common statistic cases that vary widely in the nature of the underlying pathology. We would not expect to learn much that is useful about the epidemiology of infections if we studied the distribution in a population of fever without regard to its source. Yet this has been the common practice in respect to reading. It is not therefore surprising that competent investigators have been led to contrary conclusions about the role of handedness, heredity, perceptual handicap and the like, when each has examined a heterogeneous sample of cases defined only by its reading performance.

To order our further inquiry, it is convenient to divide the sources of retarded reading into two major groups: the sociopsychological and the psychophysiological, with full realization that this dichotomy is both arbitrary and inaccurate. Given the differential distribution by social class of the complications of pregnancy and parturition, of the availability of adequate nutrition and medical care, one could equally well classify brain injury under the heading *sociophysiological*. However, the axis of classification employed in Table 2 can provide a useful basis for a preliminary examination of the types of retarded readers.

Table 2
Provisional Classification: The Sources of Reading Retardation

A. Sociopsychological Factors
   1. Quantitative and Qualitative Defects in Teaching
   2. Deficiencies in Cognitive Stimulation
   3. Deficiencies in Motivation
      a. Associated with Social Pathology
      b. Associated with Psychopathology ("Emotional")

B. Psychophysiological Factors
   1. General Debility
   2. Sensory Defects
   3. Intellectual Defects
   4. Brain Injury
   5. Specific (Idiopathic) Reading Disability

DEFECTS IN TEACHING

No one would expect a child who had not been taught to learn to read. Yet there are children in the United States who are late in beginning school, who attend irregularly, whose school year is foreshortened to conform to the farming season, and who therefore experience a significant loss of exposure to teaching. These are the children of sharecroppers and of migratory workers. Similar academic ills befall children of disorganized families who move from one tenement, and hence one school district, to another.

But even those urban or rural children of the poor who attend school more or less as required by law suffer a serious deficit in teaching. The schools they attend are likely to be overcrowded, are more often staffed by less qualified teachers, are more beset by problems of discipline to the detriment of teaching time, and employ traditional methods of teaching that, however adequate they may be for the middle class child, are highly inappropriate for the special educational needs of the disadvantaged. No less devastating is the pessimistic conviction of many teachers and many administrators that such children lack the necessary wherewithal to learn. This belief may be couched in terms of the restricted intellectual stimulation in the child's home or may be more nakedly racist in adherence to ideas of biological inferiority. Whatever the source of the conviction, it influences the performance of the teacher, the expectations he sets for the child, and the ultimate attainment in the classroom. Without a direct challenge to these conventional beliefs, educational progress will not be possible.

Under the heading of defects in teaching, every audience will expect some discussion of the "look-say" (whole word) method versus phonics. Attacks on the look-say method have their fad; they appeal to traditionalism and suggest a cheap and easy answer to contemporary problems by returning to the ways of the good old days. Such evidence as there is indicates that the average first grader learns equally well by either method. That the look-say primers have been full of drivel: "Here, Tip! Run, Jane! Look, look, look!" (Damn, damn, damn!) is not inherent in the whole word method but must be attributed to the vacuousness of the uninspired authors of these nonbooks. The excellence of the teacher and a class size small enough to permit individualization of instruction are probably more important than the choice of method. An either-or formulation is in any event absurd; a competent teacher should know the several ways of teaching reading in order to capitalize on the ability profile of the particular child. Recent information on the Initial Teaching Alphabet (ITA) suggests that it may reduce the number of nonreaders and may be particularly helpful in teaching the urban slum child.

DEFICIENCIES IN COGNITIVE STIMULATION

Although by definition the formal education of the child begins when he enters school, there has in fact been a quite extraordinary transformation in his mental apparatus during the first six years of life at home. From an only intermittently conscious organism with a limited repertoire of reflexes at birth, he has become a self-conscious, speaking, reasoning, and imaginative being. This developmental explosion accompanies a tripling of brain weight and an enormous increase in the number of connections between cells, but it is no mere unfolding of an innate process. How fast it happens and how far it goes are, within limits, a direct result of the amount and variety of patterned stimulation supplied by the environment (7).

If a child does not hear language, he will not speak. If he is exposed to a less differentiated language experience, he will speak and understand less well. The slum child has had less training in listening to sustained and grammatically complex speech, less exposure to the extensive vocabulary of our language, and less reinforcement for his own verbal efforts. He exhibits defects in auditory attention and perception, performs less well on vocabulary tests (especially when challenged by abstract words), and is less responsive to verbal instructions in the classroom (8, 9).

Many inner city children have never been more than a few blocks from their home; the museums, symphony halls, even the zoos and amusement parks of their communities are foreign territory to them. Books, magazines, even newspapers are infrequent companions; they are not often read to. Exercises with paper and pencil, puzzles, and sedentary games with formal rules are uncommon. They have been shortchanged of experiences that, for other children, serve to build concepts and set the ground for learning to learn (10). Yet their lives have, in no sense, been blank. Scrounging in the streets, dodging cars for a game of stick ball, avoiding cops, defending themselves from youthful and adult predators alike, they have had to learn the complex arts of survival in the slums. In so doing, they acquire behavior traits that *interfere actively* with the acquisition of the patterns required for success in the classroom. To note that these children are different is not to convict them of being defective. The figures from Metropolis make appallingly clear their failure to learn *as they have been taught*. This, however, is a failure of the teaching, not the children (11).

DEFICIENCIES IN MOTIVATION

Intelligence tests have been the best available single predictors of academic success, but the highest correlations obtained between I.Q. and grade averages have been on the order of 0.6. Statistically, then, "intelligence" (or whatever I.Q. tests measure) accounts at best for one third of the variance in academic performance. This is hardly surprising; we all recognize it when we choose staff members and employees, house officers and colleagues by estimating the degree of their motivation as well as their talent. Motivation, like intelligence, is shaped by the environment; in this shaping, both social class values and idiosyncratic life experiences play a role.

When parents fail to reinforce a child for good school performance or to chastise him for academic misbehavior; when they convey a belief that school success bears little relationship to ultimate occupation attainment;

when they share with the child a view of school authorities as repressive agents employed by a society hostile to their values, they provide little support for the development of achievement motivation. The beliefs on which these behaviors are predicted are not myths; they are constructed from the social reality of the slum dweller. These beliefs may lead—indeed, they do lead—to the self-perpetuation of defeat and alienation, but that does not make them untrue. The Negro high school graduate is more often unemployed and, when employed, earns less than the white graduate. Unemployment rates for young workers, white and Negro, are disproportionately high; unchecked, the crisis will grow worse as population trends lead to an increase in this age group (12). The examples of success that sustained previous generations of immigrants from abroad have been replaced by examples of failure in homes and on street corners that discourage all but the hardiest of today's domestic immigrants from farm and mine. For this, the solution will not lie in the schools but in the creation of job opportunities with equal access to all.

However, teacher attitudes may serve to consolidate a conviction of the hopelessness of it all. Educators are satisfied with less from the lower class child because they expect less; their expectations form part of the social field that molds the child and determines, in part, what he does. He arrives at school ill prepared; his initial poor performance leads to "streaming" in low ability sections; the limited teaching further retards his learning; he completes his "education" less able than others; ironically, the terminal product is used to justify the system (13). But is it not apparent that the operation of the system has guaranteed fulfillment of the prophecy? Schiffman (14) in a study of 84 elementary school children referred for placement in classes for "slow learners" because of academic failure, found that 78 percent had Wechsler performance quotients in the average or better range; yet only 7 percent of their teachers identified them as other than dull, and only 14 percent of their parents recognized their potential. Need it surprise us that 86 percent of the children rated *themselves* as dull or defective? With such a self-image, affirmed at school and at home, what shall it profit a child to try?

With or without social disadvantage, individual psychopathology is a frequent concomitant of retardation in reading. On the one hand, school difficulties are among the major complaints presented at every psychiatric clinic for children; on the other, physicians who have studied retarded readers have uniformly noted a high association with emotional disturbance (15–18). The correlation with antecedent family pathology (18) indicates that, in a substantial number of cases, the psychiatric disorder is a source of the reading problem. No single pattern of psychopathology is characteristic. Reading failure is a final common pathway for the expression of a multiplicity of antecedent disruptions in learning.

At the same time, it must be recognized that the reading difficulty is in itself a potent source of emotional distress. Embarrassed by fumbling recitations before his peers, cajoled, implored, or bullied by his parents and his teachers to do what he cannot, the retarded reader is at first disturbed and finally despondent about himself. His ineptness in reading penalizes him in all subjects and leads to his misidentification as a dullard. With class exercises conducted in what for him is a foreign language, he turns to other diversions, only to be chastised for disruptive behavior. However begun, the psychiatric disturbance and the reading disability are mutually reinforcing in the absence of effective intervention (19).

PSYCHOPHYSIOLOGICAL SOURCES

The psychophysiological sources of reading retardation can be divided into five major categories: general debility, sensory defects, intellectual defects, brain injury, and idiopathic or specific reading disability. Overlap and multiple conjunction of causes are common.

General Debility

Discussions of reading retardation do not list general debility among its causes, but this is a serious oversight. The child who is chronically malnourished and the one who is chronically ill can hardly be expected to perform adequately in school. I mention them here only to stress the importance of a thorough pediatric examination as the first step in the evaluation of any child with a learning failure.

Sensory Defects

Defects in seeing and hearing impede information transmission over the primary channels whose integration is required for reading. Visual defect leads to reading handicap only when acuity is reduced by half or more (20). With respect to hearing, however, there is increasing evidence that children with normal pure tone auditory thresholds may nonetheless do poorly at discriminating speech sounds (21) and may not be able to integrate information between sense channels, as in the task of converting auditory to visual signals (22). These deficits may stem from central nervous system pathology or from faulty perceptual experience. In either case, corrective training to minimize this source of difficulty would appear logical.

Intellectual Defects

An intellectual defect can be expected to limit reading achievement as a function of its severity. The assessment of this factor requires individual clinical examination by a competent psychologist and cannot be based upon group testing. The prognosis will, of course, vary with the nature of the underlying disorder as well as the degree of mental deficiency. However, even moderately retarded children can learn to read enough to transact the ordinary business of life, if teaching methods take into account the learning characteristics of the defective child.

Brain Injury

Children with chronic brain syndromes are at high risk for learning disabilities, though there is no simple one-to-one relationship between amount or locus of damage and ultimate academic achievement (23). The clinician should be alert to the high percentage of learning problems and to the need for special teaching techniques for children with neurological abnormalities. Occasionally children with brain tissue damage sufficient to result in mental deficiency of moderate degree are nonetheless able, in the elementary grades, to attain above average fluency in oral reading, although their comprehension of what they have read is minimal. Such instances are instructive in several respects. They serve to remind us of the variability of the clinical patterns observed in brain injured children; they indicate the complex nature of the reading process, in which word recognition and sentence comprehension are separable skills; they emphasize the importance of a thorough reading analysis in complement to a comprehensive pediatric assessment in the work up of each case of reading retardation.

Specific Reading Disability

We turn now to the important residual category of specific reading disability, also known as congenital word blindness (24), primary reading retardation (25), and developmental dyslexia (26). The adjective "specific" calls attention both to the circumscribed nature of the disability and to our ignorance of its cause. Specific reading disability may be defined as the failure to learn to read with normal proficiency despite conventional instruction, a culturally adequate home, proper motivation, intact senses, normal intelligence, and freedom from gross neurologic defect.

There are no reliable data on which to base a secure estimate of the prevalence of specific reading disability; such surveys as exist record only the extent of retardation in reading on group tests without differentiation as to cause. Clinical reports indicate a much higher rate of occurrence among boys, the male/female ratio generally exceeding 4 to 1 (26). This disproportion is similar to, but higher than, the surplus of boys among retarded readers from all causes, among children designated as academically backward (5), and among children referred to psychiatric clinics (27). Some have sought to explain these figures on the grounds of greater cultural pressure upon boys for academic success; this may account for some differential in rates of identification insofar as standards for boys may be more exacting. But it is noteworthy that boys are in general slower to acquire verbal facility and are more prone to exhibit behaviors in the early school grades that teachers label "immature." It would seem more parsimonious to relate these disproportions to the greater biological vulnerability of the male to a wide variety of ills; from the moment of conception onwards, there is a significant differential in morbidity and mortality between sexes, such that an original surplus of males is converted to its opposite by the time adulthood is attained (28, 29).

Many authorities have called to attention, as though they were diagnostic of specific reading disability, such phenomena as reversals (*was* for *saw, gril* for *girl*), mirror writing, confusion of certain letters (*b,d,p,q*), omitted or added words, perseverations, skipped or repeated lines, and the like. These very same errors occur as the normal child learns to read; what distinguishes the dyslexic is the frequency and persistence of these errors well beyond the time at which they have become uncommon in the normal.

The failure of many investigators to adhere to defined criteria for the diagnosis and to recognize the importance of the age variable accounts for some of the contradictory findings reported in the literature. It does seem that left-handedness and, more especially, delayed or inconsistent laterality occur more often among dyslexics (though many are typical dextrals), but it is quite another matter to suggest that "incomplete cerebral dominance" accounts for the reading problem. The determination of laterality is not so simple as once thought (30), nor is "brainedness" so readily to be inferred from handedness (31). The apparent association between delayed establishment of laterality and the reading defect seems more probably related to a common underlying developmental antecedent than as cause and effect. Perceptual handicaps are more often found in younger than in older dyslexics (32). This change with age may reflect the developmental course of perception (33). The older child may no longer exhibit the handicap which may have been prominent at a critical stage in the learning process and have contributed to the failure to learn to read.

We are left with the unanswered question of the nature of the defect, even if we accept the proposition that it is biological. Critchley supposes it to be due to "specific cerebral immaturity" but adds that he doubts the existence of "a structural lesion recognizable by present-day techniques" (34). Geschwind (35) has advanced the notion that there is "delayed maturation of the angular gyrus region, probably bilaterally." Geschwind argues that, since lesions of the angular gyrus in the adult result in word blindness, delay in its development might account for specific reading disability in childhood. Against this thesis is the opinion of other neurologists that pure word blindness is neither so "pure" nor so consistently associated with specific lesions as classical doctrine alleges.

THE DEVELOPMENT OF READING SKILL:
AN ACTION PROGRAM

The evidence marshalled in this paper has, I trust, persuaded you of the integral relationship between reading and intellectual development, of the appalling extent of retardation in reading among American school children, and of the multiple sources of interference to the acquisition of literacy. Permit me, in my concluding remarks, to outline the areas in which prompt social action can promote the healthy development of children. Those areas, as I see them, are (a) maternal and child health programs, (b) health and education programs for the preschool child, and (c) revised curricula and classroom conditions throughout the years of public schooling.

Maternal and Child Health Programs

At the level of primary prevention, there is a clear need for comprehensive maternal and child health programs to diminish the complications of pregnancy, childbirth, and the newborn period that lead to injury to the brain of the infant (36). Malnutrition, poor hygiene, and inadequate medical care are among the causal factors subject to control if we but have the determination to apply present knowledge and resources (37–39). Current federal legislation provides us with a splendid opportunity for progress. Medical interest will have to extend beyond vaccinations and cursory physical examinations to sensitive concern with cognitive as well as physical development. Special programs will be necessary for mothers at highest risk: the unmarried, the very young and the old, the Negro, the mother with prior history of obstetrical difficulty. It should not be tolerated that the pregnant high school student is merely dismissed from school; health care and provision for supplementary education are essential.

Preschool Programs

Preschool enrichment via Project Headstart has opened the vista of large scale efforts to foster early cognitive development. Dr. Keith Conners and I conducted a study to evaluate the results obtained by Headstart in Baltimore which enrolled some 480 children in a public school run program and 65 in a church nursery. With the assistance of Red Cross volunteers, we tested the Headstart children in the first week of the program (H_1), in its sixth and final week (H_2), and again one month later when the children entered kindergarten (H_3). At the same time (September 1965), we tested an additional 420 children from the same neighborhoods, attending the same schools, but who had not had the summer enrichment program (C). These children served as controls to permit us to determine how much, if any, change resulted from Headstart. The two tests we employed in this phase of our study were the Peabody Picture Vocabulary Test (PPVT) and the Draw-a-Person Test (DAP).

The mean scores for the Headstart children at each testing, for the controls and for the original Peabody standardization sample, are shown in Table 3. The differences between each pair of Headstart tests are statistically significant (showing steady progress), and the Headstart children were clearly superior to the controls when both entered school in September. However, despite the marked improvement, the Headstart mean scores were still well behind those for a group of five-year-old nonslum children (standard sample).

Table 3
PPVT Raw Scores for Headstart and Controls

	Headstart			*Controls*	*Standard*
Test Period	H_1	H_2	H_3	C	
Test Form	Form A	Form B	Form A	Form A	
Mean	32.63	36.83	39.74	33.65	50.22
Sigma	12.33	10.82	11.34	11.70	8.17
(N)	(424)	(423)	(413)	(402)	(133)

Differences Significant at $p < 0.0001$:
H_2 vs H_1; H_3 vs H_2; H_2 vs C; H_3 vs C
No Significant Difference Between C and H_1

Table 4 shows the mean scores on the Draw-a-Person Test for the Headstart children at each test period and for the controls. Again, the Headstart children are clearly superior to the controls in September. In these data, however, there is some evidence of change over the ten-week period in the controls in that they score higher in September than did the Headstart children in late June when they entered the program.

Table 4
Draw-a-Person Test Raw Scores for Headstart and Controls

	Headstart			*Controls*
Test Period	H_1	H_2	H_3	C
Mean	7.71	9.10	9.75	8.91
Sigma	4.79	4.20	4.41	4.98
(N)	(500)	(476)	(435)	(420)

H_2 vs H_1, p. 0.0001; H_3 vs H_2, $p < 0.01$
H_3 vs C, $p < 0.001$
H_2 vs C—No Significant Difference but
C vs H_1, $p < 0.001$

On both tests, then, there is strong evidence for significant gains attributable to the Headstart program.

Improved School Programs

If preschool enrichment is not augmented by substantial revision of traditional school services, there is little reason to anticipate significant long run benefit. None of us would expect a good diet at the age of 3 to protect against malnutrition at 6. The brain requires nourishment both biological and psychological at each stage of the life cycle; early nourishment is necessary but not sufficient to guarantee its development. The precedent shattering federal aid to education bill recognizes for the first time a national responsibility to improve the quality of education; the funds made available are but a token of what will be required ultimately. If we allow them to be used to supplant state funds or merely to be spread thinly throughout the system, no palpable changes will result. The best teachers must be attracted to slum area schools; class size must be reduced; curricula must be modified. School programs will have to be extended to include after-school tutoring and recreational activities. What I am emphasizing is capital investment in human renewal, the very principle that has paid off so handsomely in our industrial enterprise.

Permit me one final point. Most school systems introduce remedial reading instruction at the third grade or later (if they have it at all). The justification is one of economy. Of those children not reading at the end of first grade, perhaps half manage to pass muster by the end of the second grade; a few more of the remainder learn to read by standard instruction by the end of the third grade. These children are the "late bloomers," youngsters who, for unknown reasons, acquire late, but do acquire, the capacity to profit from conventional teaching. By waiting till the third grade, the school system has spared itself the cost of extra teaching for children who were going to make it on their own. This "economy," however, must be balanced against the cost to those children who, by the third grade, are deeply imprisoned in faulty learning habits, have become convinced of their ineptness, and now respond poorly to any but the most expert individual clinical instruction. Surely, this country can afford to do better by its children. It is essential that we identify the child who is not beginning to read by the second semester of the first grade, institute a careful diagnostic study, and provide the appropriate remedial education. If this means that we will be giving extra help to a child not in need of it for each child who requires it, then I urge that we do so. The surplus child will not be harmed and may be benefited; the dyslexic child will be reached at a time when the chance of success is greatest. We would not hear of delaying therapy for rheumatic fever because not every patient incurs heart disease; how then can we tolerate a view that is equivalent to saying: let us make certain the child cannot read and is really in trouble before we give him extra help? An effective program for early identification and treatment might even produce long run savings if we take into account the cost of prolonged treatment and ultimate losses in the economic productivity of the handicapped readers. But my argument places no weight on such matters. Where the healthy development of children is concerned, financial considerations are simply irrelevant.

But if we are to provide the leadership that will convince our fellow countrymen of the importance of investment in human renewal, we must first be convinced ourselves of the potential in the children we teach. We must understand that intelligence develops through experience and through challenge and is in no sense a fixed quantity (40).

The myth of immutability of intelligence has served through the ages as an intellectual barrier to social progress. Recall only the myth of the men of gold, silver, brass, and iron offered in Plato's *Republic* to persuade the citizens to accept their destiny in the state. Socrates, after attesting to the value of truth, goes on to say: "Then if anyone at all is to have the privilege of lying, the rulers of the State should be the persons . . . to lie for the public good." "How," Glaucon asks, "may we devise one of these useful falsehoods . . . ?" And Socrates responds "Citizens, we shall say to them in our tale, you are brothers, yet God has framed you differently. Some of you have the power to command, and in the composition of these he has mingled gold, wherefore also they have the greatest honor; others he has made of silver, to be auxiliaries; others again who are to be husbandmen and craftsmen he has composed of brass and iron: and the species will generally be preserved in the children." He adds: "Any meddlesome interchange between the three classes would be most mischievous to the State and could properly be described as the height of villainy."

But precisely this myth, no more mellow for all its age, is offered us today to justify the divisions of society. If we accept it, we deny to the husbandmen and the craftsmen full citizenship in our society and to that society the silver and gold they can bring to it. To every child must be given the education which alone will enable him to work to the fullest the precious ores within him. Only so can we build a true and strong republic. Only so can we build a world in which men will live as brothers.

References

1. Gray, W. S. *The Teaching of Reading and Writing.* Paris, Unesco, 1956, p. 29.
2. Gray, W. S. *The Teaching of Reading* (Burton Lecture). Cambridge, Harvard University Press, 1957, p. 2.
3. Millman, J., & Lindlof, J. "The Comparability of Fifth Grade Norms of the California, Iowa and Metropolitan Achievement Tests." *J. Educ. Measur.* 1:135, 1964.
4. Eisenberg, L. "Reading Retardation." *Pediatrics.* 37:352–365, 1966.
5. Bentzen, F. "Sex Ratios in Learning and Behavior Disorders." *Am. J. Orthopsychiat.* 33:92, 1963.
6. Miller, A. D., Margolin, J. D., & Yolles, S. F. "Epidemiology of Reading Disabilities." *Am. J. Pub. Hlth.* 47:1250, 1957.
7. Hunt, J. McV. *Intelligence and Experience.* New York, Ronald Press, 1961.
8. John, V. "The Intellectual Development of Slum Children." *Am. J. Orthopsychiat.* 33:813, 1963.
9. Deutsch, M. "The Role of Social Class in Language Development and Cognition." *Am. J. Orthopsychiat.* 35:78, 1965.
10. Harlow, H. F. "The Formation of Learning Sets." *Psychol. Rev.* 56:51, 1949.

11. Gordon, E. "A Review of Programs of Compensatory Education." *Am. J. Orthopsychiat.* In Press, 1965.
12. Freedman, M. "Perspectives in Youth Employment." *Children. 12:*75, 1965.
13. Wilson, A. B. "Social Stratification and Academic Achievement" in Passow, A. H. (ed.). *Education in Depressed Areas.* New York, Columbia University, 1963.
14. Schiffman, G. *Personal Communication.*
15. Missildine, W. H. "The Emotional Background of Thirty Children with Reading Disability." *Nerv. Child. 5:*263, 1946.
16. Fabian, A. A. "Clinical and Experimental Studies of School Children Who Are Retarded in Reading." *Quart. J. Child Behavior. 3:*15, 1951.
17. Blanchard, P. "Psychogenic Factors in Some Cases of Reading Disability." *Am. J. Orthopsychiat. 5:*361, 1935.
18. Ingram, T. T. S., & Reid, J. F. "Developmental Aphasia Observed in a Department of Child Psychiatry." *Arch. Dis. Childhood. 31:*161, 1956.
19. Eisenberg, L. "Office Evaluation of Specific Reading Disability." *Pediatrics. 23:*997, 1959.
20. Irvine, R. "An Ocular Policy for Public Schools." *Am. J. Ophth. 24:*779, 1941.
21. Goetzinger, C. P., Dirks, D. D., & Baer, C. J. "Auditory Discrimination and Visual Perception in Good and Poor Readers." *J. Otol. Rhinol. Laryngo. 69:*121, 1960.
22. Birch, H. G., & Belmont, L. "Audiovisual Integration in Normal and Retarded Readers." *Am. J. Orthopsychiat. 34:*852, 1964.
23. Eisenberg, L. "Behavioral Manifestations of Cerebral Damage in Childhood" in Birch, H. G. (ed.). *Brain Damage in Childhood.* Baltimore, Williams & Wilkins, 1964.
24. Morgan, W. P. "A Case of Congenital Word Blindness." *Brit. M. J. 2:*1378, 1896.
25. Rabinovitch, R. D., Drew, A. L., DeJong, R. N., Ingram, W., & Whithey, L. "A Research Approach to Reading Retardation." *Research Publ. A. Nerv. & Ment. Dis., Proc. 34:*363, 1954.
26. Critchley, M. *Developmental Dyslexia.* London, Heineman, 1964.
27. Bahn, A., Chandler, C., & Eisenberg, L. "Diagnostic & Demographic Characteristics of Patients Seen in Outpatient Clinics for an Entire State." *Am. J. Psychiat. 117:*769, 1961.
28. Childs, B. "Genetic Origin of Some Sex Differences Among Human Beings." *Pediatrics.* In Press, 1965.
29. Washburn, T. C., Medearis, D. N., & Childs, B. "Sex Differences in Susceptibility in Infections." *Pediatrics. 35:*57, 1965.
30. Benton, A. L. *Right-Left Discrimination & Finger-Localization: Development & Pathology.* New York, Hoeber, 1959.
31. Mountcastle, V. B. (ed.). *Interhemispheric Relations and Cerebral Dominance.* Baltimore, Johns Hopkins Press, 1962.
32. Benton, A. L. "Dyslexia in Relation to Form Perception & Directional Sense" in Money, J. (ed.). *Reading Disability.* Baltimore, Johns Hopkins Press, 1962.
33. Birch, H. G., & Belmont, L. "Audio-Visual Integration, Intelligence and Reading Ability in School Children." *Percept. & Motor Skills. 20:*295, 1965.
34. Critchley, M. 1964, *op. cit.,* p. 80.
35. Geschwind, N. "Disconnection Syndromes in Animals and Man." *Brain,* In Press, 1965.
36. Eisenberg, L. "Preventive Pediatrics." *Pediatrics. 30:*815, 1962.
37. Pasamanick, B. "Socioeconomic Status: Some Precursors of Neuropsychiatric Disorder." *Am. J. Orthopsychiat. 26:*594, 1956.
38. Scrimshaw, N. S., & Behar, M. "Malnutrition in Underdeveloped Countries." *New Eng. J. Med. 272:*137–144, 193–198, 1965.
39. Cravioto, J., & Robles, B. "Evolution of Adaptive & Motor Behavior During Rehabilitation from Kwashiorkor." *Am. J. Orthopsychiat. 35:*499, 1965.
40. Eisenberg, L. "Clinical Considerations in the Psychiatric Evaluation of Intelligence." Presented at the American Psychopathological Association. New York, February 20, 1966.

Corrective and Remedial Instruction

HELEN K. SMITH

Reading retardation may range from the complete disability of a non-reader to a lag in a single area in reading. Most retarded readers exhibit an uneven development in their reading; others lack all of the skills good readers use. Some do not have adequate word-recognition skills and cannot unlock unfamiliar words. Still others lack broad meaning vocabularies and/or comprehension skills. A few have not learned to adjust their rate of comprehension to the task at hand. Retardation, then, may occur in one, several, or all areas of reading at any grade level in school.

The problem of teaching the retarded reader is compounded by the fact that each area of reading is complex. There is much diversity among the abilities of retarded readers even in one area of reading. For example, retarded readers deficient in word-recognition skills do not always have the same difficulties. Non-readers have meager sight vocabularies and cannot read simple materials. Those who have developed an adequate sight vocabulary may not know the sounds of letters, the principles for sounds or syllabication of words, or the application of these principles. They may know the sounds of single letters but may not be able to blend them into words. In addition, they may not have had enough practice in the use of each skill and consequently are slow, laborious readers, sometimes giving so much attention to the word that they do not understand what they read. Yet, all of these students are retarded in the area of word recognition.

The principal difference in the terms *remedial* and *corrective* instruction, according to most experts in reading, appears to be in the degree of retardation. Remedial instruction is intended for those students having serious problems in reading; corrective, for those less severe. In this paper, the terms will be used synonymously.

A distinction needs to be made among the students who can be taught within the regular classes and those for whom special provisions should be made. Often students evidencing minor deficiencies or retardation in only a few skills can be instructed effectively within the classroom. For very seriously retarded readers, special classes or clinical instruction is needed. Care must be taken to separate the retarded readers from the slow learners because instructional procedures should be different for these two types of students.

CORRECTIVE AND REMEDIAL INSTRUCTION by Helen K. Smith. From *The Underachiever in Reading*, ed. H. Alan Robinson, Supplementary Educational Monograph No. 92 (1962), pp. 41–49. Published by The University of Chicago Press © 1962 by The University of Chicago. Reprinted by permission.

Because students have diverse needs and an uneven development of reading skills, individual instruction must be provided. This statement does not mean that every student must be taught one at a time. It does imply that grouping within the classroom must be flexible enough that the individual needs of each retarded reader are continuously met.

BASIC PRINCIPLES OF REMEDIAL
READING INSTRUCTION

Although retarded readers have different kinds of reading difficulties, there are a number of basic principles which are applicable to all remedial reading instruction.

1. The term *corrective and remedial reading instruction* implies that the purpose of teaching is to correct or to remedy one or more deficiencies in reading. It is not practical to begin an instructional program until the nature of the difficulty has been established. Time can be wasted; important areas of reading may be missed; others may be overemphasized.

Therefore, the first basic principle of remedial teaching is that instruction must be individualized and must be based upon a diagnosis of the reading difficulty. The teacher can obtain pertinent information about students and can locate areas of reading that have been neglected, faultily learned, or overemphasized. Diagnosis should be a continuous process during the entire instructional period. Modifications in procedures should be made from time to time with the students' changing needs.

2. Remedial instruction should begin at the level where the student can be successful. It is somewhat of a cliché to state that we need to begin where the learner is; nevertheless, this principle applies to all retarded readers, regardless of their age or grade placement.

3. The climate for remedial instruction should be one in which a student can make progress. The retarded reader needs to be accepted as a person and at his level of development. The teacher must accept the student without showing surprise, shock, or dismay. Poor readers need to be understood and accepted.

4. Emphasis in instruction should be placed upon the skills and abilities which the student does not have but which are essential for immediate success in reading. For example, we expect students to develop vocabulary and comprehension skills before they increase their rate of reading.

Sometimes teachers drill upon all reading skills whether or not the student knows and uses them. Time is of the essence to the retarded reader. It is not sufficient for him to make a year's growth in reading in one year because he will never catch up with his peers at this rate; therefore, skills which have already been learned should not be emphasized. The known can and should be used as a basis for teaching the unknown; but all stress should be placed upon mastering abilities which will help the student to move forward quickly.

5. At the same time, instruction must be balanced. For example, if overemphasis is placed upon phonetic analysis while meanings are neglected, the student is in trouble. He may have to spend so much time and energy analyzing the words themselves that by the time he has finished the sentence or paragraph he has lost all its meaning. Another student, as a result of overemphasis being placed upon oral reading, may think he must read everything orally to get meaning.

Instruction, then, must be directed toward helping the student overcome specific weaknesses while keeping the rest of the program in balance. Reading programs should not result in speedsters who do not comprehend or oral readers who glibly say words but have no idea of their meaning.

6. Much meaningful practice is essential if the newly learned reading skills are to be habituated and maintained. It is not sufficient that the students learn *about* these skills or be proficient in stating principles; they must be able to use reading skills automatically when they read. The practice must minimize isolated drill and emphasize the use of these skills and abilities in meaningful situations. For example, isolated drill in analyzing words does not insure adequate performance. Students need many opportunities to use the newly acquired word-recognition skills by reading silently and answering questions based upon the selection and in reading easy books for pleasure. In the same manner, learning the meanings of words in isolation does not benefit the student so much as studying words in context, in using them in reading and in writing, and in hearing other people use them.

7. If instruction is to be effective, it should be meaningful to the students. They should know their weaknesses, the goals of their instruction, and the avenues through which these goals are to be achieved. In addition, they should know the purpose of each lesson and how mastery of the abilities acquired will help them to become better readers. Students soon become bored with practice and drill for which they do not see a real purpose.

8. Instructional materials should be chosen in harmony with the goals of instruction and the reading levels and interests of the students. Since there is such a diversity in the needs and abilities of retarded readers, no one book is adequate for all students. Although a variety of materials is needed, there should be selectivity in the use of them. Teachers should evaluate materials in the light of the appropriateness of each for their objectives and for their students and should choose only those which will further the reading growth of their students.

At the beginning of the instructional period, materials should be sufficiently easy to permit students to have immediate success. As instruction continues, increasingly difficult materials can be used as students demonstrate that they can handle these materials. As progress is made, it is essential to maintain a balance of easy materials to insure success and more difficult ones to provide stimulation and growth. Materials should be interesting to the reader; any materials which students associate with failure in reading should be avoided.

9. Methods of instruction should be chosen in harmony with the best modes of learning for the individual child. No one remedial procedure can be recommended for all retarded readers. What is beneficial to some may be detrimental to others. For example, oral reading has a definite place in the instructional program for most students; however, it may be harmful to the slow reader who is trying desperately to read faster. If the methods chosen do not seem to work well with a given pupil, the procedures should be changed after they have been given a fair trial.

10. Remedial instruction should be well organized and systematically developed for each retarded reader. Skills should be taught sequentially and not haphazardly. For example, in the improvement of comprehension, the literal meaning must be understood before implied meanings can be interpreted.

Long-range plans, as well as daily ones, should be recorded and read occasionally by the teacher to keep instruction geared toward final goals. The original plans need not be considered permanent ones; they may need to be modified as students progress and as their needs change.

Each instructional period should be well planned. Because the attention span of retarded readers is usually short, the teacher should plan several activities for each period. They should not be chosen just as "busy work"; rather, they should be selected in harmony with the needs of the student.

11. *Success* must be the keynote of every remedial reading program. The student should experience success early and continuously. These successes should be emphasized and failures minimized. Errors made by the student should not be overlooked, but a positive attitude should be taken in correcting them. Records of progress, such as the number of words learned, the number of books read, the percentage correct on comprehension questions, and the number of words read per minute, often point out success to the students.

12. Compensations should be made for factors inhibiting growth in reading if they cannot be remedied or removed. In such instances, the teacher must recognize the problem and circumvent it by capitalizing on the students' strengths.

If referrals to specialists, such as to vision specialists, were made in the diagnosis, it is important that the instructor know the results of these referrals. For example, if the specialist has made the recommendation that the student should not be having reading instruction at this time, it is imperative that his recommendations be carried out. However, when the inhibiting factors have been corrected to the satisfaction of the specialists, reading instruction can begin. The acquisition of glasses or a hearing aid does not automatically cause the student to be a good reader. He must be taught how to read.

13. In every stage of development, the student should be given guidance in becoming an independent reader. This help should not be postponed until the student is older or until he has reached a certain reading level but should

be provided in each stage of development. He should become independent in all aspects of reading. For example, he should be able to apply principles of phonic and structural analysis independently; he should locate reference materials on his own; he should be encouraged to select leisure reading books.

REMEDIAL INSTRUCTION
IN SPECIFIC AREAS OF READING

The foregoing principles apply to remedial reading instruction regardless of the area in which deficiencies occur. Let us now consider instruction in each area of reading.

1. *Word recognition.*   Well-developed word-recognition skills are prerequisite to other reading abilities but should never be considered an end in themselves. The understanding of the printed text should always be the goal in reading, not just the mechanical naming of words. However, if students do not recognize words, they naturally can get no meaning from the selections which they read. Students reading at or below the fourth-grade level usually exhibit an uneven development in their ability to unlock words, although students who read at higher levels may also have difficulty with word-attack skills.

If the student is weak in auditory or visual discrimination or has not developed left-to-right orientation, he needs help in developing these abilities. Some experts in reading believe that these abilities should be strengthened before word-recognition skills are taught; others believe they can be developed at the same time.

The principal methods used in teaching word recognition to retarded readers are the sight, phonic, and kinesthetic methods. According to a study by Mills,[1] retarded readers profit by different methods; no one method is appropriate for all kinds of learners.

Students who do not have adequate basic sight vocabularies should receive help in this area first. The words taught for this purpose are those which comprise the majority of the words found in primary-grade materials. Later these words become the basis for phonic training. Teaching words by means of isolated drill is not desirable. More meaningful are experience stories which the learner dictates to his teacher who prepares the manuscript for him to read later. Words to be recognized instantaneously can be selected from the stories for more intensive practice. Students can also learn to recognize the basic words by reading teacher-prepared stories and interesting books written on a low vocabulary level. In addition, such instruments as the tape recorder provide opportunities for the student to see the word, to say the word, and immediately to hear the word.

Severely retarded readers who in the diagnosis do not appear to have well-developed auditory and visual aptitudes for learning to read or who have

[1] Robert E. Mills, "An Evaluation of Techniques for Teaching Word Recognition," *Elementary School Journal,* LVI (January, 1956), 221–25.

failed by other methods may achieve immediate success through the kinesthetic method developed by Fernald[2] or modifications of it. For many students, this method is slow and laborious and should not be used any longer than is necessary as it does not give the student independence in attacking unknown words.

Because it would be an impossible task for students to learn all words by sight, it is necessary that they know how to unlock unfamiliar words by learning to associate sound with the printed symbol, to apply principles of sounds to different letters and letter combinations, and to blend the sounds to form words. Meaningful approaches must be taken to help students develop such word-recognition skills. Words taken from context and studied in a systematic way are usually more meaningful and less monotonous than lists from workbooks. It is not sufficient for the student just to write the names of sounds or the rules; they need to say the words.

2. *Vocabulary.* Students may have adequate word-recognition skills but such limited vocabularies that they are seriously handicapped in their understanding of the materials which they read. They may have a meager stock of word meanings, both in breadth and depth, in their general or technical reading vocabularies. They may not be able to use context clues effectively; they may not know the meanings of affixes or roots of words and how to apply these meanings to unfamiliar words.

Although research has shown that vocabulary development cannot be left to extensive leisure reading without direction, wide reading for most students does form a basis for new contacts with words and for reinforcement of meanings of words being studied. The retarded reader, however, usually does not like to read and hence is not very likely to be reached through wide reading. As a result, it is essential that retarded readers receive direct instruction in vocabulary.

At all times the words chosen for study should be taken from meaningful context rather than from isolated lists. Unfamiliar words should first be noted in the context within which they appear and then removed from context for intensive study. It is unrealistic, however, to believe that most students can remember the meanings of words from just one contact with them. They need opportunities to meet the same word many times in a variety of contexts and to use these new words in their speaking and writing. They should hear others using them as well.

Giving the retarded reader the opportunity to learn meanings of words through varied experiences has been suggested by most experts. Both direct experiences, including language experiences, and vicarious ones should be provided. But giving the retarded reader new and satisfying experiences is not enough. New words should be introduced before the experience occurs, at frequent times during the activity, and afterward in follow-up discussions. The learner should have opportunities to use and to read the words related

[2] Grace M. Fernald, *Remedial Techniques in Basic School Subjects.* New York: McGraw-Hill Book Co., Inc., 1943.

to the experiences he is having. Misunderstandings and incorrect concepts should be clarified through discussions.

If retarded readers are not adept in the use of context clues as aids for securing meanings of words, they should be taught the various kinds as described by McCullough[3] and Artley[4] and should be given many opportunities to determine word meanings through the different kinds of context clues. In addition, they need to know when they can depend upon these clues and when it is necessary for them to consult the dictionary for the meanings. Retarded readers who are inefficient in the use of glossaries and dictionaries need practice in interpreting definitions and selecting the most appropriate meaning for the context. Use of the dictionary should not be taught for its own sake but as a tool for securing information.

3. *Comprehension.* The comprehension of ideas in passages is a complicated process which presupposes that the basic competencies in reading, such as the ability to name and to define words, are satisfactory. It requires the fusing of separate meanings into a pattern of related thoughts. All teachers have heard students say, "I always read every word of my assignments, but I don't get anything out of them." These students need instruction which will help them gain meaning from their reading.

Remediation in comprehension, as in other areas of reading, depends upon the nature of the difficulty. It is necessary for the teacher to know which comprehension skills need strengthening. Literal reading skills, such as reading for details or for a sequential order of ideas, must be understood before students are able to read for inferences or to make generalizations.

Materials for instruction in comprehension should be selected or prepared in harmony with the comprehension abilities to be taught. At first, the instructor may need to set purposes for the student, but as time progresses the student should be taught how to set his own purposes. Teachers must do more to help the retarded readers than to tell them to read for such purposes as details, comparison, and contrast, or anticipation of events; they must *show* them how to read for each purpose. Comprehension skills should be introduced and taught one at a time, but later they may be combined. The selections should be short at first, perhaps no longer than sentences or paragraphs. When students show competence in understanding these, they should be given practice in reading longer selections. Although the literal meaning must be secured first, retarded readers should learn to read for non-literal meanings as well.

Questions on the selections should be well formulated; *why* questions should overshadow the *who, what, when,* and *where* ones. Each child should be in harmony with the purposes for which students read. For example, students should not be asked questions demanding details when their purpose

---

[3] Constance M. McCullough, "Learning To Use Context Clues," *Elementary English Review*, XX (April, 1943), 140–43.

[4] A. Sterl Artley, "Teaching Word-Meaning through Context," *Elementary English Review*, XX (February, 1943), 68–74.

was to get the general import of the selection. They should correct their errors so that they do not continue making the same kinds of mistakes. Oral responses should be required as well as written ones. Discussions involving how answers were derived are helpful in clarifying any wrong concepts which have been formed. Students should learn to give their own answers rather than always to choose the best answer. At first, they may be required to select the most appropriate answers from three or four which are only slightly different. They should gradually be taught to formulate and to defend their own responses.

Students need many kinds of practice materials from a variety of sources written by different authors. Not all kinds of comprehension skills are well represented in any one source. If the same format is used throughout the book—that is, if the same kinds of selections and questions are used—students become book-wise. They can meet the requirements of this particular book but are less adept in reading other materials. No one source is sufficient for any retarded reader.

4. *Rate of reading.* Instruction to develop rate of reading should not be undertaken if there is retardation in the areas of word recognition, vocabulary, or comprehension. Often when these basic difficulties are overcome, an increase in rate of reading also occurs. However, there are some students who have no difficulties in these basic skills and yet read slowly, plodding through all materials at the same speed, regardless of the difficulty of the material or the purposes for which they are read.

The slow reader beyond the primary grades needs to be motivated to read easy materials more rapidly than he does. Sometimes this motivation comes through the use of pacing instruments, timed exercises, reading against time, and the keeping of daily records of progress.

The goal of instruction in rate of reading should be flexibility in the use of different rates; emphasis in instruction should not be just on reading faster and faster. Students should learn that some materials require thoughtful consideration and that others may be read quickly for the purpose of getting the general import.

Comprehension should be checked at all times by questions requiring general responses and not by those demanding detailed information or implications not stated in the selection. Students who are asked for such information will read more slowly to answer the questions and consequently will not achieve the goal of their instruction. Slow readers require much practice in rapid reading of easy materials both during and outside instructional periods.

Unless attention is given to the reading of study-type materials, students are likely to read them at the same pace as they do their easy reading. Materials appropriate for study with different kinds of comprehension checks should be included in each instructional period. In most cases, good readers read easy materials to get the general idea approximately twice as fast as they read study materials.

It is unwise to give rate instruction immediately after a student has made great strides in word recognition, vocabulary, and comprehension. These students should be allowed ample time—six months to one year—for practice of the newly acquired skills to gain facility in their use. After this time it may be necessary to re-evaluate rate of reading and to provide instruction directed to that end.

Much has been written concerning speed reading. Some proponents give no consideration to basic problems in reading which may be responsible for a slow rate of reading but try to push everyone to read everything with the speed of lightning. Some teachers, conversely, take the attitude that reading anything fast is wrong and will help no one to learn to read faster. Most experts in reading do not agree with either point of view; they believe rather that some students do need help in adjusting rate to the purposes for reading and the difficulty of the material. They agree that judicious decisions must be made before rate training begins and as it progresses.

5. *Interest in reading.* Retarded readers have done little or no reading for enjoyment or for information and consequently have never developed an interest in reading. Yet they are the ones who need the benefits of wide reading to reinforce the reading skills they are learning and to develop enthusiasm for books, magazines, and newspapers. They are not interested because they have never found a book they can read, much less enjoy. Many trade books of high interest and low vocabulary levels on a variety of subjects are being published today. Much guidance should be given to the retarded reader in locating a book which will give him immediate satisfaction and enjoyment. Once he has said, "This is the first time I have ever read a whole book," the chances are good that he will want the second and third books.

Retarded readers can be stimulated to read for enjoyment. As they improve their reading skills, these students have more power with which to read and consequently can find more enjoyment from their reading. Since they have not developed an interest in reading, teachers need to explore their other interests which can be broadened by reading. Teachers must also provide school time for leisure reading. Giving the retarded reader class time is an indication of the value the teacher places upon reading for enjoyment.

CONCLUDING STATEMENT

It is clear that retarded readers exhibit many kinds of difficulties in learning to read effectively. It is imperative that the teacher understand the specific skills which need to be taught or to be strengthened. Because there is much diversity among the needs of retarded readers, instruction must be individualized if progress in reading is to be achieved. The challenges in teaching retarded readers is great, but the rewards for both students and teachers are even greater.

Remedial Studies at Elementary Level:
Their Implications for Classroom Practice

ROBERT KARLIN

At the outset, permit me to state a bias for which I cannot cite much research, let alone carefully controlled investigations. It is simply this: there are no real basic differences between developmental reading and remedial reading; if differences do exist these differences are not of kind but degree. Naturally, children whose reading difficulties originate in organic dysfunction might require unique treatments. Although some of our colleagues suggest that there are more children of this type in our classrooms than we suspect, no real evidence to support this judgment—other than that these children fail to respond to help—has been found.

If we can accept this basic premise about a lack of difference between developmental and remedial reading, we might extend some of the findings of research with poor readers to typical readers. Even if we were to reject the assumption, it would not be improper, without evidence to the contrary, to suggest the *possibility* that procedures found useful with poorer readers might also be helpful with other readers.

Before we consider the findings of research with remedial readers and their classroom implications, we should note that some of them are not the products of rigorous research. Thus I prefer to look on them as suggesting trends rather than demanding convictions. Naturally, findings from even tenuous research which support our ideas strengthen convictions. We should note further that much of the research dealing with poor readers deals with factors related to their problems (laterality, for example) which does not have immediate implications for the classroom teacher. However, in spite of these noted reservations we can obtain some guidelines for working with children who have reading difficulties (and those who don't) from the results of research.

Let us now examine four aspects of our topic—evaluation, organization, methods and materials—and suggest some useful practices that emanate from studies about problem readers.

REMEDIAL STUDIES AT ELEMENTARY LEVEL: THEIR IMPLICATIONS FOR CLASSROOM PRACTICE by Robert Karlin. From *Combining Research Results and Good Practice,* Proceedings of the 11th Annual Convention of the International Reading Association, 1967, ed. Mildred A. Dawson, Volume 2, Part 2, pp. 101–08. Reprinted with permission of the International Reading Association and Robert Karlin.

EVALUATION

If we are to reduce or eliminate the reading difficulties elementary school pupils experience, we must determine what they are. In addition, we must know at what levels to offer instruction and the levels at which pupils can read books without much help from us. Most schools administer standardized reading tests for children in order to find out at what level they are reading and what their reading needs and strengths are. What does research tell us about how well these tests and their results provide us with this information?

Williams (28) sought to determine, among other things, whether there were any significant differences in the results obtained from standardized reading tests and informal inventories for normal and poor readers. She obtained data from three standardized tests and informal reading inventories based upon three reading series for pupils in the intermediate grades. She concluded that the tests placed the pupils in materials too difficult for them to use for instruction, averaging one to four years above their ability to read in books.

McCracken (19) compared the scores sixth-grade pupils obtained on a standardized reading test and a test based upon a basal reading series. He found that 93 per cent of the pupils would meet many difficulties in reading the books. On the average, standardized tests scores placed pupils about two years above levels obtained from the inventories based upon the readers.

Sipay (23) studied 200 fourth-grade pupils to discover if the results obtained from three standardized reading tests parallel those secured from an informal reading inventory. He found that all the tests overestimated the instructional level by one or more years when 96 to 99 per cent word accuracy was used as the criterion. Two of the three tests underestimated by one grade the frustration level when below 90 per cent accuracy in word recognition was used as the criterion.

Kress (14) reported a case study of a poor reader whose standardized test score was compared with the results of an informal inventory. He found that the standardized test placed the pupil at fourth grade level while second grade level was more appropriate for instructional purposes.

In a somewhat different but related study Long (17) analyzed the reading difficulties of poor elementary school readers with standardized reading tests and informal inventories and concluded that teachers generally fail to provide instruction at a sufficiently low level and in the skills required by them.

Some writers (1), (2), (12), (29) have pointed out the weaknesses of standardized reading tests—their placement of pupils at too-high levels and the limited amount of information they yield. However, another (3) prefers standardized tests to informal inventories, a second points out their limitations (25), while a third (6) suggests that both be used to obtain more accurate results about the actual reading ability of pupils.

What lessons can we learn from the foregoing? Might I suggest that we have some evidence to support the view that suitable informal reading tests will yield results which will enable us to more adequately provide reading instruction for those who need it badly. This recommendation does not preclude the use of standardized reading tests for evaluating the reading of poor readers. It merely underscores other possibilities available to us as we work with children who require special attention.

ORGANIZATION

One real problem schools face is their inability to provide special help in reading to all pupils who require it. They just do not have sufficient staff to offer what many reading people feel these pupils need—individual instruction. Is it possible to offer effective group instruction and thereby reach more children?

Lovell and others (18) in a follow-up study with 136 pupils, all of whom received remedial instruction for at least three months, found small group remedial help as effective as individual instruction.

Delacato and Delacato (7) provided group instruction for children with reading problems who previously had been tutored individually but unsuccessfully. They found that the children's attitude and reading improved and attributed these gains to the influence of group interaction.

Galotto (11) found no significant differences in results obtained by pupils who received individual or group remedial reading instruction.

Dempsey (8) compared the reading progress over a six-month period of 10 eleven- and twelve-year-old pupils, 5 of whom she taught individually and the remaining 5 in a group. She reported that on no test, standardized or informal, did one group score significantly over the other. Both groups of pupils made considerable gains in reading growth. She concluded that it is possible to group retarded readers who read on similar levels and have common reading problems.

Uncontrolled studies by others (15), (24), (26) further demonstrate the efficacy of providing group instruction in remedial reading.

The results of these studies seem to confirm the views of some reading specialists that group instruction has psychological advantages which equal the benefits derived from individual instruction. Furthermore, group instruction makes it possible for the teacher to reach many more pupils than he would otherwise be able to. Thus, classroom teachers can with confidence group their children for remedial instruction and hope to achieve results at least equal to those gained from individual teaching.

METHODS AND MATERIALS

What types of reading materials should be used to teach children with reading difficulties? Should materials for remedial reading be consistent with the interests and maturity levels of the children? The research to answer these questions is meager but some tentative answers might be found in a study which sought to compare the usefulness of basal readers and high-interest, low vocabulary trade books in a reading program for poor readers. Harris (13) randomly placed 40 fourth-, fifth- and sixth-grade pupils into one of two groups and then subdivided each group so that four groups received equal amounts of instructional time. After 57 periods of instruction, she did not find any significant difference between the two major groups in silent or oral reading achievement. She concluded that basal readers are as effective as high-interest materials for teaching poor readers.

The implications of this study are clear. We know that the reading interests of poor readers are no different from those of good readers. Use materials in whose content poor readers are interested. However, we should not assume that all pupils reject materials originally designed for younger children. These materials can be used when more desirable ones are unavailable provided teachers and children understand the purposes to which they are being put.

In a different but somewhat related study Sartain (21) sought to determine whether third-grade poor and good readers profit from workbook exercises. Neither the poor nor good readers reached a level of achievement in word recognition and comprehension significantly different from that of control groups. Some groups, however, did better than others. The investigators concluded that the learning environment of the classes rather than the materials accounted for any gains in reading.

One implication might be drawn from this study: it is not the materials you use with poor readers that count; it is what you do with the materials that makes the difference.

There have been a series of investigations whose results are mixed. These sought to determine the extent to which poor readers could improve their reading ability with instruction and/or forms of therapy. Studies by Fisher (10), Lipton (16), and Studholme (27) and others suggest that a reduction in the anxiety levels of these children facilitates learning. It seems quite clear that poor readers are more likely to prosper in classrooms with patient and understanding teachers than with critical and punishing teachers. A healthy learning climate helps to raise low self-concept, an obstacle to learning. Feelings of success can be generated by firm but sympathetic treatment as well as by growth in reading.

Other clues to teaching procedures are found in studies by Mills (20) and Roberts and Coleman (21). The former sought to determine which method—sight, phonic or kinesthetic—is best to follow for overcoming word recognition weaknesses in third-grade retarded readers. The latter sought to determine which group—normal or retarded reader—had superior visual perception and what method—visual or kinesthetic—produced better results with the groups. They found that poor readers were weaker in visual perception and improved their recognition ability when taught by visual and kinesthetic means.

We might conclude from the results of these studies that no one method of teaching word recognition skills should be relied upon with poor readers. Some learn better with one mode than another. Our chances for success are improved under conditions which give learners as many cues as possible.

Two studies by Scott (22) and Farrelly (9) with second-grade children who were poor readers produced results which indicated that a carefully planned and systematic remedial program could raise significantly the reading levels of such children. Not only do these studies suggest the desirability of instruction geared to learning levels, but also the wisdom of providing help in overcoming word recognition weaknesses *early* in pupils' school career. Too many remedial programs pick up poor readers in the middle grades—with the not unusual disappointing results.

Many reading as well as other learning specialists have suggested that meaningful learning is preferred to rote learning. A study by Catterson (5) sought to determine the validity of this recommendation. She compared the inductive method (practice in recognizing words in meaningful contexts) with the deductive method (recognizing words by applying rules). She found that her poor readers learned to recognize words better in meaningful settings than from rules. This finding supports the belief that we should help poor readers understand the processes of word attack rather than require them to memorize rules which can be forgotten easily. Meaningful learning is more efficient and lasting than meaningless learning.

Does word form have any effect on recognition? The answer to this question has significance in teaching poor readers with word recognition difficulties. Byrne (4) presented unknown words in four forms: manuscript writing, lower case typed, cursive writing and upper case typed. He found that good readers did equally well with each form. However, the poor readers missed more words that were presented in the upper case form. This form contains fewer cues than the others. The results suggest that poor readers with word recognition difficulties might benefit from exposure to word forms that approximate those found in books. The teacher can use this form in chalkboard and other writing to which these readers are exposed.

SUMMARY

As we noted at the outset, we do not have definitive results from research to guide us in helping children with reading difficulties overcome their weaknesses. More and better research in reading and learning will yield information in which we can place confidence. In the meantime, we have developed some principles that are outgrowths of theoretical models and experience. In addition, we have made some beginning efforts in research to determine if we should support these beliefs and practices. Until we obtain more conclusive data, it seems wise to use present knowledge to help children become better readers.

Bibliography

1. Austin, Mary. "Identifying Readers Who Need Corrective Reading." *Corrective Reading in Classroom and Clinic. Supplementary Educational Monographs,* Vol. XV, No. 79, Chicago: University of Chicago Press, 1953, 21.
2. Betts, Emmett. "How Well Are We Teaching Reading?" *Elementary English,* XXXVIII (October 1961), 377.
3. Bond, Guy and Tinker, Miles: *Reading Difficulties: Their Diagnosis and Correction.* New York: Appleton-Century-Crofts, Inc., 1957, 133.
4. Byrne, Robert. "The Effects of Word Form on Retention." *Reading As An Intellectual Activity,* International Reading Association Conference Proceedings, Vol. VIII, 1963, 134–136.
5. Catterson, Jane. *Inductive Versus Deductive Methods in Word Analysis in Grade Five.* Unpublished Master's Thesis, Boston University, 1959.
6. Chall, Jeanne S. "Interpretation of the Results of Standardized Reading Tests." *The Evaluation of Reading, Supplementary Educational Monographs,* Vol. XX, No. 88, Chicago: University of Chicago Press, 1958, 135.
7. Delacato, Janice F. and Carl H. "A Group Approach to Remedial Reading." *Elementary English,* XXIX (January 1952), 142–149.
8. Dempsey, Maurine. *Individual vs. Group Remedial Reading Instruction.* Unpublished Research Report, Southern Illinois University, 1964.
9. Farrelly, Mary. *The Construction and Evaluation of a Series of Lesson Plans in Phonics To Be Used With the Reluctant Readers in the Second Grade.* Unpublished Master's Thesis, Rhode Island College, 1960.
10. Fisher, Bernard. "Group Therapy With Retarded Readers." *Journal of Educational Psychology,* XLIV (October 1953), 354–360.
11. Galotto, John. *The Comparative Effectiveness of Individual Reading Therapy and Group Therapy.* Unpublished doctoral dissertation, New York University, 1962.
12. Harris, Albert. "The Diagnosis of Reading Disabilities." *Corrective and Remedial Reading,* Sixteenth Annual Conference, Pittsburgh: University of Pittsburgh, 1960, 33.
13. Harris, Anna. *The Relationship Between Reading Progress and Materials Used in Grades IV, V, and VI—A Comparison of the Effectiveness of Basic Readers versus Published High-Interest, Low-Vocabulary Materials on Reading Achievement and Attitude.* Unpublished doctoral dissertation, New York University, 1962.
14. Kress, Roy. "A Case Study of Reading Retardation—The Diagnosis and Correction." *Corrective and Remedial Reading,* Sixteenth Annual Conference, Pittsburgh: University of Pittsburgh, 1960, 87.
15. Laffey, Rose. "A Program in Remedial Reading." *Elementary English,* XXVII (April 1950), 230–239.
16. Lipton, Aaron and Feiner, Arthur H. "Group Therapy and Remedial Reading." *Journal of Educational Psychology,* XLVII (October 1956), 330–334.
17. Long, Donna Janet. *An Analysis of the Reading Difficulties of Retarded Readers in Second, Fourth and Sixth Grades.* Unpublished doctoral dissertation, State University of Iowa, 1959.
18. Lovell, K., Johnson, E. and Platts, D. "A Summary of a Study of the Reading Ages of Children Who Had Been Given Remedial Teaching." *British Journal of Educational Psychology,* XXXII (February 1962), 66–71.
19. McCracken, Robert. "Standardized Reading Tests and Informal Reading Inventories." *Education,* LXXXII (February 1962), 366–369.
20. Mills, Robert. "An Evaluation of Techniques For Teaching Word Recognition." *Elementary School Journal,* LVI (January 1956), 221–225.
21. Robert, Richard and Coleman, James. "An Investigation of the Role of Visual and Kinesthetic Factors in Reading Failure." *Journal of Educational Research,* LI (February 1958), 445–451.
22. Sartain, Harry. "Do Reading Workbooks Increase Achievement?" *Elementary School Journal,* LXII (December 1961), 157–162.
23. Scott, Mary. *A Study to Determine the Effectiveness of Teaching Reading Skills to Second-Grade Children With Reading Difficulties.* Unpublished Master's Thesis, University of Tennessee, 1959.

24. Sipay, Edward. "A Comparison of Standardized Reading Scores and Functional Reading Levels." *The Reading Teacher,* XVII (January 1964), 265–268.
25. Slesinger, Betty. "Attacking the Problem of the Retarded Reader." *Elementary English,* XXXI (March 1954), 144–145.
26. Spache, George. *Reading in the Elementary School,* Boston: Allyn and Bacon, Inc., 1964, 246.
27. Still, Jane S. "Evaluation of a Community Sponsored Summer Remedial Reading Program." *Elementary English,* XXXVIII (May 1961), 342–343.
28. Studholme, Janice M. "Group Guidance With Mothers of Retarded Readers." *The Reading Teacher,* XVII (April 1964), 528–530.
29. Williams, Joan Lee. *A Comparison of Standardized Reading Test Scores.* Unpublished doctoral dissertation, Southern Illinois University, 1963.
30. Woestehoff, Ellsworth. "Using Results of Reading Tests to Improve Instruction in Grades Four Through Six." *The Evaluation of Reading, Supplementary Educational Monographs,* Vol. XX, No. 88, Chicago: University of Chicago Press, 1958, 143.

10   Suggestions for Further Reading

There are a number of good summaries of research on the causes of reading difficulties: Guy L. Bond and Miles A. Tinker, *Reading Difficulties: Their Diagnosis and Correction* (Appleton-Century-Crofts, 1967), Chapters 5 and 6; Albert J. Harris, *How to Increase Reading Ability* (David McKay, 1970), Chapters 9–11; John Money (ed.), *Progress and Research Needs in Dyslexia* (John Hopkins, 1962). An older but equally complete summary will be found in Marjorie S. Johnson, "Factors Related to Disability in Reading," *Journal of Experimental Education,* 26 (December 1957), 1–26.

Guidelines for planning and conducting reading remediation are suggested in N. Dale Bryant, "Some Principles of Remedial Instruction for Dyslexia," *The Reading Teacher,* 18 (April 1965); Marjorie S. Johnson, "Basic Consideration in Corrective Instruction," in Marjorie S. Johnson and Roy A. Kress (eds.), *Corrective Reading in the Elementary School* (International Reading Association, 1967), 61–72; and Robert Karlin, "Characteristics of Sound Remedial Reading Instruction," in Albert J. Mazurkiewicz (ed.), *The Wide World of Reading Instruction* (Lehigh University, 1966), 138–42.

Suggestions for overcoming reading difficulties will be found in Guy L. Bond and Miles A. Tinker, *Reading Difficulties: Their Diagnosis and Correction* (Appleton-Century-Crofts, 1967), 349–89; Carl B. Smith, *Correcting Reading Problems in the Classroom* (International Reading Association, 1969); and Robert Wilson, *Diagnostic and Remedial Teaching* (Charles E. Merrill, 1967), 125–88.

A   3
B   4
C   5
D   6
E   7
F   8
G   9
H   0
I   1
J   2